HISTORICAL DICTIONARY

The historical dictionaries present essential information on a broad range of subjects, including American and world history, art, business, cities, countries, cultures, customs, film, global conflicts, international relations, literature, music, philosophy, religion, sports, and theater. Written by experts, all contain highly informative introductory essays of the topic and detailed chronologies that, in some cases, cover vast historical time periods but still manage to heavily feature more recent events.

Brief A–Z entries describe the main people, events, politics, social issues, institutions, and policies that make the topic unique, and entries are cross-referenced for ease of browsing. Extensive bibliographies are divided into several general subject areas, providing excellent access points for students, researchers, and anyone wanting to know more. Additionally, maps, photographs, and appendixes of supplemental information aid high school and college students doing term papers or introductory research projects. In short, the historical dictionaries are the perfect starting point for anyone looking to research in these fields.

HISTORICAL DICTIONARIES OF PROFESSIONS AND INDUSTRIES

Jon Woronoff, Series Editor

Historical Dictionary of Librarianship

Mary Ellen Quinn

Kenrick-Glennon

Seminary Library

Charles L. Souvay Memorial

ROWMAN & LITTLEFIELD
Lanham • Boulder • New York • Toronto • Plymouth, UK

Published by Rowman & Littlefield
4501 Forbes Boulevard, Suite 200, Lanham, Maryland 20706
www.rowman.com

10 Thornbury Road, Plymouth PL6 7PP, United Kingdom

British Library Cataloguing in Publication Information Available

Library of Congress Cataloging-in-Publication Data

Quinn, Mary Ellen, 1949–
Historical dictionary of librarianship / Mary Ellen Quinn.
 pages cm. — (Historical dictionaries of professions and industries)
Includes bibliographical references.
ISBN 978-0-8108-7807-5 (cloth : alk. paper) — ISBN 978-0-8108-7545-6 (ebook)
1. Library science—History—Dictionaries. 2. Libraries—History—Dictionaries. 3. Information science—History—Dictionaries. I. Title.
Z1006.Q56 2014
020.3—dc23
2013049443

Printed in the United States of America.

Contents

Editor's Foreword

Libraries and librarians have been with us for over two millennia. But modern librarianship has developed only over the last two centuries and rapidly evolved into its current state just in the past two decades. To say that the changes have been substantial would be a gross understatement. Once there were not even books, just tablets and parchments; now, almost unbelievably, books themselves are moving to the periphery and being replaced by electronic sources. Libraries once grew in number and expanded in size, taking pride in the quantity and quality of books on their shelves; now some libraries are closing down and others are going digital, while readers can carry a library in their laptop or Kindle. And, of course, it is no longer just a matter of librarianship and the question of just what a librarian should do, but rather of how to manage information in a growing array of formats.

This *Historical Dictionary of Librarianship* covers a long and sometimes complicated story. The chronology presents the most important events, and the introduction presents a cogent overview. The list of acronyms and abbreviations provides countless organizations and associations, including the soon-to-be familiar ALA and UNESCO. The core of the book is obviously the dictionary, an abundant and informative compilation of entries on important people, whether librarians like Melvil Dewey or philanthropists like Andrew Carnegie; places, including not only libraries but also countries and their efforts in the librarianship field; some of the more notable organizations and associations; and matters directly related to the practice of librarianship, such as classification and cataloging, becoming a librarian, and education, accreditation, and certification. There are two useful appendixes and, finally, as behooves a book on librarianship, a complete and well-organized bibliography.

This book was written by someone who is exceedingly familiar with librarianship in the United States and has a great deal of knowledge about what has been happening abroad. Mary Ellen Quinn holds an MLS and has been working in and around libraries for several decades. She was a librarian at the Jacksonville Public Library in Florida and the Chicago Public Library in Illinois. After that she moved to the American Library Association, where she became known for her work as the editor of the Reference Books Bulletin section of *Booklist*. Along the way, she has published a number of articles on library collection development and reference publishing. This reference work will certainly be welcomed by anyone who wants to know more about a profession initially not even recognized but one that we could now not be without.

Jon Woronoff
Series Editor

Acknowledgments

Much of the research for this book was done at the library at the American Library Association headquarters in Chicago. I'd like to thank the library staff—Karen Muller, Rebecca Gerber, and Valerie Hawkins—for being generous with their space, time, and resources. I'd also like to thank my husband, Ken Alexander, for being my in-home editor and giving me advice and support.

Reader's Notes

The focus of this dictionary is on librarianship as a modern, organized profession. While there is some treatment of early developments, emphasis is on the period beginning in the mid-19th century, when the first Public Libraries Act was passed in Great Britain and the first library association, the American Library Association, was formed in the United States. Although an attempt has been made to cover librarianship across the globe, the dictionary has an Anglo-American bias that reflects the available literature. Biographical coverage is representative rather than comprehensive, since many more individuals around the world have contributed to the development of librarianship than could be included in these pages.

In order to facilitate the rapid and efficient location of information and to make this book as useful a reference tool as possible, extensive cross-references have been provided in the dictionary section. Within individual entries, terms that have their own entries are in **boldface type** the first time they appear. Related terms that do not appear in the text are indicated by *See also* references. *See* refers to other entries that deal with this topic.

Acronyms and Abbreviations

AACR	*Anglo-American Cataloging Rules*
AACR2	*Anglo-American Cataloging Rules, Second Edition*
AALL	American Association of Law Libraries
AALS	Association of American Library Schools
AASL	American Association of School Librarians
ABF	Association des bibliothécaires français/French Library Association
ABGRA	Asociación de Bibliotecarios Graduados de la República Argentina/Association of Graduate Librarians of the Republic of Argentina
ABINIA	Asociación de Estados Iberoamericanos para el Desarrollo de las Bibliotecas Nacionales de Iberomérica/Association of Directors of National Libraries in Latin America
ACDF	American Committee for Devastated France
ACONDA	Activities Committee on New Directions
ACRL	Association of College and Research Libraries
ACURIL	Association of Caribbean University, Research and Institutional Libraries
ADBS	Association de professionels de l'information et de la documentation/Associations of Information and Documentation Professionals
ADI	American Documentation Institute
AFLI ·	Arab Federation for Libraries and Information
AGRICOLA	Agricultural Online Access
AIB	Associazione Italiana Biblioteche/Italian Library Association
AIBDA	Asociación Interamericana de Bibliotecarios, Documentalistas y Especialistas en Información Agrícola/ Inter-American Association of Agricultural Librarians and Documentalists
ALA	American Library Association

ALA-APA	American Library Association–Allied Professional Association
ALASA	African Library Association of South Africa
ALECSO	Arab League Educational, Cultural, and Scientific Organization
ALIA	Australian Library and Information Association
A-LIEP	Asia-Pacific Conference on Library and Information Education and Practice
ALISE	Association for Library and Information Science Education
AMBAC	Asociación Mexicana de Bibliotecarios/Mexican Association of Librarians
ANABAD	Federación Española de Asociaciones de Archiveros, Bibliotecarios, Archeóloges, Museólogos y Documentalistas/Spanish Federation of Associations of Archivists, Librarians, Archaeologists, Museologists, and Documentalists
ANKOS	Anatolian University Libraries Consortium
ARL	Association of Research Libraries
ARPANET	Advanced Research Projects Agency Network
ASCUBI	Asociación Cubana de Bibliotecarios/Library Association of Cuba
ASEAN	Association of Southeast Asian Nations
ASIS	American Society for Information Science
ASIST	American Society for Information Science and Technology
ASIS&T	Association for Information Science and Technology
ASLIB	Association of Special Libraries and Information Bureaux
BALLOTS	Bibliographic Automation of Large Library Operations Using a Time-Sharing System
BCALA	Black Caucus of the American Library Association
BEL	Board of Education for Librarianship
BIBCO	Bibliographic Record Cooperative Program
BID	Bibliothek und Information Deutschland/Library and Information Germany
BLAISE	British Library Automated Information Service
BLCMP	Birmingham Libraries Cooperative Mechanisation Project

BNB	British National Bibliography
BnF	Bibliothéque nationale de France
BOAI	Budapest Open Access Initiative
CALIS	China Academic Library and Information System
CASLIN	Czech and Slovak Library Information Network
CDNL	Conference of Directors of National Libraries
CEE	Central and Eastern Europe
CERL	Consortium of European Research Libraries
CILIP	Chartered Institute of Library and Information Professionals
CIP	Cataloging in Publication
CIPA	Children's Internet Protection Act
CLA	Canadian Library Association
CLIR	Council on Library and Information Resources
CLR	Council on Library Resources
CLSI	Computer Library Systems, Inc.
COBISS	Cooperative Online Bibliographic System and Services
COM	Computer-Output Microform
CONSAL	Congress of Southeast Asian Librarians
CONSER	Cooperative Online Serials Program
CPA	Commission on Preservation and Access
CRG	Classification Research Group
CRL	Center for Research Libraries
CUIB	Centro Universitario de Investigaciones Bibliotecológicas/ University Librarianship Research Center
DARPA	Defense Advanced Research Projects Agency
DBV	Deutscher Bibliotheksverband/German Library Association
DDC	Dewey Decimal Classification
DILL	International Master in Digital Library Learning
DL	Digital Library
DMCA	Digital Millennium Copyright Act
DPLA	Digital Public Library of America

EBLIDA	European Bureau of Library, Information, and Documentation Associations
ECIP	Electronic Cataloging in Publication
EIBM	Escuela Interamericana de Bibliotecologia/Inter-American Library School
EIFL	Electronic Information for Libraries
ERIC	Educational Resources Information Center
EU	European Union
EUCLID	European Association for Library and Information Education and Research
FADBEN	Fédération des enseignants documentalistes de l'Éducation Nationale/Federation of Teacher Documentalists in Public Schools
FAIFE	Committee on Free Access to Information and Freedom of Expression
FBI	Federal Bureau of Investigation
FEBAB	Federação Brasileira de Associações de Bibliotecários e Cietistas de Informação/Brazilian Federation of Associations of Librarians, Information Scientists, and Institutions
FESABID	Federación Española de Sociedades de Archivística, Biblioteconomía, Documentación y Museística/Federation of Spanish Societies of Archives, Libraries, Documentation, and Museology
FID	Fédération internationale d'information et de documentation/International Federation for Information and Documentation
FIRBIP	Foro Iberoamericano de Responsables Nacionales de Bibliotecas Públicas/Latin American Forum of National Public Library Directors
FRBR	Functional Requirements for Bibliographic Records
GLS	Graduate Library School
IAALD	International Association of Agricultural Librarians and Documentalists
IAML	International Association of Music Libraries, Archives and Documentation Centres
IASL	International Association of School Librarianship

IASLIC	Indian Association of Special Libraries and Information Centers
IBM	International Business Machines Corporation
ICABS	IFLA-CDNL Alliance for Bibliographic Standards
ICP	Statement of International Cataloging Principles
IFLA	International Federation of Library Associations and Institutions
IIB	International Institute of Bibliography
IIS	Institute of Information Scientists
ILIC	International Library Information Center
INFOLAC	Regional Program to Enhance Co-operation among National Development Information Systems and Networks in Latin America and the Caribbean
ISBD	International Standard Bibliographic Description
ISKO	International Society for Knowledge Organization
KALIPER	Kellogg-ALISE Information Professions and Education Renewal
KOLIS	Korean Library Information System
KORMARC	Korean Machine Readable Cataloging
LA	Library Association
LAC	Library and Archives Canada
LACAP	Latin American Cooperative Acquisitions Program
LASER	London and South Eastern Library Region
LC	Library of Congress
LCC	Library of Congress Classification
LCS	Library Circulation System; Library Computer System
LCSH	Library of Congress Subject Headings
LIASA	Library and Information Association of South Africa
LIBER	Ligue des bibliothèques européenes de recherche/League of European Research Libraries
LIBRUNAM	Libros del Sistema Bibliotecario de la UNAM
LIPER	Library and Information Professions and Education Renewal
LIS	Library and Information Science

LIWO	Library and Information Workers Organization
LQ	*Library Quarterly*
LSA	Library Services Act
LSCA	Library Services and Construction Act
LSTA	Library Services and Technology Act
MARC	Machine-Readable Cataloging
MEDLARS	Medical Literature Analysis and Retrieval System
MEDLINE	MEDLARS Online
MLA	Medical Library Association; Music Library Association
NACO	Name Authority Cooperative Program
NAL	National Agricultural Library
NASA	National Aeronautics and Space Administration
NCCP	National Coordinated Cataloging Program
NCLIS	National Commission on Libraries and Information Science
NEA	National Education Association
NLM	National Library of Medicine
NORDBOK	Nordic Literature and Library Committee
NPAC	National Program for Acquisitions and Cataloging
NSA	National Security Agency
NSF	National Science Foundation
NSFNET	National Science Foundation Network
NYPL	New York Public Library
OA	Open Access
OAS	Organization of American States
OCLC	Online Computer Library Center
OPAC	Online Public Access Catalog
OSI	Open Society Institute
OSTI	Office for Scientific and Technical Information
OWI	Office of War Information
PCC	Program for Cooperative Cataloging
PICA	Project for Integrated Catalogue Automation

PLOS	Public Library of Science
PRECIS	Preserved Context Index System
RAK	Regeln für die alphabetische Katalogisierung/Rules for Descriptive Cataloging
RBU	Répertoire bibliographique universel/Universal Bibliographic Repertory
RDA	Resource Description and Access
RISM	Répertoire international des sources musicales/International Inventory of Musical Sources
RLG	Research Libraries Group
RLIN	Research Libraries Information Network
SAB	Sveriges Allmänna Biblioteksförening/Swedish Library Association
SACO	Subject Authority Cooperative Program
SAILIS	South African Institute for Librarianship and Information Science
SALA	South African Library Association
SALALM	Seminar on the Acquisition of Latin American Library Materials
SCANUL-ECS	Standing Conference of African National and University Libraries in Eastern, Central, and Southern Africa
SCAULWA	Standing Conference of African University Libraries, Western Area
SCECSAL	Standing Conference of Eastern, Central, and Southern Africa Library and Information Associations
SCONUL	Standing Conference of National and University Libraries
SLA	Special Libraries Association
SPARC	Scholarly Publishing and Academic Resources Coalition
SRRT	Social Responsibilities Round Table
UBC	Universal Bibliographic Control
UBCIM	Universal Bibliographic Control and International MARC
UCLA	University of California at Los Angeles
UDC	Universal Decimal Classification
UN	United Nations

UNAM	Universidad Nacional Autónoma de México/National Autonomous University of Mexico
UNESCO	United Nations Educational, Scientific and Cultural Organization
UNIMARC	Universal MARC Format
USIA	United States Information Agency
USIS	United States Information Service
VDB	Verein Deutscher Bibliothekare/Association of German Librarians
VOYA	Voice of Youth Advocates
WALA	West African Library Association
WIPO	World Intellectual Property Organization
YA	Young Adult
YALSA	Young Adult Library Services Association
YMCA	Young Men's Christian Association

Chronology

ca. 2700 BCE Mesopotamia: Collections of clay tablets constitute the earliest known libraries, which grew out of temple and palace archives.

7th century BCE Assyria: Ashurbanipal's library at Nineveh is perhaps the first library for which texts are systematically collected.

3rd century BCE Egypt: The Alexandrian Library is established. Callimachos of Cyrene creates a catalog for the library around 250 BCE.

1st century BCE China: Scholar Liu Xiang begins work on the *Seven Epitomes*, the first documented Chinese catalog. **Rome:** Gaius Asinius Pollio founds the city's first public library.

6th century CE Italy: Cassiodorus establishes the Vivarium, a monastery with a library and scriptorium. Benedict of Nursia formulates a rule for monastic life that stresses the importance of books and reading.

7th century CE Syria: The first House of Wisdom, serving scholars in the Arab world, is established in Damascus.

1005 Egypt: The Dar al-Hikmah (House of Knowledge) is founded in Cairo. Its library is said to have had 600,000 volumes.

1289 France: Perhaps the first academic library, the library at the Collège de Sorbonne, is established.

1444 Italy: The San Marco Library, considered to be the first public library in Renaissance Europe, opens in Florence.

1461 France: The Royal Library, precursor to the Bibliothèque nationale de France, is established.

1473 Germany: The *Philobiblon*, written in the previous century by Richard de Bury, is issued in its first printed edition. It is one of the earliest examples of library literature.

1494 Germany: Johann Tritheim publishes *Liber de scriptoribus ecclesiasticus*, which is considered to be the first true bibliography.

1537 France: The earliest known legal deposit system is established by the Ordonnance de Montpellier.

1545 Switzerland: The first volume of Conrad Gesner's *Bibliotheca universalis*, the first general European bibliography, is published.

1560 Germany: Florian Trefler, a monk, publishes a treatise on library management.

1564 Germany: The first full-scale book trade catalog is issued by Georg Willer, a bookseller.

1595 Great Britain: Bookseller Andrew Maunsell compiles the nation's first book trade catalog.

1602 Great Britain: The Bodleian Library at Oxford opens for service.

1605 Great Britain: Francis Bacon's *Advancement of Learning* is published. It contains a system for the division of knowledge that influences library classification schemes. The Bodleian Library prints the first library catalog in English.

1620 Great Britain: The second catalog of the Bodleian catalog is published. It is the first general library catalog to be arranged in alphabetical order by authors' surnames.

1627 France: Gabriel Naudé's *Avis pour dresser une bibliothèque*, considered to be the first systematic textbook on library practice, is published.

1638 United States: The first college library in the American colonies is founded at Harvard College.

1693 United States: The first American bibliography, a catalog of the library of Reverend Samuel Lee of Boston, is issued.

1698 United States: The first documented public lending library in the American colonies opens in Charleston, South Carolina.

1710 Great Britain: The Statute of Anne, the first English copyright law, takes effect.

1723 United States: The first printed library catalog in America is prepared by librarian Joshua Gee at Harvard.

1731 United States: The Library Company of Philadelphia, the first social library, is founded.

1753 Great Britain: The British Museum, precursor to the British Library, is formed when several important private collections are merged.

1763 United States: The first medical library in America opens at the Pennsylvania Hospital in Philadelphia.

1777 Latin America: The earliest South American national library is established in Colombia.

1790 United States: The first federal copyright act is passed.

1791 France: The first national cataloging code is created to organize the books and manuscripts confiscated by the Revolutionary government.

1793 France: The Bibliothèque nationale is established as the world's first free national library.

1800 United States: The Library of Congress is established for the use of members of Congress. The first full-time librarian of Congress, George Watterson, is appointed in 1815.

1803 United States: The earliest US public library serving children, the Bingham Library for Youth, is founded in Salisbury, Connecticut.

1808 Germany: Martin Schrettinger of the Royal Library in Munich coins the term "library science."

1818 United States: State libraries are established in Illinois, New Hampshire, and New York.

1820 Germany: Friedrich Adolf Ebert of the Royal Library in Dresden writes a pioneering treatise on education for librarianship.

1821 France: The École nationale de chartes, the first school in the world for training library professionals, opens in Paris.

1833 United States: Harvard College creates the first American card catalog as a supplement to its printed catalog. The oldest free public library in the world supported by taxation opens in Peterborough, New Hampshire.

1835 United States: New York State allows school districts to use tax monies to set up and maintain school libraries.

1836 United States: The Library of the Surgeon General's Office opens in Washington, D.C. It is renamed the National Library of Medicine in 1956.

1840 Germany: *Serapeum*, the first journal devoted to librarianship, is started by Leipzig school teacher and city librarian Robert Naumann.

1841 Great Britain: Anthony Panizzi's *Rules for the Compilation of the Catalogue* for the British Museum, considered to be the first modern cataloging code, is published.

1849 United States: New Hampshire passes a bill allowing municipalities to tax themselves to set up a free public library.

1850 Great Britain: The Public Libraries Act empowers municipal authorities with a population of 10,000 or more to levy a small rate for the establishment and maintenance of a public library. Manchester is the first large city in the country to establish a free public library. **United States:** Smithsonian Institute librarian Charles Coffin Jewett's "Notices of Public Libraries in the United States of America" provides the first statistics on libraries in the nation.

1853 United States: The first distinct code of cataloging rules in the nation is compiled by Charles Coffin Jewett. The first librarians' conference is held in New York City.

1854 United States: The Boston Public Library, the first free, tax-supported public library with circulation privileges, opens its doors. At the Boston Mercantile Library, William Frederick Poole compiles a catalog which is a forerunner of the modern dictionary catalog.

1856 Spain: The Higher School of Diplomatics is established for the education of archivists and librarians. **United States:** William Frederick Poole of the Boston Public Library hires the first woman to be employed at an American library.

1860 Germany: Göttingen University appoints the first full-time academic librarian.

1861 Great Britain: Manchester Public Library opens the first children's room in Britain. **United States:** A public card catalog is instituted at the Harvard College library.

1862 United States: The Department of Agriculture Library (later the National Agricultural Library) is established.

1865 Italy: The country's earliest reported library instruction course commences at the University of Naples.

1870 Argentina: The Sarmiento Law for Public Libraries, named after President Domingo F. Sarmiento, is passed. **Italy:** Librarianship examinations are introduced. **United States:** Congress passes a law that centralizes the copyright system in the Library of Congress. The East Boston Branch, the nation's first branch library, opens in Boston.

1871 Great Britain: A woman assistant is hired at the Manchester Free Library. By 1910, there are 132 British public libraries that employ women.

1872 Japan: The first modern library in the country that is open to the public is established in Tokyo.

1873 United States: Melvil Dewey reclassifies the Amherst College Library according to his new classification scheme, the Decimal Classification.

1874 United States: The catalog of the Boston Athenaeum is published and becomes the model for the period.

1876 United States: The US Bureau of Education's special report *Public Libraries in the United States of America: Their History, Condition, and Management* presents the first official survey of public libraries. A librarians' conference takes place in Philadelphia, and the American Library Association (ALA) is founded on the final day. *American Library Journal* begins publication. Charles Ammi Cutter's *Rules for a Printed Dictionary Catalog* is published. Melvil Dewey's Decimal Classification is published.

1877 Great Britain: The Library Association is formed at close of the International Conference of Librarians in London.

1879 United States: *Index Medicus*, the first comprehensive index to medical literature, is launched.

1881 Scotland: Andrew Carnegie makes his first gift of a public library building to Dunfermline, where he was born in 1835.

1882 Great Britain: The Library Association begins publishing *Monthly Notes*. After several title changes, it becomes *The Library Association Record* in 1899. **United States:** Charles Ammi Cutter completes the printed book catalog of the Boston Athenaeum. *Poole's Index to Periodical Literature* begins publication.

1883 Canada: The first free, tax-supported public libraries in the country are established in Guelph, St. John, and Toronto. **United States:** ALA issues its first catalog rules, *Condensed Rules for an Author and Title Catalog*.

1884 United States: Columbia College establishes the School of Library Economy and names Melvil Dewey as Professor of Library Economy.

1885 Great Britain: The Library Association organizes its first examinations.

1886 International: The Berne Convention for the Protection of Literary and Artistic Works establishes a uniform copyright law to replace the need to register for copyright separately in every country. **Germany:** The first professorship in librarianship is founded at Göttingen University. **United States:** Andrew Carnegie begins a program to fund library buildings.

1887 United States: Instruction begins at the Columbia College School of Library Economy. Minerva Sanders of the Pawtucket (Rhode Island) Public Library creates the first library space designated specifically for children.

1889 United States: The College Library Section (later Association of College and Research Libraries) is established, becoming the first type-of-library division of ALA. The School of Library Economy is moved to the New York State Library.

1890 United States: The first state library agency is created as a result of the passage of the Massachusetts Library Extension Act. In Brookline, Massachusetts, Mary Bean becomes the first public librarian to open a separate children's room within a library. The New York Library Association, the first of the state associations, is established. The second library-training program in the country opens at the Pratt Institute Free Library in Brooklyn, New York. The Cleveland (Ohio) Public Library becomes the first large urban public library to offer unrestricted access to its collection.

1891 France: The *Revue des bibliotheques*, a journal of librarianship, begins publication.

1892 Japan: The Japan Library Association, the third library association in the world, is founded. **United States:** A library school opens at the Drexel Institute in Philadelphia, Pennsylvania.

1893 Germany: Prussia establishes uniform regulations for library training. **Great Britain:** The Library Association publishes *Cataloguing Rules*. **United States:** The Library Bureau begins issuing printed catalog cards and standardizes their dimension. The Department of Library Economy opens at the Armour Institute of Technology in Chicago.

1894 United States: The earliest reported children's department in a US public library opens in Denver.

1895 Belgium: The International Federation for Information and Documentation is founded. **United States:** ALA publishes the first standard list for subject headings: *List of Subject Headings for Use in the Dictionary Catalogs*. Effie Lee Power becomes the first librarian hired specifically for children's services when she joins the staff of the Cleveland Public Library.

1896 Australia: The Library Association of Australia is established. **Austria:** The country's oldest library association, the Association of Austrian Librarians, is established. **United States:** The Library of Congress moves to a new building, which, at the time, is the largest library building in the world. The National Education Association establishes a Library Section, the first organization for school librarians. *Public Libraries* is launched to meet the needs of smaller public libraries in the Midwest.

1897 Great Britain: London hosts the second international librarians' conference. **Switzerland:** The Swiss Association of Libraries and Librarians is established.

1898 China: Library reform begins with the opening of the Metropolitan University Library in Beijing, the nation's first modern academic library. **United States:** The Medical Library Association is founded in Philadelphia.

1899 Germany: The cataloging code known as the Prussian Instructions is published. **United States:** Herbert Putnam is appointed as the first experienced librarian to hold the position of librarian of Congress. The Public Archives Commission is established.

1900 Canada: The first Canadian library association, the Ontario Library Association, is founded. **Germany:** The Association of German Librarians is established. **United States:** Edward C. Williams, the first college-trained African American librarian, graduates from the New York State Library School. The first high school librarian, Mary Kingsbury, is appointed in Brooklyn, New York. The Club of Children's Librarians is established and becomes ALA's Section for Library Work with Children a year later.

1901 United States: The Library of Congress begins to distribute its cataloging to libraries in the form of cards. The first volume of the Library of Congress Classification is published. H. W. Wilson launches *Reader's Guide to Periodical Literature.* The Pratt Institute adds a course for children's librarians to its school.

1902 Canada: The first Canadian children's library opens in St. Thomas, Ontario. **Great Britain:** The Library Association begins offering courses in collaboration with the London School of Economics. **United States:** The New York State Library School becomes the first library school to require a college degree for admittance.

1903 Japan: The Japan Library Association sponsors the first library training in the country. **United States:** Andrew Carnegie makes the first grant for library education, which establishes a library school at Western Reserve University in Cleveland, Ohio.

1904 Canada: The first library course in the country is offered at McGill University. **United States:** John Cotton Dana opens a business branch at the Free Public Library of Newark, New Jersey, introducing the concept of special libraries.

1905 Belgium: The Universal Decimal Classification by Henri LaFontaine and Paul Otlet of the International Institute of Bibliography is published in Brussels. **Denmark:** The country's first library association is established. **United States:** ALA launches a review journal: *Booklist.* The Western Colored Branch opens in Louisville, Kentucky, as the first public library branch for African Americans in any American city.

1906 France: The Association of French Librarians is established. **India:** The Maharaja of Baroda begins providing subsidies to village libraries, starting the free public library movement in that country. **United States:** The first master's degree in library science (MLS) is conferred at the New York State Library School. The American Association of Law Libraries is founded.

1907 United States: The American Chemical Society launches *Chemical Abstracts*, the first modern abstracting journal.

1908 International: The Anglo-American Cataloguing Code is published in an American edition (*Catalog Rules, Author and Title Entries*) and a British edition (*Cataloguing Rules, Author and Title Entries*). **Argentina:** The country's first congress of librarians is held in Buenos Aires and results in a summer training course. **Russia:** The Society for Librarianship, the first independent Russian library association, is founded. It is active until the Russian Revolution in 1917. **Scotland:** The Scottish Library Association is founded. It is affiliated with the Library Association in 1931 and reformed as the Chartered Institute of Library and Information Professionals in Scotland in 2002. **United States:** The *American Library Association Bulletin* replaces *Library Journal* as ALA's official organ.

1909 United States: The Library of Congress begins publishing Library of Congress Subject Headings, the list of subject headings used in its catalogs. The Special Libraries Association is organized.

1910 Finland: The Finnish Library Association is formed. **New Zealand:** The Libraries Association of New Zealand (now the Library and Information Association of New Zealand Aotearoa) is founded.

1911 Canada: The Ontario Department of Education organizes the Ontario Library School, the first training for librarians in Ontario. **France:** A series of lectures sponsored by the Association of French Librarians is the country's first library training program. **India:** The first formal training course for librarians in the country is organized in the state of Baroda. **Russia:** The first Russian Congress of Librarianship takes place. **United States:** Andrew Carnegie sets up the Carnegie Corporation to provide a corporate structure for his personal giving. The first legislation providing county library service is enacted in California.

1912 India: The first library journal, *Library Miscellany*, begins publication in the English and Gujarati languages. **Netherlands:** The Netherlands Association for Librarians (later the Netherlands Association for Library, Information, and Knowledge Professionals) is formed.

1913 Norway: The Norwegian Library Association is organized. **Russia:** The first library courses are offered at Shanyavsky University in Moscow. **United States:** ALA's Roundtable of Normal and High School Librarians, the precursor to the American Association of School Librarians, holds its first meeting.

1914 Germany: The country's first regularly organized library school opens. It is intended to train women for work in popular libraries. **India:** The Andhra Pradesh Library Association, the oldest library association in the country, is organized. **Philippines:** A library training program is offered at the University of the Philippines.

1915 Brazil: The National Library in Rio de Janeiro creates the first librarians' training course in Latin America. **India:** The first formal library course conducted in any university in Asia is started at Punjab University, Lahore. **Spain:** The government of Catalonia establishes a school for librarians based on the British model. **Sweden:** The Swedish Library Association is formed. **United States:** The Association of American Library Schools (later the Association for Library and Information Science Education) is established.

1916 Mexico: The Escuela Nacional de Bibliotecarios y Archiveros provides the first formal library training in that country.

1917 Poland: The Polish Librarians' Association is formed as the Union of Polish Librarians and Archivists. **United States:** ALA's Library War Service is formed. It distributes 10 million books and magazines to military men.

1918 Denmark: The first Danish library school is organized in Copenhagen. **United States**: The National Education Association adopts the nation's first standards for school libraries.

1919 Great Britain: The first full-time School of Librarianship is established at University College, London. **United States:** ALA adopts a Code of Practice for Interlibrary Loans. The earliest young adult service is established at the New York Public Library.

1920 China: The first formal library training program in the country is established at Boone College in Wuchang. **Sweden:** The Swedish Classification System is introduced. **United States:** Standards for high school libraries are adopted by ALA and the National Education Association.

1921 Belgium: The Flemish Association for Libraries, Archives, and Documentation Centers is established in Antwerp. **Japan:** The country's first library school, the Ueno Library School, opens. It becomes the National Junior College of Librarianship in 1964.

1922 Argentina: The first school of librarianship in Latin America and the Caribbean is established at the University of Buenos Aires. **Germany:** The Union of German Popular Librarians is established. **United States:** *The Story of Mankind* by Hendrik Willem van Loon is awarded the first Newbery Medal, given for the most distinguished contribution to children's literature.

1923 Estonia: The Estonian Librarians Association is established. **France:** The Paris Library School opens, offering the country's first program to train librarians in modern American methods. **Italy:** The first formal library training program in the country is established at the University of Bologna. **Latvia:** The Latvian Library Association is established. **Philippines:** The Philippine Library Association is formed. **United States:** Charles C. Williamson's report *Training for Library Service*, commissioned by the Carnegie Corporation to examine library education, is published. The *Sears List of Subject Headings*, designed for small libraries, is published.

1924 France: An American philanthropic group opens l'Heure Joyeuse, a children's library, in Paris. **Great Britain:** The Association of Special Libraries and Information Bureaux (ASLIB) is established. **Mexico:** The Mexican Association of Librarians is founded as the Association of Mexican Librarians. **South Africa**: Johannesburg Public Library begins training classes to prepare people for the British Library Association examinations. **United States:** ALA establishes the Board of Education for Librarianship (later the Committee on Accreditation).

1925 China: The Library Association of China is founded; it is reconstituted in Taipei in 1953. The Department of Library Science at Shanghai National University, the second formal educational institution of library science in China after Boone College, is established. **Poland:** Classes for training Polish public librarians are provided at the Free University of Warsaw. **United States:** ALA begins accrediting library training programs. ALA collaborates with the National Education Association to create the first set of standards for elementary school libraries. The Hampton Institute Library School, the first school established to train African American librarians, opens.

1926 Europe: The first Nordic library conference is held. **Sweden:** The Swedish State Library School opens.

1927 International: The International Federation of Library Associations (IFLA, now the International Federation of Library Associations and Institutions) is founded. **Canada:** McGill University in Quebec obtains ALA accreditation. **Czechoslovakia:** Librarianship classes are started at Charles University in Prague.

1928 Ireland: The Library Association of Ireland is formed. The School of Librarianship in University College Dublin is established. **Japan:** The Nippon Decimal Classification is introduced. **Poland:** The First Congress of Polish Librarians takes place. **South Africa:** The first national library conference is held. **United States:** The Graduate Library School of the University of Chicago opens.

1929 India: S. R. Ranganathan, head librarian at the University of Madras, introduces a training course in the Madras Library Association headquarters, leading to the establishment of the School of Library Science at Madras University.

1930 Italy: The Italian Libraries Association is founded. **Lithuania:** The First Congress of Baltic Librarians takes place in Riga. **South Africa:** The South African Library Association is founded. **United States:** The Graduate School of Library Science awards the first doctorate in library science. **Yugoslavia:** The Association of Librarians of Yugoslavia is founded. Following World War II, there are separate associations for each of the six republics.

1931 India: S. R. Ranganathan publishes his Five Laws of Library Science. **Italy:** The Vatican Code, which is the first new cataloging code since 1908 to reflect American cataloging practices, is issued. **Lithuania:** The Lithuanian Librarians' Association is established. **United States:** The Music Library Association is founded. The Graduate Library School's journal, the *Library Quarterly*, is launched.

1932 United States: The Association of Research Libraries is established.

1933 Germany: Some 25,000 books are burned by the Nazi German Student Association. **India:** The Indian Library Association is founded during the first All-India Library Conference. S. R. Ranganathan publishes the Colon Classification. **United States:** ALA issues the first formal standards for public libraries at the national level.

1934 Australia: The Carnegie Corporation of New York commissions *Australian Libraries: A Survey of Conditions and Suggestions for Improvement* (also known as the Munn-Pitt report). **Caribbean:** The publication of Ernest A. Savage's *The Libraries of Bermuda, the Bahamas, the British West Indies, British Guiana, British Honduras, Puerto Rico, and the American Virgin Islands: A Report to the Carnegie Corporation of New York* gives impetus to library development in the region. **Italy:** A library school opens at the Vatican. **United States:** The National Agricultural Library launches the Bibliofilm Service, which uses micrographic reproduction to distribute scientific articles on a large scale.

1935 Hungary: The Association of Hungarian Librarians is founded.

1936 Cuba: The first training course for librarians is offered at the Lyceum and Lawn Tennis Club in Havana. **Great Britain:** The Association of Children's Librarians is formed. It merges with the Library Association in 1945. **United States:** The Society of American Archivists is founded.

1937 Australia: The Australian Institute of Librarians (later the Australian Library and Information Association) is established. **Great Britain:** The School Library Association is organized. **United States:** The American Documentation Institute (later the American Society for Information Science and Technology) is established.

1938 Brazil: The Paulista Association of Librarians, the country's oldest library association, is founded. **Cuba:** A national assembly of librarians is held in Havana, and the first Cuban library association is formed as a result. **Iran:** The first short course in librarianship is conducted by the Ministry of Education. **South Africa:** The country's first university-based library science program is set up at the University of Pretoria. **United States:** The Library Service Section is set up under the Works Progress Administration's Division of Service Projects to coordinate library projects. H. W. Wilson begins printing catalog cards designed primarily for school and public libraries. *Animals of the Bible: A Picture Book*, with illustrations by Dorothy P. Lathrop and text selected by Helen Dean Fish, is awarded the first Caldecott Medal, given for the most distinguished picture book for children.

1939 United States: ALA adopts the Library Bill of Rights and also adopts its first official code of ethics.

1940 Brazil: A permanent library school is established in São Paulo. **Norway:** The Norwegian School of Librarians is established. **United States:** ALA establishes the Committee on Intellectual Freedom to Safeguard the Rights of Library Users to Freedom of Inquiry; the name is shortened to Committee on Intellectual Freedom in 1947. The first volume of the Bliss Bibliographic Classification, developed by Henry Bliss, is published.

1941 United States: Andrew D. Osborn describes a "crisis in cataloging" because of adherence to traditional practices and codes.

1942 Great Britain: The Library Association's *Public Library System in Great Britain* (also known as the McColvin report) is published. **Turkey:** The first continuous training courses for Turkish librarians are offered. **United States**: The Library of Congress catalog is printed in book form, called *A Catalogue of Books Represented by Library of Congress Printed Cards, 1898–1942*.

1944 Australia: The first examinations for librarianship in the country are administered. **Ghana**: The first library training in tropical Africa is offered at Achimota College in Accra.

1945 International: United Nations Educational, Scientific and Cultural Organization (UNESCO) is established. **Ecuador:** The Ecuadorian Library Association is established. **Finland:** A library training program is offered at the School of Social Sciences in Helsinki. **Jamaica:** Nora Bateson's *Library Plan for Jamaica* is published, resulting in the creation of the Jamaica Library Service in 1948. **Guatemala:** The Library Association of Guatemala is established. **Korea:** The Chosun Library Association (later the Korean Library Association) is formed. **Hungary:** The University of Budapest offers the country's first academic training program in library science. **Mexico:** The first permanent library school, the Escuela Nacional de Biblioteconomía y Archivonomía, opens. **United States:** *School Libraries for Today and Tomorrow*, the first library standards for K–12, is published. **Uruguay:** The Library Science Association of Uruguay is established.

1946 Canada: The Canadian Library Association is founded. **Cuba:** Formal teaching of library science begins with a summer course at the University of Havana. **Egypt:** The Egyptian Libraries and Information Association, the oldest library association in the Middle East, is established as the Cairo Library Association. **Korea:** The Chosun Library Association offers the country's first library-training course.

1947 Chile: A library school is set up at the University of Chile. **Scandinavia:** The Nordic Federation of Research Librarians is founded. **United States:** The Assembly of Librarians of the Americas, the first specifically international librarians' conference in the country, is held in Washington, D.C.

1948 Caribbean: The Eastern Caribbean Regional Library School is created in Trinidad and Tobago. **Croatia:** The Croatian Library Association is founded. **Great Britain:** The Royal Society Scientific Information Conference, the first international conference devoted to the subject of scientific information, is held in London. **Guatemala:** The Library Association of Guatemala is established. **India:** The Department of Library Science at the University of Delhi establishes the country's first postgraduate library science course. **United States:** The Welch Medical Library Indexing Project, one of the earliest attempts to use machine methods for searching scientific literature, commences at Johns Hopkins University.

1949 International: UNESCO adopts a Public Library Manifesto. **Costa Rica:** The Library Association of Costa Rica is established. **Egypt:** The first institute for training librarians is organized in Cairo. **Hungary:** The first professional library science program is introduced at the University of Budapest. **Jamaica:** The Jamaica Library Association (later the Library and Information Association of Jamaica) is established. **Macedonia:** The Macedonian Library Association is established. **Spain:** The Association of Librarians, Archivists, and Archeologists is founded. **Turkey:** The Turkish Librarians' Association is founded. **United States**: The "twin codes" of cataloging (*Cataloging Rules for Author and Title Entries* and *Rules for Descriptive Cataloging in the Library of Congress*) are published. The Midwest Inter-Library Center, later called the Center for Research Libraries, is established.

1950 International: The first international conference on national bibliographic services is sponsored by UNESCO. **Bulgaria:** Library training begins at the State Institute of Library Studies. **Canada:** The University of Toronto introduces the country's first program leading to the MLS degree. **Great Britain:** The Standing Conference of National and University Libraries is established. **United States:** *The Public Library in the United States*, the general report of the Public Library Inquiry, is published.

1951 International: The International Association of Music Libraries (later the International Association of Music Libraries, Archives, and Documentation Centers) is established. **Brazil:** The Public Municipal Library of São Paulo hosts a conference on public library development in Latin America, sponsored by UNESCO and the Organization of American States. **Egypt:** The Institute of Librarianship and Archives at Cairo University, the first library school in the Arab world, is established. **Ghana:** The British Council creates the Ghana Library Board, the first public library service to black Africa. **India:** The Delhi Public Library, UNESCO's first pilot library project, is established. The University of Delhi becomes the first university in the British Commonwealth to offer a PhD in library science. **Japan:** The Japan Library School, the country's first comprehensive university-level library training program, is instituted. **Panama:** The Panamanian Association of Librarians is established. **Thailand:** Chulalongkorn University starts an undergraduate library science program. **United States**: ALA adopts new library education standards limiting accreditation to programs that grant master's degrees.

1952 Indonesia: The government sets up the Djakarta Library School.

1953 Africa: UNESCO sponsors the International Seminar on the Development of Public Libraries in Africa, held in Ibadan, Nigeria. **Argentina:** The Association of Graduate Librarians of the Argentine Republic is established. **Bulgaria:** Sofia University institutes a library science and bibliography program. **Korea, Democratic People's Republic:** The Library Association of the Democratic People's Republic of Korea is established. **Sweden:** The first Anglo-Scandinavian Public Library Conference is held. **United States:** ALA and the American Book Publishers Council publish the Freedom to Read Statement. Seymour Lubetzky's *Cataloging Rules and Principles*, a major contribution to cataloging theory, is published.

1954 Africa: The West African Library Association (WALA), the first library association in black Africa, comes into being. In 1962, WALA splits into separate organizations: the Nigerian Library Association and the Ghana Library Association. **Indonesia:** A library association is established. **Thailand:** The Thai Library Association is founded. **Turkey:** The first full-fledged library school in the Near and Middle East is established at Ankara University. **Venezuela:** A library association is launched.

1955 International: The International Association of Agricultural Librarians and Documentalists is founded. **Singapore:** The Malayan Library Group is formed. In 1965, it is divided into two organizations: the Librarians Association of Malaysia and the Library Association of Singapore. **Taiwan:** National Taiwan Normal University initiates a library training program. **United States:** The School Library Bill of Rights is issued by ALA. The School of Library Science at Western Reserve University in Cleveland, Ohio, establishes the Center for Documentation and Communication Research, the first information science research organization to be affiliated with an American library school.

1956 Bangladesh: A library association is founded. **Colombia:** The Inter-American Library School at the University of Antioquia in Medellín is started. The Colombian Association of Librarians is established. **Denmark:** The Royal School of Library and Information Science is founded. **Iceland:** Courses for library students are begun at the University of Iceland. **Israel:** The Graduate Library School of the Hebrew University in Jerusalem is established. **Pakistan:** Karachi University starts a diploma course in library science. **United States:** Passage of the Library Services Act inaugurates a wave of federal funding programs for libraries. The Ford Foundation establishes the Council on Library Resources. The first Seminar on the Acquisitions of Latin American Library Materials is held in Florida.

1957 Europe: The Scandia Plan, the first cooperative acquisitions plan for a group of countries, is launched. **Great Britain:** The first International Study Conference on Classification for Information Retrieval is held. **Kenya:** The East African Library Association is formed. **Korea:** Yonsei University begins the first full-fledged education program for librarianship. **Mexico:** The First Mexican Conference of Librarianship, Bibliography, and Exchange is held. **Nigeria:** A UNESCO-sponsored pilot public library project is launched in Enugu, Eastern Nigeria. **Pakistan:** The Pakistan Library Association is founded. **Senegal:** The first Francophone library association in Africa is organized.

1958 Bangladesh: A library science department is founded at Dhaka University. **Great Britain:** A group of professionals working primarily in scientific and technical research breaks off from the Library Association to form the Institute of Information Scientists. **Hong Kong:** The Hong Kong Library Association is formed.

1959 Arab countries: UNESCO's Regional Seminar on the Development of Libraries in Arabic-Speaking Countries is held in Beirut. **Brazil:** The Brazilian Federation of Library Associations is established. **Vietnam:** The Vietnam Library Association is founded but survives for just a few years. **United States:** ALA adopts *Standards for College Libraries.*

1960 Africa: The Hockey report, written by British Council librarian S. W. Hockey, provides a blueprint for library development in East Africa. **Asia:** UNESCO sponsors a Regional Seminar on Library Development in South Asia, held in Delhi. **Australia:** The first full-time school of librarianship opens at the University of New South Wales. **Ceylon:** The Ceylon Library Association (later the Sri Lanka Library Association) is established. **Iceland:** The Icelandic Library Association is established.**Lebanon:** The Lebanese Library Association is established. **Nigeria:** The first full-scale professional library school in tropical Africa is created at the University of Ibadan. **Trinidad and Tobago:** The Library Association of Trinidad and Tobago is started.

1961 International: IFLA sponsors the International Conference on Cataloguing Principles in Paris to try to achieve some agreement on cataloging rules. The outcome is a statement of 12 principles known as the Paris Principles. **Denmark:** The first Afro-Scandinavian Conference is held in Copenhagen. **Greece:** The first library training in the country takes place at the Young Women's Christian Association in Athens. **Paraguay:** The Association of Librarians of Paraguay is established. **Vietnam:** Hanoi Cultural University, the first university to offer library education in Vietnam, opens.

1962 Africa: UNESCO sponsors the Regional Seminar on the Development of Public Libraries in Africa at Enugu, Eastern Nigeria. **Arab countries:** UNESCO sponsors the Regional Seminar on Bibliography, Documentation, and the Exchange of Publications in Arabic-Speaking States. **Cyprus:** A library association is established. **Lebanon:** The American University Library in Beirut organizes a library course that is attended by students from Lebanon, Jordan, Kuwait, and Saudi Arabia. **United States:** Library 21, the ALA exhibit at the Seattle World's Fair, features a state-of-the-art UNIVAC Solid State 90 computer programmed to print out a portion of electronically stored text entered from a printed reference book.

1963 Cuba: *Bibliotecas*, the oldest library and information science (LIS) journal in Latin America, begins publication. **Great Britain:** The second university-based library school in the country, the University of Sheffield Postgraduate School of Librarianship, opens. **Guyana:** The Guyana Library Association is formed. **Jordan:** The Jordan Library Association is created. **Saudi Arabia:** The first university library in the Arab Gulf region is established at King Fahd University of Petroleum and Minerals. **Senegal:** The Librarian Training Center for Francophone Countries opens in Dakar. **Uganda:** The East African School of Librarianship is established at Makerere University.

1964 Africa: The Standing Conference of African University Librarians is established. In 1971–1972, it becomes two separate organizations, the Standing Conference of African University Librarians, Eastern Area, and the Standing Conference of African University Libraries, Western Area. **Ivory Coast:** UNESCO establishes a pilot public library in Abidjan. **Korea:** The Korean Library Association compiles the Korean Decimal Classification. **United States:** The National Library of Medicine launches MEDLARS, the first large-scale, computer-based retrospective search service available to the public. The University of Pittsburgh's library science program becomes the Graduate School of Library and Information Sciences.

1965 Nicaragua: The Nicaragua Association of Librarians (later the Nicaragua Association of Librarians and Related Professionals) is established. **Tunisia:** The Tunisian Association of Documentalists, Librarians, and Archivists is formed. **United States:** A conference is held at the Library of Congress to determine the requirements for a machine-readable record. The Library of Congress and the Association of Research Libraries hold a conference on the need for a national preservation program.

1966 Iran: A library association is established. A department of library science is organized at the University of Tehran. **United States:** The Library of Congress embarks on the National Program of Acquisitions and Cataloging, a worldwide acquisition and centralized national cataloging program. The first automated circulation system is installed at the Illinois State Library.

1967 International: The International Standard Book Number is introduced. *Anglo-American Cataloging Rules* (*AACR*) is published. **Africa:** The library associations of Zambia and Zimbabwe are created when the Library Association of Central Africa is dissolved. **Ethiopia:** A library association is founded. **Senegal:** The École de Bibliothécaires, Archivistes et Documentalistes opens in Dakar. **United States:** The Ohio College Library Center (OCLC, later called the Online Computer Library Center) is founded.

1968 Asia: UNESCO sponsors a Meeting of Experts on the National Planning of Library Services in Asia. **Barbados:** The Library Association of Barbados is established. **Greece:** The Greek Library Association is organized. **Iraq:** A library association is founded in Baghdad. **United States:** The Library of Congress begins publishing the *National Union Catalog of Pre-1965 Imprints*, which is completed in 1981.

1969 International: The International Meeting of Cataloging Experts is held in Copenhagen. **Asia:** The Asian-Pacific Conference on Libraries and International Development is held in Seoul, South Korea. **Caribbean:** The Association of Caribbean University, Research, and Institutional Libraries is established. **Chile:** The Chilean Library Association is established. **Great Britain:** The Birmingham Libraries Cooperative Mechanization Project, the first example of an automated library network in the nation, is created. **Malta:** The Malta Library and Information Association is established. **United States:** The Machine-Readable Cataloging (MARC) Distribution Service is launched by the Library of Congress.

1970 Asia: The Congress of Southeast Asian Librarians is formed by the library associations of Malaysia and Singapore. **Latin America:** The Latin American Association of Library and Information Science Schools is established. **Sierra Leone:** A library association is established. **United States:** The National Commission on Libraries and Information Science is created.

1971 International: IFLA adopts International Standard Bibliographic Description (ISBD) to facilitate international exchange of cataloging records. **Caribbean:** The first university-based library school in the region is established at the University of the West Indies. **Europe:** The League of European Research Libraries is founded. **Afghanistan:** The Afghanistan Library Association is established. **United States:** The National Library of Medicine launches MEDLARS Online (MEDLINE) as a selective resource for health professionals. The Alden Library at Ohio University becomes the first library in the world to perform online cataloging. Project Gutenberg, the first digital library, is founded.

1972 Fiji: The Fiji Library Association is established. **Liberia:** The first formal training for librarians is offered. **United States:** ALA's new *Standards for Accreditation* recognizes information science as an essential part of MLS programs.

1973 Great Britain: The British Library is established. **Papua New Guinea:** The Papua New Guinea Library Association is formed. Previously, it was a branch of the Library Association of Australia. **Portugal:** The Portuguese Association of Librarians, Archivists, and Documentalists is created.

1974 International: The Conference of Directors of National Libraries is established. IFLA adopts Universal Bibliographic Control. **Africa:** The Standing Conference of Eastern, Central, and Southern Africa Library and Information Associations is formed. **Arab countries:** UNESCO sponsors the Expert Meeting on the National Planning of Documentation and Library Services in Arab Countries, held in Cairo. **Cameroon:** The Cameroon Association of Librarians, Archivists, Documentalists, and Museum Curators is established. **Dominican Republic:** The Dominican Association of Librarians is founded. **Morocco:** The École des sciences de l'information is founded. **United States:** The Research Libraries Group is founded. It merges with OCLC in 2006.

1975 Asia: The library associations of Malaysia and Singapore sponsor a Conference on Universal Bibliographic Control in Southeast Asia.

1976 Belize: The Belize Library Association is founded. **Canada:** The Canadian Association of Research Libraries is established. **Germany:** A new cataloging code based on the Paris Principles is introduced. **Korea:** The Korean Library Association hosts a modified IFLA Worldwide Conference in 1976, the first time such a meeting is held in Asia.

1977 International: IFLA publishes the Universal MARC Format (UNIMARC) to facilitate the exchange of MARC records between national bibliographic agencies. **Gambia:** A library association is established. **Great Britain:** The British Library Automated Information Service, the country's first online bibliographical service, is introduced. **Liberia:** The Liberian Library Association is organized. **Malawi:** The Malawi Library Association is established.

1978 Botswana: The Botswana Library Association is established. **Lesotho:** The Lesotho Library Association is established. **Mali:** The Association of Librarians, Archivists, and Documentalists of Mali is established. **United States:** The second edition of *Anglo-American Cataloging Rules* (*AACR2*) is published.

1979 Botswana: A LIS department is established at the University of Botswana. **Canada:** The Alberta Alcoholism and Drug Abuse Commission becomes the first member of OCLC outside the United States. **China:** The Library Society of China is founded after the government gives its approval to the re-establishment of a library association. **Nepal:** The Nepal Library Association is established. **United States:** The first White House Conference on Libraries and Information Services is held. A second conference takes place in 1991.

1980 Philippines: The first IFLA conference to be held in a developing country takes place in Manila.

1981 Europe: OCLC Europe is established. **Gabon:** The Gabonese Librarians Association is formed. **United States:** The Library of Congress closes its card catalog.

1983 Antigua and Barbuda: The Library Association of Antigua and Barbuda is established. **Latin America:** The first complete Spanish print version of *AARC2* is published by the Organization of American States and the University of Costa Rica.

1984 Syria: The Libraries and Documents Association of Syria is established. **Swaziland:** The Swaziland Library Association is formed.

1985 Cuba: The Library Association of Cuba is established. **United States:** The National Science Foundation creates NSFNET, the first national academic network.

1986 Arab Countries: The Arab Federation for Libraries and Information is founded. **Brunei:** The National Library Association of Brunei is established.

1987 United States: ALA forms the Presidential Committee on Information Literacy to define the concept of information literacy and to design models for information literacy development.

1989 Germany: The International Society for Knowledge Organisation is founded at Frankfurt by Ingetraut Dahlberg. **Norway:** The world's first law concerning legal deposit of digital publications is passed. **United States:** The Association of Research Libraries publishes a study showing that, over the previous 10 years, serials expenditures in those libraries increased by around 140 percent. The University of Chicago Graduate Library School closes.

1990 Bulgaria: The Union of Librarians and Information Services Officers (later the Bulgarian Library and Information Association) is established. **Czech Republic:** The Association of Library and Information Professionals of the Czech Republic is established. **Namibia:** The Namibian Information Workers Association is established. **United States:** The Library of Congress launches the American Memory Project to make its collections available in digital form.

1991 Europe: The European Association for Library and Information Education and Research is founded as the representative of European LIS educational institutions. **Germany:** The German Library Association (East) and the German Library Association (West) unite as the German Library Association. **United States:** OCLC launches FirstSearch, designed to be used by both librarians and library patrons.

1992 International: UNESCO launches the Memory of the World project to preserve and provide access to the world's documentary heritage. **Europe:** The Consortium of European Research Libraries is organized. The European Bureau of Library, Information, and Documentation Associations is founded as an umbrella organization of national library, information, documentation, and archive associations in Europe. **France:** The École nationale supérieure des sciences de l'information et des bibliothèques is founded. **Myanmar:** The Myanmar Library Association is established. **New Zealand:** Te Rōpū Whakahau (the Māori Library and Information Workers' Association) is formed.

1993 Europe: The first BOBCATSSS Conference for LIS students and teachers in Europe is held in Hungary. **Albania:** The Albanian Library Association is established. **Italy:** A database of images is created for the Vatican Library. This is the first digital image library. **United States:** The Dewey Decimal Classification becomes available in electronic form.

1994 Armenia: The Armenian Library Association is established. **Finland:** The Helsinki Public Library becomes the first public library in the world to provide Internet service to its patrons. **Russia:** The Russian Library Association is formed.

1995 Europe: The Workshop on Education and Training of Information Specialists in Eastern Europe and CIS Countries is held in Bratislava. **Kazakhstan:** The Library Association of Kazakhstan is established. **Ukraine:** The Ukrainian Library Association is formed. **United States:** The Library of Congress establishes the Program for Cooperative Cataloging. JSTOR is founded as a not-for-profit organization whose mission is to create an archive of scholarly journal literature and to extend access to that archive as broadly as possible. The Metadata Workshop held at OCLC headquarters in Dublin, Ohio, defines a set of predefined properties for describing documents. These elements come to be known as the Dublin Core.

1996 International: The World Intellectual Property Organization (WIPO) Treaty is adopted. **Cambodia:** The Cambodian Librarians and Documentalists Association is established. **France:** The Bibliothèque nationale de France, called "the first library of the third millennium," is formally inaugurated. **United States:** ALA adds Access to Electronic Information, Services, and Networks to the Library Bill of Rights. The University of Michigan School of Information replaces the School of Library and Information Science.

1997 International: IFLA creates the Committee on Free Access to Information and Freedom of Expression to monitor intellectual freedom in libraries worldwide. **Great Britain:** The new British Library opens at St. Pancras,

London. It is the only major public building to be built in Britain in the 20th century. **South Africa:** The Library and Information Association of South Africa is founded, replacing several existing associations. **United States:** ALA launches the Spectrum Initiative to increase the diversity of the profession. The Gates Library Foundation is established to bring the Internet to libraries.

1998 International: IFLA publishes Functional Requirements for Bibliographic Records (FRBR). **United States:** The Digital Millennium Copyright Act is signed into law. The KALIPER (Kellogg-ALISE Information Professions and Education Renewal) Project, studying LIS education, begins; a report is published in 2000. The Association of Research Libraries develops the Scholarly Publishing and Academic Resources Coalition to promote open access to scholarship.

1999 International: IFLA and UNESCO adopt the School Library Manifesto. The MARC 21 format for bibliographic data is published jointly by the Library of Congress and the National Library of Canada. Electronic Information for Libraries is created as an initiative of the Open Society Institute to foster access to electronic resources in developing countries. **Azerbaijan:** The Azerbaijan Library Development Association is established. **New Zealand:** The first International Indigenous Librarians' Forum is held in Auckland.

2000 Sweden: The Swedish Library Association is founded as a result of a merger between two older groups.

2001 International: A conference sponsored by the Open Society Institute results in the Budapest Open Access Initiative. **Germany:** The migration from the German cataloging code to *AACR2* and MARC is announced. **Singapore:** The National Library Board of Singapore opens a "Totally Do-It-Yourself" library, which is run without staff but is meant to provide the same level of service as libraries with staff on-site. **United States:** Congress passes the USA Patriot Act, which allows for the seizure of library records for foreign intelligence and international terrorism investigations.

2002 International: IFLA adopts the Glasgow Declaration on Libraries, Information Services, and Intellectual Freedom. **Arab countries:** The new Library of Alexandria, the Bibliotheca Alexandrina, opens. **Europe:** The National Authority on Public Libraries in Europe is formed. **Great Britain:** The Library Association and the Institute of Information Scientists merge to form the Chartered Institute of Library and Information Professionals (CILIP).

2003 International: UNESCO adopts an Internet Manifesto prepared by IFLA. IFLA sponsors the first Meeting of Experts on an International Cataloguing Code. **Japan:** The Library and Information Professions and Education Renewal project to analyze library training is initiated. **United States:** The Supreme Court rules that the Children's Internet Protection Act, which requires libraries and schools to install Internet filters in order to retain federal funding, is not unconstitutional.

2004 Canada: The National Library of Canada is merged with the National Archives of Canada to form Library and Archives Canada. **United States:** Google announces its Book Search Library Project, with five library partners: Oxford University, Harvard University, the New York Public Library, Stanford University, and the University of Michigan.

2005 Europe: The European Library, a digital library for all of Europe, is launched. **United States:** The first iSchool conference is held at the University of Pennsylvania.

2006 Asia: The first Asia-Pacific Conference on Library and Information Education and Practice is held in Singapore. **Germany:** The Berlin School of Library and Information Science becomes the first German iSchool. **United States:** OCLC launches *WorldCat*, an international database of library holdings.

2007 Laos: The Laos Library Association is established.

2008 International: UNESCO adopts the Multicultural Library Manifesto prepared by IFLA. **Europe:** Europeana, a portal which aggregates information from European archives, libraries, museums, and audiovisual collections, is launched. **United States:** The University of Washington enters the 100 millionth bibliographic record in *WorldCat*.

2009 International: UNESCO and the Library of Congress launch the World Digital Library. The IFLA Statement of International Cataloguing Principles replaces the Paris Principles.

2010 Egypt: The Bibliotheca Alexandrina launches the Arabic Digital Library. **United States:** *RDA: Resource Description and Access* succeeds *AACR2*. The first completely bookless bricks-and-mortar library opens: the Applied Engineering and Technology Library, University of Texas at San Antonio.

2011 International: UNESCO endorses the Manifesto on Digital Libraries, which was published by IFLA in 2007. **Sweden:** Libraries begin converting from the Swedish classification scheme to Dewey Decimal Classification.

2012 Caribbean: The Dutch Caribbean Libraries Association holds its inaugural meeting in Suriname. **United States:** The New York Public Library undertakes a central branch renovation that involves moving more than two million volumes to an off-site location.

2013 Great Britain: The largest public library in Europe opens in Birmingham. **Italy:** The Vatican Library's collection of 82,000 manuscripts goes online. **United States:** The Digital Public Library of America is launched. BiblioTech, a public library offering only electronic books, opens in Bexar County, Texas.

Introduction

In the history of librarianship, 1876 was a pivotal year. The world's first association for librarians, the American Library Association (ALA), was organized, giving librarianship a formal structure, and its official journal, *American Library Journal*, provided a forum for the exchange of ideas. The precepts of emerging library practice were documented in a special report on public libraries, issued by the United States Bureau of Education. Melvil Dewey, who was a force behind ALA's founding (and whose decimal classification system also appeared in 1876), wrote in the first issue of *American Library Journal*:

> The time has at last come when a librarian may, without assumption, speak of his occupation as a profession. And, more, a better time has come—perhaps we should say is coming, for it still has many fields to conquer. The best librarians are no longer men of merely negative virtues. They are positive, aggressive characters, standing in the front rank of their communities, side by side with the preachers and the teachers. . . . The time *was* when a library was very like a museum, and a librarian was a mouser in musty books, and visitors looked with curious eyes at ancient tomes and manuscripts. The time *is* when a library is a school, and the librarian is in the highest sense a teacher, and the visitor is a reader among the books as a workman among his tools. Will any man deny to the high calling of such a librarianship the title of profession?[1]

The notion of a librarian as being simply a custodian of books was being replaced by the modern notion of a librarian as doer, and not just in the minds of the *American Library Journal*'s editorial staff. Reporting on the 12th annual ALA Conference in 1890, the *New York Times* noted that "the old idea, that any person with a liking for books, who is too unpractical or lazy to be put into any other place, is just good enough to be put in charge of the public's reading matter, is fast vanishing. The librarian of today must, besides his familiarity with books, be wide awake and 'up with the times.'"[2]

Librarianship had entered a new era, and in the United States and Great Britain during the late 19th and early 20th centuries, it passed through all the important steps that mark the development of a profession—the founding of not only the first national association and the first national-level journal but also the first professional training, the first examinations and certification (in the case of Great Britain), the first university-based professional education program, and the first accreditation of schools. Similar events were repeated around the world, albeit at different rates and to different degrees. Yet, although 1876 might be considered to mark the start of librarianship as an organized profession, the history of libraries is much older, and people have been engaged in pursuits that we recognize as librarianship for many thousands of years.

LIBRARIANSHIP IN THE ANCIENT WORLD

The first libraries were repositories for the clay tablets on which people recorded data in the ancient Near East. Rooms to store the tablets created for religious or administrative purposes existed in the temples and palaces of Mesopotamia starting in the early third millennium BCE. Among the largest archives were those found in the ruins of the royal palace at Ebla, in what is now Syria. The Ebla archives contained around 17,000 tablets. Most of them were inscribed with commercial records, but there were also tablets containing contracts; correspondence; hymns and incantations; lists arranged by subject, such as birds and fish; and bilingual dictionaries. The tablets were stored on wooden shelves that collapsed during a fire around 2200 BCE. At Sippar, a Babylonian site just south of Baghdad, Iraqi archaeologists discovered a temple library containing literary works, dictionaries, prayers, omens, incantations, astronomical records, and more, all still arranged on shelves. Substantial collections of tablets have also been discovered at other sites. In addition to providing evidence of libraries, excavations have revealed developments in library management and organization. Preservation methods included keeping tablets in underground rooms or in clay containers or wooden chests. The most primitive catalogs were simply lists identifying each tablet by its incipit (first few words of text), but later listings contained bibliographical details such as the number of tablets on which a book was contained, the incipit, a brief description, and the name of the author. Individuals identified as "masters of the book" or "keepers of the book" or "keepers of the tablet," among other variations, were responsible for the records and must have received the same rigorous training as the scribes. Their specific duties are unknown, however.

The palace library established by Ashurbanipal (ca. 668–630 BCE) at Nineveh was one of the largest in the ancient world and the first one that has been documented as being systematically assembled and organized. Ashurbanipal's agents traveled throughout Assyria and even into foreign lands to gather written records. The library contained not only administrative and legal records but also divinatory, lexical, literary, magical, and medical texts, many translated into Assyrian from their original languages. The collection was arranged by subject matter in different rooms, and each room had a tablet near the door that listed the general contents. The tablets themselves were kept on shelves in earthen jars. Each tablet had a tag indicating the jar, shelf, and room where it belonged. More than 30,000 cuneiform tablets and fragments from the library survive, most of them housed at the British Museum or the Iraq Department of Antiquities.

The papyrus employed by the ancient Egyptians for recording information was much more fragile than clay, so the existence of ancient Egyptian libraries is based solely on textual or archaeological sources. Houses of Life, which were attached to temples throughout Egypt, functioned as libraries in that they were the places where sacred texts were stored. Some lists of titles have been found inscribed on temple walls. The largest House of Life, built by Rameses II around 1300 BCE, was said to have held some 10,000 scrolls. The scribes of the Houses of Life were expected to be learned men, and their duties may have included writing, copying, and authenticating documents.

Libraries were in existence in Greek-speaking countries as early as the sixth century BCE. The famous library of Aristotle, who is often considered to be the first large-scale book collector in the West, was just one of numerous private libraries in Athens. Inscriptions and excavations show that there were public libraries in cities throughout the Hellenistic world. Libraries were often part of the gymnasia that served as centers for social and intellectual pursuits as well as training centers for participants in public games. Perhaps the best-known library from antiquity is the Alexandrian Library, which was established in Alexandria, Egypt, in the third century BCE. The library may have been started at the suggestion of the Greek scholar Demetrius of Phalerum, who was familiar with the school founded in Athens by Aristotle. Under the first two Ptolemies, the Alexandrian Library became the main center of scholarly work in the Greco-Roman world. The library was public in the sense that it was open for use, but only by an elite group of scholars. The directors of the library were themselves well-known scholars, beginning with Zenodotos of Ephesus.

Callimachus of Cyrene, a poet who worked in the Alexandrian library from around 260 BCE until his death in 240 BCE, compiled a classified subject listing entitled *Tables of Persons Eminent in Every Branch of Learning, Together with a List of Their Writings*. The list is better known as the *Pinakes*, possibly named after the tablets that contained bibliographic information about the rolls of papyrus stored in the library. Callimachus divided works into a number of classes, first poetry and prose, and then smaller categories, such as dramatic poets, lyric poets, philosophers, orators, and so on. Within these categories or tables, works were arranged alphabetically by author. For each author, brief biographical information was provided. Some critical and historical remarks were also included. This was followed by a list of the author's works in alphabetical order. The *Pinakes* has been called the first catalog (and Callimachus is sometimes referred to as the first cataloger), although it is not clear whether the *Pinakes* was actually a catalog of library holdings or a bibliography of Greek literature based on library holdings. In either case, it seems to have occupied 120 scrolls, although only a few excerpts survive. By the beginning of the second century BCE, there were other comprehensive libraries, including one at the Temple of Athena at Pergamum. In purpose and design it may have been modeled on the library at Alexandria, and it was said to have contained 200,000 papyrus rolls in 32 BCE.

In Rome, private libraries were considered an important part of civilized life. Seneca wrote that a library ranked with a bathroom as a necessary ornament of a home. Cicero, who declared that if a person had a garden and a library he had everything he needed, had a permanent library in each of his 18 villas in Italy. Educated slaves often served as librarians; Cicero's librarian, Tyrannion, was a slave until he was able to buy his freedom.

Among the civic monuments in Rome and in the provincial cities were public libraries that were built by wealthy donors to celebrate their own success. Julius Caesar planned to build a public library in Rome that would rival the one in Alexandria, and he enlisted the scholar Marcus Terentius Varro to gather materials for a library that would house as complete a collection as possible of Greek and Latin texts. Though the project came to an end with Caesar's death, plans for a public library were later brought to fruition by writer and politician Gaius Asinius Pollio, who formed a library in the Temple of Liberty on the Aventine Hill and opened it to the public in 37 BCE. The library had two sections, one for works in Greek and one for works in Latin. After he became emperor, Augustus built two more libraries along the same lines, using men who had been trained in the Greek East to organize them. The precedent Augustus created for imperial patronage of public libraries was followed by subsequent rulers, and by the fourth century CE, there may have been as many as 29 public libraries in Rome. Emperor Claudius formalized library administration under an official of the imperial civil service. The titles held by the staff of each library would include *bibliothecarius*, or librarian; *librarius*, whose duties might include cataloging, copying, restoring texts, and translating; and *vilicus*, who might be a clerk or custodian.

The only surviving library of the classical era is the private library of more than 2,000 scrolls discovered in the ruins of the Villa of the Papyri in Herculaneum, which was buried when Vesuvius erupted in 79 CE. Although the scrolls, which contain mostly Greek philosophical works, were badly charred (early excavators thought they were lumps of charcoal), they were not destroyed. The fact that someone may have been in the process of moving the scrolls to safety has led to speculation that the house's main library has yet to be discovered.

The scroll was the dominant form of book in the ancient world, but both the Greeks and Romans used wooden tablets for short documents. The Romans are often credited with inventing the codex, beginning with sheets of papyrus or parchment that were bound together to form personal notebooks. The earliest evidence for the use of the codex for a literary work appears in the writings of the poet Martial in the first century CE. The codex had a number of advantages for libraries. Whereas several scrolls were often required for a longer work, in codex form the work could be contained in a single volume. The codex was more durable, easier to transport, and easier to store. The codex had a spine, on which information about a work could be written; and, eventually, the codex had page numbers, which made it easier to find information within the work. Gradually, the codex replaced the scroll in the West, and between the fourth and the eighth centuries, many works were converted to codex from scroll.

Around 378, Ammianus Marcellinus wrote that the libraries of Rome were like tombs, forever closed. As the Roman Empire disintegrated, scholarly institutions such as libraries disappeared. The establishment and development of libraries outside Western Europe continued, although information about them is scarce. Constantinople had three great libraries: the Imperial library founded by Constantine between 330 and 336; the library of the Academy, a university founded in the fifth century; and the library of the Patriarch, which housed theological materials. The fortunes of all of these libraries fluctuated over the centuries until the destruction that was caused first by the Crusaders in 1204 and then by the Turks in 1453.

The earliest evidence of organized libraries in China dates to the seventh century BCE. References to an imperial library began to appear during the Han dynasty, which ruled from 206 BCE to 220 CE. The first catalog of the imperial collection was created in the first century BCE by Liu Hsiang, and the first Chinese classification system was created by his son, Liu Hsin. The invention of paper is traditionally attributed to the Chinese in the early part of the second century BCE. From China, paper traveled west in the eighth century to the Arabs, who then introduced it to Europe.

LIBRARIES IN THE MIDDLE AGES

In medieval Europe, it was primarily the monasteries that undertook scholarly activity and maintained what might be termed libraries. Two important sixth-century developments laid the foundation for monastic libraries in the West. Flavius Aurelius Cassiodorus, a retired civil servant, founded a monastery at Vivarium in southern Italy. There, he established a library and encouraged his monks to cultivate learning and to study the classics. He also instructed the monks about how to handle, copy, correct, and repair manuscripts in order to preserve texts. Cassiodorus's contemporary, Benedict of Nursia, founded the Benedictine monastic order and laid down rules that called for each monk to spend part of the day reading religious texts. For this, the monks needed books and a place to store them. Cassiodorus and Benedict set a pattern for the medieval library and scriptorium that would endure until the Renaissance.

Monastery libraries might simply be book presses or chests; a common word for library was *armarium*, which referred to the chest. Separate rooms for libraries did not appear regularly until the 14th century. There are some documents describing the duties of the monk in charge of the library, but there is nothing to suggest that anyone was specially trained for the job. The role of the monk who served as librarian was not a complicated one. Once a year, the librarian read aloud from a list the titles of all the books that had been lent in the previous year and the names of the monks who had borrowed them. The monks would then return the books and be provided with new ones. If not all the books on the librarian's list were accounted for, a search would be made. A monk was required to borrow and read just one book a year. Collections were small, ranging from a few dozen to several hundred volumes. Collections of more than 1,000 books were rare. Libraries expanded their collections and replaced defective books through copying, and it was not unusual for books to be loaned for that purpose, even between libraries that were far apart. Catalogs, which date from the ninth century, were inventory lists written on sheets of parchment. To deter theft, books were often chained to desks, lecterns, or shelves. Chained libraries were fairly common into the 18th century, long after the invention of printing made books less rare, and a few chained libraries still exist. The library at Hereford Cathedral in England, built in 1611, is one of the largest surviving examples, with all its chains, rods, and locks intact.

The great age of monastic libraries and scriptoria lasted from the eighth until the 12th centuries. Monasteries were not the only places where one might find a library, however. The Irish scholar Alcuin, who was the librarian of the cathedral library in York, helped Charlemagne establish an extensive court library at Aachen in the eighth century, and some small private libraries existed as well. Libraries could also be found in the schools that were attached to cathedrals in cities such as Canterbury in England and Notre Dame in France. With the revival of urban and commercial life in the 12th century, cathedral schools began to supplant the often geographically remote monasteries as intellectual centers, and book production began to pass into the hands of lay scribes and book dealers. The pace of library development quickened, fuelled by a growing interest in secular learning, the manufacture of cheaper and more portable books, and the rise of the universities. The earliest of these was created when a charter was granted to a group of students and teachers in Bologna, Italy, in 1158. By 1300, there were almost 20 universities in Western Europe. Few of them started out with libraries. Instead, small collections might be found in individual colleges or faculties. Perhaps the first central university library was the one established at the Sorbonne at the University of Paris. In 1257, French theologian Robert de Sorbon founded the Collège de Sorbonne for instructing theology students, and the college received his collection of manuscripts when he died in 1274. By 1290, the collection contained more than 1,000 volumes. The most important works were kept chained in a room that was open for use, while other, less important works were kept in another room and were allowed to circulate. The library's catalog listed holdings in a hierarchical subject arrangement, from the most important category, scripture, to the least important, the liberal arts.

Another notable medieval university library, the library at Oxford University, began as a collection of books that were stored in chests. The chests were replaced by a room built above a church early in the 14th century by Thomas Cobham, the Bishop of Worcester. A chaplain was appointed to take care of the library and say prayers for Cobham's soul. In the 15th century, the university decided that new, larger quarters were needed in order to house the sizeable collection of manuscripts donated by Humfrey, Duke of Gloucester. All of the manuscripts were gone and the bookshelves sold by the mid-1550s, but Duke Humfrey's library was refurbished by Thomas Bodley, starting in 1598, to create the Bodleian Library.

By 1500, there were more than 75 universities in Western Europe. Their libraries represented a shift away from the monastic function of copying and preserving manuscripts and toward a new emphasis on supporting study and research. This shift occurred at about the same time as the revival of interest in ancient Greek and Roman literature that helped to ignite the Renaissance. A few free town libraries also made their appearance in England, France, and Germany. The world's oldest national library, France's Bibliothèque nationale, had its roots in the 14th century, when King Charles V established a royal library. Although the manuscripts inherited by the king provided the library's foundation, he enlarged the collection and made it accessible to all of the members of his court. Many of its more than 1,200 volumes were in French.

Outside Western Europe, libraries flourished in the Muslim world after the Arab conquest and were commonplace in mosques, royal palaces, and homes. Bayt al-Hikmah, or the House of Wisdom, was established in Baghdad in the ninth century to house the caliph's growing collection of Greek, Persian, and Sanskrit texts. In addition to being a depository for books, it became a center for translation and scholarly research. Similar institutions sprang up in other cities. Cairo's Dar al-Hikmah (House of Knowledge), founded in 1005, was said to have had 600,000 volumes in its library. The library established in Cordoba, Spain, in the 10th century was reported to have had around 400,000 volumes and a staff of 500. Many of the libraries in the Muslim world were destroyed by Christian crusaders beginning in the 11th century, or during the Mongol raids in the 13th century.

Further east, libraries were a feature of Buddhist monasteries in China, India, and Japan. Sacred texts were stored in sutra repositories, or revolving cabinets, until stitched books began to replace scrolls around 972. These books required different library housing and were often stored in large wooden chests. Libraries sometimes included living quarters for librarians and their assistants.

GREAT LIBRARIES OF THE RENAISSANCE

During the Renaissance, new libraries were created as a result of the efforts of humanist scholars to seek out and acquire classical manuscripts, many of which moldered in once-distinguished monasteries. One of the most active book hunters, Poggio Bracciolini, visited the famous monastery of St. Gall in Switzerland in 1416 and found books confined to a dungeon and covered with dust and filth. One of the earliest collectors was Petrarch, who conceived the idea of donating his manuscripts to the Republic of Venice in order to make them available for public use. Petrarch's plan was never realized, however, and it was left to Cosimo de' Medici to become the first great library founder of the Renaissance. The collection amassed by Florentine bookseller Niccolò di' Niccoli served as the foundation for the San Marco Library, which opened under Cosimo's sponsorship in a Dominican convent in 1444. The library was the first architectural space designed for the use and study of books. It was also the first public library in Florence. (It is sometimes called the first public library in modern Europe as well, but the same claim is made about other libraries.) The San Marco Library contained the most comprehensive collection of Latin and Greek classical authors available in Italy at the time. Another avid book collector, Tommaso Parentucelli, acted as Cosimo's librarian, cataloging the collection and drawing up a book selection guide that served as a model for other bibliophiles. The contents of the San Marco Library were combined with the Medici's private library to form the Biblioteca Laurenziana, which opened in 1571 in a building designed by Michelangelo.

The acquisition of books was part of a program to enhance a family's prestige, and a number of rulers in addition to the Medici established notable libraries. Federigo da Montefeltro, Duke of Urbino, established a scriptorium which employed several dozen scribes to copy all the known works in Latin, or in Greek translated into Latin. As his librarian, he employed Federigo

Veterani, whose duties included keeping the books arranged and easily accessible, protecting them from dampness and vermin as well as keeping them out of the hands of "ignorant, dirty, and tasteless persons," and courteously explaining the beauty of their handwriting and illustrations. Consisting of more than 1,000 manuscripts, the duke's library was bequeathed to the citizens of Urbino, but it became part of the Vatican Library in the 17th century. In Cesena, Prince Novello Malatesta created the Malatestiana, which opened in 1452. It is the oldest working library in the world still housed in its original building. The Biblioteca Marciana, the first civic library in Italy, was formed when the Greek scholar and churchman Basilios Bessarion gave his collection of several hundred manuscripts to the Republic of Venice in 1468.

When Tommaso Parentucelli became Pope Nicholas V in 1447, he decided to make his collection of Greek, Hebrew, and Latin manuscripts available for the "common convenience of the learned." The project was furthered by Pope Sixtus IV, who installed the collection in a newly restored suite of rooms and appointed Bartolmeo Platina in 1477 as the first formal Vatican librarian. By 1481, the Vatican Library contained around 3,500 volumes and was considered to be the largest library in the Western World.

Some of the men employed by the Medicis and others to furnish their libraries are described as librarians, but they had more expansive roles. They advised, traveled, negotiated, and searched everywhere for manuscripts, while organizing and supervising the work of copyists, translators, and illuminators. One example was Vespasiano da Basticci, who spent 14 years building the Duke of Urbino's collection. Vespasiano's business was to obtain manuscripts, have them transcribed, and sell the copies to collectors. He operated the largest manuscript-copying enterprise in Europe and counted Cosimo de' Medici among his customers. He also had a hand in building the Vatican Library collection, and he carried on a brisk trade in manuscripts with England, Germany, Hungary, and Portugal. His bookshop in Florence was a gathering place for many of the great humanists of the day. Like many of the great Renaissance collectors, Vespasiano was no lover of printed books. In his description of the Duke of Urbino's library, he wrote with satisfaction that the duke would have been ashamed to have a printed book in his collection. As the printed book began to supersede the manuscript, Vespasiono retired to write *Lives of Illustrious Men of the Fifteenth Century*, which provides brief biographies of a number of his distinguished clients.

North of the Alps, the Biblioteca Corviniana in Hungary was second only to the Vatican Library in terms of size. Its founder, Matthias Corvinus, who ruled Hungary and Croatia from 1458 to 1490, wanted his library to outshine that of every other monarch, and he employed copyists and purchasing agents in Italy and elsewhere to expand his collection. It has been estimated that the number of volumes in the library was probably between 2,000 and 2,500, including a few printed books. The library was neglected after the king's death, and the collection was later dispersed. The few books, called Corviniae, that still exist today are scattered in libraries around the world. In 2005, efforts began to create a digital reconstruction of the Corviniana collection as part of UNESCO's Memory of the World project.

LIBRARIES IN THE 16TH AND 17TH CENTURIES

The introduction of movable type in the 1450s brought new economies to the production of books, making them much more affordable and assuring a wide distribution not only of titles, but of multiple identical copies. As the number of books increased, their value diminished, so chaining was no longer necessary. New tools evolved to deal with the resulting flood of available knowledge. Swiss-born physician, botanist, linguist, and zoologist Conrad Gesner published what has been called the first modern bibliography, *Bibliotheca universalis*, beginning in 1545. *Bibliotheca universalis* was the first attempt to produce a comprehensive record of authors' works, and the first bibliography organized according to a system of classification. The first comprehensive catalog of the book trade was issued in Germany in 1564 in connection with the Frankfurt Book Fair. Andrew Maunsell, an English draper turned bookseller, published what is considered to be the first true national bibliography, *Catalogue of English Printed Bookes*, in 1595. Maunsell created his bibliography because he feared that many of the books that had been printed in England were in danger of being lost and forgotten.

Library collections grew more quickly following the invention of printing and required more specialized skills to organize and manage. In 1560, Florian Trefler, a German monk, published what may be the first treatise on library management, commenting in his introduction on the difficulty of finding books in a library that had no catalog. He devised a scheme of classification and call numbers, and recommended a catalog with five parts: an alphabetical author index, a shelf list, a classified subject index, an alphabetical index to the classes, and a list of books not shelved in the main collection. This was a considerable advance from the simple inventory list arranged by broad category.

Prominent men continued to build impressive collections. The libraries of a number of Renaissance princes fared better than the Corviniana, and several provided the foundation for national libraries. In France, the enactment in 1537 of history's first legal deposit legislation, requiring printers and booksellers to deposit with the royal librarian a copy of any book printed in the kingdom, was an important step in the transition of the royal library from private collection to national institution. The wording of the law makes clear the concern for safeguarding books that might otherwise be lost. In Vienna, the collection of manuscripts and books that the Hapsburgs had been amassing since the 13th century was turned into a well-organized institution by Dutch scholar Hugo Blotius, who was appointed as the first official librarian in 1575. The Bavarian court library (later the Bavarian State Library) in Munich, Germany, was founded in 1558 and was greatly expanded when Duke Albrecht V purchased the collection of bankrupt Augsburg merchant Johann Jakob Fugger in 1571. Fugger's collection numbered around 12,000 volumes, and his bankruptcy was caused in part by his passion for books.

Martin Luther was a supporter of libraries, and at his urging, municipal libraries appeared in a number of German towns. In Italy, the Biblioteca Angelica was established in 1605 when churchman Angelo Rocca gave his collection to the convent of the Augustins de Camerino to create a library accessible (twice daily except Thursdays) to anyone who wanted to use it. It is the oldest public library in Rome. The Biblioteca Ambrosiana was established in Milan by Cardinal Federico Borromeo, who wanted to create a library that would support the Counter-Reformation. To assemble the collection, the cardinal appealed to religious and secular leaders and monasteries for donations, and sent agents across Western Europe, Greece, and Syria to make purchases. The library opened in 1609 and was available to anyone capable of using the collection of 12,000 books and 9,000 manuscripts.

Cardinal Richelieu, King Louis XIII's chief minister, established a large library in Paris and appointed scholar and physician Gabriel Naudé as his librarian. Naudé made the Bibliothèque Mazarine into one of the most extensive and important private libraries in Europe, with a collection of 40,000 volumes. In 1643, the Mazarine was opened to the learned public, making it the first public library in France.

Naudé's views on how the library of a wealthy private collector should be assembled and organized were expressed in *Advis pour dresser une bibliothèque* (*Advice on Establishing a Library*), the first systematic, comprehensive treatise on librarianship, which was published in 1627. His first recommendation was to consult with other collectors and to acquire copies of the catalogs of other libraries. He suggested an encyclopedic approach to the selection of books, including works by all principal authors, ancient and modern, well-known or obscure, secular or religious. A variety of viewpoints should be represented, and controversial and esoteric subjects should not be ignored. In addition to books, libraries should collect dissertations, pamphlets, and manuscripts of classical authors preceding the invention of movable type. Libraries should be located away from noisy streets and should be well-lit, comfortably (but not expensively) furnished, and equipped with pens, paper, ink, and other useful supplies. The collection should be arranged under subjects that reflect the university curriculum and should be kept on open shelves. There should be two catalogs, one arranged by author and one arranged by subject. Finally, the librarian should be a learned and honorable person and should receive a decent salary.

Naudé was particularly impressed by the Bodleian Library, which opened at the University of Oxford in 1601 through the efforts of English statesman Thomas Bodley. A few years earlier, Bodley had offered to restore Oxford's old library quarters, which had fallen into disuse. He provided shelves and seats and also endowed the library with an annual income. The collection was built through donations and purchases on the continent, as well as through the arrangement Bodley made in 1610 with the Stationer's Company (the printers' guild), which brought into the library a copy of every book printed by a member of the company. The library was "public" in the sense that it was open to the graduates and faculty of any of the Oxford colleges. Undergraduates were barred.

In 1601, Bodley appointed a young scholar, Thomas James, as his library keeper. According to the job description provided in the library's statutes, the library keeper must be a graduate and a linguist, with no outside distractions (such as marriage). He was responsible for recording donations of books or money, arranging the holdings, preparing catalogs, and seeing that the books and other holdings were in good condition. He was to be on hand during service hours except for seven days off every quarter, when some other able graduate could fill in. An assistant should be capable of finding and issuing requested books. A servant was responsible for cleaning the books and the library. The keeper's post would be secure except in the case of heinous offense or gross insufficiency. Bodley's letters to James reveal further details about what was considered to be the library keeper's duty: identifying books to be purchased, preparing the catalog, making materials available to scholars, and preventing the development of mold in the books. James complained frequently about the workload but nevertheless stayed at the library until 1620. The Bodleian catalog of 1605 has been called the first printed general catalog of a public library, but it was essentially a shelf list. The catalog of 1620 was the first general library catalog that served primarily as a finding aid. Arranged in a single sequence by authors' surnames and by catchwords for anonymous works, it was a milestone in catalog arrangement.

That the library at Oxford played an important role in the advancement of learning was noted by Scottish clergyman John Dury in *The Reformed Librarie-Keeper* (1650), among the earliest books on library organization. Appointed as deputy keeper of the king's library after the overthrow of Charles I, Dury believed that librarians should be more than mere custodians. Instead, his ideal library keeper is busy cataloging the collection, corresponding and trading books with learned men in order to increase the collection, and meeting with the faculty. Libraries in colleges and universities were Dury's chief concern. Another clergyman, Thomas Bray, wanted to put reading in the hands of a broader group. In order to provide impecunious clergymen with the books they needed for their work, Bray solicited donations to establish 80 parochial lending libraries in England and Wales, many in rural areas. He also established 39 libraries in North America. The Bray libraries, which were meant to be used by the laity as well as by the clergy, have been called the first lending libraries. Yet another clergyman, James Kirkwood, proposed a different approach in *An Overture for Establishing Bibliothecks in Every Paroch throughout the Kingdom*, published in 1699. His idea was that parish libraries in Scotland should be supported by a tax on the ministers and landlords of the parishes. Kirkwood is sometimes called the father of free libraries. More than 70 small libraries were established in Scotland according to his plan, but they fell into disuse after his death in 1709.

While parish and church libraries were often the only providers of public access to books in rural areas, other libraries might be available to people living in towns. A small number of town libraries existed in England, France, and Germany before 1500, but more appeared following the Reformation. Some of these were municipal reference libraries formed for the purposes of administration. Others were endowed by individual benefactors or groups of benefactors. One of most important of the early English town libraries was Chetham's Library in Manchester, England, established in 1653 under the will of Humphrey Chetham, a prosperous wool merchant. A full-time librarian was appointed in 1656 at a salary of £10 a year plus food and accommodation. Chetham's Library was originally a chained reference library containing mostly theological books and intended for use by scholars, but it rapidly evolved into an institution similar to a public library, and, in fact, claims to be the oldest public library in the English-speaking world.

Across the Atlantic, libraries were established by religious institutions in Latin America beginning in the 16th century. In Canada, the Collèges des Jésuites de Québec opened the first college library in North America in 1635. The first library in the American colonies, Harvard College Library, was established in 1638.

LIBRARIES FROM 1700 TO 1850

In the 18th century, noted scholars were appointed to oversee court libraries such as the one at Wolfenbüttel, which was the seat of the court of the Duchy of Brunswick in Germany. This library was first set up in 1572 and had grown to around 135,000 volumes by 1666, the year it was opened to the public. Although he is better known as a philosopher, Gottfried Wilhelm Leibniz was employed as the library's director from 1690 to 1716. When the library needed new quarters, Leibniz designed one of the first freestanding, purpose-built library buildings. He also emphasized the importance of a fixed budget and careful cataloging.

Germany was also the home of the most important of the new universities founded during the Enlightenment. The University of Göttingen, which opened in 1737, was the first university to be conceived of as a research university rather than as a teaching institute. The university library was meant to serve working scholars by acquiring the books that scholars were most likely to need and instituting liberal policies for their use. The collection began with the donation of a 9,000-volume private library and had reached more than 200,000 volumes by the time American scholars visited it early in the 19th century. The Harvard College library held only around 30,000 volumes at the time.

The rise of national libraries in Europe corresponded with the growth of secular monarchies and nationalism. The British Museum was formed in 1753 when several important private collections were merged. The Imperial Public Library, now the Russian National Library, was founded in St. Petersburg in 1795. More than 20 countries, most of them in Europe, had national libraries by 1800. The earliest South American national libraries were established in Colombia in 1777 and in Ecuador in 1792. Almost all of the countries in Europe and Latin America had national libraries by end of the 19th century. In the United States, the Library of Congress, which is regarded as the national library, was created in 1801. The oldest national library in the world, the French royal library, became the Bibliothèque nationale during the French Revolution.

With the spread of literacy came book clubs, reading groups, literary societies, debating societies, periodical reading rooms, and similar entities that sprang up in Northern Europe and North America. The demand for reading material led to new types of libraries, called social libraries. Because they served a broad readership, social libraries are considered to be a bridge between older, more exclusive libraries and modern public libraries. Among the most common types of social libraries were subscription libraries, which were membership associations. In some cases, members owned the collection, and in other cases, individuals paid a fee to use the collection but did not own it. Although there were subscription libraries for the clergy in Great Britain in the 17th and early 18th centuries, the first secular subscription libraries were established in Scotland beginning in the 1740s. Several reading societies combined to found the first English subscription library in Liverpool in 1753, and subscription libraries soon appeared in other cities. The first such library in London, the London Library, was created in 1786. These libraries catered to the middle class, and some of them acquired their own buildings. The first example of a social library in America, the Library Company of Philadelphia, was formed in 1731 by Benjamin Franklin and a group of associates. It was a nonprofit shareholder organization that acquired popular as well as more serious literature for circulation among members. Louis Timothee was employed as the librarian in 1732, but he resigned a year later, and Franklin served as librarian until a replacement was found.

Another type of social library was the commercial circulating library. While private subscription libraries emphasized serious reading, circulating libraries, which developed from the lending libraries of booksellers, gave prominence to fiction and appealed more to popular taste. The first circulating library was created by Allan Ramsay in Edinburgh in 1725. Although there is evidence that booksellers had been lending books since the mid-1600s, Ramsay was the first to create a circulating library specifically intended for rental. Circulating libraries could soon be found in London and other English cities and towns. Some were very small, while others had extensive catalogs and advertised nationwide. It has been estimated that England had more than 1,000 circulating libraries by 1800, many of them located in popular vacation destinations such as Brighton and Bath. London had 26 circulating libraries in 1800. William Rind of Annapolis, Maryland, is credited with opening the first circulating library in the American colonies in 1762. One of the largest American circulating libraries, operated by French-born bookseller Louis Alexis Hocquet de Caritat of New York, claimed to have more than 30,000 volumes in 1800.

Other social libraries were created and supported specifically to benefit the working class. For example, the Ledhills Reading Society was established for lead miners in Scotland in 1741.The Birmingham Artisans' Library, founded in England in 1797, charged its members one penny per week and was a forerunner of the libraries that were set up in mechanics' institutes beginning in the 1820s. By 1850, there were more than 800,000 volumes in 702 mechanics' institute libraries in England, Ireland, Scotland, and Wales. In the United States, apprentices' libraries, which provided wholesome reading material to young men who were emigrating to the cities to find work, were common. The Mechanics Apprentices' Library Association, established in Boston in 1820, is thought to be the first apprentices' library in the world. There were also mercantile library associations for clerks. One of the largest and most successful of these, the Mercantile Library Association of New York City, was founded in 1820 and was the fourth largest library in the United States by 1871. As the 19th century progressed, social libraries expanded to other parts of the country and were joined by agricultural libraries, county libraries, railroad libraries, hotel reading rooms, sewing circle libraries, YMCA libraries, ladies' club libraries, and many other kinds. These libraries met the reading needs of a wide variety of people and were considered to be "public" in that they were not privately owned. After the Civil

War, however, a new definition of a public library began to take hold. Social libraries were displaced by, and many social libraries merged with, new libraries that were free, publically supported, and open to all.

THE PUBLIC LIBRARY MOVEMENT

In 1850, Smithsonian Institution librarian Charles Coffin Jewett published the first public library statistics. Appended to a Smithsonian Institution Board of Regents Report, *Notices of Public Libraries in the United States of America* contained statistics on 694 libraries, including state libraries, theological seminary libraries, mercantile libraries, college libraries, school libraries, historical society libraries, ladies' club libraries, and libraries of many other stripes. Most of these libraries were "public" only in a limited sense. Many served a particular clientele. Many had closed stacks and were open during inconvenient hours. Although free libraries existed in some towns, they tended to be privately founded and funded. However, industrialization, urbanization, and educational reform helped fuel a movement toward libraries that were publically funded and open to all. The modern public library movement began with the passage in 1850 of Great Britain's Public Libraries Act, empowering municipal authorities to levy a small rate for the establishment and maintenance of a public library. One of the arguments against the passage of the act was that ratepayers, who would come from the middle and upper classes, would be supporting a service that only the working class would use. Another was that people who had more knowledge were more difficult to manage. The many compromises that were made in order to turn the act into law meant that British public libraries developed slowly. Progress was more rapid in the United States, where the modern public library movement was launched by the opening of the Boston Public Library in 1854.

In both Great Britain and the United States, public libraries were seen as part of the system of mass education, providing the means of continuing instruction after people left school. Steel magnate-turned-philanthropist Andrew Carnegie was so convinced of the role libraries played in self-improvement that he funded the construction of more than 2,400 libraries in Great Britain, the United States, and other parts of the world. In the United States, Carnegie's benevolence helped stimulate the movement toward municipal support, since the communities that received Carnegie libraries were required to contribute an annual sum of 10 percent of the money donated to build collections and hire staff.

Based on democratic principles and untrammeled by the need to safeguard old and valuable materials, a public library model began to emerge in the United States. Tax-supported public libraries welcomed people of all classes (although not, until later, of all races). Stacks were open, hours were extended, children's services were provided, books were allowed to circulate, and trained librarians were in charge. This model was soon adopted in Great Britain and Scandinavia. Although the division between the scholarly library and popular book collection persisted elsewhere in Europe, publically supported libraries were a reality in most European countries before World War I. In the 20th century, the American model of librarianship that grew out of public library movement was instituted elsewhere in the world, often with the support of agencies such as the Carnegie Corporation of New York, the Rockefeller Foundation, and the United Nations. In many countries, the modern library movement is said to have begun with the introduction of American library ideas. Questions have been raised, however, as to whether the American model is universally relevant and sustainable.

THE RISE OF THE LIBRARY PROFESSIONAL

Until about the middle of the 19th century, the role of the librarian was seen as being chiefly custodial. However, a body of specialized library knowledge was beginning to form around the need to organize a growing number of printed materials. Several important catalog codes appeared in the 19th century, which for that reason is sometimes referred to as "the century of codes." These codes, among them *Rules for the Compilation of the Catalogue*, created for the British Library Museum in 1841, and Charles Ammi Cutter's *Rules for a Printed Dictionary Catalog*, published in 1876, helped lay the foundation for the idea that librarianship required special skills and expertise. Librarians also began to claim an expanded role for themselves as libraries assumed a greater importance in the context of the many social and cultural changes taking place during the 19th century.

One of the first signs that librarians had begun to think of themselves as having a distinct occupation was the librarians' conference held at the University of the City of New York (later New York University). More than 80 librarians convened to discuss topics such as the indexing of periodicals and the need for cataloging standards. Although the conference had few concrete results, it set a precedent for the second conference that took place 23 years later in Philadelphia and resulted in the founding of ALA. With a formal organization in place, librarians were increasingly defined by their own expert knowledge, training, literature, and standards.

The period from 1876 to 1923, the year in which the landmark report *Training for Library Service* (better known as the Williamson report) was published, has been called the "Dewey era" of American librarianship because of the way that Melvil Dewey shaped the early development of the library profession. During this period, education for librarianship was influenced by Dewey's emphasis on practical training. Dewey also encouraged women to become librarians, and by 1920, women accounted for more than 88 percent of the 15,297 librarians listed in the US census. The preponderance of women and the emphasis on the technical aspects of librarianship came to be seen as damaging to the profession. The Williamson report, which was commissioned by the Carnegie Corporation of New York, was highly critical of librarianship's focus on details and techniques rather than on principles. Based on recommendations made in the report, including that librarians be provided with advanced education rather than training, the Graduate School of Library Science was established at the University of Chicago in 1926. New standards approved by the ALA Council in 1951 recognized the master's degree in library science as the entry-level degree in the United States and limited ALA accreditation to master's degree programs.

The example of professionalization in the United States was followed by librarians in other nations. A year after the founding of ALA, the Library Association of the United Kingdom (now the Chartered Institute of Library and Information Professionals, CILIP) was established at the International Conference of Librarians in London. The third professional library association was founded in Japan in 1892. By 1910, there were professional associations in Austria, Belgium, Denmark, Finland, France, Germany, Scotland, and New Zealand. The first library association in Latin America was founded in Mexico in 1924. The South African Library Association, the first library association in Africa, was founded in 1930. A number of foreign students came to the United States to study librarianship, but education gradually became available in other countries as well. Formal training, as opposed to occasional short courses, was organized in Canada in 1904 and in India in 1915. In Great Britain, the London School of Librarianship was established at University College in 1919. Professional journals began to appear: the *Revue des bibliothèques* was published in France starting in 1891. The national-level associations were joined by other types: the Special Libraries Association was founded in 1909, and the International Federation of Library Associations and Institutions (IFLA) was organized in 1927. IFLA has played an important role in the development of librarianship worldwide, often in partnership with the United Nations Educational, Social, and Cultural Organization (UNESCO).

LIBRARIANS IN THE INFORMATION AGE

Technology first entered libraries in the 1930s in the form of business machines, which were seen as a way to free librarians from the drudgery of routine work. Subsequently, technology began to present librarians with ways to address some of the pressing problems related to growth. In 1944, Fremont Rider estimated that if the Yale University Library continued to grow at its current rate, by 2040 it would "have approximately 200,000,000 volumes, which will occupy over 6,000 miles of shelves."[3] He proposed his invention, the microcard, as a solution. In the 1960s, computers offered a way of dealing with the storage problems created by the ever-growing amount of published scholarship; in fact, by 1967, Jesse Shera wrote that, thanks to computers, the storage problem was solved.[4] Further advances in information and communication technology have meant that digital information can be disseminated with ease: physical and geographic boundaries have become far less important; information resources can be shared in multiple locations; and controlled access to information resources has given way to unmediated electronic access.

Despite its transformative benefits, technology has raised fundamental questions about the value of library collections and space, the relevance of library services, and the role of the librarian. Shera noted in "Librarians against Machines" that librarians were caught off guard and were "quite unprepared for the intrusion of a new technology that has been known variously as documentation, information science, automation, and information storage and retrieval, despite the fact that the storing and retrieving of recorded knowledge had been the librarian's unique responsibility for many centuries."[5] Andrew Abbott, writing 20 years later in *The System of Professions*, noted that computers required "near-total standardization in descriptive cataloging and indexing, which deeply invaded the area of judgment that made librarians professional."[6] Librarians, who once had an exclusive hold on information, had lost their "physical custody of cultural capital,"[7] as Abbott put it. Librarianship responded to these changes beginning in the 1970s by moving away from its focus on libraries and library services and repositioning itself first as library and information science (LIS) and then as information studies. By the end of the 20th century, librarianship had become more interdisciplinary, expanding its knowledge base and incorporating concepts from information environments that went beyond traditional library settings. Librarianship had also become more global, with bodies such as the European Union and IFLA working to develop cross-border LIS educational cooperation and promote joint recognition of qualifications. A number of developments in the first decades of the 21st century offer examples of the ways in which traditional information services such as libraries are being transformed. In 2001, the National Library Board of Singapore opened a "Totally Do-It-Yourself" library, which was run without staff but was meant to provide the same level of service as libraries with staff onsite. Beginning in 2002, a number of public library buildings in London, England were closed and replaced by retail-inspired "Idea Stores." In 2004, the National Library of Canada was merged with the National Archives of Canada to form Library and Archives Canada, part of the growing convergence of the cultural heritage institutions: libraries, archives, and museums. In 2010, as part of a pattern to move higher-education library collections online, the first completely bookless bricks-and-mortar library in the United States, the Applied Engineering and Technology Library, opened at the University of Texas at San Antonio. The University of Chicago's new library, which opened in 2011, has a completely automated book storage and retrieval system managed by robotic cranes. A Pew Research Center report released in 2012 revealed that in the previous year, "the number of those who read e-books increased from 16% of all Americans ages 16 and older to 23%. At the same time, the number of those who read printed books in the previous 12 months fell from 72% of the population ages 16 and older to 67%."[8] In an article published in the *New Republic* in 2012, David Bell noted that "there are now far more books available, far more quickly, on the iPhone than in the New York Public Library."[9] In 2013, the Vatican Library's collection of 82,000 manuscripts went online, continuing the trend of digitizing and providing open access to the world's documentary heritage. Also in 2013, BiblioTech, a public library offering only electronic books, opened in Bexar County, Texas. Five key trends in the new global information environment were identified in the 2013 IFLA Trend Report: the expansion and, at the same time, limitation of who has access to information; the democratization and disruption of learning; the redefinition of the boundaries of privacy and data protection; the empowerment of new voices and groups; and the transformation of the global information economy.[10] The future of librarianship will depend on the ability not only to adapt to, but to be at the forefront of, transformations in the way information is acquired, accessed, evaluated, disseminated, and preserved.

NOTES

1. Melvil Dewey, "The Profession," *American Library Journal* (September 30, 1876), 5–6.
2. "Librarians of America," *New York Times*, September 13, 1890.
3. Fremont Rider, *The Scholar and the Future of the Reference Library: A Problem and Its Solution* (New York: The Hadham Press, 1944), 12.
4. Jesse Shera, "Librarians against Machines," *Science* 156 (May 12, 1967), 746.
5. Ibid., 748.

6. Andrew Abbott, *The System of Professions*: *An Essay on the Division of Expert Labor* (Chicago: University of Chicago Press, 1988), 220.

7. Ibid., 217.

8. Lee Rainie and Maeve Duggan, "E-book Reading Jumps; Print Book Reading Declines," Pew Internet and American Life Project, December 27, 2012. http://libraries.pewinternet.org/2012/12/27/e-book-reading-jumps-print-book-reading-declines/.

9. David A. Bell, "The Bookless Library," *New Republic* 243 (August 2, 2012), 31–36.

10. *Riding the Waves or Caught in the Tide? Navigating the Evolving Information Environment* (The Hague: IFLA, 2013).

A

ACADEMIC LIBRARIES. What may be the first central academic library was organized at the **Sorbonne** in Paris, **France**, in 1289. In **Great Britain**, libraries were founded in the universities of Oxford and Cambridge in the 13th century, followed by those of the Scottish universities in St. Andrews, Aberdeen, Glasgow, and Edinburgh in the 15th and 16th centuries.

The Harvard College Library, established in 1638, was the first library in the British colonies in America and was followed by the College of William and Mary, Yale College, the College of New Jersey (later Princeton University), and King's College (later Columbia University). As in Europe, collections grew largely through donations. The colonial colleges followed a classical model of education, meaning students relied on textbooks and had little need for libraries, which were barely accessible in any case. The job of the librarian, who might be a recent graduate, a junior faculty member, a college president, or even a janitor, was part-time and chiefly custodial. This model persisted well into the 19th century; the academic librarians who attended the **Librarians' Conference of 1853** operated the library as an extra duty.

Europe, on the other hand, had a tradition of scholarly librarianship, and beginning in the 1870s, several European countries introduced professional examinations and **certification** for university librarians. In **Germany**, the Göttingen University Library appointed the first full-time professional academic librarian in 1860. George Ticknor and other Americans who traveled to Europe were impressed by the library at Göttingen, which had over 200,000 volumes at a time when the collection at Harvard numbered 30,000. Americans were also impressed by the Göttingen model of advanced scholarship. Although Harvard University and Yale University had already established graduate schools, Johns Hopkins University, which opened in 1876, was the first American institution of higher learning to establish a program based on Göttingen's example.

An expanded and diversified curriculum, changes in teaching methods, and the growing number of graduate programs called for a library that would offer more materials and better access. Like **public libraries**, academic libraries in the **United States** opened their stacks, liberalized their lending policies, and extended their hours. Harvard University provided 82 hours of library service per week in 1896, up from 48 in 1876. The increasingly complex problems related to maintaining academic libraries created a need for full-time librarians, who began to see themselves as a distinct group. The founding of the **American Library Association (ALA)** in 1876 gave impetus to a growing professional awareness, although the public-library focus of ALA meant that academic librarianship was sometimes relegated to a secondary role. A College Library Section (now the **Association of College and Research Libraries, ACRL**) was formed within ALA in 1889 to address academic librarians' concerns.

In the 20th century, university library collections grew to such an extent that librarians began to see size as a major concern. The need to control growth was one of the factors leading to the development of plans for cooperative acquisitions. College library collections, on the other hand, were found to be inadequate. As a result of a study published in the 1930s, the **Carnegie Corporation of New York** awarded 83 grants to college libraries for improvement of book collections. The Carnegie Corporation also supported the development of standards. ALA published the first authoritative purchasing guide, Charles B. Shaw's *A List of Books for College Libraries*, in 1931, followed by Foster E. Mohrhardt's *A List of Books for Junior College Libraries* in 1937. Numerical standards for book collections, staffing patterns, salaries, and book funds adopted by ALA were later incorporated into *Standards for College Libraries*, which was adopted in 1959. *Standards for Junior College Libraries* was adopted in 1960. *Standards for University Libraries* was prepared by ACRL and the **Association of Research Libraries (ARL)** in 1972; by that time university library standards had already been produced in **Canada**, Germany, and Great Britain. *Standards for Libraries in Higher Education* superseded earlier US standards in 2011. The standards developed for academic libraries in the United States have influenced the international standards.

Beginning in the 1960s, advances in technology led to the **automation** of acquisitions, **cataloging**, circulation, and processing. In the 1980s, libraries began to install online public access catalogs (OPACs). Librarians also began to turn their attention to the growing availability of online systems and electronic databases. Changes in teaching methods and scholarly communication, the move to electronic books and journals, and the mass digitization of rare books, manuscripts, and archival materials have led to a decline in annual building-based statistics and a fundamental shift from a model based on ownership to one based on access. The first completely bookless bricks-and-mortar library in the United States, the Applied Engineering and Technology Library at the University of Texas at San Antonio, opened in 2010.

In the early days of the academic library movement in the United States, most librarians functioned under the control of faculty members, who generally assumed responsibility for book selection and collection development. The change from bachelor's degree to master's degree as the professional credential for librarianship influenced the status of the academic librarian, as did the establishment of doctoral programs in the field. Subject specialization in libraries expanded following World War II, and librarians gradually assumed primary responsibility for selection and collection management, further helping them in their quest for professional recognition. The ACRL, the Association of American Colleges (now the Association of American Colleges and Universities), and the American Association of University Professors issued a joint statement on faculty status of academic librarians in 1972.

In many countries, academic librarians have low status and low pay, in part because library education is primarily at the undergraduate level. Academic library issues such as the adoption and use of information technologies, cooperation and resource sharing, and the shift from a materials-oriented to a user-oriented focus are similar across the globe, with the differences being that, in some countries, development has moved at a slower pace.

See also BODLEIAN LIBRARY; CENTER FOR RESEARCH LIBRARIES (CRL); EDUCATION FOR LIBRARIANSHIP; FARMINGTON PLAN; METCALF, KEYES D. (1889–1983); RESEARCH LIBRARIES GROUP (RLG); SCHOLARLY PUBLISHING AND ACADEMIC RESOURCES COALITION (SPARC); SERIALS CRISIS; UNDERGRADUATE LIBRARIES.

ACCREDITATION. In the United States, the **American Library Association (ALA)** began accrediting **library science** programs in 1925. In 1923, the **Carnegie Corporation of New York** encouraged professional accreditation in a number of fields, including librarianship, and this, along with the Carnegie-funded **Williamson report** (1923) examining the state of the 15 existing library schools, prompted ALA to form the **Board of Education for Librarianship (BEL)** in 1924. Among the first programs in the United States to be accredited were those at the Carnegie Library of Atlanta, the Los Angeles **Public Library**, the New York Public Library, the **Pratt Institute**, the University of Illinois, and the University of California at Berkeley. In 1925 and 1933, the BEL produced minimum standards for library training programs. More complete *Standards for Accreditation*, adopted in 1951, stipulated that library schools must be associated with institutions of higher learning and made the master's degree the credential for entering the profession. In 1956, the BEL was replaced by the ALA Committee on Accreditation, which issued revised standards in 1972 and 1992. The standards adopted in 1992 came at a time when many schools were reinventing themselves. Some had dropped the word *library* from their names, and some were even questioning whether ALA accreditation was still relevant. The 2008 *Standards for Accreditation of Master's Programs in Library and Information Studies* reaffirmed the core competencies laid out in the 1992 standards. In 2013, there were 63 ALA-accredited programs in the United States, **Canada**, and Puerto Rico.

McGill University in Quebec sought and obtained ALA accreditation in 1927, setting a precedent for the rest of Canada. In **Great Britain**, the **Library Association (LA)** began accrediting programs in the 1970s after dropping its system of direct examination of individual candidates. Outside the United States and most other English-speaking countries, accreditation is generally the job of government or government-funded agencies.

See also APPRENTICESHIP; CERTIFICATION; EDUCATION FOR LIBRARIANSHIP.

ADULT EDUCATION. Public libraries in the **United States**, **Great Britain**, and elsewhere were outgrowths of 19th-century social and educational reform. Providing a way for people to continue their education after they left school was seen as a part of the library's core mission. The **Carnegie Corporation of New York** funded William S. Learned's *The American Public Library and the Diffusion of Knowledge* (1924), which called for the library to become a university for the community and provided the basis for the formation of the **American Library Association (ALA)** Commission on the Library and Adult Education (later the Board on Library Adult Education) and the 1926 publication of the ALA report *Libraries and Adult Education*. Adult education programming was also stimulated by Alvin Johnson's *The Public Library—A People's University*, published in 1938. Examples of adult education activities included a **reader's advisory service** and, on a larger scale, the **Reading with a Purpose**, Great Books, Great Issues, and American Heritage programs. *Adult Education Activities in Public Libraries*, a study published by ALA in 1954, found that a majority of the libraries surveyed were involved to some degree in helping adults continue their education. This survey was later updated by ALA's Adult Services in the Eighties project. Margaret E. Monroe's classic *Library Adult Education: The Biography of an Idea* (1963) describes the development of public library services tied to adult education.

See also THE FICTION QUESTION.

AFRICA. Although libraries existed in Africa as early as the 16th century in centers of scholarship such as Timbuktu, the early development of modern libraries is closely linked to the colonial period. Colonial administrators created cultural libraries as well as special libraries to support research in agriculture, medicine, and other areas. Society, club, subscription, and **public**

libraries were established by Asian and European settlers. Agencies such as the **Carnegie Corporation of New York** and the **British Council** also played a role in library development. The Carnegie Corporation provided grants for libraries in British West Africa in the 1930s, and the British Council created reading rooms in East Africa in the 1940s and 1950s.

The library services that developed in East and Anglophone West Africa following independence were based on British and American models, with support from foreign aid agencies and consultants. Development in former Belgian, French, Portuguese, and Spanish colonies was generally slower. The Gold Coast Library Board (later the **Ghana Library Board**), created in 1950, was the first public library service to black Africa and became a model for other African library laws. In East Africa, a blueprint for library development was provided by the 1960 report *Development of Public Library Services in East Africa*, also known as the Hockey report for its author, British Council consultant Sydney W. Hockey. Several countries set up national public library services, with a central headquarters coordinating a network of branches and mobile units. After the ambitious planning of the 1950s and 1960s, libraries began to deteriorate. A lack of government support and a weak publishing industry contributed to the decline. **Academic libraries** became dependent on donors, and although donor funding has brought about some progress, a 2004 Carnegie-funded study of academic libraries found overcrowding, inadequate infrastructure, and outdated materials. The public library sector, which has received little attention from funders, struggles with minimal technology, inadequate space, small and outdated collections, and insufficient and poorly paid staff. Moreover, traditional library service meets the needs of a very small percentage of the population. Since the 1980s, there have been a number of critiques of the attempt to adapt Western librarianship to Africa. The Kenya National Library Service's use of camels to transport library materials to isolated groups of people is an example of a new approach to library services. Railway carriages, donkey carts, bicycles, and boats have been tried in other countries. Zimbabwe's Rural Libraries and Resources Development Project works to create a more sustainable public library model by establishing and supporting libraries in partnership with rural communities.

In 1944, the British Council, in cooperation with the governments of Nigeria, Ghana, and Sierra Leone, set up a library school in Accra, Ghana, to prepare students for the British **Library Association (LA)** examination. The school closed after one year because it was thought that there was no demand for libraries. A full-time professional model of **education** emerged from the **International Seminar on the Development of Public Libraries in Africa**, sponsored by the **United Nations Educational, Scientific and Cultural Organization (UNESCO)** and held in Ibadan, Nigeria, in 1953. One result of the seminar was the opening of the Carnegie-sponsored library school in

Ibadan in 1959. The seminar also led to the formation of the **West African Library Association (WALA)**. The first library school for French-speaking Africans, the Librarian Training Center for Francophone Countries, opened in Dakar, Senegal, in 1963. The East African School of Librarianship (later the East African School of Library and **Information Science**, EASLIS) was established at Makerere University in Kampala, Uganda, in 1963. Formal training was also launched in the 1960s in Ethiopia, Nigeria, and Zambia. By the 1980s, a few schools had introduced master's degree programs. EASLIS introduced a PhD program in the 2004–2005 academic year.

WALA and the **East African Library Association (EALA)**, which was founded in 1957, were regional organizations, but eventually these were dissolved as librarians in individual countries formed associations of their own. The Standing Conference of African University Libraries was formed in 1964 and later split into the Standing Conference of African National and University Libraries in Eastern, Central, and Southern Africa (SCANUL-ECS) and the Standing Conference of African University Libraries, Western Area (SCAULWA).

See also HARRIS, WILLIAM JOHN (1903–1980); SOUTH AFRICA.

AFRICAN AMERICANS IN LIBRARIANSHIP. African American contributions to librarianship began with Daniel A. P. Murray, an employee at the **Library of Congress (LC)** from 1871 to 1923, who assembled an important collection of books and pamphlets by black authors. In 1900, Edward C. Williams, the first formally trained African American librarian in the **United States**, graduated from **New York State Library School**. Another important figure in the early history of African Americans in librarianship was **Thomas Fountain Blue** of the Louisville (Kentucky) Free **Public Library**. Blue headed the library's **Western Colored Branch**, which opened in 1905, and later the Colored Department, which opened in 1914. He also established an **apprentice** class to train African Americans for library work, the first such program in the South. Other cities such as Atlanta, Houston, Knoxville, Nashville, and Memphis sent their black branch librarians to Louisville to be trained. Around 40 people, all of them **women**, completed the program before it was terminated in 1921.

The growing awareness of the need to provide library service to African Americans created a push to prepare African Americans for library work. In 1925, with support from the **Carnegie Corporation of New York** and the Julius Rosenwald fund, the **American Library Association (ALA)** established a school for training African American librarians at the Hampton Institute in Virginia. After the **Hampton Institute Library School** closed in 1939, Carnegie and Rosenwald funds supported the launch of a new school, the **School of Library Service, Atlanta University** in 1941. A second school opened in 1941 at North Carolina College for Negroes (now North Carolina Central University).

After graduating from library school, African American librarians still faced a long struggle for acceptance and equality. Black librarians were generally only hired to work in black institutions, meaning that even those who left the South for their training had to return in order to find a job. Discriminatory practices often kept African Americans from fully participating in professional meetings. Jim Crow laws excluded black librarians from joining state and local library associations. At the 1936 ALA meeting in Richmond, Virginia, Virginia laws prohibited African Americans from hotel rooms and meals. Although ALA had made arrangements with host hotels to ensure that all delegates could use the same entrance, African Americans had to sit in reserved sections in the meeting rooms. Following the conference, and after criticism from the library press, ALA adopted a policy not to convene again in a city where all librarians could not meet as equals. It was not until the Miami Beach conference in 1956 that ALA met again in the South. In 1954, in a move to desegregate state chapters, ALA banned states from having more than one chapter, and in 1962 adopted the Statement on Individual Membership, Chapter Status, and Institutional Membership, requiring state chapters to certify compliance with ALA policies on member rights. As a result, chapters in Alabama, Georgia, Louisiana, and Mississippi withdrew. In 1964, Savannah (Georgia) State College librarian **E. J. Josey**, who had not been allowed to attend a Georgia library conference meeting at which an ALA staff member was the principal speaker, offered a resolution that prevented ALA officers and staff members from attending segregated state chapter conferences. This resolution led to the integration of library associations in several southern states.

Josey was the first male African American president of ALA, serving from 1984 to 1985. He founded the **Black Caucus** of ALA in 1970 and edited the landmark *Black Librarian in America* (1970) and *Black Librarian in America Revisited* (1994). He was just one of a number of trailblazers following in the steps of Murray, Williams, and Blue. **Virginia Proctor Powell Florence** became the first African American woman to complete a professional **education** program in librarianship when she received her degree from the Carnegie Library School of Pittsburgh in 1923. In 1940, **Eliza Atkins Gleason** was the first African American to receive a doctoral degree in librarianship. In 1976, **Clara Stanton Jones** became the first African American to serve as ALA president. Robert Wedgeworth became the first black executive director of ALA in 1972.

A sense that ALA was reluctant to move on issues that mattered to black librarians prompted a group of them to meet at the 1970 ALA Midwinter Meeting to discuss common concerns. The Black Caucus was formed as a result. African American librarians continued to struggle with a lack of career opportunities, however. Although fellowships under Title II-B of the Higher Education Act of 1965 boosted the number of professional librarians from minority groups in the 1970s and 1980s, few African Americans held positions at a policy-making level. African Americans made up 5.1 percent of the total number of librarians in 2010.

See also AFRICAN AMERICANS, LIBRARY SERVICE TO; BAKER, AUGUSTA B. (1911–1998); DELANEY, SADIE PETERSON (1889–1958).

AFRICAN AMERICANS, LIBRARY SERVICE TO. In principle, African Americans had free access to the **public libraries** that proliferated in the western and northern states in the late 19th and early 20th centuries. However, in the South, where most blacks lived at the time, libraries were slower to develop, and blacks were barred by law from entering most of them. What library services were provided for blacks were found in separate reading rooms, separate branches of libraries, or completely separate library buildings. In 1903, the Cossit Library in Memphis, Tennessee, made an arrangement with an African American normal school, the Lemoyne Institute, to provide a librarian and books for black readers if the school provided the space. A library intended to serve the entire black population of Galveston, Texas, was set up in an addition to a high school building in 1904. The Charlotte Public Library for Colored People, which opened in Charlotte, North Carolina, in 1905, was separate from the Charlotte Public Library and had its own governing board. The year 1913 saw the opening of the Colored **Carnegie Library** in Houston, Texas, founded and administered by black Houstonians. African Americans established an independent library in Savannah, Georgia. The Louisville (Kentucky) Free Public Library was at the forefront of the African American library movement, having established the **Western Colored Branch**, the first African American branch library, in 1905. A second branch, the Eastern Branch, opened in 1914. The library then established a Colored Department, which was completely staffed and administered by African Americans. However, several large cities, among them Atlanta, Birmingham, Dallas, Mobile, Nashville, and New Orleans, provided no public library service to blacks as late as 1913.

In the absence of local action, philanthropy often provided the impetus for library service to African Americans. In 1910, James S. Gregory of Marblehead, Massachusetts, set up a traveling library service called the Marblehead Libraries, based on lists of titles solicited from black schools. The **Carnegie Corporation of New York** built facilities in Mississippi, Missouri, Tennessee, Texas, and elsewhere. The General Education Board, which was funded by the **Rockefeller Foundation**, supported the building of black college libraries. The Julius Rosenwald Fund set up county demonstration libraries with the stipulation that the model libraries be open to all. The Carnegie Corporation, the Julius Rosenwald Fund, and the General Education Board were also instrumental in establishing professional education for black librarians.

In 1913, William F. Yust, former head of the Louisville Free Public Library, delivered an address at the **American Library Association (ALA)** conference at Kaaterskill, New York, that was perhaps ALA's first substantive discussion related to African American library service. In 1922, ALA formed the Work with Negroes Round Table, which, at its first meeting, was presented with the results of a survey developed by **Ernestine Rose** of the 135th Street Branch in New York City. A questionnaire had gone out to 122 institutions inquiring about library service to African Americans and the presence of African Americans on library staffs. While libraries in all western states and most midwestern states reported free access for blacks, few southern libraries allowed access. Another survey on library service to African Americans and the need for training for African American librarians was conducted by **Louis Shores** of Fisk University in 1928. Questionnaires were sent to over 80 cities with large African American populations, and of the 74 libraries that responded, only 31 provided any service for African Americans. In 1940, **Eliza Atkins Gleason** reported in *The Southern Negro and the Public Library* that only 20 percent of African Americans in the South had access to public library services. In 1961, ALA amended the **Library Bill of Rights** to include a statement that no one should be denied access to libraries because of race. Yet, the ALA report *Access to Public Libraries*, published in 1963, found that although direct discrimination was limited to 16 southern states, indirect discrimination occurred throughout the country. Some within ALA opposed the association's intervening in civil rights issues, while others criticized it for not doing enough to promote freedom of access. It was because of the civil rights movement rather than the efforts of librarians that library segregation finally came to an end.

See also AFRICAN AMERICANS IN LIBRARIANSHIP.

AGUAYO, JORGE (1903–1994). Jorge Aguayo, considered the founder of **library science** education in **Cuba**, was born in Havana on December 4, 1903. After receiving degrees from the University of Havana, he took a position at the university's general library. In 1941, Aguayo received a fellowship from the **Rockefeller Foundation** to study at Columbia University's Library School, and when he returned to the University of Havana, he brought with him modern library tools and procedures related to **cataloging** and **classification**. He was also involved in early library training programs, and directed the formal teaching of library science that began with summer courses in 1946. He was a founder of the University of Havana's library science school, which opened in 1950. In 1959, he became director of the

General Library, University of Havana. Aguayo had a hand in library development throughout **Latin America**. He wrote several cataloging manuals that were used in Latin American library schools. He came to the **United States** in 1960 and was the director of the Columbus Memorial Library at the Organization of American States (OAS) until his retirement in 1973.

AHERN, MARY EILEEN (1860–1938). A pioneer of the **public library** movement, Mary Eileen Ahern was born on a farm in Indiana on October 1, 1860, and graduated from Central Normal College in Danville, Indiana, in 1881. The years she spent as a teacher sparked her interest in libraries, and she worked at the Indiana State Library for several years, becoming state librarian in 1893. When her two-year term ended in 1895, she enrolled in the Department of Library Economy at the **Armour Institute** in Chicago. Before she completed the one-year course, she was offered the editorship of a new journal, *Public Libraries*, to be published by the Chicago office of **Melvil Dewey**'s **Library Bureau**.

As *Public Libraries* editor, Ahern made information about the emerging profession of librarianship more widely available. She encouraged **women** to enter the profession and encouraged workers in small and rural libraries to participate in professional activities. She organized the Indiana State Library Association and was active in the **American Library Association (ALA)**, the Illinois Library Association, and other professional organizations. She also took an interest in **school** librarianship and **international** library cooperation.

ALBANY LIBRARY SCHOOL. *See* NEW YORK STATE LIBRARY SCHOOL.

ALEXANDRIAN LIBRARY. The largest library in antiquity, the Alexandrian Library was established around 300 BCE by Ptolemy I (ruled between 305 and 282 BCE) and enlarged by his successor, Ptolemy II (282–246 BCE). It was housed near the royal palace in the Museum (that is, temple to the Muses) of Alexandria, Egypt. The library was intended to be an international research center for use by the scholars whom Ptolemy lured to Alexandria, by creating a place where they could live and work without being bothered by daily concerns. The library's collection included Greek literature along with translations of important works in other languages, acquired in various ways. One way was to seize books and manuscripts from all travelers arriving in Alexandria, and to keep those items not already in the library's collection, compensating their owners with copies. Prominent scholars were hired as library directors and often had to tutor the royal children as well. The first director, Zenodotus, introduced a **classification** scheme, perhaps based on methods that Aristotle worked out for his own collection. As far as is known, Zenodotus is the first to have used alphabetical order as a means of organization. **Callimachos** of Cyrene, appointed to the library in 260 BCE (although it is not certain whether he was ever the library's director), compiled a **catalog** called the *Pinakes* (full title: *Tables of Persons Eminent in Every Branch of Learning Together with a List of Their Writings*), sometimes described as the first library catalog. The library's demise came gradually. Fire may have destroyed a large part of the collection in 48 BCE, and the area of the city in which the Museum was located was destroyed in 272 CE, although a smaller supplementary library survived until 391 CE, when it was demolished and burned. The Bibliotheca Alexandrina, the new Library of Alexandria, opened in 2002, on or near the site of the original.

AMERICAN ASSOCIATION OF LAW LIBRARIES (AALL). The AALL was established at the American Library Association (ALA) Annual Conference in Narragansett, Rhode Island, in 1906. The driving force behind the new association was A. J. Small, law librarian of the Iowa State Library, who had issued a call to other state and law librarians to come together to discuss the possibility of forming an organization. Small served as the president of AALL from 1906 to 1908. AALL launched its official publication, *Index to Legal Periodicals and Law Library Journal*, in 1908; these continued as a combined publication until 1936, after which time they were published separately. A full-time staff and headquarters were set up as a result of an expansion plan carried out in the 1930s. In 2013, AALL had more than 5,000 members.

AMERICAN DOCUMENTATION INSTITUTE (ADI). *See* ASSOCIATION FOR INFORMATION SCIENCE AND TECHNOLOGY (ASIS&T).

AMERICAN LIBRARIES. *American Libraries* is the flagship magazine of the **American Library Association (ALA)**. It was preceded by the *Bulletin of the American Library Association*, which was started in 1907 in order to publish association proceedings. The name was changed to *ALA Bulletin* in 1939 and to *American Libraries* in 1970.
See also LIBRARY JOURNAL.

AMERICAN LIBRARY ASSOCIATION (ALA). ALA is the leading professional association of **public** and **academic** librarians and libraries in the **United States**. The idea of forming an association was discussed at the **Librarians' Conference** held in New York City in 1853, but more than 20 years went by before the idea became a reality. On April 22, 1876, a letter from James Yates, a public librarian in **Great Britain**, was printed in Frederick Leypoldt's "Library and Bibliographical Notes" column in *Publishers Weekly*, commenting on the fact that, although other groups were convening at the Centennial Exhibition in Philadelphia, no meeting of librarians had been planned. In May 1876, Leypoldt, **Richard Rogers Bowker**, and **Melvil Dewey** began organizing a librarians' meeting to take place in Philadelphia in October of that year. On October 6, 1876, delegates formed ALA, creating the first formal structure for librarianship. **Justin Winsor** was elected president and Dewey was elected secretary and treasurer. Dewey, Winsor, and the several vice presidents were named to act as an executive board and were charged with drawing up a constitution. *American Library Journal*, which was launched in 1876 by Bowker, Dewey, and Leypoldt, served as the association's first official organ. The first headquarters were in Boston, in rooms that also housed the **Library Bureau**, Dewey's library supplies business. In 1909, the headquarters moved to Chicago and opened with the first salaried executive officer and paid staff.

In its early years, ALA was dominated by Dewey and by men of the older generation of librarians, such as Winsor and **William Frederick Poole**. Among the association's early achievements was the publication of a new edition of *Poole's Index to Periodical Literature*. ALA was also instrumental in the appointment of **Herbert Putnam** as librarian of Congress in 1899. In 1889, the College Library Section (now the **Association of College and Research Libraries, ACRL**) became the first type-of-library division. A unit for library trustees became the first type-of-activity division in 1890. Other specialized units followed. The publishing board, which ALA had created in 1886, launched a review journal, *Booklist*, in 1905. ALA made the *Bulletin of the American Library Association* its official organ in 1908.

ALA has held an annual conference since 1876, and, in 1908, began holding an annual business meeting, the Midwinter Meeting. In the course of its history, the association has been organized into what were known at different times as departments, divisions, and most recently separate associations, within the overall structure. In 2011, ALA had nearly 60,000 members, 11 membership divisions, 37 standing committees, and 18 roundtables.

See also ACCREDITATION; ADULT EDUCATION; AFRICAN AMERICANS IN LIBRARIANSHIP; AFRICAN AMERICANS, LIBRARY SERVICE TO; *AMERICAN LIBRARIES*; AMERICAN LIBRARY IN PARIS; ASHEIM, LESTER E. (1914–1997); ASSOCIATION FOR LIBRARY AND INFORMATION SCIENCE EDUCATION (ALISE); BATCHELDER, MILDRED L. (1901–1998); BENJAMIN FRANKLIN LIBRARY; BLACK CAUCUS OF THE AMERICAN LIBRARY ASSOCIATION (BCALA); BOARD OF EDUCATION FOR LIBRARIANSHIP (BEL); BOOKS FOR CHINA; CATALOGING AND CATALOGS; CENSORSHIP; CHILDREN'S LIBRARY SERVICE; COOPERATIVE ACQUISITIONS PROJECT FOR WARTIME PUBLICATIONS; CUBA; EDUCA-

TION FOR LIBRARIANSHIP; ELMENDORF, THERESA WEST (1855–1932); THE FICTION QUESTION; FREEDOM TO READ STATEMENT; GAY, LESBIAN, BISEXUAL, AND TRANSGENDER ROUND TABLE; INTELLECTUAL FREEDOM; INTERNATIONAL LIBRARIANSHIP; LIBRARY BILL OF RIGHTS; LIBRARY OF CONGRESS (LC); LIBRARY WAR SERVICE; MILAM, CARL H. (1884–1963); PARIS LIBRARY SCHOOL; PROGRESSIVE LIBRARIANSHIP; PUBLIC LIBRARY INQUIRY; *RDA: RESOURCE DESCRIPTION AND ACCESS*; READING WITH A PURPOSE; REFORMA; SCHOOL LIBRARIES; UNIONIZATION; YOUNG ADULT (YA) LIBRARY SERVICE.

AMERICAN LIBRARY IN PARIS. Following World War I, the American Library in Paris was founded under the auspices of the **American Library Association (ALA)**. The library, which opened in May 1920, contained a collection of books that had been sent to American troops in Europe as part of the Library War Service. The collection was organized by Library War Service staff using American methods, which were new to most of Europe at the time. Many of the library's staff members were American librarians with temporary assignments. The American Library in Paris became a subscription library after ALA ceased paying for its operation in November 1920. Through its services and its role as the home of the **Paris Library School**, the library was instrumental in introducing modern librarianship to **France**. It remained open during World War II and remains open today as the largest English-language lending library on the European continent.

AMERICAN LIBRARY JOURNAL. See LIBRARY JOURNAL.

AMERICAN SOCIETY FOR INFORMATION SCIENCE (ASIS). *See* ASSOCIATION FOR INFORMATION SCIENCE AND TECHNOLOGY (ASIS&T).

AMERICAN SOCIETY FOR INFORMATION SCIENCE AND TECHNOLOGY (ASIS&T). *See* ASSOCIATION FOR INFORMATION SCIENCE AND TECHNOLOGY (ASIS&T).

ANDERSON, EDWIN HATFIELD (1861–1947). Edwin Hatfield Anderson was born in Zionsville, Indiana, on September 27, 1861. He graduated from Wabash College, Crawfordsville, Indiana, in 1883. After spending several years teaching and writing, he attended the **New York State Library School** in Albany, New York, while also working as a librarian at the Young Men's Christian Association (YMCA). In 1891, he joined the staff of the Newberry Library in Chicago as a cataloger. The following year, he became the librarian of the Carnegie Free Library in Braddock, Pennsylvania, and in 1895, he assumed the librarian's post at the new Carnegie Library of Pittsburgh. In 1906, Anderson was appointed director of the New York State Library and the New York State Library School, succeeding **Melvil Dewey**. In 1908, he became assistant director at the New York **Public Library** (NYPL) under John Shaw Billings, and in that capacity convinced **Andrew Carnegie** to provide funds for the NYPL School, which opened in 1911. Anderson was elected director of the library in 1913 and served in that post until his retirement in 1934. He was president of the **American Library Association (ALA)** from 1913 to 1914.

ANGLO-AMERICAN CATALOGING CODE. See ANGLO-AMERICAN CATALOGING RULES (AACR).

ANGLO-AMERICAN CATALOGING RULES (AACR). The origin of the *Anglo-American Cataloging Rules*, the first and most widely used multinational descriptive cataloging code, lies in an early cooperative effort between the **American Library Association (ALA)** and the **Library Association (LA)** of **Great Britain**. In 1893, ALA's "Condensed Rules for an Author and Title Catalogue" were first published in *Library Journal*. In 1900, ALA appointed a committee to look into revising the rules to make them more compatible with the rules of the **Library of Congress (LC)**. Around the same time, the LA began work on a revision of its own cataloging rules, which had been published in 1893. It was **Melvil Dewey** who suggested that the two associations work together, and an agreement to cooperate was reached in 1904. The resulting *Anglo-American Cataloging Code* was published in 1908 in an American edition (*Catalog Rules, Author and Title Entries*) and a British edition (*Cataloguing Rules, Author and Title Entries*). World War II put an end to discussions between the two associations about revising the code. In 1941, ALA published a preliminary second edition of the American rules, followed by *ALA Cataloging Rules for Author and Title Entries* in 1949. Because so many American libraries were using LC catalog cards, ALA also adopted *Rules for Descriptive Cataloging in the Library of Congress*, published the same year.

In the 1950s, British and American librarians began to work together again to revise the codes that had been issued in 1949. The Statement of Principles (commonly known as the **Paris Principles**), adopted at the **International Conference on Cataloging Principles** in 1961, helped shape the new *AACR*, which were published in two versions, North American and British, in 1967. In addition to becoming the code for libraries in North America and **Canada**, *AACR* formed the basis for codes that were developed in many other countries. In 1974, representatives from Canada, Great Britain, and the **United**

States met to establish a plan for the second edition. Among the goals was a reconciliation of British and North American versions into a single text. *Anglo-American Cataloging Rules, Second Edition* (*AACR2*) appeared in 1978, published jointly by ALA, the Canadian Library Association, and the Chartered Institute of Library and Information Professionals (CILIP), as the LA was called by this time.

AACR2 was revised in 1988, 1998, and 2002. Work on a major revision, to be called the *Anglo-American Cataloging Rules, Third Edition*, began in 2004. *AACR2* had come under criticism as being inadequate for the new kinds of resources that had appeared after it was adopted, and the committee charged with its revision decided to take a completely new approach. The result, ***RDA: Resource Description and Access***, was published in 2010.

See also FUNCTIONAL REQUIREMENTS FOR BIBLIOGRAPHICAL RECORDS (FRBR).

APPRENTICESHIP. When **Melvil Dewey** opened the first formal library school in 1887, apprentice-style programs were among the most common forms of library training in the **United States**. Apprenticeships were offered by large **public libraries** as well as by some **academic libraries**. In public libraries, these programs often took the form of short courses that combined practical experience with coursework, for the purpose of training the library's own staff. The public libraries in Brooklyn, Chicago, Detroit, Los Angeles, New York, and St. Louis were among those providing such training. In 1879, Dewey unsuccessfully floated the idea of an organized apprenticeship program under the auspices of the libraries that were already involved in training, with one central library school for the completion of studies.

Apprentice courses continued even as more library schools opened. Some libraries still preferred to train their own assistants, and some could not afford to pay the salaries that library school graduates might expect. The lack of library schools on the West Coast was one of the factors that led to opening the Library Training School at the Los Angeles Public Library to visiting librarians and library assistants in 1915. By the 1920s, librarians generally accepted the necessity for some form of professional training. The publication of the **Williamson report** in 1923 and the creation of the **Board of Education for Librarianship (BEL)** of the **American Library Association (ALA)** in 1924 marked the beginning of a shift away from technical training accomplished through apprenticeship and toward the establishment of academic programs affiliated with educational institutions.

See also ACCREDITATION; CERTIFICATION; EDUCATION FOR LIBRARIANSHIP.

ARAB COUNTRIES. The earliest Islamic libraries were mosque libraries. Numerous private libraries were founded by caliphs and scholars. Great libraries were part of institutions such as the Bayt al-Hikma (House of Wisdom), established in Damascus in the seventh century; and Dar al-Hikmah (House of Knowledge), established in Cairo in 1005. Such institutions functioned as centers for translating books into Arabic and for original scholarly research, and scholars were put in charge of them. Some libraries were very large; the library in Cairo was said to have had 600,000 volumes. Many libraries were destroyed by accidental fire or during times of instability, but the greatest destruction came from the Mongol raids in the 13th century. Since then, libraries in Arab countries have drawn on different influences, including not only the medieval Islamic traditions but also newer American and European practices. The Egyptian Library Association, formed in 1946, helped usher in modern librarianship when it spearheaded the establishment of the first library school in the Arab world at Cairo University in 1951. For a number of years, this was the only librarianship training in the region other than short courses.

In 1946, the **United Nations Educational, Scientific and Cultural Organization (UNESCO)** began sending experts to the Arab region to provide advice on a variety of library activities. UNESCO also began granting fellowships for librarians from Arab countries to study abroad. In 1952, UNESCO and the government of Egypt established a Regional Fundamental **Education** and Training Production Center, which included a library demonstration and training program. UNESCO also organized a series of regional meetings on library issues in Arabic countries, beginning with the Regional Seminar on the Development of Libraries in Arabic-Speaking Countries, held in Beirut in 1959. These meetings emphasized the need for professional training. By 1988, there were undergraduate programs in Egypt, Iraq, Libya, Morocco, Saudi Arabia, and Sudan, and postgraduate training programs in Egypt, Iran, Morocco, and Saudi Arabia. Cairo University offered both a master's degree and a PhD beginning in 1956. The Arab Federation for Libraries and Information (AFLI), established in 1986, has worked to improve library and **information science** (LIS) education and to encourage the establishment of national professional associations.

The number of libraries in Arab countries grew in the middle of the 20th century, spurred by an expansion in education. In Egypt, for example, the **public library** movement benefited from the government's emphasis on mass education in the 1950s. Libraries did not have adequate support, however, and development was further slowed by the lack of national planning, effective library legislation, and library cooperation. In 1980, there were only eight library associations in the region and very few professional library journals. There was also a critical shortage of trained librarians, despite the development of library education.

Issues related to **cataloging** and **classification** have been a particular challenge for Arab libraries. For example, Arab libraries did not adopt **Library of Congress Subject Headings (LCSH)** because the headings do not provide in-depth coverage of topics of interest to Arabic speakers. Similarly, Arab libraries did not adopt American **Machine-Readable Cataloging (MARC)** standards, because MARC could not support the input and display of Arabic script. Instead, beginning with King Fahd University of Petroleum and Minerals in Saudi Arabia in the 1980s, libraries automated by "Arabizing" various Western library software systems. Attempts to develop an ARABMARC system, beginning in 1977, have not succeeded. Although developments in library **automation** helped raise awareness of the need to establish and maintain a regional common ground while also conforming to international practices and standards, libraries in the Arab world in the early 21st century continue to be hampered by a lack of bibliographic tools, standardization, and technical infrastructure.

See also ARAB LEAGUE EDUCATIONAL, CULTURAL, AND SCIENTIFIC ORGANIZATION (ALECSO); EL SHENITI, EL SAYED MAHMOUD (1920–1995).

ARAB LEAGUE EDUCATIONAL, CULTURAL, AND SCIENTIFIC ORGANIZATION (ALECSO). Established by the Arab League in 1970 and headquartered in Tunisia, ALECSO has played a prominent role in the development and promotion of librarianship and library services in **Arab countries**. It has sponsored professional meetings, including several Arab Bibliographical Conferences. It has also sponsored regional training courses, and has published and translated works on **library science** and **documentation**. ALECSO has been instrumental in the Arabization of the **Dewey Decimal Classification (DDC)** and **International Standard Bibliographic Description (ISBD)** and in the drafting of an Arabic subject heading list.

ARGENTINA. Argentina has a long **public library** history. The Buenos Aires Public Library (later the National Library) was established in 1810, more than a decade before the University of Buenos Aires. A more wide-ranging public library movement started in the 1870s with the passage of the Sarmiento Law for Public Libraries, named after President **Domingo F. Sarmiento** and inspired by similar legislation in North America. The Sarmiento Law, in turn, became the model for library statutes in other **Latin American** countries. By 1876, Argentina had 182 public libraries. In 1908, the country's first professional meeting of librarians initiated a summer training course. In 1922, a course for librarians was created at the University of Buenos Aires, the first such course in Latin America. The Museo Social Argentino began library training in 1936 and, after a reorganization under

Carlos Victor Penna in the 1940s, introduced modern techniques. Most library training takes place at the undergraduate level. Argentina has a number of professional library associations, among them the Association of Graduate Librarians of the Republic of Argentina/Asociación de Bibliotecarios Graduados de la República Argentina (ABGRA), which was founded in 1953.

See also BORGES, JORGE LUIS (1899–1986).

ARMARIUS. The monk in charge of the library in a medieval **monastery** was sometimes called the *armarius*. It was his duty to take care of the books, which were often kept in an *armarium* (cabinet or chest). The *armarius* might also be in charge of the scriptorium, where manuscripts were copied.

ARMOUR INSTITUTE. The Armour Institute in Chicago was a technical training school established in 1893. Modeled after the **Drexel Institute** and the **Pratt Institute**, the Armour Institute offered training in library work. The program, directed by **Katharine L. Sharp**, was the first library school in the Midwest. In 1897, the school was transferred to the University of Illinois and began to grant a bachelor's degree in **library science**.

See also EDUCATION FOR LIBRARIANSHIP; SCHOOL OF LIBRARY ECONOMY.

ASADULLAH, KHALIFA MOHAMMAD (1890–1949). Considered to be one of the architects of the library movement in **India** and Pakistan, Khalifa Mohammad Asadullah was born on August 6, 1890 in Lahore, which was part of British India at the time. He was among the students in the first library training class organized at the University of Punjab, and in 1916, he became the first qualified librarian at the Government College, Lahore. This was followed by jobs at the Mohammedan Anglo-Oriental College of Aligarh and at the Imperial Secretariat Library in New Delhi. In 1930, he was appointed librarian of the Imperial Library (now the National Library of India) in Calcutta, the second Indian and the first Muslim to hold the position. He remained there for 17 years, during which time he instituted a library training program. He was one of the founding members of Indian Library Association, which was established in 1933, and he served from 1933 to 1947 as its first secretary. He left the Imperial Library in 1947 and migrated to Pakistan, becoming the first prominent librarian to opt to serve the government of the newly created nation.

ASHEIM, LESTER E. (1914–1997). Lester E. Asheim was born in Spokane, Washington, on January 22, 1914. He received a BA in Librarianship from the University of Washington in 1937. After World War II, he enrolled in the **Graduate Library School (GLS)** at the University of Chicago and received a PhD in 1949. He joined the faculty in 1948 and was dean from 1952 to 1961. From 1961 to 1971, he worked at the **American Library Association (ALA)**, first as director of the International Relations Office and then as director of the Office for Library **Education**. There, he produced a statement, "Library Education and Manpower," that proposed a hierarchy of training and education for all library personnel. Also called the Asheim paper or statement, it was officially adopted by ALA on June 30, 1970, and, with a few revisions, has remained a major ALA policy document. Asheim returned to the University of Chicago in 1971. In 1975, he accepted a faculty position at the University of North Carolina. His article "Not **Censorship** but Selection," published in *Wilson Library Bulletin* in 1953, is considered a classic article on **intellectual freedom**.

ASIA. *See* ASIA, SOUTHEAST; CHINA; INDIA; JAPAN.

ASIA-PACIFIC CONFERENCE ON LIBRARY AND INFORMATION EDUCATION AND PRACTICE (A-LIEP). The first A-LIEP was organized in 2006 by the Library and **Information Science** (LIS) departments of the National Technical University of Singapore and the University of Malaya. Twenty-one countries were represented. This was possibly the first LIS conference focusing on the **Asia**-Pacific region, and it led to greater regional collaboration and cooperation among LIS educators and researchers. The fifth A-LIEP was held in Thailand in 2013.
    See also CHINA; JAPAN.

ASIA, SOUTHEAST. Although the history of libraries in Southeast Asia dates back thousands of years, many aspects of the modern era of librarianship have their roots in colonial occupation. The first **public library** in Singapore, the Singapore Library (later the Raffles Library and Museum), was founded by British expatriates and opened to the public on a subscription basis in 1845. In the Philippines, the American Circulating Library, opened in 1899 for the use of American soldiers and sailors, was turned over to the government in 1901 and became part of the Philippine National Library. The Dutch built libraries in Indonesia as tools to control what was published and read. Most libraries in Vietnam developed along French lines, with an emphasis on preservation of the collection for use by scholars.

    The first library training program in Southeast Asia was organized by Americans James Alexander Robertson and Mary Polk in the Philippines in 1914. The Philippine Library Association (now the Philippine Librarians Association) has been in existence since 1923 and serves as an umbrella for all the library associations (nearly 30) in the country. Training for librarians in Thailand began in 1951 at Chulalongkorn University under the auspices of the Fulbright Foundation, and several librarians who had completed the program founded the Thai Library Association in 1954. The Malayan Library Group, founded in 1955, later became the Library Association of Singapore and the Librarians Association of Malaysia. A Vietnam Library Association was originally founded in 1959 and was reinstituted in 2006. The Indonesian Library Association was formed in 1973 with the merger of the Indonesian Association of Special Libraries and the Indonesian Library, Archive, and **Documentation** Association. With the formation of the Laos Library Association in 2007, a professional library group existed in every country in the region. Brunei became the latest Southeast Asian country to set up a Library and **Information Science** (LIS) program, which was established in 2000. Graduate-level **education** is not available in all Southeast Asian countries, and there are no formal library training programs in Cambodia, Laos, or Myanmar. In 2010, there were just 15 professionally trained librarians in Laos and four in Cambodia.

The **academic libraries** of Malaysia, the Philippines, Singapore, and Thailand are the most developed in the region. Singapore has an innovative public library system for its urban population. In several countries, rural public library services are a focus, and mobile library networks are extensive. Library **automation** began in the 1980s, with Malaysia and Singapore taking the lead. Overall, library development has been uneven, and Cambodia, Laos, and Myanmar, in particular, lag behind. The Asia Foundation and the **United Nations Educational, Scientific and Cultural Association (UNESCO)** are among the organizations that have worked to advance library development in the region.

Beginning with the formation of the **Congress of Southeast Asian Librarians (CONSAL)** in 1970, regional cooperation has played an increasingly significant role, and librarians in Southeast Asia have worked on collaborative projects related to bibliographic control, digitization, information networking, and LIS education.

See also ASIA-PACIFIC CONFERENCE ON LIBRARY AND INFORMATION EDUCATION AND PRACTICE (A-LIEP).

ASSEMBLY OF LIBRARIANS OF THE AMERICAS. The Assembly of Librarians of the Americas, the first specifically international librarians' conference held in the **United States**, was organized in 1947 by the US State Department and the **Library of Congress (LC)**, in cooperation with the Pan American Union, the **American Library Association (ALA)**, and other bodies. Representatives from libraries and archives in every country in **Latin America** except Honduras, along with librarians from **Canada**, the Philippines, and the United States met from May 12 to June 7 at the LC to discuss library development and library relations. Among the Assembly's outcomes were increased inter-American cooperation, Spanish editions of the **Dewey Decimal Classification (DDC)** and the ***Anglo-American Cataloging Rules (AACR)***, and recommendations for training requirements for Latin American librarians.

ASSOCIATION FOR AMERICAN LIBRARY SCHOOLS (AALS). *See* ASSOCIATION FOR LIBRARY AND INFORMATION SCIENCE EDUCATION (ALISE).

ASSOCIATION FOR INFORMATION SCIENCE AND TECHNOLOGY (ASIS&T). ASIS&T was founded on March 13, 1937, as the American **Documentation** Institute (ADI), an organization made up of individuals nominated by and representing affiliated scientific and professional societies, foundations, and government agencies. Its founder, Watson Davis, was the head of Science Service, a news service designed to popularize science and disseminate scientific knowledge to the general public. ADI's initial interest was the development of microfilm as an aid to information dissemination. The organization's name was changed to the American Society for **Information Science** (ASIS) in 1968, the American Society for Information Science and Technology (ASIST) in 2000, and the Association for Information Science and Technology (ASIS&T) in 2013.

See also INTERNATIONAL FEDERATION FOR INFORMATION AND DOCUMENTATION (FID).

ASSOCIATION FOR LIBRARY AND INFORMATION SCIENCE EDUCATION (ALISE). The foundation for ALISE was created in 1911, when a group of library school faculty who were meeting at the **American Library Association (ALA)** conference formed the Round Table of Library School Instructors. The Round Table voted to form a permanent organization, the Association of American Library Schools (AALS), in 1915. The new association set some early standards for library **education**, but this function was taken over by ALA following the publication of the **Williamson report** in 1923. AALS began publishing *Journal of Education for Librarianship* (now *Journal for Education in Library and Information Science*) in 1959. The association's name was changed to Association for Library and **Information Science** Education in 1983. In 2012, ALISE had 500 members and more than 60 institutional members, mostly in the **United States** and **Canada**.

See also KELLOGG-ALISE INFORMATION PROFESSIONS AND EDUCATION RENEWAL PROJECT (KALIPER).

ASSOCIATION OF CARIBBEAN UNIVERSITY, RESEARCH AND INSTITUTIONAL LIBRARIES (ACURIL). ACURIL was founded as the Association of **Caribbean** Research and Institute Libraries in 1969, at a conference sponsored by the Association of Caribbean Universities. Headquartered in San Juan, Puerto Rico, ACURIL has three official languages—English, French, and Spanish—and includes **school, public,** national, **academic,** and special libraries from countries in the Caribbean basin together with mainland countries that border the Caribbean Sea and the Gulf of **Mexico.**
See also CUBA; LATIN AMERICA; MEXICO.

ASSOCIATION OF COLLEGE AND RESEARCH LIBRARIES (ACRL). The **American Library Association**'s **(ALA)** largest division, ACRL is a national organization of **academic** and research libraries and librarians. ACRL got its start in 1889, when 13 librarians attending the ALA Annual Conference in St. Louis recommended that a section be formed for college libraries. The first meeting of the College Library Section was held at the Annual Conference at the White Mountains of New Hampshire the following year, with 15 librarians in attendance. In 1897, the name was changed to the College and Reference Library Section, and in 1923, the section adopted its own bylaws. The movement toward a stronger professional organization, which had begun in the 1920s, culminated in 1938 with the approval of bylaws that transformed the section into an autonomous association. In response, the ALA Council ratified a new constitution that included provisions for the creation of self-governing divisions. ACRL was recognized as ALA's first division on May 1, 1940.
See also COUNCIL ON LIBRARY AND INFORMATION RESOURCES (CLIR); OPEN ACCESS (OA) MOVEMENT.

ASSOCIATION OF RESEARCH LIBRARIES (ARL). ARL was founded in 1932 by the directors of several large North American university and research libraries in order to facilitate cooperation and to address common problems. There were 42 charter members. In 1962, a secretariat was established in Washington, D.C., with a grant from the National Science Foundation (NSF), and ARL expanded to 72 members. By 2012, membership had increased to 126 **academic,** government, and **public libraries** in North America.
See also COOPERATIVE ACQUISITIONS PROJECT FOR WARTIME PUBLICATIONS; OPEN ACCESS (OA) MOVEMENT; RESEARCH LIBRARIES GROUP (RLG); SCHOLARLY PUBLISHING AND ACADEMIC RESOURCES COALITION (SPARC); SERIALS CRISIS.

ASSOCIATION OF SPECIAL LIBRARIES AND INFORMATION BUREAUX (ASLIB). In the mid-1910s, the government of **Great Britain** began to sponsor information bureaus that were set up within companies to collect and disseminate technical and scientific data. A movement to coordinate this activity led to a conference in 1924 that was attended by librarians from information bureaus and special libraries. ASLIB was formally organized in 1926. In the 1930s, ASLIB became aligned with the international **documentation** movement, and during World War II, it played an important role in addressing problems related to the flow of scientific, industrial, and military information. ASLIB was liquidated in 2004, and in 2010 was acquired by MCB Group, the holding company for Emerald Group Publishing Limited. It is now known as ASLIB: The Association for Information Management.

See also INFORMATION SCIENCE; LIBRARY ASSOCIATION (LA).

ATKINSON, HUGH C. (1933–1986). Hugh Atkinson was born on November 27, 1933, in Chicago, Illinois. Following his graduation from the University of Chicago's **Graduate Library School (GLS)**, he held positions at Pennsylvania Military College and the State University of New York at Buffalo. In 1967, he moved to Ohio State University, where he was instrumental in the creation of an online **catalog** and circulation system based on short records. The Library Circulation System (LCS, later the Library Computer System) was one of the first online library circulation programs, intended to further cooperation among libraries by making circulation information for a given library available throughout a library network. Atkinson next implemented LCS at the University of Illinois at Urbana-Champaign, where he became university librarian in 1976. He also oversaw the creation of the multitype Illinois LCS network, which became the most developed statewide library system of its time. The **American Library Association (ALA)** Hugh C. Atkinson Memorial Award for contributions by an academic librarian in the areas of library **automation** or management was established in his honor.

ATLANTA UNIVERSITY SCHOOL OF LIBRARY SERVICE. See SCHOOL OF LIBRARY SERVICE, ATLANTA UNIVERSITY.

AUSTIN, DEREK WILLIAM (1921–2001). Derek William Austin was born in London, England, on August 11, 1921. After serving in World War II, he received a grant to attend library school, and he was elected a Fellow of the **Library Association** in 1950. He worked in **public libraries** in **Great Britain** until 1963, when he was appointed as subject editor of the **British National Bibliography (BNB)**. From 1967 to 1969, he also worked under the auspices of the **Classification Research Group** to develop a new bibliographic **classification** scheme. Although no new scheme materialized, Austin applied the general principles formulated during the project to the creation of a new subject index for the BNB, the Preserved Context Index System (PRECIS), which was also adopted in **Australia**, **Canada**, and elsewhere. Although the BNB replaced PRECIS in 1996, Austin's system has continued to influence indexing practices. After the BNB became part of the **British Library** in 1974, Austin was appointed as the head of the library's Subject Systems Office.

AUSTRALIA. The first libraries in Australia were subscription libraries, which began to appear as early as the 1820s. Free **public library** service was established beginning with the opening of the Melbourne Public Library in Victoria in 1856. Public libraries were also opened in the capitals of other newly created colonies, but they were, in fact, state libraries with a primary mission of providing **reference service**. They also administered government subsidies, which supported the subscription-based libraries in the mechanics' institutes that had been set up based on the model created in **Great Britain**. Some of the Australian mechanics' institute libraries persisted well into the 20th century. In part because of the continued existence of such libraries, the development of free, locally supported public libraries was slow. The establishment of a professional association also proceeded in fits and starts. The Library Association of Australia, founded in 1896, held several conferences before it was dissolved in 1902. It was succeeded by the Australian Library Association in 1928.

The year 1934 was a watershed in the history of Australian librarianship. In that year, the **Carnegie Corporation of New York** commissioned Ralph Munn, director of the Carnegie Library of Pittsburgh, and Ernest R. Pitt, head of the State Library of Victoria, to undertake a study of Australian libraries. Their landmark report, *Australian Libraries: A Survey of Conditions and Suggestions for Improvement* (also known as the Munn-Pitt report), harshly condemned the institute libraries and called for the creation of public libraries along American and British lines. It also recommended the establishment of an association that would administer exams and maintain a register of qualified librarians. As a result of the report, the Australian Library Association went out of existence in the 1930s, to be replaced by the Australian Institute of Librarians in 1937. The report also gave rise to a grassroots Free Library Movement, as well as to the passage of a series of Library Acts that made provisions for free public library service. Despite its slow beginnings, the public library movement developed rapidly beginning in the last quarter of the 20th century, and by 2008, every community in Australia, including remote rural and Aboriginal communities, had free public library service.

John Wallace Metcalfe, a key figure in Australian librarianship, started the practice of formal library training in the late 1930s, with a series of courses held within the Public Library of New South Wales. In 1941, the Australian Institute of Librarians (the name of which was changed to Library Association of Australia in 1949) set up its Board of Examination and **Certification**, and in 1944 administered its first exams. Training schools were established in the major state libraries to prepare employees and others wishing take the exams. The first full-time Australian School of Librarianship (now the School of Information, Library, and Archive Studies) opened in 1960 at the University of New South Wales, with Metcalfe as its director. Library training programs were also created at a number of technical colleges. The Library Association of Australia (now Australian Library and Information Association, ALIA) phased out its examination system in the 1960s and began accrediting courses at the librarian and library technician levels.

See also McCOLVIN, LIONEL R. (1896–1976).

AUTOMATION. Library automation began with the circulation system. The first charging machine, the Dickman Book Charger, was put on the market in 1927, and the first electronic machine, the Gaylord Electric-Automatic Book Charger, was introduced in 1932. In the 1930s, some libraries began to experiment with punch cards. The cards were used with equipment manufactured by International Business Machines Corporation (IBM), and IBM decided to look for a library to automate with state-of-the-art techniques. The system developed for the Montclair (New Jersey) **Public Library** in 1940 consisted of punch book cards and borrower cards and a device called a record control unit, which was wired to a keypunch machine. Other libraries tried photocharging, which created a photographic record of circulation transactions; and audiocharging, which involved dictating information into a microphone and recording it on a disc. Automation did not begin to have a real impact, however, until the arrival of minicomputers and machine-readable records, especially the standardized **Machine-Readable Cataloging (MARC)** developed by the **Library of Congress (LC)**. Beginning in the 1960s, computers significantly changed not only circulation but also acquisitions, **cataloging**, and serials control.

Faster processing speeds, increased storage, and lower hardware costs helped pave the way for important advances in the late 1960s and 1970s. Several pioneering local automation projects were created, among them Ohio State University's Library Circulation System (LCS) and Stanford University's **Bibliographic Automation of Large Library Operations using a Time-sharing System (BALLOTS)**. Another significant trend was the evolution of computer-based bibliographic service centers (called bibliographic "utilities") such as the online union catalog implemented by the **Online**

Computer Library Center (OCLC), offering access to large databases of ready-to-use cataloging records. OCLC, the **Research Library Information Network (RLIN)**, and other computer-based networks quickened the pace of library automation in the **United States** because it was easier and less expensive for libraries to join networks than to develop their own systems. Finally, commercial automated library systems became available; in the mid-1970s, Computer Library Systems, Inc. (CLSI) was the first company to sell a computer-based circulation control system.

These early developments in automation were applied to backroom operations, but local computer-generated catalogs began to appear in the 1960s. The computer-output microform (COM) catalog was widely adopted in the 1970s. A few institutions, Ohio State University Libraries being one of the first, introduced an online public access catalog (OPAC). OPAC development accelerated in the 1980s and led to integrated systems in which the public-access catalog was just one component of a larger online system.

Searching for and retrieving information was another service-related library function that became increasingly automated, beginning in the 1960s. The American Chemical Society was an early leader in the use of computer technology to organize and disseminate information. Large-scale retrieval systems and services began to emerge. In 1964, the **National Library of Medicine (NLM)** launched the Medical Literature Analysis and Retrieval System (MEDLARS). The Educational Resources Information Center (ERIC) was established by the US Department of Education in 1967. Many of the early databases were produced by government agencies and were limited to government use, but in 1972, the first commercial, nongovernmental database was made publicly available by Dialog, an online search service that had been developed by Lockheed. Publishers of printed **bibliographies**, indexes, and other works used by libraries started to automate their processes, enabling them not only to produce print products more efficiently but also to feed computer-readable databases. Access to databases was accelerated in the 1980s by the introduction of CD-ROM, which library patrons could use on their own instead of having to rely on librarians as intermediaries.

In 1969, the Advanced Research Projects Agency Network (ARPANET) became the first network to use a single communications link to communicate with more than one machine. In 1986, ARPANET was replaced by the National Science Foundation Network (NSFNET), which formed the backbone of the Internet and opened the way for the World Wide Web in the 1990s. Networked technologies made it possible for libraries to share catalogs and to include in their catalogs digital resources held both internally and externally. This was a major step in the evolution of library automation from transforming behind-the-scenes technical operations to transforming the way libraries and their users connect, and in moving libraries from a model based on ownership to one based on access.

Libraries in northern Europe began to automate in the 1970s. Although regional, national, and linguistic fragmentation initially hampered European automation efforts, the development of regional and national networks such as the Project for Integrated Catalogue Automation (PICA) in the Netherlands and the London and South Eastern Library Region (LASER) network in **Great Britain** helped to promote cooperation and standardization. The trend in Europe since the 1990s has been to connect library systems across borders. The slower pace of library automation in some areas of the world has contributed to a digital divide. The Andrew W. Mellon Foundation and the Open Society Foundations have spearheaded projects to support library automation in **Eastern Europe**, and the **United Nations Educational, Scientific and Cultural Organization (UNESCO)** has played a role in library automation in **Asia** and **Latin America**.

See also AVRAM, HENRIETTE D. (1919–2006); BIRMINGHAM LIBRARIES COOPERATIVE MECHANISATION PROJECT (BLCMP); KILGOUR, FREDERICK G. (1914–2006).

AVRAM, HENRIETTE D. (1919–2006). Library **automation** pioneer Henriette Avram was born in New York City on October 7, 1919. In 1952, with no college degree and little previous work experience, she was given a job at the National Security Agency (NSA) as a systems analyst and programmer. Following positions at the American Research Bureau and Datatrol, an early software company, she joined the **Library of Congress (LC)** in June 1965 and was assigned to come up with an automated **cataloging** format. To that end, she developed and implemented the **Machine-Readable Cataloging (MARC)** pilot project, which culminated in the launch of the MARC Distribution Service in 1969. In addition to working to ensure that MARC would be adopted nationwide, she contributed to the development of international standards for cataloging. She culminated her career at LC as associate librarian for collections, directing 1,700 employees.

See also WOMEN IN LIBRARIANSHIP.

B

BACON, FRANCIS (1561–1626). English statesman and philosopher who is known as the creator of the scientific method. He also developed an outline of knowledge based on the principle that all intellectual pursuits are rooted in three faculties: memory (history), imagination (poetry), and reason (philosophy). Many subsequent **classification** schemes were based on Baconian principles, including the **Dewey Decimal Classification (DDC)**.

BAIN, JAMES, JR. (1842–1908). Canadian library leader James Bain was born on August 2, 1842, in London, England. His family, originally from Scotland, moved to Toronto, **Canada**, in 1846. Starting in his youth, Bain worked among books, first at his father's Toronto bookshop, then for publishers in **Great Britain** and Canada. In 1883, he was appointed the first chief librarian of the new Toronto **Public Library**, which opened in 1884 in a renovated building. During his tenure, he opened four branch libraries and built a major collection of Canadian history and literature. In 1903, he sought and received a grant from **Andrew Carnegie** for a new main library building and three additional branches. Bain was a founding member of the Ontario Library Association and served as its first president from 1901 to 1902. The James Bain Medallion is awarded each year to an outstanding library board member in Ontario.

BAKER, AUGUSTA B. (1911–1998). Augusta Baker was born in Baltimore, Maryland, on April 1, 1911. In 1934, she became the first **African American** to receive a **library science** degree from the Albany (New York) State Teachers College. When she was hired in 1937 by **Anne Carroll Moore** as an assistant to the **children's** librarian at the 135th Street Branch in Harlem, it was the start of a 37-year career at New York **Public Library** (NYPL). In 1939, she founded the James Weldon Johnson Memorial Collection of books, presenting unbiased, well-rounded portrayals of African Americans that became the basis for the groundbreaking **bibliography** *Books about Negro Life for Children*. Baker was promoted to Assistant Coordinator of Children's Services and Storytelling Specialist in 1954 and in 1961 became Coordinator of Children's Services. Her retirement from NYPL in 1974 was followed by a second career as the University of South Carolina's storyteller-in-residence. The annual Augusta Baker's Dozen, a storytelling festival, was established in her honor. The University of South Carolina's Thomas Cooper Library houses the Augusta Baker Collection of Children's Literature and Folklore.

See also WOMEN IN LIBRARIANSHIP.

BALLOTS. *See* BIBLIOGRAPHIC AUTOMATION OF LARGE LIBRARY OPERATIONS USING A TIME-SHARING SYSTEM (BALLOTS).

BARKER, TOMMIE DORA (1888–1978). Tommie Dora Barker was born on November 15, 1888 in Rockmart, Georgia. She attended Agnes Scott College and graduated from the **Carnegie** Library School of Atlanta in 1909. After working in Alabama, she returned to Atlanta and took a job at the Carnegie Library of Atlanta, becoming its director in 1915. From 1915 to 1930, she was also director of the library's training school, which became affiliated with Emory University in 1925. In 1930, she began the phase of her career for which she is perhaps best known when she was appointed the **American Library Association (ALA)** regional field manager for the South, overseeing the Rosenwald Fund's county library demonstrations, among other projects. Her book *Libraries of the South: A Report on Developments, 1930–1935* was the first survey of the condition of libraries in the region. In 1936, Barker returned to the Emory Library School as director, a position she held until retiring in 1954.

See also WOMEN IN LIBRARIANSHIP.

BATCHELDER, MILDRED L. (1901–1998). Mildred L. Batchelder was born on September 7, 1901, in Lynn, Massachusetts. She received a BA from Mt. Holyoke College in 1922, followed by a BLS from the **New York State Library School** in 1924. After working as a **children's** librarian, she joined the staff of the **American Library Association (ALA)** in 1936 as the first **school library** specialist, and in 1938, she became head of the School and Children's Library Division. In 1957, her title became Executive Secretary of the Children's Service Division and the **Young Adult** Services Division. Throughout her career, Batchelder fostered school library development and school–**public library** cooperation, advocated for library services for children who were underserved, and pioneered internationalism in children's literature. She strongly believed that the translation of foreign-language children's books would increase global understanding. The Batchelder Award, created in 1966 (the year of her retirement), is presented each year to an American publisher for translation of a book originally published in a foreign language in another country.

See also WOMEN IN LIBRARIANSHIP.

BATTLE OF THE BOOKS. In **Great Britain**, a controversy known as the Battle of the Books erupted in the 19th century over the question as to whether open access should be allowed in **public libraries**. Most librarians were opposed to open access, but by the 1890s, a number of prominent librarians had begun to campaign for its wider adoption. By the 1920s, all British public libraries had opened their shelves.

See also BROWN, JAMES DUFF (1862–1914).

BELPRÉ, PURA (1899–1982). Pura Belpré was born in Cidra, Puerto Rico, on February 2, 1899 (or 1903). After studying for a year at the University of Puerto Rico, she relocated to New York City in 1920. In 1921, she became the first Puerto Rican to be hired by the New York **Public Library** (NYPL) when she took a job as the Hispanic assistant at the branch at 135th Street in Harlem. In 1925, she enrolled in the library school at NYPL and studied storytelling, which became an important part of her library work. In 1929, she was transferred to the 115th Street Branch, and later to the 110th Street Branch, to work with the growing Puerto Rican population. After her marriage in 1943, Belpré devoted her time to storytelling and writing. In 1960, she returned to NYPL and was appointed Spanish **Children's** Specialist. She continued her outreach to the Puerto Rican community following her retirement in 1968. The Pura Belpré Award, established in 1996, is presented each year to a Latino/Latina writer and illustrator of a book for children.

See also WOMEN IN LIBRARIANSHIP.

BENJAMIN FRANKLIN LIBRARY. In 1941, the **American Library Association (ALA)** was asked by the government of the **United States** to operate an American-style **public library** in **Mexico** City. The Benjamin Franklin Library, or Biblioteca Benjamín Franklin, was dedicated on April 13, 1942, its name chosen in part because Franklin was an admired figure in **Latin America**. Modeled on the **American Library in Paris**, the Benjamin Franklin Library was intended to promote cultural relations between Mexico and the United States and to showcase American librarianship. The US government provided money for staff salaries, equipment, and books. ALA contributed technical advice, nominated the director, and assisted with book selection. In addition to housing a collection of American books and periodicals, the library offered a wide range of cultural activities, including English-language classes. ALA ceased its involvement in 1947, but the library has continued to play an important role in strengthening relations between libraries in Mexico and the United States.

See also INTERNATIONAL LIBRARIANSHIP; OVERSEAS LIBRARIES PROGRAMS.

BIBLIOGRAPHIC AUTOMATION OF LARGE LIBRARY OPERATIONS USING A TIME-SHARING SYSTEM (BALLOTS). BALLOTS was an integrated technical processing system developed at Stanford University. One of a number of online systems implemented by research libraries in the **United States** during the early 1970s, it had an impact on American librarianship because of its adoption by the **Research Libraries Group (RLG)** as the basis for the **Research Libraries Information Network (RLIN)**.

See also AUTOMATION; BIBLIOGRAPHY.

BIBLIOGRAPHY. The term *bibliography* refers to the study of books. Enumerative (or systematic) bibliography is the listing of books according to some plan, and it developed as a way to control recorded information. The librarians of antiquity were primarily bibliographers. One of the best known was the Greek poet **Callimachos**, who worked at the **Alexandrian Library** in the third century BCE. He compiled the *Tables of Persons Eminent in Every Branch of Learning Together with a List of Their Writings* (better known as the *Pinakes*), which served as both a bibliography and a **catalog** of the library's holdings. The catalogs of medieval **monasteries** attest to the continuing effort to enumerate the books contained in large collections, or, in a few cases, in several collections.

Bibliographies began to develop as entities separate from library catalogs after the invention of moveable type. Johann Tritheim, the abbot of a German monastery, is credited with compiling the first true bibliography, and for that reason he has been called the father of bibliography. His *Liber de scriptoribus ecclesiasticus* (1494) lists around 7,000 ecclesiastical works, arranged chronologically by their authors and indexed by the authors' Christian names. He published a second bibliography, focusing on German authors, in 1495. Another important early bibliography is *Biblioteca universalis*, which was compiled by Swiss zoologist **Conrad Gesner** and published beginning in 1545. Rather than restricting himself to works related to a particular field, such as theology, Gesner sought to take a more universal approach by listing every author who had written in Greek, Latin, and Hebrew. Gesner's is the first example of a classified bibliography, and of a bibliography that includes descriptions of books. It is divided into two parts: a listing of approximately 1,800 authors and their works and a listing of the works arranged under 21 subject headings. Gesner provided short biographical data for each author, along with indications of printing places and dates, printers, and editors of the works, most of which he had examined during visits to libraries in **Germany** and **Italy**. Another bibliography based largely on firsthand examination was John Bale's 1548 listing of the writers of England, Scotland, and Wales, which was one of the first attempts to record a national literature. Bibliographies related to subjects such as medicine and law also began to appear.

Another type of bibliography that developed during this period came from the book trade and listed books that were available for sale. The first full-scale book catalog was issued in 1564 by Georg Willer, a bookseller in Augsburg, and was intended to provide advance information on books that would be available at book fairs. It was issued regularly until 1627 and had numerous imitators. The first comprehensive book trade catalog in **Great Britain**, *Catalogue of English Printed Bookes*, was published by English bookseller Andrew Maunsell in 1595. Library catalogs continued to serve as bibliographic guides, and the first **Bodleian Library** catalog, which was the first general library catalog to be printed in Europe, appeared in 1605.

American bibliography began in 1693 with the catalog of the library of Reverend Samuel Lee of Boston, whose books were being offered for sale. The first American college library catalog, that of Harvard College, appeared in 1723. The **Library Company of Philadelphia** published a catalog of its holdings in 1757, and other **social libraries** followed suit. The first book trade bibliography in the **United States** was published by Boston booksellers in 1804. Although it listed just 1,138 books and was discontinued after the first issue, it helped lay the groundwork for tools for booksellers and librarians, such as the *Publishers' Trade List Annual*, started by Frederick Leypoldt in 1873, and the *Cumulative Book Index*, started by **H. W. Wilson** in 1898. Among other notable examples of the bibliographies that began to appear in the 19th and early 20th centuries are Joseph Sabin's *Dictionary of Books Relating to America from Its Discovery to the Present Time*, first published in 1868 and continued by **Wilberforce Eames**; and **Charles Evans**'s *American Bibliography: A Chronological Dictionary of All Books, Pamphlets, and Periodical Publications Printed in the United States of America from the Genesis of Printing in 1639 Down to and Including the Year 1820, with Bibliographical and Biographical Notes*, published beginning in 1903.

Just as the explosion in the number of books led to a substantial increase in the number of bibliographies, the growth of libraries led to an increase in both the number of library catalogs and the attention paid to organizing them. There was also a growing sense that a unified approach to cataloging was needed. As early as 1850, **Charles Coffin Jewett** of the Smithsonian Institution library called for a centralized cataloging agency, which would not only create efficiency but would be the means of publishing a bibliography of library holdings in the United States.

During the 19th and 20th centuries, interest in national bibliography grew, especially as 'legal deposit legislation made it easier to acquire bibliographic control of a country's publications. National bibliographies began in **Russia** in 1907, in Germany in 1913, and in **Japan** in 1948. The **British National Bibliography (BNB)** was established in 1949, the **Indian** National Biography in 1958, the Kenya National Bibliography in 1980, the **Brazil** Bibliography in 1983, and the **China** National Bibliography in1998. National libraries serve as the official bibliographic centers in many countries, not only creating and publishing the national bibliography but also processing and distributing bibliographic records for all libraries to use. The United States is one of a handful of countries that do not have a national bibliography (nor does the United States have an official national bibliographic center, although the **Library of Congress [LC]** performs many of the functions of a national bibliographic agency).

The structure of national bibliographic services throughout the world has been greatly influenced by international conferences, beginning with the 1950 Conference on the Improvement of Bibliographic Services, which was sponsored by the **United Nations Educational, Social and Cultural Organization (UNESCO)**. This was followed in 1977 by the International Congress on National Bibliographies, sponsored by UNESCO and the **International Federation of Library Associations and Institutions (IFLA)**. In 1998, the International Conference on National Bibliographic Services affirmed that the national bibliography is a major instrument in ensuring a full recording of the national published heritage and achieving bibliographic control.

In 1895, two Belgian lawyers, Henri LaFontaine and **Paul Otlet**, conceived the idea of a master bibliography of all the world's knowledge. Their project, at first called the Universal Bibliographic Repertory and later renamed the Mundaneum, was a catalog assembled by cutting information from printed library catalogs and other sources and pasting it on cards, the number of which eventually grew to more than 12 million. Otlet began to speculate about technological solutions to managing the sheer volume of paper, but it took the arrival of the computer age and the introduction of **machine-readable cataloging (MARC)** and bibliographic networks such as the **Online Computer Library Center (OCLC)** to bring the idea of a universal bibliography closer to reality. Since the 1970s, IFLA has supported **universal bibliographic control** through the creation of standards to facilitate the exchange of bibliographic records.

See also INTERNATIONAL STANDARD BIBLIOGRAPHIC DESCRIPTION (ISBD).

BIBLIOTHÈQUE NATIONALE DE FRANCE (BNF). Considered to be the first real national library, **France**'s Bibliothèque nationale originated in 1520, when King Francis I established the Royal Library at Fontainebleau and appointed humanist scholar Guillaume Budé as his *maître de librarie*. The Royal Library was later transferred to Paris. The first **legal deposit** system, which required that a copy of every published book be deposited in the king's library, was introduced in 1537. In the 18th century, the library was opened to the general public once a week for two hours. During the **French Revolution**, the Royal Library became the Bibliothèque nationale. In the 1990s, much of the collection was moved to a new building, the Bibliothèque François Mitterand, which became part of a new administrative entity called the Bibliothèque nationale de France (BnF), encompassing both the new library and the old Bibliothèque nationale. The new library was controversial because of its design, which called for storing books in glass-walled towers where they would be exposed to sunlight. Wood panels were later installed behind the glass in order to protect the books. It was also controversial because it broke from the scholarly tradition of French librarianship in order to serve the general public as well as researchers. Proclaimed as "the first library of the third millennium," it was France's largest postwar cultural project.

See also CAIN, JULIEN (1887–1974); DELISLE, LÉOPOLD VICTOR (1826–1910).

BILLINGS, JOHN SHAW (1838–1913). John Shaw Billings was born on April 12, 1938, in Allensville, Indiana. After graduating from Miami University, Oxford, Ohio, in 1857, he studied medicine and served as a field surgeon and hospital administrator during the American Civil War. In 1864, he was assigned to the Surgeon General's office in Washington, D.C., and over the course of 30 years, he became a leading expert on public hygiene, hospital construction, sanitary engineering, medical and vital statistics, and medical **bibliography**. He turned the small library of the Surgeon General's office into the nation's foremost medical library, now the **National Library of Medicine (NLM)**. In the 1870s, he initiated two pioneering finding guides, the *Index Catalogue* and the *Index Medicus*. Shaw retired from the army in 1895, and in 1896, he became the first director of the New York **Public Library**. He consolidated two major as well as numerous smaller existing libraries, initiated a branch library system, and persuaded **Andrew Carnegie** to contribute funds for building a central library, which opened in 1911. Billings was president of the **American Library Association (ALA)** from 1901 to 1902.

See also PUBLIC LIBRARIES IN THE UNITED STATES OF AMERICA.

BIRMINGHAM LIBRARIES COOPERATIVE MECHANISATION PROJECT (BLCMP). Funded by **Great Britain**'s Office of Scientific and Technical Information, BLCMP was created in 1969 to develop a system that would allow three libraries (Birmingham **Public Libraries** and the libraries of the University of Aston and Birmingham University) to cooperatively use **machine-readable** bibliographic records produced by the **British National Bibliography (BNB)** and the **Library of Congress (LC)**. A computer-generated union **catalog** of the three participating libraries was produced in 1972. BLCMP was the first example of an automated library network in Britain and it gained national importance as other libraries became interested in the project.

BISHOP, WILLIAM WARNER (1871–1955). Academic library leader William Warner Bishop was born on July 21, 1871, in Hannibal, Missouri. Having received bachelor's and master's degrees from the University of Michigan, he taught Greek for several years before deciding to pursue a library career, first at Princeton University, and then at the **Library of Congress (LC)**. He accepted a position as librarian at the University of Michigan in 1915 and served as president of the **American Library Association (ALA)** from 1917 to 1918. Throughout his career, he made significant contributions to the concept of the academic research library as well as to **international** library cooperation. As the **Carnegie Corporation of New York**'s chief consultant on matters related to libraries and librarianship, he chaired the Corporation's Advisory Group on College Libraries. He also played a leading role in the founding of the **International Federation of Library Associations and Institutions (IFLA)**, serving as its president from 1931 to 1936, and in the reorganization of the **Vatican** Library.

BLACK CAUCUS OF THE AMERICAN LIBRARY ASSOCIATION (BCALA). The BCALA was formed in 1970 as a result of an invitation from librarian and civil rights activist **E. J. Josey** to **African American librarians** to meet at the **American Library Association (ALA)** Midwinter Meeting. The purpose was to call attention to the need for ALA to fulfill its responsibilities to minority groups in librarianship and in the nation at large. The first meeting of the BCALA took place at the 1970 ALA Annual Conference in Detroit, and a formal Statement of Purpose was ratified at the Annual Conference in Dallas in 1971. In 1992, the BCALA held its first national conference in Columbus, Ohio, with the theme "Culture Keepers: Enlightening and Empowering Our Communities."

See also PROGRESSIVE LIBRARIANSHIP.

BLISS BIBLIOGRAPHIC CLASSIFICATION. The last of the library **classification** schemes that appeared in the late 19th and early 20th centuries was created by **Henry Bliss** for the library of the City College of New York. An outline appeared in *Library Journal* in 1910, but it was not until after the publication of *A System of Bibliographic Classification* in 1935 that other libraries began to adopt it. The full edition was published in four volumes (1940–1953). The City College Library continued to use Bliss's system until 1967, and the system is still used in some British **academic** and special libraries. A radically revised version, called *BC2*, was published beginning in 1977.

See also COLON CLASSIFICATION; DEWEY DECIMAL CLASSIFI-CATION (DDC); LIBRARY OF CONGRESS CLASSIFICATION (LCC); UNIVERSAL DECIMAL CLASSIFICATION (UDC).

BLISS, HENRY EVELYN (1870–1955). Henry Bliss was born on January 29, 1870, in New York City. He attended the City College of New York but left without obtaining a degree. In 1891, he returned to City College as deputy librarian and remained there for nearly 50 years. Dissatisfied with the **Dewey Decimal Classification (DDC)** and **Library of Congress Classifica-tion (LCC)** systems, in 1908 he reorganized the City College collection using his own scheme, the **Bliss Bibliographic Classification**, which has been called the last of the important general **classification** schemes. Bliss also wrote two theoretical works on the organization of knowledge: *The Organization of Knowledge and the System of the Sciences* (1929) and *The Organization of Knowledge in Libraries and the Subject-Approach to Books* (1934).

BLUE, THOMAS FOUNTAIN (1866–1935). Thomas Fountain Blue was born in Farmville, Virginia, on March 6, 1866. He attended Hampton Normal and Agricultural Institute and Richmond Theological Seminary. In 1905, he was appointed librarian of the **Western Colored Branch** of the Louisville (Kentucky) Free **Public Library** and thus became a pioneer in library ser-vices to **African Americans**. A second branch, the Eastern Colored Branch, opened in 1914, and Blue was put in charge of that facility as well. In 1919, he became head of the Louisville Free Public Library's new Colored Depart-ment. Blue developed an **apprenticeship** program, which, until 1925, was the only program in the South for training black librarians and was consid-ered a national model. An active member of the **American Library Associa-tion (ALA)**, he was the only African American in attendance at the 1922 conference in Detroit, and his paper on the Western Colored Branch training program made him the first African American to deliver a speech at an ALA conference.

BOARD OF EDUCATION FOR LIBRARIANSHIP (BEL). In 1923, **Charles C. Williamson** was commissioned by the **Carnegie Corporation of New York** to examine library **education**. As a result of his report *Training for Library Service* (commonly known as the **Williamson report**), the **American Library Association (ALA)** formalized the BEL, which was charged with the evaluation and reorganization of library training, service, and **certification**. The BEL was replaced by the Committee on **Accreditation** in 1956.

BODLEIAN LIBRARY. In 1597, English diplomat and scholar **Thomas Bodley** offered to use his considerable fortune to restore and endow the old library quarters at Oxford University. The refurbished library opened in 1602. Bodley employed an agent to purchase books from the continent and hired Thomas James as librarian at a salary of 23 pounds a year. Bodley's letters to James reveal what he considered to be a librarian's duties: keeping records of donations, identifying books to be purchased, preparing a **catalog**, making materials available to scholars, and preventing the development of mold. The relationship between Bodley and James was frequently contentious. James felt overworked and underpaid, and was finally allowed to have an assistant in 1604. His request for permission to marry was at first refused, however, since Bodley considered that marriage would be a distraction.

The catalogs James compiled grew out of Bodley's frustration over not being able to determine what books were in the library and are considered milestones in catalog history. The 1605 catalog, the first general catalog to be printed in Europe, was in the same order as the books on the shelves. There, the arrangement was by size, then by university faculty (arts, theology, medicine, and law), and then by author. The second catalog, compiled in 1620, was the first general library catalog to be arranged alphabetically by author. The third published catalog, issued in 1674 when Thomas Hyde was the librarian, introduced the principle of selecting only one form of an author's name. It is better known, however, for the cataloging guidelines contained in its preface. The 1674 catalog and its successor, printed in 1738, were widely distributed and influenced cataloging practice in colonial America as well as in Europe.

See also ACADEMIC LIBRARIES; GREAT BRITAIN.

BODLEY, THOMAS (1545–1613). Thomas Bodley was born on March 2, 1545, in Exeter, England. After graduating from Oxford University in 1563, he became a fellow of Merton College. In 1576, he began a diplomatic career and traveled widely until his retirement from public life in 1597. In 1598, Bodley offered to restore Oxford's old library quarters (called Duke Humfrey's library after its original donor), which had been established in the previous century but had since fallen into disuse. He provided shelves and seats, and also endowed the library with an annual income. Although Bodley rarely visited the library, which opened in 1602, he was very involved in its operations. He filled his letters to his librarian, Thomas James, with instructions about acquisitions, **cataloging** and **classification**, preservation, and more. At his instigation, James compiled the first general library catalog to be printed in Europe. In 1610, Bodley made arrangements with the Stationers' Company (the printers' guild) to send the **Bodleian Library** a copy of every new book printed, the precursor to **legal deposit** agreements.

BOGLE, SARAH COMLY NORRIS (1870–1932). Sarah Comly Norris Bogle was born in White Deer Mills, Pennsylvania, on November 17, 1870. After attending the University of Chicago, she earned a certificate from the library school at the **Drexel Institute** in 1904. Following jobs at the Juniata College Library (where she was director) and Queensborough **Public Library,** she began working at the **Carnegie** Library of Pittsburgh in 1910, where she soon became head of the already nationally known **Children's** Department and director of the Carnegie Training School for Children's Librarians. In 1920, Bogle moved to Chicago to work for the **American Library Association (ALA).** As assistant secretary to **Carl Milam,** she played a key role in the funding and development of the **Paris Library School.** She traveled extensively, representing ALA at various international conferences. She was also involved in advancing library **education.** The Bogle Pratt International Library Travel Fund, sponsored by the Bogle Memorial Fund and the Pratt Institute School of Information and **Library Science,** is awarded each year to an ALA personal member to attend his or her first international conference.
See also WOMEN IN LIBRARIANSHIP.

BOOKLIST. Booklist is the review journal of the **American Library Association (ALA).** It was started in 1905 as a buying list of recent books, intended to assist librarians in making selection decisions. **Andrew Carnegie** provided funds to underwrite the publishing costs. The first issue, dated January–February 1905, included 108 titles, all suggested by librarians. *Booklist* was ALA's first serial publication, because *Library Journal,* which had served as the association's official organ since 1876, was published from the offices of *Publishers Weekly.*

BOOKS FOR CHINA. Many libraries and library collections in **China** were destroyed following the Japanese invasion of China in 1937. T. L. Yuan, the chairman of the Chinese Library Association, who was also the director of the National Library in Beijing, wrote to the **American Library**

Association (ALA) to ask if it would organize a committee to collect book donations for Chinese libraries. ALA's Committee on **International** Relations responded by announcing a Books for China campaign in 1938. Because of the military situation in China and elsewhere, the first shipment did not arrive until 1947. The materials in the first shipment were purchased by ALA with a grant from the US State Department, but other agencies also purchased or donated books and periodicals. In 1946, the Books for China program was expanded to include the Philippines.

BOONE LIBRARY SCHOOL. The Boone Library School, the first institution for training librarians in **China**, was established at Boone College, a small mission school in Wuchang, in 1920. Having created the Boone College Library in 1910, **Mary Elizabeth Wood** introduced an American-style **library science** program with the help of two Boone graduates, **Samuel T. Y. Seng** and Thomas C. S. Hu, whom she had arranged to send to the **United States** to study at the Library School of the New York **Public Library**. The Boone Library School opened with six students and Wood, Shen, and Hu as teachers. In the years that followed, the faculty comprised librarians from the United States and **Canada**, as well as Chinese scholars. In 1929, the school became a separate undergraduate institution. By 1949, it had trained nearly 500 professional librarians. The Boone Library School was absorbed by Wuhan University in 1952.

See also EDUCATION FOR LIBRARIANSHIP.

BORGES, JORGE LUIS (1899–1986). Jorge Luis Borges was born in Buenos Aires, **Argentina**, on August 24, 1899. Most of his education took place in Europe, where his family lived from 1914 to 1921. His first collection of poetry was published in 1923. Although better known as a writer, Borges was also a librarian. He worked at a branch of the Buenos Aires Municipal Library from 1937 to 1946, chiefly as a cataloger, and he wrote many of his short stories when his **cataloging** tasks were done. He was appointed director of the National Library in 1955, although by that time he was blind. He worked to make the library a cultural center while also using it as a place to pursue his literary career. When former Argentinian president Juan Perón returned from exile in **Spain** in 1973 and was elected president for a second time, Borges resigned. A number of his stories, especially "The Library of Babel" (1941), explore ideas related to the philosophy of librarianship, and he is considered by some to be the theoretical father of the World Wide Web.

BOSTON ATHENAEUM. The Boston Athenaeum first opened its doors in 1807. Like many other so-called **public libraries** of the time, it was a membership library, supported largely by the sale of shares and open to members of the public who were subscribers. In 1849, it moved from a house that had been purchased 40 years before to a newly constructed building on Beacon Street. By that time, the collection had grown to nearly 50,000 books. The 1874 **catalog**, begun in 1856 by **William Frederick Poole** and completed by **Charles Ammi Cutter**, became the model for the period. In 1853, a proposal to consolidate the library with the new **Boston Public Library** was voted on and defeated. Although the public library movement heralded the end of most subscription libraries in the **United States**, the Boston Athenaeum has survived to the present day.

See also SOCIAL LIBRARIES.

BOSTON PUBLIC LIBRARY. The Boston Public Library was the first large, municipally supported, freely accessible **public library** in the **United States**. In the 1840s, several prominent Bostonians, including Charles Ticknor, a Harvard professor, and Edward Everett, a clergyman, convinced the Boston city fathers to establish a public library. Ticknor, in particular, believed that such a library could be a force for social and political stability by supporting the education of the general public rather than by serving the narrower interests of scholars. Boston mayor Josiah Quincy Jr. and financier Joshua Bates made large donations. The library opened on March 20, 1854, in a former schoolhouse, with a collection of 16,000 volumes. Its opening gave a major impetus to the public library movement. In 1858, the library moved to a building on Boylston Street and, in 1895, to a new building in Copley Square.

BOSTWICK, ARTHUR ELMORE (1860–1942). Arthur Elmore Bostwick was born in Litchfield, Connecticut, on March 8, 1860. He received a PhD in physics from Yale University and worked in **reference** publishing for several years. He joined the staff of the New York **Public Library** (NYPL) in 1895. After serving as director of the Brooklyn Public Library from 1899 to 1901, he returned to NYPL as head of the circulating department. He was president of the **American Library Association (ALA)** from 1907 to 1908, and in 1909, he was appointed director of the St. Louis (Missouri) Public Library. In 1925, ALA sent Bostwick to **China** in response to a request from the Chinese Association for the Advancement of Education, which had asked for a delegate to provide guidance on introducing a modern library system. His seven-week visit, during which he met with librarians and dignitaries in a number of cities, had a considerable impact on public library development in China. He remained director of the St. Louis Public Library until 1938 and then stayed on as associate librarian until his death.

See also INTERNATIONAL LIBRARIANSHIP.

BOWKER, RICHARD ROGERS (1848–1933). Richard Rogers Bowker was born September 4, 1848, in Salem, Massachusetts. After graduating from the City College of New York in 1868, he worked as a journalist and bookseller. In 1873, he began work at Frederick Leypoldt's *Publishers Weekly*, which he subsequently bought from Leypoldt in 1878. In 1876, Bowker joined Leypoldt and **Melvil Dewey** to launch ***Library Journal*** and to plan the national meeting in October of that year that led to the formation of the **American Library Association (ALA)**. Throughout his career, Bowker continued to support the library profession through his publications and the many articles and editorials he wrote for *Library Journal*. He was an active member of ALA, and although he refused to serve as president because he was not a librarian, he was made honorary president late in life. He also played a role in the establishment of the Brooklyn **Public Library**, the organization of the American Book Trade Association, the passage of **copyright** legislation, and the appointment of **Herbert Putnam** as librarian of Congress.

BRADSHAW, LILLIAN MOORE (1915–2010). Lillian Moore Bradshaw, the first **woman** in the **United States** to head a big-city library system, was born in Hagerstown, Maryland. She earned a bachelor's degree from Western Maryland College and, in 1938, a master's degree in **library science** (MLS) from **Drexel** University. She worked in libraries in Utica, New York, and Baltimore, Maryland, before joining the staff of the Dallas (Texas) **Public Library** in 1946. She was appointed director of the Dallas Public Library in 1962, the first woman to hold the position. During her tenure as director, a new central library was constructed and 18 of the library's 25 branches were built. She continued to serve in city government after her retirement in 1984. Bradshaw served as president of the **American Library Association** (ALA) from 1971 to 1972. She was also known as an advocate for **intellectual freedom**.

BRAY, THOMAS (1656–1730). Church of England clergyman Thomas Bray was born in Shropshire, England. He graduated from Oxford University in 1675. A handbook based on his methods of teaching in the parish to which he was assigned brought him to the attention of church leaders, and in 1695, he was selected to oversee the work of clerics in new parishes in colonial Maryland. Because most of the clerics could not afford to buy the books they needed in order to instruct their parishioners, Bray decided to provide libraries that would loan books to the clergy and the laity. He issued a public appeal and ultimately established 39 libraries in North America, some with over 1,000 volumes. He also established 80 parochial lending libraries in **Great Britain**. Bray's plan for lending books was novel at the time. Although the Bray libraries gradually disappeared after his death, they are considered to be forerunners of **public libraries**.

BRAZIL. As with other countries in **Latin America**, the first Brazilian libraries were those established by religious houses. Brazil's National Library, founded in 1810, had its origins in the library of the Portuguese royal family, who were seeking refuge from Napoleon's troops. In 1915, the National Library began operating Brazil's first library training course, which was modeled after the **École nationale des chartes** in **France**. A course organized in the 1930s by **Rubens Borba Alves de Moraes**, director of the Municipal Library of São Paulo (today the Mario de Andrade Library), helped introduce North American concepts and techniques. An American-style training course was also offered at the Mackenzie Institute library in São Paulo. A permanent library school was established in São Paulo in 1940 with support from a **Rockefeller Foundation** grant administered by the **American Library Association (ALA)**. Another important development was the opening of the first branch of the Biblioteca Infantil, a library for children, in São Paulo in 1936. In 1962 came the first legislation officially acknowledging as librarians those individuals who graduated from recognized library schools. The first postgraduate course in librarianship, not only in Brazil but in Latin America, was implemented in 1970 by the Brazilian Institute of **Bibliography** and **Documentation** in conjunction with the Federal University of Rio de Janeiro. As of 2010, Brazil had a significant number of schools of library and **information science** (LIS) compared to other countries in Latin America. Study at the undergraduate level is the most common. The majority of librarians work in special and university libraries.

There are numerous professional library associations in Brazil. The oldest, the Paulista Association of Librarians, was founded in 1938 upon the graduation of the first class of librarians in São Paulo. Librarians meeting at the Second Brazilian Congress of Librarianship and Documentation in 1959 founded the Brazilian Federation of Library Associations (FEBAB, now the Brazilian Federation of Associations of Librarians, Information Scientists, and Institutions) to coordinate the work of the various regional associations. FEBAB has been the sponsor of the Brazilian Congresses of **Library Science** and Documentation since 1959.

BRETT, WILLIAM HOWARD (1846–1918). William Howard Brett was born on July 1, 1846, in Braceville, Ohio. After serving in the Civil War, he completed two years of college before settling in Cleveland. He spent the next 10 years working as a salesman at a bookstore. His reputation as an expert on books led to his appointment as head of the Cleveland **Public Library** in 1884. He was a leader in library innovation, reclassifying the collection using the **Dewey Decimal Classification (DDC)** and introducing open-shelf access and branch libraries. Brett was also a pioneer in **children's library service**, hiring the country's first children's librarian, **Effie Louise Power**, in 1895 and establishing a children's room in 1898. In 1896, he began publishing an index to periodicals which later became *The Reader's Guide to Periodical Literature*. He also played a key role in the founding of the library school at Western Reserve University and served as its first dean. He was president of the **American Library Association (ALA)** from 1896 to 1897.

BRIET, SUZANNE (1894–1989). Known as "Madame **Documentation**" for her contributions to the movement, Suzanne Briet was born in Paris, **France**. She attended the École de Sèvres, which trained **women** to be secondary school teachers, and taught in Algeria for several years. In 1924, after placing first on the national library examinations, she was one of the first three women hired by the **Bibliothèque nationale**, where she modernized the bibliographic and **reference services**. She became active in the emerging documentation movement, cofounding the Union française de organismes de documentation in 1931 and playing a role in planning a training program for documentalists. In 1950, she was named founding director of the Institut national des techniques de la documentation. Her classic work *What Is Documentation?* (1951) is an important text in the theory of **information science**.

BRITISH COUNCIL. The British Council was created in the British Foreign office in 1934. Following World War II, it opened libraries throughout the world based on the model of a British lending library, as part of its charge to build cultural and educational relationships between **Great Britain** and other countries. It also supported **public library** development, most notably in **Africa** and the **Caribbean**. Beginning in the 1980s, the Council began to focus on other activities, such as teaching English to fee-paying students. After 2000, the British Council repositioned its traditional library services as Knowledge and Learning Centers.

See also INTERNATIONAL LIBRARIANSHIP; OVERSEAS LIBRARIES PROGRAMS.

BRITISH LIBRARY. Great Britain's national library, the British Library, originated with the creation of the British Museum by an Act of Parliament in 1753. The British Museum was intended to be a repository for the collections of Hans Sloane (physician to George II and president of the Royal Society), Robert and Edward Harley, and Robert Cotton. Sloane's collection alone included around 40,000 books and 3,500 manuscripts, as well as botanical, zoological, and other specimens. The collection of the Royal Library was added in 1757, and the British Museum Library was opened to the public in 1759. **Anthony Panizzi** became Keeper of Printed Books in 1837, and, in addition to adding significantly to the collection, he compiled a **catalog** that was the basis for the first modern code for author and title entry. The British Museum Library, the National Central Library, and the National Lending Library for Science and Technology were merged to form the British Library in 1973. They were joined by the **British National Bibliography (BNB)** and the Office for Scientific and Technical Information in 1974, the **India** Office of Library and Records in 1982, and the British Institute of Recorded Sound in 1983.

See also AUSTIN, DEREK WILLIAM (1921–2001); RESEARCH LIBRARIES GROUP (RLG).

BRITISH MUSEUM LIBRARY. See BRITISH LIBRARY.

BRITISH NATIONAL BIBLIOGRAPHY (BNB). The British National **Bibliography** (BNB) was established in 1949 in response to recommendations made by **Lionel McColvin** in his 1942 survey (known as the McColvin report) of **public libraries** in **Great Britain**. McColvin determined that **catalogs** produced by individual libraries were uneconomical and incomplete, and he proposed the creation of a weekly list of full catalog records of new books on which library catalogs could be based. The Council of the British National Bibliography was established in March 1949, and the new national bibliography commenced full operations in 1950. It consisted of weekly lists of all books and first issues of new serial titles published in Britain, cataloged in accordance with the *Anglo-American Cataloging Code* and classified according to **Dewey Decimal Classification (DDC)**. Author/title indexes were provided every four weeks, and the lists were cumulated into an annual volume. A BNB **catalog card** service was started in 1956. BNB **Machine-Readable Cataloging (MARC)** service began in 1969, and BNB MARC records were made available online with the introduction of the British Library Automated Information Service (BLAISE) in 1977. The BNB became part of the **British Library** in 1974.

See also AUSTIN, DEREK WILLIAM (1921–2001).

BROWN, JAMES DUFF (1862–1914). British library leader James Duff Brown was born on November 6, 1862, in Edinburgh, Scotland. After working as a bookseller, he applied for a position as library assistant at the new Mitchell Library in Glasgow and began working there in 1876. In 1888, he was appointed the first librarian at Clerkenwell, one of the London parishes that were setting up municipal libraries. In 1889, he produced a **dictionary catalog** for the library based on the one created by **Edward Edwards** at Manchester **Public Library** in the 1850s. Brown's attendance at the **American Library Association (ALA)** conference in Chicago in 1893 prompted him to establish an open-shelves policy at Clerkenwell, which was a controversial innovation in **Great Britain** at that time. In 1905, he was appointed head of the new public library at Islington. His book *Manual of Library Economy*, first published in 1903, was for many years the basic textbook of public library practice in Britain. He also influenced the development of librarianship as founder of the *Library World* (later *New Library World*). His Subject **Classification**, which was published in 1906, was adopted by many British libraries and was still in use in some libraries in the late 1960s.

See also BATTLE OF THE BOOKS; LIBRARY ASSOCIATION (LA).

BRUNET CLASSIFICATION SYSTEM. In 1810, French bibliographer Jacques-Charles Brunet published a bibliographical dictionary, *Manuel du libraire et de l'amateur des livres*. In it, he presented a **classification** system based on one that had been created for Paris booksellers in the 17th century. There were five main classes: history, jurisprudence, literature, science and arts, and theology, each with a number of subdivisions. The system, sometimes referred to as the French system, is still used in part by the **Bibliothèque nationale**. It also influenced classification at the **British Museum Library**. Brunet's scheme became part of 19th-century classification in the **United States** after being introduced at the Harvard College Library in 1830. It was adopted by a number of other US libraries, including the **Library Company of Philadelphia**.

BUTLER, PIERCE (1886–1953). Pierce Butler was born on December 19, 1884, in Clarendon Hills, Illinois. He received an MA and a PhD from Dickinson College, Pennsylvania, and a PhD from Hartford Theological Seminary, Connecticut. In 1916, he joined the staff of the Newberry Library in Chicago and became head of the order department as well as bibliographer and custodian of the John M. Wing Foundation on the History of Typography and the Printed Book. In 1928, he was appointed part-time lecturer on the history of books and printing at the **Graduate Library School (GLS)** at the University of Chicago, and he became a full-time faculty member there in

1931. His *Introduction to Library Science* (1933) introduced the idea of librarianship as a science and is considered a landmark in the development of library thought. Despite his emphasis on quantitative social science techniques, he began to argue for a more humanistic approach to librarianship later in his career.

C

CAIN, JULIEN (1887–1974). Considered to be one of the most prominent European national library directors of the 20th century, Julien Cain was born in Montmorency, **France**, on May 10, 1887. He studied at the École du Louvre and worked as a history teacher, editor, and government official before being appointed head of the **Bibliothèque nationale** in 1930. He oversaw numerous renovations of the library as well as the establishment of a microfilm department and a national record library. The Catalogue Room, which he established in 1935, was conceived as a national center for **documentation** and **bibliography**, and marked the beginning of cooperation with other libraries in France. Cain's tenure at the library was interrupted when he was removed from his post by the Vichy government because he was Jewish. He was arrested by the Nazis in 1941 and deported to Buchenwald in 1944. After World War II, he was able to resume his duties at the Bibliothèque nationale, and he was also appointed to oversee the new national library service. In addition to his contributions to French librarianship, Cain was known as a leader in **international** library cooperation.

CALLIMACHOS (c. 305–240 BCE). Callimachos of Cyrene was a poet and scholar who worked in the **Alexandrian Library** from around 260 BCE until his death in 240 BCE. He is sometimes called the first cataloger because of the **classified** subject listing that he compiled, the *Pinakes*, based on the Alexandrian Library collection. The full title was *Tables of Persons Eminent in Every Branch of Learning, Together with a List of Their Writings*. Divided into several classes of poetry and prose and then arranged alphabetically by author, the *Pinakes* influenced other **catalogs** in the Greco-Roman world.

CANADA. Library development in Canada was in many ways similar to that of the **United States**. Private and college libraries existed from an early date; the Collèges des Jésuites de Québec opened the first college library in North America in 1635. The first Canadian subscription library was launched in 1779. Additional **social** and subscription libraries sprang up as the population grew in the 19th century. In general, public library development occurred earlier in Ontario than elsewhere in Canada; the first provincial free libraries act was passed in Ontario in 1882. In 1883, the first free, tax-supported **public libraries** were established in St. John, Guelph, and Toronto. As in the United States, **Andrew Carnegie** gave impetus to the public library movement by donating 125 library buildings to communities across Canada from 1901 to 1917.

Toronto University opened the first specifically designed **academic library** building in Canada in 1892, followed by McGill University in 1893. In 1904, McGill University librarian **Charles Gould** offered a three-week summer course in librarianship, based on the precepts of **Melvil Dewey**. This was the first such course in Canada. A four-week course was provided at the Ontario Library School, formed in 1911. In 1927 McGill University instituted a full-year program with the aid of a **Carnegie Corporation of New York** grant. At the request of the Ontario Department of Education, the University of Toronto established a library school (replacing the Ontario Library School) in 1927, and offered a full-year course in 1928. Both the McGill and Toronto schools sought **accreditation** from the **American Library Association (ALA)**, creating a precedent for other Canadian library **education** programs to follow. A French-speaking school opened at the University of Montreal in 1937. Toronto introduced the first Canadian program leading to a master's degree in **library science** (MLS) in 1950 and the first PhD program in 1971. In 1965, McGill launched a two-year MLS program, which became the Canadian standard in 1968. Canada also has a number of library technician programs, the first having been established in 1962.

The formation of the Ontario Library Association, following the 1900 ALA conference in Montreal, was a stepping stone to the founding of the Canadian Library Association (CLA). Professional groups were also organized in other Canadian provinces between 1911 and 1932. Although the Carnegie-funded report *Libraries in Canada: A Study of Library Conditions and Needs* (1933) concluded that it would be impossible to form a Canadian library association because of financial constraints, Canadian librarians attending the ALA Annual Conference in Montreal in 1934 organized the Canadian Library Council. In 1945, the Council resolved to take preliminary steps to form the CLA, which was incorporated in 1947. In 2011, the CLA abolished its divisions (Canadian Association of College and University Libraries, Canadian Association for **School Libraries**, Canadian Association of Public Libraries, Canadian Association of Special Libraries and Information Services, and Canadian Library Trustees Association) and replaced them with member-driven networks.

The National Library of Canada was formed in 1953 to serve as the national repository for Canadian culture, scholarship, and publishing. In 2004, the National Library merged with the National Archives to form Library and Archives Canada (LAC).

See also ANGLO-AMERICAN CATALOGING RULES (AACR); BAIN, JAMES, JR. (1842–1908); CLASSIFICATION; RDA: RESOURCE DESCRIPTION AND ACCESS; SMITH, LILLIAN H. (1887–1983).

CARIBBEAN. Subscription and commercial circulating libraries existed in the Caribbean during the 18th and much of the 19th centuries. The **public library** movement started to gain momentum in the 1840s, with several British colonies passing public library legislation. Early in the 20th century, Barbados, St. Lucia, Dominica, St. Vincent, Trinidad, and Guyana built public libraries with **Carnegie Corporation of New York** funds. Library development in the region was given further impetus by **Ernest A. Savage**'s *The Libraries of Bermuda, the Bahamas, the British West Indies, British Guiana, British Honduras, Puerto Rico, and the American Virgin Islands: A Report to the Carnegie Corporation of New York* (1934). Financial assistance from the Carnegie Corporation led to the establishment of the Eastern Caribbean Regional Library in Trinidad and Tobago in 1941. The Eastern Caribbean Regional Library School was created in 1948, based on the syllabus and examinations of the **Library Association (LA)** of **Great Britain**.

In Jamaica, the government requested Canadian librarian Nora Bateson to formulate a strategy for libraries, which was published as *Library Plan for Jamaica* (1945). The Jamaica Library Service, created in 1948, was developed in accordance with Bateson's recommendations and included a network of public and **school library** services. The Jamaica Library Association (now Library and Information Association of Jamaica) was formed in 1949. While the British model of librarianship was dominant in most of the English-speaking countries in the Caribbean, close proximity to the **United States** brought American influences as well. Elsewhere in the region, Dutch, French, and Spanish patterns prevailed.

The first **academic library** in the Caribbean came with the establishment of the University of the West Indies in 1948. In 1969, the **Association of Caribbean University, Research, and Institutional Libraries (ACURIL)** was formed as part of a movement to link libraries in the Dutch-, English-, French-, and Spanish-speaking territories. The **United Nations Educational, Scientific and Cultural Organization (UNESCO)** supported the first Department of Library Studies (now Department of Library and Information Studies), which was created at the Mona, Jamaica, campus of the University of the West Indies in 1971 and serves 15 English-speaking countries.

See also CUBA.

CARNEGIE, ANDREW (1835–1919). Andrew Carnegie was born in Dunfermline, Scotland, on November 25, 1835. In 1848, his family emigrated to the **United States** and ended up in Pittsburgh, Pennsylvania. Determined to escape from poverty, Carnegie worked his way up from bobbin boy to telegraph operator to a superintendent at the Pennsylvania Railroad. After the Civil War, he turned his attention to iron and then to steel, organizing the first of his steel works in 1873. At about the same time, he embarked on a career of philanthropy, with his support for libraries being perhaps the best-known result. In 1881, he gave the gift of a **public library** building to Dunfermline. By 1917, there were more than 1,600 **Carnegie libraries** in the United States, along with more than 800 libraries in other parts of the world. Carnegie wealth also provided funds for Carnegie Hall, Carnegie Mellon University, the Carnegie Endowment for International Peace, and numerous other organizations. In 1901, Carnegie sold his company to J. P. Morgan for $480 million and retired from business to devote himself to full-time philanthropy. By the time of his death in 1919, Andrew Carnegie had given away about $350 million.

See also CARNEGIE CORPORATION OF NEW YORK.

CARNEGIE CORPORATION OF NEW YORK. In 1911, **Andrew Carnegie** established a trust, the Carnegie Corporation of New York, to distribute his wealth. The corporation's library program carried on his legacy of support for libraries. At first, this support was primarily in the form of gifts of **public library** buildings, but attention later turned to **education**. Reports commissioned from economist Alvin S. Johnson in 1916 and from librarian **Charles C. Williamson** in 1918 focused on the need for better-trained library staff. The **Williamson report**, in particular, was a landmark, resulting in a radical retooling of library education and training. In addition to endowing and supporting library schools, the corporation sought to strengthen the profession by supporting the activities of the **American Library Association (ALA)**. Carnegie funds were also used for library service to rural areas, library service to **African Americans** in the South, and other similar types of programs. Until 1941, the corporation spent around $830,000 per year on public libraries and librarianship in the **United States**. From 1930 to 1943, several million dollars were allocated to support college libraries. Since World War II, the focus of the corporation in the United States has been on grants for central services provided by ALA, the **Library of Congress (LC)**, and other entities, as well as on grants to individual libraries for special initiatives. Beginning in the 1920s, the corporation gave impetus to the public library movement outside the United States, using the part of the endowment that was earmarked for British dominions and colonies such as **Australia**, **Canada**, and **South Africa**. Since the 1990s, the Carnegie Corporation's library-related activities have centered on sub-Saharan **Africa**.

See also ACADEMIC LIBRARIES; ACCREDITATION; CARIBBEAN; CARNEGIE LIBRARIES; CENTER FOR RESEARCH LIBRARIES (CRL); COUNCIL ON LIBRARY AND INFORMATION RESOURCES

(CLIR); EAMES, WILBERFORCE (1855–1937); FARMINGTON PLAN; GRADUATE LIBRARY SCHOOL (GLS); HAMPTON INSTITUTE LIBRARY SCHOOL; INTERNATIONAL SEMINAR ON THE DEVELOPMENT OF PUBLIC LIBRARIES IN AFRICA; *LIBRARY QUARTERLY* (*LQ*); LIBRARY WAR SERVICE; PUBLIC LIBRARY INQUIRY; READING WITH A PURPOSE; SCHOOL OF LIBRARY SERVICE, ATLANTA UNIVERSITY.

CARNEGIE LIBRARIES. Andrew Carnegie made his first gift of a **public library** building in 1883, in his birthplace, Dunfermline, Scotland. From then until 1919, he and the **Carnegie Corporation of New York** gave $56 million to build 2,509 libraries. Of these, 1,681 were built in the **United States** and 828 were established in other countries, primarily **Great Britain** and Ireland but also **Australia**, **Canada**, the **Caribbean**, Fiji, and New Zealand. In the United States, the donation of a library typically began with a letter written by the applicant to James Bertram, Carnegie's secretary, who then sent a list of questions. Once an application was approved, Carnegie provided funds only for the building. The recipient had to provide the site and agree to contribute an annual sum equaling 10 percent of the donated money to build collections and hire staff, thereby creating a tradition of shared government support of public libraries. The size of the grant was based on population size. Initially, communities that met the requirements were free to choose their own designs. Beginning in 1908, however, Bertram required that architectural plans be submitted for approval. A copy of his pamphlet containing minimum standards and six model floor plans was sent to every community that received a grant. Carnegie grants were a major factor in the expansion of public libraries, and the need for trained staff for those libraries contributed to the development of the library profession.

CARNOVSKY, LEON (1903–1975). Leon Carnovsky was born on November 28, 1903, in St. Louis, Missouri. After graduating from the University of Missouri in 1927, he received training in library work at the training school of the St. Louis **Public Library**. In 1929, he entered the newly created **Graduate Library School (GLS)** at the University of Chicago, receiving his PhD and joining the GLS faculty in 1932. In addition to teaching, Carnovsky edited the *Library Quarterly* from 1943 to 1961. He was well known for his many publications, especially on **intellectual freedom** and on public libraries. He was also a consultant for the **American Library Association (ALA)** and the **United Nations Educational, Scientific and Cultural Organization (UNESCO)** on library matters around the world, and a report he wrote for UNESCO led to the establishment of the Graduate Library School of the Hebrew University in Jerusalem in 1956. Carnovsky retired from the University of Chicago in 1971.

CATALOG CARD. The first library **catalog** cards may, in fact, have been playing cards. Curators of the new state-owned collections in **France**, formed as a result of the **French Revolution**, were instructed to use playing cards (which at the time were blank on one side) to record details about each item. The earliest known reference to a catalog card (or slip, as it was called) in the **United States** was made by the librarian of Harvard College Library in 1840, and a handwritten slip system was in place at Harvard by 1848. In order to increase their durability, the slips were pasted onto cards of uniform size, which were kept in wooden drawers. By the end of the 19th century, card catalogs were a common feature in libraries, replacing the printed book catalog. In 1877, the **American Library Association (ALA)** adopted a uniform size for the catalog card: three by five inches. The **Library of Congress (LC)** began printing standard-size cards for its own collection in 1898. In 1901, LC began its Card Distribution Service, supplying printed cards to other US libraries. Libraries that subscribed to this service could use the LC bibliographic records as their own records, or at least as the foundation for their own records.

Outside the United States, card-distribution services were set up by the Centralized Cataloging Bureau of the Soviet Union, the **British National Bibliography (BNB)**, and the Swedish Royal Library, to give just a few examples. LC began to mechanize its service in the late 1960s. In the last quarter of the 20th century, computerized catalogs made the card catalog and the catalog card itself obsolete. LC closed its card catalog in 1981.

CATALOGING AND CATALOGS. Cataloging was one of the first tasks (and for a long time the only specialized task) associated with librarianship, and the practice and the profession have developed together. There is archeological evidence of library catalogs going as far back as the seventh century BCE, but, with a few exceptions, cataloging remained rudimentary until the modern era. The typical medieval catalog was an inventory list, compiled without a system. Broad subject arrangement was the general pattern. As the publishing industry, book collections, and libraries began to grow (especially after the invention of movable type), methods of bibliographic control evolved, and innovations such as alphabetical arrangement and the addition of indexes and cross-references were introduced. The **Bodleian Library** Catalog of 1620 is considered to be the first modern library catalog. Designed to be a practical finding aid for students, it was arranged in a single sequence organized by authors' surnames and by catchwords for anonymous works. The Bodleian catalog of 1674 added the principle that only one form of an author's name was to be used.

So many major works on cataloging and **classification** were created during the 19th century that it is sometimes called the century of codes. The first of these emanated from the **British Museum Library**, where Sir **Anthony Panizzi** compiled 91 *Rules for the Compilation of the Catalogue*, published in 1841. Smithsonian librarian **Charles Coffin Jewett** drew heavily on these rules when he drew up the first distinct code of cataloging rules in the **United States**, published in 1853. While previous codes had been created for particular libraries, Jewett's idea of uniformity to support a national catalog helped lay the groundwork for future catalog development in the United States and elsewhere. Another major contribution came from **Charles Ammi Cutter**, whose work at the **Boston Athenaeum** helped him formulate *Rules for a Printed Dictionary Catalog* (1876). The most comprehensive code of the period, it codified the practice of entry by author, title, subject, and form; the use of cross-references; and the use of subject terms (rather than words taken from a book's title) for subject headings.

Although some steps had been taken toward cooperation and uniformity, American libraries at the end of the 19th century could still choose from among numerous codes. The survey conducted in 1893 by W. C. Lane of the Boston Athenaeum found wide variation in the cataloging rules that were used and how they were applied. The 1898 publication of the **Library of Congress (LC)** catalog on cards, followed by the 1901 agreement between the **American Library Association (ALA)** Publishing Board and LC, by which LC would print and distribute **catalog cards** for current books, made it more economical to follow one standard. In 1908, cooperation between American and British catalogers resulted in the *Anglo-American Cataloging Code*, based on Cutter's *Rules* plus accommodation to LC practice. In 1941, ALA published its own revision of the 1908 code, prompting Andrew D. Osborn's landmark paper **"The Crisis in Cataloging"** (1941), which was widely circulated. In 1949, ALA published a new code, *ALA Cataloging Rules for Author and Title Entries*. Because so many American libraries were using LC catalog cards, ALA also adopted LC's *Rules for Descriptive Cataloging*. The two sets of rules were meant to be used together.

In 1951, **Seymour Lubetzky** of LC was approached by ALA to examine the 1949 code. He recommended that future editions be based on broad principles rather than on particular instances. Lubetzky's *Code of Cataloging Rules* (1953) was the basis for a draft statement of principles for a possible international code presented at the **International Conference on Cataloging Principles**, held in Paris in 1961. The Statement of Principles (also known as the **Paris Principles**) adopted at that conference influenced the *Anglo-American Cataloging Rules* (*AACR*), published in 1967, as well as the cataloging codes of a number of other countries. Bibliographic control on an international level was further aided by the development of unique identifiers such as the International Standard Book Number (ISBN) and standards such as **International Standard Bibliographic Description (ISBD)**.

Automation has played a significant role in standardization and cooperation. The introduction of **Machine-Readable Cataloging (MARC)** standards allowed libraries to easily share bibliographic record information, and the development of major bibliographic utilities such as the **Online Computer Library Center (OCLC)** made it easier to retrieve records created by other libraries. Further steps toward increasing the ability to share cataloging information worldwide were taken at a series of Meetings of Experts on an International Cataloging Code, held from 2003 to 2007 and sponsored by the **International Federation of Library Associations and Institutions (IFLA)**, resulting in the Statement of International Cataloging Principles. The increasing costs associated with cataloging have led to cooperative ventures such as the **Program for Cooperative Cataloging (PCC)**, which is administered by LC.

In 1974, representatives from ALA, the **British Library**, the Canadian Library Association, the **Library Association (LA)**, and LC began work on *Anglo-American Cataloging Rules, Second Edition* (*AACR2*), which appeared in 1978. Planning for a third edition led to a decision in 2005 to take a new approach, leading to the publication of *RDA: Resource Description and Access* in 2010. Designed as a new cataloging code for the digital environment, RDA is built on internationally shared cataloging principles, standards like ISBD, and the new conceptual models of **Functional Requirements for Bibliographic Records (FRBR)**.

See also CATALOGING IN PUBLICATION (CIP); CHÁVEZ CAMPOMANES, MARIA TERESA (1890–1981); DICTIONARY CATALOG; INTERNATIONAL MEETING OF CATALOGING EXPERTS; MANN, MARGARET (1873–1960); NATIONAL PROGRAM FOR ACQUISITIONS AND CATALOGING (NPAC); VATICAN CATALOGING RULES.

CATALOGING IN PUBLICATION (CIP). In 1958, the **Library of Congress (LC)** began an experiment called Cataloging-in-Source to make **cataloging** data for books available prior to publication. More than 1,000 titles from 157 publishers were cataloged before the experiment was discontinued. It was succeeded in 1971 by the CIP program, whereby LC staff created bibliographic records for forthcoming books that were most likely to be acquired by libraries in the **United States**, based on galleys received from publishers. More than 6,000 titles from 200 publishers were processed during the first year. By the end of 2011, the output had grown to an average of 54,000 titles per year from more than 5,000 publishers. Electronic Cataloging in Publication (ECIP) went into operation in 2000. In 2004, the LC launched the ECIP Cataloging Partnership Program, in which other libraries share in the creation of cataloging data. ECIP fully replaced the paper-based CIP in 2007. By making information about a title available prior to publication, CIP facilitates book ordering as well as cataloging. Similar programs have been implemented by national libraries worldwide.

See also UNIVERSAL BIBLIOGRAPHIC CONTROL (UBC).

CENSORSHIP. Resisting censorship has become one of the core tenets of librarianship, but earlier generations of librarians in the **United States** saw themselves more as guardians of books (and, as the **public library** movement developed, arbiters of taste) than as champions of **intellectual freedom**. In 1908, **American Library Association (ALA)** president **Arthur Bostwick** declared that librarians had a duty to protect readers from immoral books, and the idea of providing access to literature that uplifted and improved the reader held sway for several decades.

In the 1930s, the library profession began to consider its stance on censorship and intellectual freedom, prompted in part by attempts, including some made by librarians, to ban and even burn John Steinbeck's *The Grapes of Wrath*. In 1938, the Board of the Des Moines (Iowa) Public Library approved a Bill of Rights for the Free Public Library, which provided the model for the Library's Bill of Rights (later called **Library Bill of Rights**), adopted by ALA in 1939. The ALA Committee on Intellectual Freedom to Safeguard the Rights of Library Users to Freedom of Inquiry was formed in 1940 (the name was shortened to Committee on Intellectual Freedom in 1947). At the 1953 Annual Conference, ALA adopted the **Freedom to Read Statement**, which reaffirmed the principles of intellectual freedom as embodied in the Library Bill of Rights. At the same time, there was growing debate within the profession about the possibility of reconciling intellectual freedom and social responsibility. In 1956, following several censorship episodes in California, the California Library Association joined with the School of Librarianship at Berkeley to conduct a study of censorship. *The Climate of Book Selection: Social Influences on School and Public Libraries* (1958), also known as the Fiske report, showed that the majority of librarians reported incidents in which the controversial nature of an author or book resulted in a decision not to buy, despite the fact that librarians supported the freedom to read. Later studies have shown that librarians continue to practice self-censorship when it comes to controversial materials.

The ALA Office of Intellectual Freedom, established in 1967, documents attempts to remove materials from library shelves. Such incidents are often local, but librarians in the United States have also faced (and sometimes participated in) censorship sponsored by the government. During World War I, many librarians used the Army Index of allegedly harmful books to purge their collections. During World War II, there was another drive to remove or label books that were considered subversive, and during the Cold War, librarians working **overseas** were investigated and censored by Senator Joseph McCarthy for allegedly putting pro-Communist books in US Information Agency libraries. In 2000, the US Congress enacted the **Children's** Internet Protection Act (CIPA), which required libraries and schools to install Internet filters in order to retain federal funding. Although ALA filed a lawsuit to overturn CIPA, it was upheld by the US Supreme Court in 2003.

Elsewhere in the world, state censorship has turned librarians into servants of ideology and has even led to the destruction of libraries and books. Thousands of books were burned by the Nazis in **Germany**. Libraries became political tools in **China, Cuba,** and the **Soviet Union** under Communist rule. In the 1990s, mayors in some cities in southern **France** took control of library acquisitions in order to promote the National Front. In 1997, the **International Federation of Library Associations and Institutions (IFLA)** created the Committee on Freedom of Access to Information and Freedom of Expression (FAIFE) to monitor intellectual freedom in libraries worldwide.

See also LIBRARY AWARENESS PROGRAM.

CENTER FOR RESEARCH LIBRARIES (CRL). In 1949, 10 large university libraries in the midwestern **United States** launched the Midwest Inter-library Corporation as a centralized storage space for little-used materials. The site for a building was donated by the University of Chicago, and the **Carnegie Corporation of New York** and the **Rockefeller Foundation** provided grants for construction. In addition to accepting deposits of research materials from its members, the Midwest Inter-library Corporation began to acquire serials, government and legal documents, microforms, dissertations, and other types of publications that were costly or difficult to obtain. In the 1960s, the geographic restrictions on membership were removed and the name was changed to the Center for Research Libraries. There are now more than 250 members, consisting mostly of American and **Canadian** colleges and universities.

See also ASSOCIATION OF RESEARCH LIBRARIES (ARL).

CENTRAL AND EASTERN EUROPE (CEE). *See* EUROPE, CENTRAL AND EASTERN.

CERTIFICATION. In many countries, individual librarians are certified by government agencies. National systems for examination and certification were introduced in **Italy, France,** and Prussia before the end of the 19th century. In a few countries, the certifying body is the library association. In

Great Britain, for example, the **Library Association (LA)** was authorized by Royal Charter to hold national examinations leading to certification. In 1882, proposals for three certificates based on examinations were approved, and the first examinations were held in 1885. Librarians in **Africa** and elsewhere were able to sit for the examinations and obtain qualification even when there was no library school or library association in their own country. The system of overseas examinations ended in 1964. The LA began accrediting programs in the 1970s after dropping its system of direct examination of individual candidates, and it currently combines an **accreditation** and a certification program.

In the **United States** and **Canada**, the **American Library Association (ALA)** accredits library **education** programs rather than certifying individuals. In his 1923 report *Training for Library Service* (also known as the **Williamson report**), **Charles C. Williamson** recommended a national system of certification for librarians in the United States, but this was rejected by ALA, which chose to focus on training instead. There is, however, some certification at the local level and within certain specializations. **School library** media specialists are generally certified by states. The **Medical Library Association (MLA)** established a credentialing program in 1949. ALA inaugurated the Certified **Public Library** Administrator program for library managers in 2006, and, in 2010, established the Library Support Staff Certification program for paraprofessionals. Both programs are voluntary and are administered by the American library Association–Allied Professional Association (ALA-APA).

CHARTERED INSTITUTE OF LIBRARY AND INFORMATION PROFESSIONALS (CILIP). *See* LIBRARY ASSOCIATION (LA).

CHÁVEZ CAMPOMANES, MARIA TERESA (1890–1981). Maria Teresa Chavéz Campomanes was born on August 1, 1890, in Pueblo de los Angeles, **Mexico**. She studied at the School for Librarians in Mexico City and continued her **education** at the **Pratt Institute** in Baltimore, Maryland. She worked at the New York **Public Library** and the **Library of Congress (LC)** before returning to Mexico. She was one of the founders of the Escuela Nacional de Biblioteconomía y Archivonomía, as well as the College of **Library Science** at the Universidad Nacional Autónoma de México (UNAM). She taught **cataloging** for many years, and her manuals on cataloging and **classification** became standard texts.

CHICAGO, UNIVERSITY OF, GRADUATE LIBRARY SCHOOL. *See* GRADUATE LIBRARY SCHOOL (GLS).

CHILDREN'S LIBRARY SERVICE. Children's library service as it is generally understood originated in American and British libraries. **Great Britain** took the lead in formalizing the provision of books for children in the 1850 **Public Libraries Act**, although it was not until 1861 that the Manchester **Public Library** opened the first separate children's room. Early examples of library service for children in the **United States** include Sunday **school libraries** and individual efforts such as the Bingham Library for Youth, established by Caleb Bingham in Salisbury, Connecticut, in 1803. The idea of children's librarianship began to take shape with William I. Fletcher's report "Public Libraries and the Young," appearing in the US Bureau of Education's *Public Libraries in the United States of America* (1876), which argued against age restrictions. Service to children became a topic of discussion in *Library Journal* and at conferences of the fledgling **American Library Association (ALA)**. In the 1880s, Minerva Sanders, librarian at the Pawtucket (Rhode Island) Free Public Library, pioneered the extension of full library privileges to children and created the first designated children's library space. In 1890, the first separate children's reading room opened in Brookline, Massachusetts.

Public library service to children developed rapidly in the 1880s and 1890s as part of the public library's educational mission. Boston, Denver, Omaha, Pittsburgh, Philadelphia, San Francisco, Seattle, and other cities opened children's reading rooms. By the end of the 19th century, space for children was a common feature in libraries. Surveys conducted by **Caroline Hewins** and others helped to document and influence the emerging role of librarians working with the young. ALA held its first general discussion of library work with children at the Annual Conference in 1897. The Club of Children's Librarians was established at the ALA Annual Conference in Montreal in 1900 and a year later, it became the Section for Library Work with Children (precursor of the Association of Library Service to Children).

Staffing and staff training were key elements in the professionalization of library work with children. In 1895, Cleveland (Ohio) Public Library became the first to install a librarian, **Effie Louise Power**, specifically for children's services. In 1896, **Anne Carroll Moore** was hired to oversee the new children's room at the **Pratt Institute** in Brooklyn, New York. In 1898, **Frances Jenkins Olcott** became the first director of children's work when she was hired to supervise the children's department at the **Carnegie** Library of Pittsburgh. The Pratt Institute led the way in training when it added a course for children's librarians in 1899. A class started by the Carnegie Library of Pittsburgh in 1900 to train assistants for its children's rooms was expanded to a two-year Training School for Children's Librarians in 1901. Special classes for children's librarians were also organized at public libraries in Brooklyn, Cleveland, and elsewhere.

The availability of children's literature was essential to children's librarianship, and tools were created to help librarians promote literature of good quality. Caroline Hewins's *Books for the Young: A Guide for Parents and Children* (1882) was the first widely circulated **bibliography** of children's books. The *Children's Catalog*, first published by **H. W. Wilson** in 1909, helped to set standards for children's collections in libraries, as did review journals such *Booklist* (begun in 1905) and *The Horn Book* (begun in 1924). The **Newbery Medal**, established in 1922, and the **Caldecott Medal**, established in 1938, contributed further to the development of criteria for evaluating children's books.

In Britain, as in the United States, the growth of public libraries and the establishment of a professional association, the **Library Association (LA)**, helped lay the foundation for children's librarianship. Early public library leaders such as **Stanley Louis Jast** and **W. C. Berwick Sayers** were enthusiastic about the American model of outreach, programming, and open access to books. Some countries, while adopting aspects of the American model, have experimented with different approaches. In **India**, for example, several university libraries have children's sections. India also has a library devoted exclusively to children, the Library of the Children's Book Trust in New Delhi. Other examples of stand-alone children's libraries are the **l'Heure Joyeuse** in Paris, **France**; the Miracle Libraries in **Korea**; and the Osu Children's Libraries in Ghana. The International Youth Library, founded in Munich, **Germany**, in 1949, serves as a research center for international children's literature. Recent trends in children's librarianship include extending services to babies and toddlers (and their parents and caregivers), and borrowing elements from museums, playgrounds, and theme parks to create children's library spaces. In some countries, however, library service to children has not progressed much beyond the reading room stage. Since the 1950s, the **International Federation of Library Associations and Institutions (IFLA)** and the **United Nations Educational, Scientific and Cultural Organization (UNESCO)** have played an active role in furthering library service to children in developing countries.

See also BAKER, AUGUSTA B. (1911–1998); BATCHELDER, MILDRED L. (1901–1998); COLWELL, EILEEN HILDA (1904–2002); HENNE, FRANCES E. (1906–1985); SMITH, LILLIAN H. (1887–1983); YOUNG ADULT (YA) LIBRARY SERVICE.

CHINA. The history of organized librarianship in China can be traced to the first century BCE, when the first **catalog** of the imperial library was created and the first Chinese library **classification** system, known as the Seven Epitomes, was devised. During the Han dynasty (206 BCE–220 CE), the imperial library was established and opened to scholars. One of the curators, Hsun Hsu (213–289), created a classification system that was the standard for more than 2,000 years and is still used for older Chinese writings. The foundational texts of Chinese **library science** were written in the 12th century by Cheng Ju (1078–1144) and Zheng Qiao (1103–1162).

Traditionally, libraries were seen as storehouses open only to the elite, but Western-style concepts of the library's educational role, put forward by Chinese reformers, were an important influence on China's first modern **academic library**, now the Beijing University Library, which opened in 1898. Leaders of the next wave of reform, the New Culture movement, also supported library modernization. The government's mass education program following the founding of the Republic of China contributed to an increase in the number of libraries.

American library practices were spread to China by **Mary Elizabeth Wood**, who opened the **Boone Library** in Wuchang in 1911. Wood sent two students to the **United States** to study library science, and when they returned, they helped found the Boone College Department of Library Science, the first formal training program for Chinese librarians. Wood was also instrumental in getting the US Congress to resolve that some of the funds from the Boxer Rebellion indemnity payments be used for the establishment and maintenance of **public libraries** in China. In addition, she played a role in getting the **American Library Association (ALA)** to send St. Louis (Missouri) Public Library director **Arthur E. Bostwick** as a delegate to China to provide guidance on introducing a modern library system. Bostwick's seven-week visit in 1925 was part of the New Library movement promoting American concepts of librarianship, especially with regard to public libraries. A number of Chinese students studied librarianship in **Japan**, the Philippines, and the United States. The Chinese Library Association was founded in 1925, and China was one of the founders of the **International Federation of Library Associations and Institutions (IFLA)** in 1927.

Library development came to a halt during the period that started with the outbreak of the Sino-Japanese War in 1937 and ended with the establishment of the People's Republic of China in 1949. The new government considered libraries to be useful propaganda tools and replaced American influence with Russian models. The **Soviet Union** sent experts to China to promote Soviet library ideas, and Chinese librarians went to the Soviet Union to study. Acquisition of English-language materials stopped, as did the use of tools such as the **Dewey Decimal Classification (DDC)** and **Library of Congress Classification (LCC)**. Contacts with IFLA were suspended. The era of Soviet influence ended in 1959, when relations between China and the Soviet Union broke down. This was followed by the isolation of China from the West. During the Cultural Revolution (1966–1976), libraries became ideological battlefields, library **education** came to a standstill, librarians were denounced, and books were destroyed. After the Cultural Revolution there was a severe shortage of qualified librarians. With the government's modernization program came a new emphasis on improving library services and training skilled staff. The Library Society of China, successor to the Chinese Library Association, was founded in 1979 and joined IFLA in 1981. This period also saw the reform of cataloging practices and the beginning of **automation**. The Chinese Library Classification was first published in 1975 and is used in most Chinese libraries. In 1981, the National Library of China, which plays an important role in bibliographic control and library automation and networking, began to subscribe to **Machine-Readable Cataloging (MARC)** tapes. In 1983, China agreed to adopt *Anglo-American Cataloging Rules (AACR)*, **International Standard Bibliographic Description (ISBD)**, and **Library of Congress Subject Headings (LCSH)** for classification of Western-language materials. In 1989, the Chinese Machine-Readable Cataloging format became the standard for cataloging Chinese-language materials, and the 1990s saw further progress in the standardization and networking of library services. The Chinese government launched a nationwide academic library cooperative, the China Academic Library Information System (CALIS), in 1998. Libraries have been collaborating to build the China Academic **Digital Library** Information System (CADLIS) since 2002.

From 1949 to 1979, there were only two library and **information science** (LIS) programs in China, but the huge increase in the number of libraries in the 1980s led to a growth in LIS education, such that there were 58 LIS programs by 1987. Most library science instruction is provided at the undergraduate level. In 1992, reflecting a shift in emphasis from LIS to information management, Beijing University updated its curriculum and changed the name of its program to Department of Information Management. Other institutions followed suit. At the end of the 20th century, more than half of LIS graduates were employed as information professionals in better-paying private companies and industries rather than in libraries.

See also BOOKS FOR CHINA; CENSORSHIP; LIU, GUOJUN (1899–1980); SENG, SAMUEL T. Y. (1883–1976).

CLAPP, VERNER WARREN (1901–1972). Verner Warren Clapp was born on July 3, 1901, in Johannesburg, **South Africa**. His family left South Africa a few years later, settling in Poughkeepsie, New York. Clapp graduated from Trinity College in Connecticut and studied philosophy at Harvard. When he took a summer job at the **Library of Congress (LC)** in 1922, it was the beginning of a 33-year career that culminated in a position as chief assistant librarian starting in 1947. Among his many other accomplishments, he started the **Cooperative Acquisitions Project for Wartime Publications** program that enabled the library to acquire two million European publications. In 1956, he left the LC to chair the **Council on Library Resources**

(CLR) and served as its president from 1956 to 1967. He also chaired a library mission to **Japan** to help found the National Diet Library, where the Clapp Collection of books and other library science materials are housed.

CLASSIFICATION. Since ancient times there have been numerous examples of library classification systems, but these were primarily specialist and in-house creations. It was not until the 19th and early 20th centuries that more general systems covering all subjects came into being. Examples include the **Dewey Decimal Classification (DDC)**, the **Library of Congress Classification (LCC)**, and the **Universal Decimal Classification (UDC)**, sometimes called the Brussels Classification. The most familiar is DDC, devised by **Melvil Dewey** and published in 1876. In 1893, **Charles Ammi Cutter** published the first parts of his **Expansive Classification**, and although his system was not widely adopted, it influenced the LCC scheme, which was designed by **J. C. M. Hanson** and **Charles Martel** beginning in 1898. The UDC, published in 1905, was originally planned as a French translation of DDC but ended up being a more detailed adaptation.

A new phase in classification started with the development of faceted systems that relied on synthesis rather than on enumerative or hierarchical structure. **Indian** librarian **Shiyala Ramamrita Ranganathan**, whose writings form the basis of modern classification theory, developed the **Colon Classification**, first published in 1933. Like UDC, the Colon Classification allows much more detailed content indexing. Another faceted system, the **Bliss Bibliographic Classification**, was developed by **Henry Bliss** and published from 1940 to 1953. Although it never caught on in the **United States** because DDC and LC were so well established, the Bliss Bibliographic Classification was popular in British libraries.

In the United States, LCC is used by most **academic** and research libraries, many having switched from DDC beginning in the 1950s. DDC is most common in **public** and **school libraries**, although in recent years, some libraries have experimented with other ways to organize their collections in order to make them more user-friendly. DDC and LC are the most widely used classification systems worldwide. DDC has been translated into 30 languages and has formed the basis for such national schemes as the Swedish Library Classification and the Nippon Decimal Classification, introduced in the 1920s; the Finnish Public Library Classification, approved in 1936; and the **Korean** Decimal Classification, developed in the 1940s. Some countries use modified versions of the LC. For example, **Canada** has developed special schemes within LC for Canadian history, literature, and law. The Regensburg Classification system, created at the Regensburg University Library in **Germany** in the 1960s, is similar to LC in many respects. The Library-Bibliographic Classification developed in the **Soviet Union** and the Chinese Library Classification are additional examples of systems originating in other countries. There are also various subject and type-of-material schemes, such as those created by the **National Library of Medicine (NLM)** and the US Government Printing Office.

See also BACON, FRANCIS (1561–1626); CALLIMACHOS (c. 305–240 BCE); CATALOGING AND CATALOGS.

CLASSIFICATION RESEARCH GROUP (CRG). The CRG, which made significant contributions to **classification** and **information science** theory in **Great Britain**, was an outgrowth of the Royal Society Conference on Scientific Information held in London in 1948. Following the conference, a committee was formed to examine problems related to classification of scientific information. After meeting for a few years, the committee invited several librarians to participate, and the CRG was formally organized in 1952. Consisting of a small working group described as "enthusiasts," the CRG was heavily influenced by the work of **S. R. Ranganathan** and was closely aligned with the British **documentation** movement and the **Association of Special Libraries and Information Bureaux (ASLIB)**. Among its activities was an ultimately unsuccessful project funded by NATO to develop a new general classification scheme. More recently, the CRG has been involved in the revision of the **Bliss Bibliographic Classification**.

See also AUSTIN, DEREK WILLIAM (1921–2001); FARRADANE, JASON (1906–1989); VICKERY, BRIAN CAMPBELL (1918–2009).

COLON CLASSIFICATION. In 1933, **Indian** librarian and **library science** theoretician **Shiyala Ramamrita Ranganathan** introduced the Colon **Classification** system as a reaction against the **Dewey Decimal Classification (DDC)**, which he felt was too inflexible. Colon Classification begins with traditional main classes but breaks the classes down into their basic elements, called facets. These facets are combined to form a complete class number describing an item at a very detailed level. The name Colon Classification comes from the colons used to connect the pieces of a class number. Although Colon Classification was never widely adopted, Ranganathan's principles influenced many existing schemes, including later editions of the DDC.

See also BLISS BIBLIOGRAPHIC CLASSIFICATION; CLASSIFICATION RESEARCH GROUP (CRG); LIBRARY OF CONGRESS CLASSIFICATION (LCC); UNIVERSAL DECIMAL CLASSIFICATION (UDC).

COLUMBIA SCHOOL OF LIBRARY ECONOMY. *See* SCHOOL OF LIBRARY ECONOMY.

COLWELL, EILEEN HILDA (1904–2002). Eileen Hilda Colwell, known as the doyenne of **children's** librarianship in **Great Britain**, was born on June 16, 1904, at Robin Hood's Bay, Yorkshire. She studied librarianship at University College, London. In 1926, she became one of the first children's librarians in Britain when she was given a temporary part-time job organizing a library service for children in Hendon, a suburb of London. Finding no books or even a building in Hendon, she set up a service using donated books and space in local schools. Once a library building was constructed, she became the permanent children's librarian, a post she held for 40 years. She introduced book talks, story hours, and other activities that were unusual in Britain at the time and were widely copied. She was instrumental in the formation in 1937 of the Association of Children's Librarians (later the Youth Library Section of the **Library Association**). She also established at a course at University College that for a number of years was the only theoretical training in children's librarianship available in Britain.

See also WOMEN IN LIBRARIANSHIP.

CONFERENCE OF DIRECTORS OF NATIONAL LIBRARIES (CDNL). Organized in 1974, CDNL is an independent organization consisting of the chief executives of national libraries. It was established to facilitate discussion and to promote understanding and cooperation on matters of common interest worldwide. CDNL works closely with the National Libraries section of the **International Federation of Library Associations and Institutions (IFLA)**, and its annual meeting takes place in conjunction with the annual IFLA conference.

See also UNIVERSAL BIBLIOGRAPHIC CONTROL (UBC).

CONGRESS OF SOUTHEAST ASIAN LIBRARIANS (CONSAL). Inspired by the establishment of the Association of Southeast Asian Nations (ASEAN), the library associations of Malaysia and Singapore organized the first Conference of Southeast Asian Librarians in Singapore in 1970. The conference was attended by representatives from Cambodia, Indonesia, Malaysia, Philippines, Singapore, Thailand, and South Vietnam, and resulted in the formation of CONSAL. In 2012, library associations and librarians from Brunei, Cambodia, Indonesia, Laos, Malaysia, Myanmar, Philippines, Singapore, Thailand, and Vietnam were CONSAL members. CONSAL focuses on cooperation in librarianship, **bibliography**, **documentation**, and related activities in the region. It also works to promote ties between Southeast Asian librarians, library schools, and library associations, as well as other regional and international organizations.

See also ASIA, SOUTHEAST.

CONSORTIUM OF EUROPEAN RESEARCH LIBRARIES (CERL). CERL was formed in 1992 to promote cooperation between research libraries in order to preserve and improve access to Europe's printed heritage. Among its projects is the Heritage of the Printed Book Database, which integrates catalog records from major European and North American research libraries for items of European printing from the hand-press period (c. 1455–c. 1830).

See also LEAGUE OF EUROPEAN RESEARCH LIBRARIES/LIGUE DES BIBLIOTHÈQUES EUROPÉENNES DE RECHERCHE (LIBER).

COOPERATIVE ACQUISITIONS PROJECT FOR WARTIME PUB-LICATIONS. In 1945, the **American Library Association (ALA)**, the **Association of Research Libraries (ARL)**, and the **Library of Congress (LC)** established the Cooperative Acquisitions Project for Wartime Publications, the first major cooperative acquisitions program. The goal was to obtain for American libraries important works that had been published in Europe just prior to and during World War II. More than two million items were acquired by LC agents and were distributed among the cooperating libraries.

See also FARMINGTON PLAN.

COPYRIGHT. The first known example of a copyright was granted by the Senate of Venice in 1469. The first copyright law, the Copyright Act of 1709 (also known as the Statute of Anne, after Queen Anne), was enacted in **Great Britain**. In the **United States**, the first federal copyright law, protecting books, maps, and charts, was enacted in May 1790. Administration of copyright law was transferred to the **Library of Congress (LC)** in 1870. Until the late 19th century, copyright laws applied only to domestic works, but in 1886, the Berne Convention for the Protection of Literary and Artistic Works established a uniform copyright law to replace the need to register the copyright separately in every country. The United States signed on to the Berne Convention in 1988, and 165 countries were signatories as of 2012. An administrative bureau set up by the Berne Convention in 1893 became the World Intellectual Property Organization (WIPO) in 1967. WIPO, which has been an agency of the United Nations (UN) since 1974, administers 25 intellectual property treaties. The WIPO Copyright Treaty was adopted in 1996 in order to address issues related to information technology and the Internet. In the United States, the WIPO Treaty is implemented by the Digital Millennium Copyright Act (DMCA) of 1998.

DMCA and other recent legislation reflect an overall trend to strengthen copyright law and its enforcement, but limitations and exceptions to copyright laws help to achieve a balance between the rights of copyright owners and the rights of individuals to access and use information. An example of an exception in US copyright law is the fair use doctrine, which allows reproduction of a work for teaching, scholarship, research, and other purposes. However, exceptions that enabled libraries to preserve and make available works in the print era have not kept pace with changes in the way information is created and delivered. In 2012, the **International Federation of Library Associations and Institutions (IFLA)** produced a Treaty Proposal on Copyright Limitations and Exceptions for Libraries and Archives in order to guide members of WIPO in updating limitations and exceptions for libraries and archives worldwide.

COUNCIL ON LIBRARY AND INFORMATION RESOURCES (CLIR). CLIR began as the Council on Library Resources (CLR), which was established by the Ford Foundation in 1956 as a nonprofit, grant-making foundation. Louis B. Wright, director of the Folger Library in Washington, D.C., had approached the foundation about funding an organization that would address issues related to scholarly libraries. **Verner Warren Clapp**, one of the top administrators at the **Library of Congress (LC)**, became CLR's first president. Among the activities that received support from CLR were the publication of the *Union List of Serials* (1965); the launch of *Choice*, the review journal of the **Association of College and Research Libraries (ACRL)**; and the implementation of the **Machine-Readable Cataloging (MARC)** pilot project. In addition, CLR provided grants for the development of the **Online Computer Library Center (OCLC)** and other bibliographic utilities. Other initiatives include the **Digital Library** Federation and the Global Digital Libraries Collaborative. CLR has also played a role in preservation, establishing the Commission for Preservation and Access (CPA) in 1986. In 1997, CLR was merged with CPA to become the Council on Library and Information Resources (CLIR).

See also INFORMATION SCIENCE; INTERNATIONAL CONFERENCE ON CATALOGING PRINCIPLES.

COUNCIL ON LIBRARY RESOURCES (CLR). *See* COUNCIL ON LIBRARY AND INFORMATION RESOURCES (CLIR).

"THE CRISIS IN CATALOGING". In 1940, a committee appointed by librarian of Congress Archibald MacLeish to assess the library's operations reported the presence of a large and growing backlog of unprocessed materials. Andrew D. Osborn, head of the **cataloging** department at Harvard University, was asked to write an article to publicize some of the committee's findings and recommendations. His paper, entitled "The Crisis in Cataloging," was presented before the American Library Institute and later published in the *Library Quarterly* (October 1941). Osborn was highly critical of the traditional approach to cataloging, with its over-reliance on specific rules rather than on broader principles. Osborn's paper helped to bring about a shift in cataloging theory and practice in the **United States**.

See also ANGLO-AMERICAN CATALOGING RULES (AACR).

CRUNDEN, FREDERICK MORGAN (1847–1911). Frederick Morgan Crunden was part of the first generation of American librarians who saw themselves primarily as managers rather than as scholars. He was born on September 1, 1847, in Gravesend, England, and his family moved to St. Louis, Missouri, when he was still a child. He worked as a teacher after receiving BA and MA degrees from Washington University. In 1877, Crunden became the librarian of the Public School Library Society of St. Louis, a subscription library that had been created in 1865, and he presided over its establishment as the St. Louis **Public Library** in 1893. Under Crunden's leadership, the St. Louis Public Library was particularly known for its services to children and immigrants. Crunden was an early member of the **American Library Association (ALA)**, which he joined in 1878, and he served as its president from 1889 to 1890.

CUBA. In Cuba, modern library development was ushered in by the construction of a new library building on the campus of the University of Havana in the 1930s. Through the initiative of the assistant director, **Jorge Aguayo**, the library introduced American models of librarianship, such as the **dictionary catalog**, the **Dewey Decimal Classification (DDC)**, and **Library of Congress (LC)** printed cards. The first training course for librarians was offered at the Lyceum and Lawn Tennis Club, a women's club that opened a **public library** and sponsored literacy campaigns. A national assembly of librarians was held in November 1938, and the first Cuban library association was formed as a result. Formal teaching of librarians started in 1946 at the University of Havana with a summer course that was the precursor to the Escuela de Bibliotecarios, which opened in 1950.

After the Revolution, many professional librarians left the country, and some aspects of American-style librarianship were replaced by other models. The public library movement, which had not gained much steam before the Revolution, was given a boost by the new government's literacy push and the creation of a national public-library network. A school opened in 1971 to train people for work in bookstores and publishing houses, as well as libraries and archives. The Library Association of Cuba/Asociación Cubana de Bibliotecarios (ASCUBI) was established in 1985. Libraries in general have suffered following the **United States** embargo and the withdrawal of Soviet aid.

In 1998, Berta Mexidor, an economist, launched the Independent Libraries in Cuba Project to give Cuban readers unrestricted access to books, magazines, documents, and other publications not provided by state institutions. By 2001, the number of independent libraries had grown to 82. The independent librarians, most of whom were academicians or journalists, were fired from government jobs and, in some cases, detained. The movement set off a debate about the appropriate response from the **American Library Association (ALA)** and the **International Federation of Library Associations and Institutions (IFLA)**. The debate culminated in a 2004 resolution to support and assist the Cuban library community in safeguarding free access to information, and a continued call for the elimination of the US embargo and for lifting travel restrictions that limit professional exchanges.

See also ASSOCIATION OF CARIBBEAN UNIVERSITY, RESEARCH AND INSTITUTIONAL LIBRARIES (ACURIL).

CUTTER, CHARLES AMMI (1837–1903). Charles Ammi Cutter was born in Boston on March 14, 1837. He graduated from Harvard College in 1855 and entered Harvard Divinity School, where he was appointed librarian in 1857. In 1860, he became **cataloging** assistant to Ezra Abbott in the Harvard Library, where he and Abbott collaborated on a new catalog using index cards rather than printed volumes. In 1868, he was elected librarian at the **Boston Athenaeum**, where he produced the first major modern **dictionary catalog**. His *Rules for a Printed Dictionary Catalog* became part of the **United States** Bureau of Education's report on *Public Libraries in the United States of America: Their History, Condition, and Management*, which was published in 1876. Cutter's *Rules*, issued in a second edition in 1889, a third edition in 1891, and a posthumous fourth edition in 1904, served as the authority on which many subsequent cataloging codes were based. While at the Boston Athenaeum, Cutter also developed his **Expansive Classification**, which helped shape the **Library of Congress Classification (LCC)**. Conflicts with the Athenaeum's trustees led to Cutter's resignation in 1893. His next appointment was as librarian of the new Forbes Library in Northampton, Massachusetts. Cutter served as president of the **American Library Association (ALA)** from 1887 to 1889.

See also INTERNATIONAL CONFERENCE OF LIBRARIANS, 1877.

D

DAHL, SVEND (1887–1963). Svend Dahl was born in 1887 in Copenhagen, **Denmark**. He began studies in zoology at the University of Copenhagen, and then starting in 1907 was employed as an assistant, first at the Royal Library and then at the University of Copenhagen Library, returning to the Royal Library in 1911. He was appointed to the committee that prepared the first Danish **public library** law in 1920. Dahl then became library inspector. In 1925, he was appointed director of the Copenhagen University Library, which he modernized by extending hours and adding new services. In 1953, he became the national librarian of Denmark. Among Dahl's many writings is *Handbook of Library Science* (1912), the first modern Nordic guide to librarianship. The fourth edition appeared in three volumes between 1957 and 1960, with specialists from all five Nordic countries as contributors. In 1950, Dahl helped launch *Libri: International Library Review* (now *Libri: International Journal of Library and Information Services*).

DANA, JOHN COTTON (1856–1929). John Cotton Dana, an important figure in the **public library** and special library movements in the **United States**, was born in Woodstock, Vermont, on August 19, 1856. He received an AB from Dartmouth College in 1878 and then moved to Denver, Colorado, for health reasons. After working around the United States as a surveyor, lawyer, newspaper editor, preacher, and construction supervisor, he returned to Denver, where an article he wrote in 1889 for the *Denver Arbitrator* on the quality of public education led to his appointment as the first librarian of the Denver School District (which later became the Denver Public Library). He introduced a number of innovations, including extended hours, open shelves, a **children's** room, and marketing of the library. He also created a business collection, as well as a medical collection that later became the Denver Medical Library. In 1898, he moved to Massachusetts to supervise the City Library of Springfield and in 1902 became librarian of the Free Public Library of Newark, New Jersey, making it one of the most successful urban public libraries in the United States. He founded a business library in Newark's business district, the first of its kind, and founded the **Special Libraries**

Association (SLA) in 1909. Although Dana was involved with the American Library Association (ALA), even serving as president from 1895 to 1896, he was also one of its most vocal critics. Two awards have been established in his honor: the John Cotton Dana Library Public Relations Award of ALA and the John Cotton Dana Award of SLA.

DELANEY, SADIE PETERSON (1889–1958). A pioneer in the use of books as therapy, Sadie Peterson Delaney was born in Rochester, New York, on February 26, 1889. After graduating from the College of the City of New York in 1919, she received training at the library school of the New York Public Library. She then began work at the 135th Street Branch in Harlem. In 1924, she became the librarian at the Veterans Administration Hospital in Tuskegee, Alabama, and spent the rest of her career working with hospitalized black veterans. Within a year after her arrival, the collection had grown from 200 volumes to 4,000 books for patients and 85 books for medical staff. Her pioneering use of bibliotherapy became internationally known. She and her assistants consulted with the medical staff to get patient case histories and then tailored library services to meet each patient's needs. She also instituted literary societies, clubs, story hours, and book discussions that were broadcast over the radio. In 1934, she set up a special department for the blind.

See also AFRICAN AMERICANS IN LIBRARIANSHIP; WOMEN IN LIBRARIANSHIP.

DELISLE, LÉOPOLD VICTOR (1826–1910). Léopold Victor Delisle was born in Valognes, France, on October 24, 1826. He studied at the École nationale des chartes from 1846 to 1848. In 1852, he was appointed as an assistant in the department of manuscripts at the Bibliothèque nationale, and he rose through the ranks to become the director of the library in 1874. Delisle's career as a librarian was firmly grounded in the French tradition of scholarship, and he was a noted expert in the study of manuscripts. At the same time, he was an effective administrator. He reorganized the library's collection, introduced a methodical system of cataloging, and oversaw the production of a printed catalog, the first volume of which appeared in 1897. His retirement in 1905 marked the end of more than 50 years of service to France's national library.

DENMARK. The oldest library in Denmark, University Library, was founded in 1482. The Royal Library was founded in 1648. These libraries have been under a common administration since 1943. The public library movement had its roots in small parish libraries and subscription libraries created in the 19th century. The state began to make grants to public libraries in the 1880s. Andreas Schack Steenberg, a grammar school teacher, furthered public library development by taking a keen interest in English and American libraries and disseminating ideas about them in articles and books. In 1920, the Danish Parliament passed the first Public Library Act.

The first professionally trained Danish librarians were educated in the **United States**. The first Danish library school was organized in Copenhagen in 1918, with training intended only for qualification as a public librarian. When the Royal School of Library and **Information Science** was founded in 1956, replacing the older program, training was extended to prepare individuals to work in research and **academic libraries** as well.

Denmark's first library association, formed in 1905 to promote popular book collections, merged with another group of library supporters in 1919 to become the Danish Library Association. Today, it primarily represents public libraries. A number of librarians split from the Danish Library Association to form the Danish Union of Librarians, which is a national professional association as well as a trade union. Another organization, the Danish Research Libraries Association, was founded in 1978. In 1990, these and other Danish library organizations formed the Library Umbrella to provide a collective voice at the national and international level.

See also DAHL, SVEND (1887–1963); SCANDIA PLAN.

DEWEY DECIMAL CLASSIFICATION (DDC). In 1876, **Melvil Dewey**, then assistant librarian at Amherst College, published a booklet entitled *A Classification and Subject Index for Cataloguing and Arranging the Books and Pamphlets in a Library*, which became known as the Dewey Decimal Classification. The system contained 10 main classes subdivided decimally to form a total of 1,000 categories, numbered 000–999. The division of subject classes was based on an earlier **classification** system devised around 1870 by William Torrey Harris, superintendent of the St. Louis Public Schools, for the St. Louis (Missouri) Public School Library. The first use of DDC in a large general library occurred in 1877, when Josephus Larned used it to organize the collection of the Buffalo (New York) Young Men's Association Library. The second (1885) edition of DDC expanded on the first and also set the notational pattern for subsequent editions. Dewey supervised revisions through the 13th until his death in 1931. Forest Press, publisher of DDC beginning in 1911, became a division of the **Online Computer Library Center (OCLC)** in 1988, and DDC has been available in electronic form as well as print since 1993. WebDewey, the Web-based version, was first released by OCLC in 2000. An abridged edition has been published since 1894 to meet the needs of smaller libraries. The 23rd edition of DDC was published in 2011.

See also BLISS BIBLIOGRAPHIC CLASSIFICATION; COLON CLAS-SIFICATION; LIBRARY OF CONGRESS CLASSIFICATION (LCC); UNIVERSAL DECIMAL CLASSIFICATION (UDC).

DEWEY, MELVIL (1851–1931). Melvil Dewey, often referred to as the father of modern librarianship, was born on December 10, 1851, in Adams Center, New York. In 1870, he enrolled at Amherst College in Massachusetts and later began working in the college library. Upon his graduation in 1874, he was hired to manage the library and reclassify its collections. In 1876, he published the **Dewey Decimal Classification (DDC)**. That same year, he helped organize the conference of librarians that resulted in the formation of the **American Library Association (ALA)**, and he served as its first secretary from 1876 to 1891. He was also a cofounder and the first editor of *American Library Journal* (later *Library Journal*). In 1881, he established the **Library Bureau**, a library and office supplies company.

Dewey became chief librarian at Columbia College in 1883, and in 1887 he opened the Columbia **School of Library Economy**, the first library school. The curriculum reflected his pragmatic approach and his emphasis on the technical rather than on the theoretical aspects of librarianship. He admitted 17 **women** to the first class of 20, which angered the Columbia College trustees. He moved the library school to Albany, New York, in 1889, after accepting an appointment as state librarian and secretary to the regents of the University of the State of New York. In 1890, he was one of the founders of the New York Library Association. He served as ALA president from 1890 to 1891 and again from 1892 to 1893.

Dewey was a controversial figure. In addition to his conflicts with the Columbia College trustees, his business practices caused difficulties. In 1895, he and his wife founded the Lake Placid Club, a recreation and rest club for librarians, social workers, and teachers; in 1905, he was forced to resign as state librarian because the club's restrictive admission policy allowed no Jews to be admitted. In 1906, he was forced out of active participation in ALA, in part because of reports of sexual harassment. He moved permanently to Lake Placid, where he set up a foundation to carry out reforms in library practice such as metric conversion and simplified spelling. He then moved to Florida with his second wife, and in 1926, he established a southern branch of the Lake Placid Club, with the same restrictive policies. He died in Florida on December 26, 1931.

See also CLASSIFICATION; INTERNATIONAL CONFERENCE OF LIBRARIANS, 1877; NEW YORK STATE LIBRARY SCHOOL; *PUBLIC LIBRARIES IN THE UNITED STATES OF AMERICA*.

DHLOMO, HERBERT ISAAC ERNEST (1903–1956). South African poet, dramatist, journalist, political activist, and librarian, Herbert Dhlomo was born on February 26, 1903, near Pietermaritzburg in the Natal Province of South **Africa**. After training as a teacher at Adams College, he worked as a teacher and journalist. In 1937, he was selected from among 61 applicants to be the librarian-organizer of the Carnegie Non-European Library Service, which the **Carnegie Corporation of New York** had set up to provide library service to black Africans. Dhlomo was responsible for organizing and selecting books for various library centers; training the local volunteer staff of African helpers; lecturing and advising on reading material; and arranging literary readings, debates, and other activities at the local centers. He worked as a journalist after leaving his position with the Non-European Library Service in 1940. During the course of his career he wrote more than a dozen plays and hundreds of poems in addition to numerous articles.

DICTIONARY CATALOG. Introduced in the **United States** in the 19th century, the dictionary **catalog** is one in which all entries and cross-references are displayed in one alphabetical sequence. **Charles Ammi Cutter** is considered to have created the first major example when he was the librarian at the **Boston Anthenaeum**. Although it was replaced by the Online Public Access Catalog (OPAC) in the 1990s, the principles of the dictionary catalog have continued to influence library cataloging.

DIGITAL LIBRARY (DL). The **International Federation of Library Associations and Institutions (IFLA)** defines DLs as collections of digital resources available online, created and managed according to internationally accepted collection development principles, and supported by services that make them easily accessible to users. A significant event in DL history occurred in 1993, when the National Science Foundation (NSF)/Defense Advanced Research Projects Agency (DARPA)/National Aeronautics and Space Administration (NASA) Research in Digital Libraries Initiative funded six DL projects. Since then, the number of DLs has exploded, and researchers from many disciplines have been drawn into DL research. The early idea of the DL was a system to provide access to digitized books and other text documents. The DL has since evolved into something much more media-rich, dynamic, collaborative, and personalized.

Some DLs represent the effort of a single institution. Others, such as HathiTrust, have resulted from cooperation among several institutions. Project Muse and JSTOR are nonprofit organizations that have created DLs by licensing content from scholarly publishers. Google has created a DL (Google Books) by digitizing more than two million books from the collections of a number of libraries worldwide. A growing number of countries have national digital libraries; the Digital **Public Library** of America (DPLA) was launched in 2013. Among large-scale regional projects is the European Library, which offers access to the collections of 48 national libraries and leading research libraries in Europe. The Bibliotheca Alexandria opened the Arabic Digital Library in 2010. At the international level, the World Digital Library, developed by the **Library of Congress (LC)** and supported by the **United Nations Educational, Cultural and Scientific Organization (UNESCO)**, was launched in 2009 to make available significant primary materials from cultures around the world. IFLA, whose Manifesto on Digital Libraries was published in 2007, is involved in establishing DL standards and guidelines. Several other organizations, including the Digital Library Federation, which is a program of the **Council on Library and Information Resources (CLIR)**, and the DELOS Association for Digital Libraries, which was funded in part by the European Commission, promote work on DL issues.

DLs have raised key questions about the traditional library's broader purpose. The first digital-only public library in the **United States** opened in Texas in 2013, providing more than 100 e-readers and access to more than 10,000 e-books, but no physical books. DLs have also contributed to a rethinking of the traditional functions of the librarian. The DELOS Digital Library Manifesto addresses the question of the librarian's place in the DL world and suggests several possible roles: the end-user librarian, who acts as the front-end for the library client; the digital librarian, who decides the policies regulating the DL; and the system librarian, who manages the DL software. The evolution and growth of DLs has led to new educational programs. An example is the International Master in Digital Library Learning (DILL), which is a cooperative project of Oslo University College in **Norway**, Tallinn University in Estonia, and Parma University in **Italy**. In the United States, Virginia Polytechnic Institute and State University, which is home to the Digital Library Research Laboratory, has collaborated with the University of North Carolina, Chapel Hill, to develop a DL curriculum.

DIX, WILLIAM SHEPHERD (1910–1978). William Shepherd Dix, a leader in American **academic** librarianship, was born in Winchester, Virginia, on November 19, 1910. He attended the University of Virginia and worked as an English teacher for a number of years before receiving a PhD in literature at the University of Chicago. In 1947, he became an English instructor at Rice Institute in Houston, Texas, and a year later was asked to assume directorship of the library there. As chairman of the **Intellectual Freedom** Committee of the **American Library Association (ALA)** from 1951 to 1953, he was one of the principal authors of the landmark **Freedom to Read** statement. In 1953, he became librarian at Princeton University and held that position until he retired in 1975. His appointment in 1955 to the

United States Commission to the **United Nations Educational, Cultural and Scientific Organization (UNESCO)** led to his becoming one of the most-traveled American librarians. In the 1960s, he was instrumental in the passage of legislation that provided funding for the **National Program for Acquisitions and Cataloging** of the **Library of Congress (LC)**. Dix was president of ALA from 1969 to 1970.

DOCUMENTATION. Documentation was a new concept of bibliographic organization developed by **Paul Otlet** and others at the International Institute of **Bibliography** (later the **International Federation for Information and Documentation, FID**) in Brussels in the late 19th century. *Document* was a term that Otlet coined for any source of information, whether in the form of text, image, or object, that could be indexed and used for study. *Documentation* was used to describe any activity related to the collection, description, preservation, organization, retrieval, reproduction, and dissemination of documents. Later, it came to refer primarily to the handling of scientific and technical information. In continental Europe, documentation emerged as a distinct profession with its own techniques and training. Documentation was transported to the **United States** by Watson Davis, who founded the American Documentation Institute (later the **Association for Information Science and Technology, ASIS&T**) in 1937. In **Great Britain** and the United States, **information science** began to replace documentation in the 1950s.

See also BRIET, SUZANNE (1894–1989).

DOWNS, ROBERT B. (1903–1991). Robert B. Downs was born on May 25, 1903, in Downsville, North Carolina. After attending the University of North Carolina, he received a master's degree in **library science** (MLS) at Columbia University. He directed the libraries at Colby College, the University of North Carolina, and New York University before taking over as director of the Library and Library School at the University of Illinois in 1943, a position he held until 1971. After World War II, he made numerous trips abroad as a consultant to libraries and library schools in Afghanistan, **Mexico, Turkey,** and elsewhere. He served as president of the **American Library Association (ALA)** from 1952 to 1953. *Books That Changed the World*, one of his many publications, was translated into 14 languages. The Robert B. Downs **Intellectual Freedom** Award was established by the University of Illinois Graduate School of Library and **Information Science** in his honor.

DREXEL INSTITUTE. The Drexel Institute, a technical training school, opened in Philadelphia, Pennsylvania, in 1891. A library training program directed by **Melvil Dewey**'s student Alice B. Kroeger was established a year later with a class of 10 members. Together with the **Pratt Institute** in Brooklyn, New York, and the **Armour Institute** in Chicago, this was one of the first library training schools to be organized after the creation of the **School of Library Economy** at Columbia College. It is now the College of **Information Science** and Technology at Drexel University.

See also EDUCATION FOR LIBRARIANSHIP; UNITED STATES.

DZIATZKO, KARL (1842–1903). German library leader Karl Dziatzko was born on January 27, 1842, in Neustadt, Upper Silesia, which was then part of Prussia. After studying at the University of Breslau and the University of Bonn, he spent several years as a teacher. In 1872, he was appointed director of the University Library of Breslau. He introduced a number of reforms, among them a revision of the **catalog** that became a model for other universities in **Germany** and the basis for the **Prussian Instructions**, first published in 1899. In 1886, he was appointed to the world's first professorship of **library science** at the University of Göttingen, and was a key figure in the reform of Prussian librarianship that took place under Friedrich Althoff, the Prussian Minister of Culture. He was also instrumental in founding the Association of German Librarians in 1900. His collection of 550 items on library science, the book trade, libraries, and related topics was purchased by the University of Illinois Library in 1905.

E

EAMES, WILBERFORCE (1855–1937). Known as the dean of American bibliographers, Wilberforce Eames was born on October 12, 1855, in Newark, New Jersey. Early jobs in bookstores helped fuel his interest in **bibliography** and book collecting. In 1885, he took a position at the Lenox Library in New York City and was elected as head of the library in 1893. When the Lenox Library merged with the New York **Public Library** (NYPL) in 1895, he became part of the NYPL staff. He was named bibliographer of NYPL in 1916. Eames is best known for his continuation of *Dictionary of Books Relating to America from Its Discovery to the Present Time*, which bibliographer and bookseller Joseph Sabin had begun compiling in 1868. Sabin completed some 13 volumes before his death in 1881. Eames took up where Sabin left off, producing six volumes from 1884 to 1892, at which time other obligations forced him to set the project aside. Work resumed in 1927, this time with support from the **Carnegie Corporation of New York** and the Bibliographical Society of America and with the addition of a full-time editor, and the 29-volume *Dictionary* was completed in 1936.

See also EVANS, CHARLES (1850–1935).

EAST AFRICAN LIBRARY ASSOCIATION (EALA). EALA was founded in Nairobi, Kenya, in 1957, thanks in part to the efforts of the president of the **Australian** Library Association. There is no evidence of indigenous **African** participation until 1960. Branches of the association were later established in Kenya, Tanganyika (now Tanzania), and Uganda, and the first biennial conference was held in Nairobi in 1966. Librarians from the participating countries formed their own associations in the 1970s but agreed to retain the biennial conference, which is now the Standing Conference of Eastern, Central, and Southern Africa Library and Information Associations (SCECSAL).

See also WEST AFRICAN LIBRARY ASSOCIATION (WALA).

EASTMAN, LINDA ANNE (1867–1963). The first **woman** to head a major metropolitan **public library** in the **United States**, Linda Anne Eastman was born on July 17, 1867, in Oberlin, Ohio. She began working as an assistant at the Cleveland (Ohio) Public Library in 1892. In 1896, **William Howard Brett**, the library's director, offered her a position as vice librarian, and she became the library's director when Brett died in 1918. In addition to overseeing the completion of the new main library, she established a special travel section, a business information bureau, and services for the blind. She is also known for her writings on **children's** librarianship. Eastman taught at Western Reserve University's School of **Library Science** from 1904 to 1937 and was president of the **American Library Association (ALA)** from 1928 to 1929.

EBERT, FRIEDRICH ADOLF (1791–1834). German library theorist Friedrich Adolf Ebert was born at Taucha, near Leipzig, on July 9, 1791. He received a degree from the University of Leipzig in 1813 and was given a job at the university's library. While still a student, he wrote a work in which he declared that the only way to improve the condition of libraries was to pay librarians enough to enable them to devote their whole time to library service instead of having to supplement their incomes with outside work. In 1814, he was appointed to the Royal Library at Dresden. His pioneering treatise on **education for librarianship**, *Die Bildung des Bibliothekars*, written in 1820, was based in part on the premise that libraries should be organized in such a way as to provide maximum service to the public. Ebert's ideas helped pave the way for the development of professional librarianship in **Germany** later in the 19th century.

ÉCOLE NATIONALE DES CHARTES. The École nationale des chartes (or National School of Paleography and Archival Science) was founded in 1821 to train scholars in organizing the materials that had been amassed by the government as a result of confiscations during the **French Revolution**. A degree of *archiviste paléographe* has been awarded since 1829. The school is the oldest institution in Europe that specializes in archival sciences, and for more than a century, it remained the only formal library **education** program in **France**.

EDUCATION FOR LIBRARIANSHIP. Until late in the 19th century, training for librarianship generally took place on the job, sometimes as part of an **apprenticeship** program. In the **United States**, the push for better training was driven by the rapid growth in the number of **public libraries** that was brought about by **Andrew Carnegie**'s program for funding library construction. In 1879, **Melvil Dewey** wrote in *Library Journal* about the lack of professional education and proposed to establish a library school. In 1887, after three years of planning, he opened the **School of Library Economy** at Columbia College in New York City. By 1900, there were library training programs offered at the **New York State Library** in Albany, New York (the location to which the Columbia school was moved in 1889), the **Pratt Institute** in Brooklyn, the **Drexel Institute** in Philadelphia, and the **Armour Institute** in Chicago. All were run by Dewey graduates and were based on his model of efficiency and standardization. A number of large public libraries also offered formal courses, which in many cases expanded upon training developed for the library's own staff. For example, the training class founded at the Los Angeles Public Library in 1891 was reorganized as the Library School of the Los Angeles Public Library in 1914. By 1919, there were 15 programs in the United States. The length of the program, the type of degree or certificate, and the admission requirements all varied. In 1906, the school at Albany conferred the first master's degree in **library science** (MLS) and remained the only school to award a master's degree until the 1920s.

In 1903, the **American Library Association (ALA)** Committee on Library Training made the first systematic survey of education for librarianship, gathering information on the nine schools that were open at the time, as well as various summer schools and training classes. The committee's report, published in 1905, recommended that two or three years of college work be required for admission to library school, and that at least one-third of the instructors have received training in a recognized library school. In 1907, the **Association of American Library Schools (AALS)** held its first meeting at the ALA conference in Asheville, North Carolina. AALS assumed responsibility for setting standards for library schools, until that function was taken over by the ALA **Board of Education for Librarianship (BEL)** in 1925.

The BEL had been created following the publication of the **Williamson report** in 1923. This report had its origins in an earlier study commissioned by the **Carnegie Corporation of New York** in 1916. The corporation asked economist Alvin S. Johnson to evaluate its investment in public libraries. Johnson focused on the need for staff that was better trained, and **Charles C. Williamson**, an economist who taught at the New York Public Library School, was then hired to carry out a study of library education, which he conducted from 1919 to 1921. In his report, Williamson called for drastic changes, including advanced education for librarianship instead of technical training. The Williamson report set library education in the United States on a new course, resulting in the end of library schools outside an **academic** setting, the emergence of **accreditation**, and the founding of the University of Chicago **Graduate Library School (GLS)** in 1928.

In the years following the Williamson report, there were three different types of accredited programs in the United States: schools that required a bachelor's degree for admission to a program leading to a master's degree (Type I); schools that required a bachelor's degree and gave a one-year course, resulting in a second, five-year, bachelor's degree (Type II, the most common); and schools that did not require a bachelor's degree or four years of college (Type III). In 1951, the ALA Council approved new standards for accrediting library education programs, requiring completion of an undergraduate degree for admission to ALA-approved schools. By 1970, there were more than 70 accredited master's degree programs in the United States and **Canada**, thanks in part to federal programs supporting education and library expansion. The number of doctoral programs also increased. Whereas only 100 doctorates in librarianship had been awarded up to the end of the 1940s (almost all of them from the University of Chicago), the number grew to over 1,000 in the 1970s. However, declining enrollment led to the closure of 17 library and **information science** (LIS) programs, among them the University of Chicago program, which closed in 1991, and the Columbia University program, which closed in 1992. From 1998 to 2000, the **Kellogg-ALISE Information Professions and Education Renewal Project (KAL-IPER)** conducted the most comprehensive examination of LIS education since the Williamson report, identifying a number of significant trends, including a modification and expansion of the curriculum to educate other types of information professionals.

In Europe, the first formal library training program, the **École nationale des chartes**, was founded in Paris, **France**, in 1821. University-level library education was first offered in **Italy** in 1865. In **Germany**, the first library science chair was established at Göttingen University in 1886. These and other continental European programs were based on scholarly traditions and included courses on the history of the book, the art of printing, and the management of archives. In **Great Britain**, the **Library Association (LA)** created a system of **certification** based on examinations beginning in 1885, and the first full-time school of librarianship was established in 1919. The British model of first or undergraduate degrees in librarianship and the American model of postgraduate education can be found in various combinations worldwide. Education and training for librarianship is offered primarily at the undergraduate level in **Latin America**, the **Caribbean**, and the Middle East, although some postgraduate programs exist. In **Africa** and **Asia**, LIS education ranges from a certificate to the PhD. In Europe, the majority of schools offer postgraduate as well as undergraduate degrees. In some countries, such as Germany, graduate and postgraduate education tends to be specialized, while in others, such as Britain, it tends to be more generalized. The **European Association for Library and Information Education and Research (EUCLID)** was founded in 1991 as the representative of European

LIS educational institutions. LIS schools in the European Union (EU) have been working toward the goals laid out in the Bologna Declaration of 1999, which calls for internationalization and cooperation across the educational systems of all EU members.

A major trend in the second half of the 20th century was the integration of information science into library education. In 1964, the library science program at the University of Pittsburgh was the first to add "information" to its name, and, by 1996, the roster of ALA-accredited programs contained no schools of library science only. More recently, some LIS programs have broadened their scope by evolving into interdisciplinary information schools. In 1995, the University of California, Berkeley, changed the name of its program to School of Information Management Systems, and in 1998 elected to no longer pursue accreditation by ALA. Similar changes are occurring in other countries, resulting in education that is more diverse but less clearly focused on libraries and library services.

See also AFRICAN AMERICANS IN LIBRARIANSHIP; BOONE LIBRARY SCHOOL; FAIRCHILD, MARY SALOME CUTLER (1855–1921); HAMPTON INSTITUTE LIBRARY SCHOOL; INTER-AMERICAN LIBRARY SCHOOL; iSCHOOLS; OLCOTT, FRANCES JENKINS (1873–1963); PARIS LIBRARY SCHOOL; PLUMMER, MARY WRIGHT (1856–1916); SCHOOL OF LIBRARY SERVICE, ATLANTA UNIVERSITY; SHARP, KATHARINE L. (1865–1914); WOMEN IN LIBRARIANSHIP.

EDWARDS, EDWARD (1812–1886). Edward Edwards, who helped found the modern **public library** movement in **Great Britain**, was born in London, England, on December 14, 1812. The son of a bricklayer, he appears to have been self-taught, but a pamphlet that he wrote on the administration of the British Museum led to a position as an assistant at the **British Museum Library**, beginning in 1839. While still at the museum, he became active in the movement to establish free public libraries, and his writings on the subject resulted in his giving evidence before parliamentary committees that prepared the way for the passage of the **Public Libraries Act** in 1850. Edwards was then offered the position of head of the Manchester Free Library, the first important municipal library opened under the new act. After leaving his position in 1858, he continued to write while finding employment primarily as a cataloger in Oxford. Among his many works is *Memoirs of Libraries* (1859), a history of libraries since earliest times.

EDWARDS, JOHN PASSMORE (1823–1911). Like **Andrew Carnegie**, John Passmore Edwards was an important benefactor to **public libraries** in **Great Britain**. He was born in Blackwater, Cornwall, on March 24, 1823, and he became a successful publisher of newspapers and periodicals. Once his fortune was made, he decided to spend it on causes related to the welfare of the working class. He saw public libraries as part of this program and provided building funds and books for approximately 30 libraries between 1892 and 1900. Most of the libraries were located in Cornwall, but some were established in working-class districts of London.

EDWARDS, MARGARET ALEXANDER (1902–1988). Margaret Alexander Edwards, a leader in the development of library services to **young adults,** was born on October 23, 1902, on a farm near Childress, Texas. She received a BA from Trinity University, Waxahachie, Texas, in 1922 and worked for a time as a teacher of English and Latin. Later, she moved to New York City and received an MA in Latin from Columbia University (she returned to Columbia to receive a BS in **Library Science** in 1937). She joined the staff at the Enoch Pratt Free Library in Baltimore, Maryland, and in 1933 was assigned to work with teenagers for a few hours each day, an assignment which became a full-time position in 1937. As the coordinator of young adult (YA) library service until 1962, Edwards transformed the collection, established YA collections in each of the library's branches, instituted outreach programs, and developed a training program for the staff. She created the Margaret A. Edwards Trust, to be administered by the **American Library Association (ALA)** and intended to explore ways to promote reading among YAs. Among the projects sponsored by the trust are the Alex Award for adult books with teen appeal and the MAE Award for Best Literature Program for Teens. Edwards's book, *The Fair Garden and the Swarm of Beasts*, first published in 1969, is considered a classic in the field of YA services.

See also WOMEN IN LIBRARIANSHIP.

EL SHENITI, EL SAYED MAHMOUD (1920–1995). Prominent Egyptian librarian El Sayed Mahmoud El Sheniti was born in Alexandria, Egypt, on November 25, 1920. He earned a BA from Cairo University in 1940, a higher diploma in social sciences from Alexandria University in 1953, and a PhD in **library science** from the University of Chicago in 1960. Among other positions, he was the librarian at Alexandria University Library and at the American University in Cairo Library, as well as the administrator of the Egyptian National Library and Archives. He was a professor in the Department of Library, Information, and Archives of the Faculty of Arts, Cairo University. In addition, he contributed to a number of projects of the **United Nations Educational, Social and Cultural Organization (UNESCO)**, and from 1966 to 1974, he was a member and chairman of the UNESCO International Advisory Committee for Libraries, **Documentation**, and Archives. He presided over the Egyptian Library, Information, and Archives Association from 1964 until his death.

See also ARAB COUNTRIES.

ELECTRONIC INFORMATION FOR LIBRARIES (EIFL). Created in 1999 as an initiative of the Open Society Institute (OSI), EIFL is an independent foundation that supports the wide availability of electronic resources for library users in transition and developing countries. It began by advocating for affordable access to commercial e-journals for academic and research libraries in **Central and Eastern Europe (CEE)**. As of 2013, EIFL runs programs related to consortium management, **copyright**, licensing, **open access**, and other issues in over 60 countries in **Africa, Asia**, Europe, and **Latin America**.

ELMENDORF, THERESA WEST (1855–1932). Theresa West Elmendorf was born on November 1, 1855, in Pardeeville, Wisconsin. In 1877, she took a position at the Young Men's Association in Milwaukee, a library that formed the basis for the Milwaukee **Public Library**. Elmendorf worked at the Milwaukee Public Library after it opened in 1878, becoming its deputy director in 1880 and its director in 1892. In 1896, she moved to Buffalo, New York, where her husband had been appointed director of the Buffalo Public Library. She became the vice librarian at the Buffalo Public Library following her husband's death in 1906, and she worked there until she retired in 1921. Elmendorf was the first **woman** to be elected president of the **American Library Association (ALA)**, serving from 1911 to 1912.

EUROPE. *See* DENMARK; EUROPE, CENTRAL AND EASTERN; FINLAND; FRANCE; GERMANY; GREAT BRITAIN; ITALY; NORWAY; RUSSIA; SPAIN; SWEDEN.

EUROPE, CENTRAL AND EASTERN. The former Eastern bloc countries, the independent states in the former Yugoslavia, and the Baltic states of Estonia, Latvia, and Lithuania constitute the region known as Central and Eastern Europe (CEE). Some of these countries have rich and very old library traditions. The founding in 1348 of the first university in central Europe, Charles University in Prague, laid the foundation for the establishment of university libraries. The library of the Kraców Academy (known today as the Jagiellonian University) in Poland was founded in 1364. One of the greatest libraries of the Renaissance, the Bibliotheca Corviniana, was created in the 15th century by Matthias Corvinus, King of Hungary and Croatia. One of the largest libraries in Europe during the 18th century was the Zaluski

Library, established in Warsaw, Poland, by Andreas and Joseph Zaluski and opened to the public in 1748. The collection was confiscated by the **Russians** in 1794 and became part of the Russian Imperial Public Library. Some of the materials were returned to Poland in the 1920s, only to be destroyed by German troops in 1944. The National Széchényi Library of Hungary began with the collection donated to the Hungarian people by Count Ferenc Széchényi in 1802.

As in much of the rest of Europe, a variety of nongovernmental, often grassroots, institutions such as parish libraries, **school libraries**, public reading rooms, and municipal libraries sprang up during the 19th century. Romania had a **public library** law as early as 1864. In Bulgaria, a unique institution called the *chitaliste* began to appear in the 1850s. Combining a library and cultural center, *chitaliste* could be found in every town and village and are still a part of Bulgarian culture. Modern library practice was introduced in a few countries. In Hungary, for example, Ervin Szabó was influenced by the American and British public library model when he reorganized the Metropolitan Library in Budapest, starting in 1904.

The oldest library association in the region, the Polish Librarians' Association, was established in 1917 and was a founding member of the **International Federation of Library Associations and Institutions (IFLA)**. Library associations were established in Yugoslavia (with separate sections in Croatia, Serbia, and Slovenia) in 1930 and in Hungary in 1935. There were library associations in Estonia and Latvia starting in 1923, and in Lithuania beginning in 1931. The Congress of Baltic Librarians was formed in 1930 and met several times before Soviet occupation began in 1940. Classes for training Polish public librarians were provided at the Free University of Warsaw beginning in 1925, and a graduate library school was established in Poland in 1945. Librarianship classes at Charles University in Prague, initiated in 1927, created the first generation of trained Czech and Slovak librarians. The first professional **library science** program in Hungary was introduced at the University of Budapest in 1949. In Bulgaria, Sofia University established a library science and **bibliography** program in 1953. As of 2013, Albania is the only CEE country that does not have a library school.

Many library collections in the region were destroyed during World War II. Others were seized by the Nazis and eventually made their way to museums and libraries in the Soviet Union. After the war, libraries came under state control, following the Soviet model, and librarianship became ideologized. In the Baltic countries, many library materials, including the bulk of national literature, were removed from the shelves and put into restricted collections. Even in countries where libraries were well organized and well supported, modernization was hindered by international isolation and the fact that most information technology was unavailable or unaffordable. With the collapse of Communism and the end of centralized state planning and financing, libraries had to adjust to new political, social, and economic realities. State **censorship** came to an end, but so did state subsidies. Existing library networks broke down, and many libraries were forced to reduce their services or even to close. The former Yugoslavia went through a decade of civil wars, and in 1992, Serbian forces set fire to Bosnia's National and University Library, destroying an estimated 90 percent of the collection.

In the 1990s, CEE countries began to invest heavily in information infrastructure, including library **automation**. A number of philanthropic foundations, along with the European Union (EU), stepped in to help CEE libraries catch up with those in Western Europe and the **United States**. The Andrew W. Mellon Foundation, focusing on research and **academic libraries** in Czechoslovakia, Hungary, and Poland, provided support for the training of librarians in modern library techniques and management, the acquisition of Western materials, and the introduction or improvement of library automation systems. From 1990 to 1997, more than 80 libraries received funding from the Mellon Foundation for automation projects. Support for automation, preservation, and training came from the Open Society Foundation created by George Soros, who began his philanthropic career in the 1980s by distributing photocopiers to libraries in Hungary. Since 2000, the Bill and Melinda Gates Foundation has awarded grants to public libraries in Bulgaria, Latvia, Lithuania, Poland, and Romania to provide free access to computers and the Internet. International funds enabled CEE librarians to travel abroad and be exposed to modern standards and services, and also helped to motivate libraries to develop national and regional networks for interlibrary cooperation. Among the regional networks are Cooperative Online Bibliographic System and Services (COBISS), which was developed as a shared **cataloging** system for Yugoslavian libraries in 1987 and is now in use in Bulgaria, Slovenia, and most of the Western Balkan countries; and the Czech and Slovak Library Information Network (CASLIN), which was financed by the Mellon Foundation.

CEE countries began to modernize their library and **information science** (LIS) curricula in the 1990s, shifting away from a traditional model based on preservation and bibliographical studies. In 1994, the **European Association for Library and Information Education and Research (EUCLID)**, IFLA, and the **United Nations Educational, Scientific and Cultural Organization (UNESCO)** organized the Workshop on Education and Training of Information Specialists in Eastern Europe and CIS Countries, held in Bratislava, Slovakia, to establish training needs and priorities. Since 2000, member countries of the EU have based their LIS curriculum reforms on the Bologna Process, which aims for uniformity in European higher **education**.

See also ELECTRONIC INFORMATION FOR LIBRARIES (EIFL).

EUROPEAN ASSOCIATION FOR LIBRARY AND INFORMATION EDUCATION AND RESEARCH (EUCLID). Founded in 1991, EUCLID is an organization of European schools of library and **information science** (LIS). Its goal is to promote European cooperation within LIS **education** and research. Among EUCLID's projects are the BOBCATSSS conference, organized each year by students from an LIS school in **Central or Eastern Europe** and students from an LIS school in Western Europe.

EUROPEAN BUREAU OF LIBRARY, INFORMATION AND DOCU-MENTATION ASSOCIATIONS (EBLIDA). Headquartered in The Hague, EBLIDA is an umbrella association for library, information, **documentation**, and archive associations and institutions in Europe. It was founded in 1992 by a group of national library associations in the face of new policy and legislative initiatives that would have impacted core library functions. Among its objectives are promoting the interests of the library and **information science** profession at the European level.

EVANS, CHARLES (1850–1935). Charles Evans was born in Boston, Massachusetts, on November 13, 1850. He began his library career at the **Boston Athenaeum** at the age of 16. Subsequently, he held positions at the Indianapolis (Indiana) **Public Library**, the Enoch Pratt Free Library in Baltimore, the Newberry Library in Chicago, and elsewhere, but he is best-known as a bibliographer. While employed as a librarian, he began compiling a chronological, annotated list of early American imprints, and in 1902, he decided to devote himself to the task full time. The first volume of *American Bibliography: A Chronological Dictionary of All Books, Pamphlets, and Periodical Publications Printed in the United States of America from the Genesis of Printing in 1639 Down to and Including the Year 1820, with Bibliographical and Biographical Notes* appeared in 1903. After working on the project for a number of years, Evans revised his initial plan to include publications up to 1820 and settled on 1800 instead. By the time of his death, he had completed coverage of most of 1799. The project was finished under the sponsorship of the American Antiquarian Society, and a supplement was published in 1970. Evans's work is considered to be the foundation of American bibliography. *See also* EAMES, WILBERFORCE (1855–1937).

EXPANSIVE CLASSIFICATION. Expansive Classification was a **classification** system designed by **Charles Ammi Cutter**, based on the system he had devised for the **Boston Athenaeum**. Expansive Classification consisted of a series of seven increasingly complex schedules suited for libraries, from the smallest to the largest. Part of the system involved the use of alphabetic tables, which became known as Cutter numbers, to abbreviate the names of authors. The first six expansions were published in 1893. Cutter was still working on the seventh when he died in 1903. Although the Expansive Classification was never widely adopted, it laid the groundwork for **Library of Congress Classification (LCC).**

See also CATALOGING AND CATALOGS.

F

FAIRCHILD, MARY SALOME CUTLER (1855–1921). Library educator Mary Salome Cutler Fairchild was born in Dalton, Massachusetts, on June 21, 1855. She graduated from Mount Holyoke Female Seminary in 1875 and taught there until she was hired by **Melvil Dewey** as a cataloger at the Columbia College library. She taught **cataloging** at the **School of Library Economy** founded by Dewey in 1887 and then went with him when he transferred the school to **Albany**, New York, in 1890. As vice director, she took over the school's day-to-day operations and helped define the curriculum, which became a model for other library training programs. Fairchild chaired the committee to organize the **American Library Association (ALA)** exhibit at the 1893 **World's Columbian Exposition**. In 1899, she organized the New York State Library for the Blind. She also wrote numerous articles and was a frequent lecturer on library-related topics.

See also WOMEN IN LIBRARIANSHIP.

FARMINGTON PLAN. The Farmington Plan for cooperative acquisitions was developed in the 1940s to address deficiencies in foreign coverage in **United States** research libraries. The plan took its name from the town in Connecticut where the Librarian's Council of the **Library of Congress (LC)** held its first planning meeting (1942). Sponsored by the **Association for Research Libraries (ARL)**, with support from the **American Library Association (ALA)**, the **Carnegie Corporation of New York**, the **Rockefeller Foundation**, and others, the plan was intended to ensure that at least one copy of every new foreign book of possible research interest was acquired by an American library and made available for use by other libraries. The focus of the first effort in 1947 was on Western European publications, but the scope was later expanded. The Farmington Plan was terminated in 1972.

See also COOPERATIVE ACQUISITIONS PROJECT FOR WARTIME PUBLICATIONS.

FARRADANE, JASON (1906–1989). Jason Farradane, who is said to have coined the phrase *information science*, was born Jason Lewkowitsch in Poland on September 29, 1906. An emigrant to England, he adopted the name Farradane in honor of two British scientists: Michael Faraday and J. B. S. Haldane. In 1929, he received a degree in chemistry at what is now Imperial College in London and began working as a chemist and documentalist. He put himself in the vanguard of the emerging field of information science when he presented a paper entitled "The Scientific Approach to Documentation" at the Royal Society Scientific Information Conference in 1948. He was an early member of the **Classification Research Group (CRG)**, which was formed as a result of the conference, and he contributed to **classification** theory by developing what he called the "relational theory" of indexing. In 1958, he was instrumental in establishing the Institute of Information Scientists (which united with the **Library Association** in 2002 to form the Chartered Institute of Library and Information Professionals) to act as a professional body for information workers. He also established an educational program for information science at the Northampton College of Advanced Technology (now City University, London) in 1961. This was the first such program in **Great Britain**. Farradane joined the faculty of the college in 1963 and served as the director of its Center for Information Science beginning in 1966.

THE FICTION QUESTION. One of the debates that emerged in the early years of the library profession was what came to be called "the fiction question," or, in **Great Britain**, the "great fiction question." **Public** librarians saw it as part of their mission to elevate the masses, and they feared that fiction would have a deleterious effect. In the **United States**, library leaders such as **William Frederick Poole** and **Ainsworth Rand Spofford** were in favor of putting novels in library collections, but they wanted librarians to act as arbiters of taste, steering readers toward the "best" literature. In 1881, the **American Library Association (ALA)** compiled a list of 28 authors whose works were questionable on moral or literary grounds, among them Horatio Alger, Wilkie Collins, and E. D. E. N. Southworth. The debate continued into the 20th century, ending when public demand gradually led to an increase in popular fiction on library shelves.
See also CENSORSHIP.

FINLAND. The history of Finnish **academic libraries** began with the establishment of the Academy of Turku in 1640. The academic library system in Finland began to grow in the 19th century when a number of teachers' colleges were founded, and it expanded again in the 20th century with the establishment of polytechnics. Finland traces the origin of its **public library**

movement to the reading societies and libraries founded by elite (mostly Swedish-speaking) citizens for their own use and the "people's libraries" established for the benefit of the poor. The growth in the number of people's libraries in the last half of the 19th century was due in no small part to the Society for Popular Enlightenment, which was organized in 1874 to produce good literature at affordable prices and to support the people's library movement. The society was heavily influenced by American library ideas, and its activities paved the way for the creation of the State Library Bureau in 1921.

Before World War II, short training courses were the only training available for librarians in Finland. Courses for Swedish-speaking librarians were arranged by the Friends of the Swedish Elementary School, which did much to promote library services for the Swedish-speaking population. Helle Kannila, chief of the State Library Bureau, started a one-year diploma program at the School of Social Sciences in Helsinki in 1945. The first Nordic chair in Library and **Information Science** (LIS) was established at the University of Tampere in 1971. The Finnish Library Association was founded in 1910; most of its members are part of the public library sector. The Finnish Research Library Association, established in 1929, was the first Finnish institutional member of the **International Federation of Library Associations and Institutions (IFLA)**.

Finland is widely considered to have the most well-developed public library system in the world. The first Library Act, passed in 1928, established regular state support for public libraries, and although the responsibility for arranging library and information service was shifted to the local authorities in the 1990s, the government continues to direct public library policy. **School libraries** have been less of a priority. Both academic and public library networks are available to all Finnish citizens free of charge.

See also SCANDIA PLAN.

FIVE LAWS OF LIBRARY SCIENCE. In 1931, **Indian** librarian and theoretician **Shiyala Ramamrita Ranganathan** proposed the Five Laws of Library Science as the basic principles of library work. The laws are:

1. Books are for use.
2. Every reader his [or her] book.
3. Every book its reader.
4. Save the time of the reader.
5. The library is a growing organism.

FLEXNER, JENNIE MAAS (1882–1944). A pioneer in **reader's advisory service**, Jennie Maas Flexner was born on November 6, 1882, in Louisville, Kentucky. Her career as a librarian began when she took a job at the Louisville **Public Library** in 1905. In 1908, she entered the Library School at Western Reserve University in Cleveland, Ohio. Returning to Louisville, she took charge of the library's training program and became head of the circulation department. Her book *Circulation Work in Libraries* (1927), the first book on library circulation, became a standard text. In 1928, she was hired by the New York Public Library to establish a Readers' Advisory Office, which opened in 1929 and mainly served immigrants and the unemployed. She coauthored *Readers' Advisory Service* (1934) with Sigrid Edge. Her other books include *Readers' Advisors at Work: A Survey of Development in the New York Public Library* (1941) and *Making Books Work: A Guide to the Use of Libraries* (1943).

See also WOMEN IN LIBRARIANSHIP.

FLORENCE, VIRGINIA PROCTOR POWELL (1897–1991). The first **African American woman** to receive a library degree, Virginia Proctor Powell Florence was born on October 1, 1897, in Wilkinsburg, Pennsylvania. Unable to find a job as a teacher after graduating from Oberlin College, Ohio, in 1919, she worked as a beautician in Pittsburgh, Pennsylvania, and then applied for admission to the Pittsburgh **Carnegie** Library School. At that time, only one other African American had received a formal library **education**: Edward C. Williams, who had graduated from the **New York State Library School** in 1900. She was admitted to the Pittsburgh Carnegie Library School, although she was not allowed to interact with white library patrons during her practical work. She graduated in 1923, and, after working for a time at the New York **Public Library**, she became the first African American to take the New York State high **school** librarian's examination (1927). She worked in high schools in Brooklyn, New York; Washington, D.C.; and Richmond, Virginia, until she retired.

FRANCE. In France, as elsewhere in Europe, almost all early libraries were found in **monasteries** until the rise of the universities. The library at the **Sorbonne** was established in the 13th century. What is considered to be the first **public library** in France, the Bibliothèque Mazarine, was established in the 17th century. The Royal Library, which originated in the 14th century, became the **Bibliothèque nationale** during the **French Revolution**. Materials confiscated from religious and private libraries during the Revolution were assigned first to new secondary schools and then, after 1803, to municipal libraries. Although these libraries were open to the public, they met scarcely any needs except those of the learned, as British public library advocate **Edward Edwards** noted in 1869. Even today these libraries hold valuable state collections. The role of French librarians was to a large extent defined by the need to preserve and maintain this national legacy of ancient records for use by scholars. The general public could make use of the hodgepodge of *bibliothèques populaires* that opened in Paris in the 19th century.

Modern public library development began thanks to the efforts of reformers such as **Eugène Morel** of the Bibliothèque nationale, who admired the service orientation of public libraries in the **United States** and **Great Britain**. The Association of French Librarians/Association des bibliothècaires français (ABF) was founded in 1906 and defined librarianship in terms of public service as well as scholarly research. Following World War I, the American Committee for Devastated France (ACDF) provided support to Jessie Carson, a librarian on leave from the New York Public Library, to set up several model public libraries in Aisne. ACDF also provided funding and trained personnel for the **American Library in Paris**, which opened in 1922. **L'Heure Joyeuse**, a **children's** library launched in Paris in 1924 by an American philanthropic group, contributed further to the diffusion of modern library concepts. World War II brought innovation to a halt, and, following the war, libraries in France lagged behind those in similar countries in terms of number, staffing, and collection size.

The weakness of public libraries led to the creation of parallel services, some run by religious groups. A coordinating agency for libraries was formed in 1945 and some libraries were opened that were aimed at encouraging reading by the public at large, but it was not until the 1960s, when rapid urbanization and school expansion created more demand for libraries, that the French government began to take an interest in library development. Public libraries received more attention as a result of government decentralization in the 1970s. An effort to upgrade **academic library** buildings and collections began in the 1980s. At the same time, French librarianship began to shift toward a more user-oriented focus. The term *médiathèque* was adopted to differentiate the new model of public libraries from the *bibliothèques* of the past.

The **École nationale des chartes**, founded in 1821, remained the only formal library training program in France for more than a century. The creation of professional examinations and **certification** for university librarians coincided with the expansion of universities in the 1880s and was the first step in professionalizing academic librarianship. The ABF sponsored the first courses in modern librarianship, consisting of a series of lectures delivered by Eugène Morel. Following World War I, the **American Library Association (ALA)** established the **Paris Library School**, which operated from 1923 to 1929 and trained the first generation of public librarians in France. Some training was also offered by the Paris municipal library system, l'Heure Joyeuse, and the Institut Catholique de Paris. Librarians are now trained primarily at the École nationale supérieure des sciences de l'information et des bibliothèques, which was founded in 1992.

The ABF is currently the country's largest library association. Information and **documentation** specialists belong to the Association des professionals de l'information et de la documentation (ADBS), founded in 1963. **School libraries**, called documentation and information centers, are staffed by teacher-librarians, many of whom belong to the Fédération des enseignants documentalistes de l'Éducation Nationale (FADBEN).

In 1988, President François Mitterand proposed the construction of a new national library, which it was hoped would relieve some of the space problems suffered by university libraries, in particular. It was also hoped that the library would inaugurate a new age of French librarianship by introducing cutting-edge technologies and revising its mission. Unlike the old Bibliothèque nationale, which preserved rare and archival material for scholarly use, particularly in the humanities, the new library was intended to offer a broader range of materials and services and would be open to the general public. The library was planned with two separate levels: one serving the general public and the other serving academic researchers. The public reading room opened in 1996, and the research library opened in 1998. A few days after the completion of the area set aside for scholars, the library was shut down by a library workers' strike, brought on in part because the automated system that was supposed to deliver books to researchers failed to operate properly and workers had to hand-carry books over long distances. The library was also beset by controversy over its cost overruns and its design, which originally called for books to be stored in glass buildings without regard for the damaging effects of sunlight. Despite its problems, the BnF ushered in greater cooperation between libraries in France and other countries.

See also BRIET, SUZANNE (1894–1989); CAIN, JULIEN (1887–1974); DELISLE, LÉOPOLD VICTOR (1826–1910); HENRIOT, GABRIEL (1880–1965); NAUDÉ, GABRIEL (1600–1653).

FREEDOM TO READ STATEMENT. In May 1953, the **Intellectual Freedom** Committee of the **American Library Association (ALA)** collaborated with the American Book Publishers Council (now the Association of American Publishers) to hold a Freedom to Read conference at the Westchester Country Club in Rye, New York. Discussions formed the basis for the Freedom to Read statement, which was endorsed by ALA at that year's Annual Conference. The statement was amended on January 28, 1972; January 16, 1991; July 12, 2000; and June 30, 2004. The Freedom to Read Statement is one of the primary documented expressions of ALA's intellectual freedom principles.

See also CENSORSHIP; LIBRARY BILL OF RIGHTS.

FRENCH REVOLUTION. During the French Revolution, materials confiscated from religious houses and the nobility (estimated to be about 10 million books) became the property of the state and were taken to temporary storehouses (*dépôts littéraires*), where staff members were to record details about each item on cards. The cards were then to be sent to an office in Paris. Although plans for a national union catalog never materialized, the instructions issued by the government for **cataloging** the confiscated libraries constituted the first national code for descriptive cataloging. Many of the confiscated books made their way to the **Bibliothèque nationale**. Others were eventually assigned to municipal libraries where they would be available to the general public, although in fact it was primarily scholars who used them.
See also FRANCE.

FUNCTIONAL REQUIREMENTS FOR BIBLIOGRAPHICAL RECORDS (FRBR). FRBR is a conceptual model for structuring bibliographic databases. It was the work of a committee formed by the **International Federation of Library Associations and Institutions (IFLA)** in 1991. The purpose was to define the requirements for bibliographic records in relation to a wide variety of media and the needs of a wide range of users, taking full advantage of the capabilities of digital technology. FRBR is based on the entity-relationship database model that describes the attributes of entities and the relationships among them. Implementation was slow after it was published in 1998, in part because of the challenges of applying it to existing data. However, FRBR has influenced **cataloging** codes as well as a number of bibliographic databases and systems.
See also RDA: RESOURCE DESCRIPTION AND ACCESS.

G

GAY, LESBIAN, BISEXUAL, AND TRANSGENDER ROUND TABLE. The **American Library Association**'s **(ALA)** Gay, Lesbian, Bisexual, and Transgender Round Table had its origins in the Task Force on Gay Liberation, which, when it was formed in 1970, was the first openly gay and lesbian group established as part of a professional association. The name of the group was changed to Gay and Lesbian Task Force in 1986; to Gay, Lesbian and Bisexual Task Force in 1995; and to Gay, Lesbian, Bisexual, and Transgender Round Table in 1999.

See also PROGRESSIVE LIBRARIANSHIP.

GERMANY. University libraries were established in Germany beginning in the 14th century. Professional librarianship in Germany began to take shape in the great court libraries that arose beginning in the 16th century in Dresden, Munich, and elsewhere, but trained professional librarians did not emerge until 19th-century reforms brought an increased need for efficient library management and organization. Munich court librarian **Martin Schrettinger** and Dresden court librarians **Friedrich Adolph Ebert** and Julius Petzholdt were among those who made important contributions to **library science** theory.

Several significant developments took place in the late 19th and early 20th centuries, including the establishment of a library science chair at Göttingen. With its well-defined acquisitions principles and its liberal policies regarding use, the Göttingen University library served as a new model for scholarly libraries. Regulations for library training in Prussia were issued in 1893, and a **cataloging** code, the **Prussian Instructions**, was issued in 1899. A number of these developments were the work of Friedrich Althoff, an official in the Prussian Ministry of Culture, and **Karl Dziatzko**, the first professor of library studies at Göttingen. The Association of German Librarians/Verein Deutscher Bibliothekare (VDB), representing **academic** and research librarians, met for the first time in 1900. The Deutsche Bücherei, founded in Leipzig in 1912 by the Association of the German Book Trade, provided a central point for the acquisition of all German-language publications.

Reading circles, reading societies, and commercial lending libraries that were formed beginning in the 18th century were the precursors of the **public libraries**. Many cities established libraries for the general public in the 19th century, and a modern public library movement began to take shape under the influence of developments in the **United States**. In the 1840s, the facilities that made books available to working people in the United States so impressed a visiting German historian, Friedrich von Raumer, that when he returned to Berlin, he established a number of people's libraries, or Volksbibliotheken, which were partially supported by the city. The only German librarian to attend the 1893 **World's Congress of Librarians** in Chicago returned to Germany and launched the Bücherhallenbewegung (Book Hall Movement). Examinations for service in popular libraries began in Prussia in 1909, and public librarians formed their own association in 1922. As the public library movement expanded, two different concepts emerged, leading to the "direction dispute" that broke out in 1912. One group believed the public library should embrace liberal selection policies and leave it to the public to decide what to read. Another group, under **Walter Hofmann**, director of the city public libraries in Leipzig and founder of the German School for Popular Librarianship, believed in the need to transmit cultural values through strictly controlled selection policies and guidance from the librarian. The dispute dominated German librarianship until the Nazi era, and it was only after 1945 that public libraries made the transition to modern practices, allowing free access to the stacks.

More than 22 million books were lost during World War II, and many scholarly libraries were completely destroyed. After the war, libraries in East and West Germany followed their own paths, but the reunification of Germany in 1990 meant the reunification of librarianship as well. Efforts were made to bring the university and public libraries of the former German Democratic Republic up to West German standards. The State Library in Berlin combined with the Deutsche Bücherei in Leipzig and the Deutsche Bibliothek in Frankfurt am Main to form the German National Library. In 1991, the German Library Association (East) and the German Library Association (West) united as the German Library Association/Deutscher Bibliotheksverband (DBV). Library and Information Germany (Bibliothek und Information Deutschland, BID) is an umbrella organization uniting the DBV, the VDB, and other groups of information professionals. **Education** for library work is offered at both the university and the polytechnic level. In 2006, the Berlin School of Library and **Information Science**, formed when the programs at the Free University of Berlin and Humboldt University of Berlin merged following reunification, became the first German **iSchool**.

See also CENSORSHIP; MILKAU, FRITZ (1859–1934); *SERAPEUM.*

GESNER, CONRAD (1516–1565). Conrad Gesner, a physician and naturalist who made important contributions to **bibliography**, was born on March 26, 1516, in Zurich, Switzerland. He received a doctorate in medicine from the University of Basel and was appointed professor of physics at the Collegium Carolinum (later University of Zurich). In 1554, he became chief town physician of Zurich. In addition to being a physician, he was a botanist, linguist, and zoologist. Because of his *Historiae Animalium*, which appeared in six volumes starting in 1551, he is considered one of the founding fathers of zoology. He made his contribution to librarianship with *Biblioteca universalis*, published beginning in 1545. Consisting of a list of all of the writers that he could identify who had written in Greek, Latin, and Hebrew, and also their works, it employed the first major systems of bibliographical description and **classification**.

GHANA LIBRARY BOARD. The passage of the Gold Coast (as Ghana was then called) Library Ordinance in 1949 led to the establishment of the Ghana Library Board, the first national library service in sub-Saharan **Africa** and the first **public library** service to black Africans. The board took over the Aglionby Library (which had been established by the Anglican bishop of Accra) and also the **British Council**'s mobile library service to create a central public library in Accra. The Ghana Library Board served as a model for other African public library services.
See also WEST AFRICAN LIBRARY ASSOCIATION (WALA).

GLEASON, ELIZA ATKINS (1909–2009). Eliza Atkins Gleason was born on December 15, 1909, in Winston-Salem, North Carolina. Following her graduation in 1930 from Fisk University, her first library job was at the Louisville Municipal College for Negroes in Louisville, Kentucky. She attended library school at the University of Illinois and the University of California at Berkeley and continued her studies at the University of Chicago **Graduate Library School (GLS)**, where in 1940, she became the first **African American** to be awarded a PhD in **library science**. Her dissertation was published in 1941 as *The Southern Negro and the Public Library*. Gleason was the founding dean of the **School of Library Service, Atlanta University**, which opened in 1941. In 1942, she became the first African American to serve on the **American Library Association (ALA) Council**. Gleason returned to Chicago after World War II and continued her work in library **education**. The Eliza Atkins Gleason Book Award is presented by the Library History Round Table of ALA every third year to recognize the best book written in English in the field of library history.
See also WOMEN IN LIBRARIANSHIP.

GOULD, CHARLES H. (1855–1919). Canadian library leader Charles H. Gould was born on December 6, 1855. in Groveton, New Hampshire. His family moved to Montreal when he was a child, and he graduated from McGill University in 1877. He worked in the family flour milling business until 1892, when he was appointed the first full-time librarian at McGill University's Redpath Library, which had been donated by Montreal sugar magnate Peter Redpath. Before assuming his position, Gould spent a year traveling to Europe and the **United States** to study modern library administration. His efforts to have the **American Library Association (ALA)** meet in **Canada** came to fruition with the 1900 conference in Montreal. Gould was one of the organizers of the Ontario Library Association, the first Canadian library association. In 1904, he introduced the first library training program in Canada, laying the foundations for the McGill Library School. He served from 1908 to 1909 as the first Canadian president of ALA. By the time of his death, the Redpath Library had the largest collection in Canada.

GRADUATE LIBRARY SCHOOL (GLS). The GLS at the University of Chicago was created as a direct result of the Carnegie-funded **Williamson report** on library **education**. Following the publication of the report in 1923, the **Carnegie Corporation of New York** solicited suggestions for the establishment of a graduate library school that would be part of a university and pledged one million dollars in support. The University of Chicago was selected from among a number of contenders. GLS opened in 1928, its primary purpose being to conduct research, leaving it to other library schools to provide practical training. The first dean, George Alan Works, was succeeded by **Louis Round Wilson** in 1932. Among other notable faculty members in the foundational years were **Lester Asheim**, **Pierce Butler**, **Leon Carnovsky**, and **Douglas Waples**. Research findings were communicated in the *Library Quarterly*, launched in 1931, and in the monographic series University of Chicago Studies in **Library Science**, which started in 1933. GLS awarded the first doctorate in library science to Eleanor Upton in 1930.

Although controversial at first, the GLS model of research driven by scientific inquiry marked a shift in the direction of American library education and was key in developing library science as a discipline. The school stopped accepting admissions in 1989.

See also GLEASON, ELIZA ATKINS (1909–2009); HENNE, FRANCES E. (1906–1985).

GREAT BRITAIN. University libraries in Great Britain started as small collections of donated books that began to appear in the records of Oxford and Cambridge universities in the 14th century and St. Andrews University in Scotland in the 15th century. The number of colleges and universities expanded during the 19th century, but most of them relied on gifts and endowments for their financing and had few resources to devote to libraries. **Public libraries** had their antecedents in the coffee house book clubs, periodical reading rooms, miners' and mechanics' libraries, literary societies, circulating libraries (especially the famous Mudie's Select Circulating Library, founded in 1842) and other **social libraries** that sprang up as literacy rates increased.

Modern library development began in 1850 with the passage of the **Public Libraries Act**. At first, the act applied only to England and Wales, but it was extended to Scotland and Ireland in 1853. Library development was slow because the act set population requirements for the towns that were empowered to finance free public libraries and imposed limitations on the tax the towns could levy. As a result, many towns relied on benefactors such as **John Passmore Edwards**, who built 24 libraries in London and elsewhere, and **Andrew Carnegie**, who provided more than 380 communities with grants for library buildings between 1897 and 1913.

Only about 75 towns had adopted the Public Libraries Act by 1877, the year that the **Library Association (LA)** (now the Chartered Institute of Librarians and Information Professionals, CILIP) was formed. In 1885, the LA established the first examinations for library certificates and organized summer schools, correspondence courses, and other forms of **education**. Beginning in 1902, courses were provided in London in collaboration with the London School of Economics. In 1919, with the help of a grant from the Carnegie United Kingdom Trust, the first full-time School of Librarianship was established at University College, London. Beginning in 1927, the Scottish Library Association and other independent regional associations joined with LA to form a single group. The LA's monopoly on examination and **certification** along with its public library focus (created through the energies of public library leaders such as **James Duff Brown**, **Louis Stanley Jast**, and **Ernest Savage**) were among the factors that led to friction with **academic** librarians. Ultimately, academic librarians formed the **Standing Conference of National and University Libraries** (SCONUL, now the Society of College, National, and University Libraries). Other professional associations include the **Association of Special Libraries and Information Bureaux (ASLIB)**, established in 1926, and the School Library Association, established in 1937. The School Library Association represents teachers who run **school libraries**, while LA's School Libraries Section, also founded in 1937, supports certified librarians in schools.

In 1941, **Lionel R. McColvin**, city librarian of Westminster, was asked by the LA to survey the current conditions and future needs of public libraries. *The Public Library System in Great Britain: A Report on Its Present Condition and Proposals for Post-War Reorganization* (also known as the McColvin report) was completed in 1942 and had a profound impact on librarianship in Britain. McColvin called for the establishment of a national body with responsibility for libraries and a reduction in the number of local library authorities. It was not until the passage of the Public Libraries and Museums Act in 1964, however, that local authorities were required to adhere to standards and deliver comprehensive service. On the academic library side, the publication in 1963 of the Report on Higher Education (also known as the Robbins report) was followed by an expansion of higher education and, as a consequence, new library buildings, larger library budgets, and more staff. The second university-based library school in the country, the University of Sheffield Postgraduate School of Librarianship, opened in 1963. By 1970, a number of other universities had established their own schools of librarianship and had begun to offer diplomas and degrees. As a result, the LA ended its examinations in the 1970s and began accrediting programs instead.

Automation in Britain began to occur in the 1960s. The newly created Office for Scientific and Technical Information (later the Research and Development Branch of the British Library) funded a number of automation projects, including the **Birmingham Libraries Cooperative Mechanisation Project** and the South West University Libraries Systems Cooperative Project, and it also supported a feasibility study into requirements for British **Machine-Readable Cataloging (MARC)**. The Scottish Libraries Cooperative Automation Project was started in 1973. The British Library Automated Information Service (BLAISE), the first online bibliographical service in Britain, was launched in 1977. Other important late 20th-century developments include the merger of the British Museum Library with several other national library institutions in 1973 to form the **British Library**. The publication in 1993 of a report by the Joint Funding Councils' Libraries Review Group (popularly known as the Follett report), a major review of higher education libraries, led to more than 100 new academic library building projects.

See also ANGLO-AMERICAN CATALOGING RULES (AACR); AUSTIN, DEREK WILLIAM (1921–2001); BACON, FRANCIS (1561–1626); BATTLE OF THE BOOKS; BODLEIAN LIBRARY; BODLEY, THOMAS (1545–1613); BRAY, THOMAS (1656–1730); BRITISH COUNCIL; BRITISH NATIONAL BIBLIOGRAPHY (BNB); CATALOGING AND CATALOGS; CHILDREN'S LIBRARY SERVICE; CLASSIFICATION RESEARCH GROUP (CRG); COLWELL, EILEEN HILDA (1904–2002); EDWARDS, EDWARD (1812–1886); FARRADANE, JASON (1906–1989); GREENWOOD, THOMAS (1851–1908); INFORMATION SCIENCE; INTERNATIONAL CONFERENCE OF LIBRARIANS, 1877; NICHOLSON, EDWARD WILLIAMS BYRON (1849–1912); PANIZZI, ANTHONY (1797–1879); SAYERS, WILLIAM CHARLES BERWICK (1881–1960); VICKERY, BRIAN CAMPBELL (1918–2009).

GREEN, SAMUEL SWETT (1837–1918). Public library leader Samual Swett Green was born on February 20, 1837, in Worcester, Massachusetts, and graduated from Harvard Divinity School in 1864. His library career began in 1867, when he was appointed a trustee of the Worcester Free Public Library in place of his recently deceased uncle, the library's founder. In 1871, Green became the library's director, and over the next 38 years he introduced innovations that are a fundamental part of modern library service. For example, under his leadership, the Worcester Free Public Library became the first public library in New England to be open on Sundays. On the basis of his paper "The Desirableness of Establishing Personal Intercourse and Relations between Librarians and Readers," delivered at the conference of librarians in Philadelphia in 1876, he is credited with founding library **reference service**. He was also a strong proponent of cooperation between public libraries and schools.

See also UNITED STATES.

GREENE, BELLE DA COSTA (1879–1950). Belle da Costa Greene was born Belle Marion Greener in Washington, D.C., on November 26, 1879. Her first position was in the Princeton University Library, where she developed her interest in rare books. In 1905, she was hired by J. Pierpont Morgan to organize and **catalog** his growing collection of books, prints, and drawings. In addition to being Morgan's private librarian, she was his primary advisor, often traveling abroad to acquire additional books, manuscripts, classical texts, historical art, prints, incunabula, and cultural artifacts. Greene worked at the Morgan Library for more than 40 years, becoming its director when it was established as a public institution in 1924.

See also UNITED STATES; WOMEN IN LIBRARIANSHIP.

GREENWOOD, THOMAS (1851–1908). Described as the apostle of free **public libraries** in **Great Britain**, Thomas Greenwood was born in Cheshire, England, on May 9, 1851. He made his fortune in publishing, but the time he spent in public libraries in Manchester and other towns while working as a traveling salesman helped to turn him into a staunch advocate of free public libraries. He wrote and lectured in support of libraries and worked to encourage municipalities to adopt the **Public Libraries Act**. His book *Free Public Libraries: Their Organization, Uses, and Management* (1886), had a significant influence on Britain's public library movement. To encourage the professionalization of librarianship, he assembled a collection of around 10,000 bibliographies, library **catalogs**, book-sale catalogs, rare book specimens of early printing and binding, and texts on historical bibliography and library economy. This collection was presented to the Manchester Public Library in 1904.

H

HAMPTON INSTITUTE LIBRARY SCHOOL. The opening of the Hampton Institute Library School in Virginia in 1925 was the culmination of a search by the **American Library Association (ALA)** to find a school that would take on the job of training **African American librarians** in the South. **Louis Round Wilson** of the University of North Carolina had been sent by ALA to investigate possible locations for the library school, and although Fisk, Howard, and Tuskegee universities were also contenders, Hampton Institute was selected. Among the reasons for its selection was the fact that, even though it was a black school, it allowed a biracial faculty. This meant that qualified whites could be hired to teach, an important consideration when there were so few trained black librarians. The quality of Hampton's library and the eminence of many of its graduates were also factors. The **Carnegie Corporation of New York**, the **Rockefeller Foundation**'s General Education Board, and the Julius Rosenwald Fund provided support. Florence Rising Curtis was appointed as the Library School's director.

Hampton opened as a junior undergraduate school, but entrance requirements were raised to three years of approved undergraduate work in 1929, and to graduation from a four-year institution in 1934. The school awarded a bachelor's degree in **library science** and graduated 138 librarians, providing many black colleges with their first professionally trained staff. Despite Hampton's successes, however, discussions were being held among library and philanthropic leaders as early as 1931 about moving the school elsewhere. Among the concerns were Hampton's lack of a central location and the fact that Hampton Institute was a vocational school. The Hampton Library School closed in 1939. The **School of Library Service, Atlanta University**, was established to replace it in 1941.

See also EDUCATION FOR LIBRARIANSHIP.

HANSON, JAMES CHRISTIAN MEINICH (1864–1943). J. C. M. Hanson was born in **Norway** on March 13, 1864, and emigrated to the **United States** at the age of nine. After attending Luther College in Decorah, Iowa, and Concordia Theological Seminary in St. Louis, Missouri, he pursued graduate studies at Cornell University. In 1890, he became a cataloger at the Newberry Library in Chicago, where he met **Charles Martel**. In 1893, Hanson became head cataloger for the University of Wisconsin, and in 1897, he was appointed chief of the Catalog Department at the **Library of Congress (LC)**. Martel joined him at LC the same year and together they began work on what became the **Library of Congress Classification (LCC)** system. Hanson also oversaw the start of LC's **catalog card** distribution program. In 1910, he left LC for the University of Chicago Library and was later appointed to the faculty of the new **Graduate Library School (GLS)**. In 1928, he took a leave of absence to lead the **Vatican** Library reorganization funded by the **Carnegie** Endowment for International Peace. Hanson retired in 1934.

See also CLASSIFICATION.

HARRIS, WILLIAM JOHN (1903–1980). Regarded as the father of Nigerian librarianship, William John Harris was born in Oamaru, New Zealand, in 1903. After studying in **Great Britain** and graduating from Oxford University in 1929, he became a librarian at the University of Otago in New Zealand. In 1948, he was appointed head of the library of the first post-secondary institution in Nigeria: University College in Ibadan. In addition to organizing the library, he took steps to remedy Nigeria's lack of a publishing infrastructure and a national **bibliography**. He also played an active role in developing Nigerian librarianship. He was a founding member and first president of the **West African Library Association (WALA)**, and he was instrumental in the creation of the Institute of Librarianship in Ibadan in 1959. This was the first library training program in Anglophone West **Africa**. Following his retirement from Ibadan in 1968, Harris became a professor of **library science** at the University of Ghana and a librarian at the Mid-West Institute of Technology, Benin (now the University of Benin). The John Harris Library at the University of Benin was named in his honor.

HENNE, FRANCES E. (1906–1985). Frances E. Henne was born on October 11, 1906, in Springfield, Illinois. After receiving BA and MA degrees from the University of Illinois, she moved to New York to pursue a **library science** degree at Columbia University. She became an instructor in school librarianship at the **New York State Library School** in 1937. In 1939, she was invited to teach at the University of Chicago **Graduate Library School (GLS)**, making her the first **woman** to be a member of the faculty. While at the University of Chicago, she received her doctorate degree and was instrumental in the establishment of the Center for **Children's** Books and the *Bulletin of the Center for Children's Books*. In 1954, she joined the faculty of the School of Library Service at Columbia University. A champion of **school libraries**, Henne made a significant contribution to the development of school library standards. She wrote *Standards for School Library Programs*, published by the **American Library Association (ALA)** in 1960, and she coordinated the drafting of revised standards, published in 1969. The Frances Henne Award is presented each year by the American Association of School Librarians (AASL).

HENRIOT, GABRIEL (1880–1965). Archivist and librarian Gabriel Henriot was born in Paris, **France**, on January 18, 1880. He attended the **École nationale des chartes**, the national school for archivists, as well as the École des hautes études and, in 1905, was appointed librarian of the Bibliothèque historique de la ville de Paris. In 1920, he became director of the Forney Library, a special library where he instituted a number of reforms. He served as president of the Association des bibliothécaires français (ABF) from 1925 to 1927. In 1928, while attending the International Congress of Librarians and Booklovers in Prague, he presented a proposal that led to the founding of the **International Federation of Library Associations and Institutions (IFLA)**. For that reason, he is sometimes referred to as IFLA's spiritual father. He also became heavily involved in advancing library **education** in France. After teaching at the **Paris Library School**, he created a municipal library school, and, when that closed, a training program at the private Institut Catholique, which he directed for 25 years.

L'HEURE JOYEUSE. L'Heure Joyeuse is a **children's** library in Paris, **France**. It was opened in the Latin Quarter on May 24, 1924, by the Book Committee on Children's Libraries, an American philanthropic group that had set up a similar library in Brussels a few years earlier. The first director, Claire Huchet, was succeeded by her assistant, Marguerite Gruny, niece of **public library** advocate **Eugène Morel**. The user-oriented model put in place at l'Heure Joyeuse ushered in a new era of **public** librarianship in France. The staff pioneered open shelves, story hours, annotated bibliographies, and more. Children of all classes were welcome. Gruny retired in 1968, having served as director for more than 30 years. The library moved to new quarters in 1974.

HEWINS, CAROLINE M. (1846–1926). Children's library service pioneer Caroline M. Hewins was born in Roxbury, Massachusetts, on October 10, 1846. She worked at the **Boston Athenaeum** from 1866 to 1867 under **William Frederick Poole**, then spent some time taking classes at Boston University and teaching. In 1875, she took a post as librarian at the Young Men's Institute of Hartford, Connecticut, a subscription library that later became Hartford's **public library**. There, she developed a program of service to children. In 1882, she inaugurated a series of reports, "Reading for the

Young," that were based on national surveys designed to determine what was being done to encourage a love of reading. That same year, publisher Frederick Leypoldt invited her to compile *Books for the Young: A Guide for Parents and Children*, which became a widely used and influential selection tool. She was one of the founders of the Connecticut Library Association as well as the Club of Children's Librarians, the precursor of the **American Library Association (ALA)** section on children's librarianship.

See also WOMEN IN LIBRARIANSHIP.

HOFMANN, WALTER (1879–1952). Influential German librarian Walter Hofmann was born in Dresden on March 24, 1879. He worked as an engraver until he was commissioned by the wife of a wealthy manufacturer to plan, organize, and manage a **public library** for Dresden-Plauen (a district of Dresden), despite the fact that he had no library training or experience. In 1913, he was hired to organize a library system for the city of Leipzig. As city librarian, he promoted ideas that were part of a larger movement to reform **adult education**, including the notion that only "authentic" literature was appropriate for libraries, and that, because readers were not qualified to choose what to read, they should receive books from the librarians' hands rather than being allowed open access to the shelves. A believer in centralized library operations, Hofmann established the German Center for Popular Libraries in 1913. In addition to providing services such as centralized purchasing and bookbinding, the center included **Germany**'s first library school, which opened in 1914 to train librarians for work in popular libraries. Another one of his projects, the Institute of Reading Studies, was set up during the 1920s. His book *Die Lektüre der Frau* (1931), based on the results of the institute's research, was the first systematic study on reading behavior of a defined group of readers. Hofmann was dismissed from his post by the Nazis in 1937.

THE HORN BOOK. The oldest magazine in the **United States** for reviewing **children's** literature, *The Horn Book* was founded in Boston, Massachusetts, in 1924 by Bertha Mahony Miller and Eleanor Whitney Field, proprietors of the Bookshop for Boys and Girls. The shop had been opened in 1916 as a project of the Women's Educational and Industrial Union. When the shop was sold in 1936, *The Horn Book* became an independent enterprise.

I

INDIA. Although India's library tradition dates back several thousand years, the seeds of modern library development were sown in the 19th century when a number of college and **public libraries** were established, some by states and some by missionaries. The free public library movement got its start in 1906 when the Maharaja of Baroda (sometimes referred to as the **Andrew Carnegie** of India) began providing subsidies to village libraries. The Maharaja had been impressed by the libraries he had seen during his travels in the **United States,** and he invited William Alanson Borden, who had trained under **Charles Ammi Cutter** and taught at the Columbia **School of Library Economy**, to organize a free public library system. Appointed director of the state libraries in 1910, Borden established an extensive network consisting of a central library and branches, started a library training program, organized a librarians' club, launched a library journal (*Library Miscellany*), and designed a **classification** scheme for Indian libraries using elements from the **Dewey Decimal Classification (DDC)** and Cutter's **Expansive Classification**. Another American, Asa Don Dickinson, was appointed librarian of Punjab University, Lahore, and in 1915 started the second library training course in India. Dickinson also initiated the second Indian publication on **library science**, *The Punjab Library Primer.*

The first modern universities were opened in India in 1857, and the first university library building was constructed on the University of Calcutta campus in 1873. Many of the colleges that existed in India did not have libraries until the Indian University Act (passed in 1904) mandated that colleges maintain libraries and that books be lent to students. The University of Madras began a three-month certificate course in librarianship in 1929. In 1937, this changed to a one-year graduate diploma course, which served as a model for the development of library science **education** in the country. The Department of Library Science at the University of Delhi established the first postgraduate library science course in 1948 and awarded the country's first PhD in library science in 1957. In 2010, there were 178 schools offering a bachelor's degree in library and **information science** (the most common), 78 offering a master's degree, and 63 offering a PhD. However, there is no statutory body to **accredit** programs according to an international standard.

Most of the handful of public libraries that existed in India prior to the 1950s had closed shelves and charged subscription fees. In 1951, the **United Nations Educational, Scientific and Cultural Organization (UNESCO)**, in collaboration with the government of India, established the Delhi Public Library. Intended as a model for the development of free and accessible public libraries in all of **Asia**, it contained such modern library services as a **children's** department (rare in Asia at the time) and a Braille section, as well as branch and mobile services. The government of India appointed a committee in 1957 to recommend a plan for public libraries. The Sinha Committee report, named after its chair, K. P. Sinha, called for free library service for every citizen, comprehensive state library laws, and library cooperation. However, its recommendations were not implemented. A National Policy on Library and Information Systems was formulated in 1985 but was never approved. There is still no national public library legislation, and development has been uneven because some states have not enacted library laws.

India has a number of professional library associations. The oldest, the Andhra Pradesh Library Association, was formed in 1914 to establish a statewide system of libraries similar to the one set up in Baroda. The largest association, the Indian Library Association, was founded in 1933 during the All-India Library Conference. The Indian Association of Special Libraries and Information Centers (IASLIC) was founded in 1955, modeled after the **Association of Special Libraries and Information Bureaux (ASLIB)**. **Shiyala Ramamrita Ranganathan**, who was instrumental in founding the Indian Library Association, played a key role in shaping the concepts of Indian librarianship and also influenced library theory worldwide.

See also ASADULLAH, KHALIFA MOHAMMAD (1890–1949).

INFORMATION SCIENCE. Many researchers who study the history of information science trace its roots to the start of the **documentation** movement and the founding of the International Institute for **Bibliography** (later the **International Federation for Information and Documentation, FID**) in 1895. Documentation itself derived many of its principles from work done in the 19th century by librarians. However, unlike traditional librarianship, which focuses on books on library shelves, documentation focuses on the **classification**, storage, and retrieval of information in any form. FID's counterpart in the **United States**, the American Documentation Institute (later the **Association for Information Science and Technology, ASIS&T**) was established in 1937 and directed its attention toward the use of microfilm as a tool for storing and retrieving information.

Following World War II, the huge number of technical reports generated by the British and the Americans for military purposes, together with several hundred tons of captured German documents, resulted in an enormous stockpile of information. The development of information science was spurred by the push to organize, retrieve, and disseminate this information; by increased government funding for Cold War research and development; and by the emergence of new technologies, especially computers. Research into computers was directly influenced by the article "As We May Think," written by Vannevar Bush and published in *The Atlantic* monthly (1945). In it, Bush, head of the US Office of Scientific Research and Development, envisioned an information system, the *Memex*, that would store all the articles, reports, correspondence, and other documents that an individual scientist would need. Bush's paper was followed by the Royal Society Scientific Information Conference (held in London in 1948), the first international conference devoted to the subject of scientific information. By the time of the second conference, the International Conference on Scientific Information, held in Washington, D.C., in 1958, it was clear that information science was developing into a discipline distinct from documentation. Documentation's replacement by information science in the United States was reflected in the name change from American Documentation Institute to American Society for Information Science (ASIS) in 1968.

Although information science and **library science** were initially at odds, librarians such as **Ralph Shaw**, **Jesse Shera**, and **Mortimer Taube** made important contributions to the convergence of the two fields. The 1963 Conference on Libraries and **Automation**, sponsored by the **Council on Library Resources (CLR)**, the **Library of Congress (LC)**, and the National Science Foundation (NSF), was held to initiate a dialogue between librarians and information scientists on the relationship between library operations and computer technology. The launch of the **National Library of Medicine**'s **(NLM)** Medical Literature Analysis and Retrieval System (MEDLARS) in 1964 and of LC's **Machine-Readable Cataloging (MARC)** in 1968 served as early examples of successful applications of information science to libraries.

In 1955, the School of Library Science at Western Reserve University in Cleveland, Ohio, which had offered a documentation course as early in 1949, established the Center for Documentation and Communication Research, the first information science research organization to be affiliated with a library school in the United States. In 1964, the University of Pittsburgh became the first institution to change the name of its library science program to Library and Information Sciences (LIS). In 1965, the American Documentation Institute sponsored the Working Symposium on **Education** for Information Science (known as the Airlie Conference), and it was not long before information science courses became a regular part of the library science curriculum.

In **Great Britain**, the first information science course was established by **Jason Farradane** at Northhampton College of Advanced Technology (later City University, London) in the 1960s. Farradane was also the founder of the Institute of Information Scientists, which later united with the **Library Association (LA)** to form the Chartered Institute of Library and Information Professionals (CILIP).

INTELLECTUAL FREEDOM. Intellectual freedom as an abiding principle of librarianship received its first official endorsement when the Library's Bill of Rights (later renamed the **Library Bill of Rights**) was adopted by the **American Library Association (ALA)** in 1939. In 1940, ALA established the Committee on Intellectual Freedom to Safeguard the Rights of Library Users to Freedom of Inquiry (shortened to Committee on Intellectual Freedom in 1947). The Office of Intellectual Freedom was established in 1967 to implement the policies of the Committee on Intellectual Freedom and the ALA Council that are related to intellectual freedom issues.

In 1997, the **International Federation of Library Associations and Institutions (IFLA)** created the committee on Freedom of Access to Information and Freedom of Expression (FAIFE) to monitor intellectual freedom in libraries worldwide. IFLA adopted the Statement on Libraries and Intellectual Freedom in 1999. The IFLA Internet Manifesto and the Glasgow Declaration on Libraries, Information Services and Intellectual Freedom were adopted in 2002.

See also CENSORSHIP; FREEDOM TO READ STATEMENT; KRUG, JUDITH FINGERET (1940–2009).

INTERAMERICAN LIBRARY SCHOOL. The Interamerican Library School/Escuela Interamericana de Bibliotecologia (EIBM) at the University of Antioquia in Medellín, Colombia, opened in 1957. It was intended to provide university-level training to prepare Colombians for library work and also to serve as a regional training center for librarianship in **Latin America**. The **Rockefeller Foundation** provided support until 1970. The school conducted several important studies related to librarianship in Latin America and, in the 1960s, developed the first set of standards, known as the Medellín standards, for Latin American library schools.

See also EDUCATION FOR LIBRARIANSHIP.

INTERNATIONAL ASSOCIATION OF MUSIC LIBRARIES, ARCHIVES AND DOCUMENTATION CENTRES (IAML). The idea of an international music library association grew out of the first international meeting for music libraries, which was held in Florence, **Italy**, in 1949 in order to address problems in music scholarship and musical documentary heritage brought on by World War II. The IAML was formally established in Paris, **France**, in 1951, with support from the **United Nations Educational, Scientific and Cultural Organization (UNESCO)**. One of its primary goals was the establishment of a new **bibliography** of musical sources, the International Inventory of Musical Sources/Répertoire international des sources musicales (RISM), which documents music manuscripts from the earliest times through the early 19th century. In 2013, IAML had around 2,000 individual and institutional members in more than 40 countries.

See also MUSIC LIBRARY ASSOCIATION (MLA).

INTERNATIONAL ASSOCIATION OF SCHOOL LIBRARIANSHIP (IASL). The IASL was founded in Jamaica in 1971. Its purpose is to encourage **school library** development worldwide; to promote the **education** of school librarians, teacher librarians, and media specialists; and to promote research and publication related to school librarianship.

INTERNATIONAL CONFERENCE OF LIBRARIANS, 1877. Following the American conference of librarians that led to the founding of the **American Library Association (ALA)** in 1876, a British librarian, **Edward Williams Byron Nicholson**, called for a similar meeting to be held in London. The conference, which took place in October 1877, included among its 218 delegates representatives from **Australia**, Belgium, **Denmark**, **France**, **Germany**, Greece, and **Italy**, as well as **Great Britain**. Seventeen Americans attended, among them **Charles Ammi Cutter**, **Melvil Dewey**, **Samuel Swett Green**, **William Frederick Poole**, and **Justin Winsor**. A major outcome of the conference was the founding of the **Library Association (LA)** of the United Kingdom. A second international library conference held in London in 1897 drew more than 600 participants.

INTERNATIONAL CONFERENCE ON CATALOGING PRINCIPLES. Held in Paris in 1961 under the auspices of the **International Federation of Library Associations and Institutions (IFLA)**, the International Conference on **Cataloging** Principles was convened by the **United Nations Educational, Scientific and Cultural Organization (UNESCO)**, funded by the **Council on Library Resources (CLR)**, and attended by delegates from 53 countries and 12 international organizations, as well as by 104 observers. The purpose was to discuss the principles on which **bibliographies** and library catalogs should be based. The **Paris Principles**, issued as a result of the discussions, had an effect on cataloging codes around the world and provided the basis for the development of international standards.

See also INTERNATIONAL MEETING OF CATALOGING EXPERTS.

INTERNATIONAL FEDERATION FOR DOCUMENTATION. *See* INTERNATIONAL FEDERATION FOR INFORMATION AND DOCUMENTATION (FID).

INTERNATIONAL FEDERATION FOR INFORMATION AND DOCUMENTATION (FID). Originally called the International Institute of **Bibliography** (IIB), FID was founded in Brussels in 1895 by Henri La Fontaine and **Paul Otlet**. Its purpose was to promote a worldwide approach to bibliographical **classification**. IIB published the **Universal Decimal Classification (UDC)** from 1904 to 1907. The name of the organization was changed to International Institute of **Documentation** in 1931, to International Federation for Documentation in 1937, and to International Federation for Information and Documentation in 1986. At the time of its centennial in 1995, FID was an organization with members in 93 countries, with a stated purpose of developing and facilitating global and integrated programs, activities, and networks. FID was dissolved in 2000.

See also ASSOCIATION FOR INFORMATION SCIENCE AND TECHNOLOGY (ASIS&T); INFORMATION SCIENCE.

INTERNATIONAL FEDERATION OF LIBRARY ASSOCIATIONS AND INSTITUTIONS (IFLA). IFLA is an **international** body representing the interests of library and information services and their users. At the International Congress of Librarians and Book Lovers held in Prague in 1926, French librarian **Gabriel Henriot** proposed the creation of a standing international library committee, with members elected by national library organizations. On September 30, 1927, representatives from library associations in 15 countries who were attending the British **Library Association**'s **(LA)** 50th anniversary conference in Edinburgh signed a resolution to form the International Library and Bibliographical Committee. In 1929, the name was changed to International Federation of Library Associations, and statutes that had been prepared by **Carl H. Milam** of the **American Library Association (ALA)** were adopted. In 1947, IFLA and the **United Nations Educational, Scientific and Cultural Organization (UNESCO)** reached a formal agreement regarding mutual cooperation. In 1962, a UNESCO grant established IFLA's central secretariat.

In the 1970s, IFLA established regional sections for **Africa**, **Asia** and Oceania, and **Latin America** and the **Caribbean**. Since then, there has been a steady increase in participation from developing countries. As of 2010, IFLA had more than 1,600 members in 150 countries. It is headquartered in The Hague.

See also CATALOGING AND CATALOGS; CENSORSHIP; CONFERENCE OF DIRECTORS OF NATIONAL LIBRARIES (CDNL); COPYRIGHT; DIGITAL LIBRARY (DL); FUNCTIONAL REQUIREMENTS FOR BIBLIOGRAPHICAL RECORDS (FRBR); INTELLECTUAL FREEDOM; INTERNATIONAL CONFERENCE ON CATALOGING PRINCIPLES; INTERNATIONAL STANDARD BIBLIOGRAPHIC DESCRIPTION (ISBD); KOREA; MACHINE-READABLE CATALOGING (MARC); OPEN ACCESS (OA) MOVEMENT; PUBLIC LIBRARIES; SCHOLARLY PUBLISHING AND ACADEMIC RESOURCES COALITION (SPARC); SCHOOL LIBRARIES; UNIVERSAL BIBLIOGRAPHIC CONTROL (UBC).

INTERNATIONAL LIBRARIANSHIP. International librarianship was defined in 1974 by the International and Comparative Librarianship Group of **Great Britain**'s **Library Association (LA)** as activities conducted by institutions, organizations, groups, or individuals of two or more nations on behalf of library services and librarianship. An early landmark in the history of international librarianship is the 1877 **International Conference of Librarians** in London, which 16 Americans attended. Sixteen years later, several foreign governments sent representatives to the **World Congress of Librarians** held in Chicago. Other international gatherings took place before the 19th century came to a close.

The **American Library Association**'s **(ALA)** Committee on International Relations was created in 1900, and during World War I, the **Library War Service** program raised ALA's international profile. ALA contributed further to the internationalization of librarianship as a profession by opening the **Paris Library School** in 1924. The founding of the **International Federation of Library Associations and Institutions (IFLA)** in 1928 gave international librarianship an organized structure.

International travel in the 19th century was the catalyst for the modern library movement in a number of countries, and from their beginning, library schools in the **United States** had a contingent of foreign students. St. Louis (Missouri) **Public Library** director **Arthur Bostwick** visited **China** in 1925, becoming the first of the more than 500 individuals who had served as American library consultants to Asian libraries by 1967. ALA's first International Relations Office was established in 1943 with support from the **Rockefeller Foundation**. The US government initiated a number of library-related programs as part of its diplomatic strategy to promote democracy during and after World War II, inviting ALA to open and operate libraries in several **Latin American** capitals and sending American librarians to the Pacific region under the auspices of the US Office of War Information. The **British Council** sent librarians to postcolonial **Africa** and the **Caribbean** to study the condition of libraries there. ALA and the Rockefeller Foundation provided professional and financial assistance for new library schools in **Asia**, and American librarians were often recruited to teach. Other examples of international librarianship range from exchanges of publications to support for libraries through monetary grants and book donations, such as the Books for Europe program in the 1920s and the **Books for China** program in the 1930s. The **United Nations Educational, Scientific and Cultural Organization (UNESCO)** has contributed to library development on an international level since its founding in 1945.

A number of international associations were founded beginning in the 1950s, including the International Association of Agricultural Librarians and **Documentalists (IAALD)** and the **International Society for Knowledge Organization (ISKO)**. Regional associations such as the **Congress of Southeast Asian Librarians (CONSAL)** and the Nordic Literature and Library Committee (NORDBOK) were established, as were meetings such as the Anglo-Scandinavian Public Library Conference, the **Japanese**–United States Conference on Libraries and **Information Science** in Higher Education, and the China–United States Conference. The International Library Information Center (ILIC) at the University of Pittsburgh was created in 1964 to serve as a training and research center in the field of international librarianship. Under the leadership of Harold Lancour, the University of Pittsburgh also pioneered the internationalization of library **education** by bringing faculty from different countries to teach there in the 1960s. The Mortenson Center for International Library Programs was founded at the University of Illinois in 1986 to strengthen international ties among libraries and librarians. The ALA Book Fellows program, which operated from 1986 to 1998, performed a similar function. The Arizona Library Association became a leader in promoting international librarianship on a state level when it created the International Librarianship Round Table in 1988.

The internationalization of library education continues to be an important trend. In Europe, schools of library and information science (LIS) are working to standardize the curriculum across European Union (EU) members. IFLA has sponsored research that examines LIS education standards worldwide and evaluates issues related to determining the equivalency and reciprocity of LIS qualifications among different countries.

See also BENJAMIN FRANKLIN LIBRARY; EUROPEAN ASSOCIATION FOR LIBRARY AND INFORMATION EDUCATION AND RESEARCH (EUCLID); OVERSEAS LIBRARIES PROGRAMS; SHARIFY, NASSER (1925–2013).

INTERNATIONAL MEETING OF CATALOGING EXPERTS. The International Meeting of **Cataloging** Experts was held in Copenhagen, **Denmark**, in 1969 to discuss questions arising from the **Paris Principles** approved in 1961. The participants developed the **International Standard**

Bibliographic Description (ISBD) to facilitate international exchange of cataloging records. A follow-up meeting held in Grenoble in 1973 resulted in the publication of two documents: a standard edition for monographic publications (ISBD [M]) and a set of recommendations for serial publications (ISBD [S]).

See also INTERNATIONAL CONFERENCE ON CATALOGING PRINCIPLES; UNIVERSAL BIBLIOGRAPHIC CONTROL (UBC).

INTERNATIONAL SEMINAR ON THE DEVELOPMENT OF PUBLIC LIBRARIES IN AFRICA. Held at the University of Ibadan in Nigeria in 1953, the **United Nations Educational, Cultural and Scientific Organization (UNESCO)** International Seminar on the Development of **Public Libraries** in **Africa** was a landmark in the history of African librarianship. The four-week meeting was attended by 29 participants from 16 countries north and south of the Sahara, as well as from **Great Britain** and **France**. Just six of the participants were African. One result of the seminar was a study commissioned by the **Carnegie Corporation of New York** and conducted by Harold Lancour to assess the library needs of West Africa. His report stressed the necessity for professional library training and led to the opening of the library school in Ibadan in 1959. National schools were also started in Accra and Dakar. Another outgrowth of the seminar was the establishment of a pilot public library in Enugu, Nigeria. The seminar also resulted in the establishment of the **West Africa Library Association (WALA)** in 1954 and the National Library of Nigeria in 1964.

INTERNATIONAL SOCIETY FOR KNOWLEDGE ORGANIZATION (ISKO). ISKO is the leading international society for the organization of knowledge. Founded in 1989, its mission is to advance conceptual work in knowledge organization in all kinds of forms, and for all kinds of purposes, such as databases, libraries, dictionaries, and the Internet. In addition to its international body, ISKO has 12 regional chapters in **Asia**, Europe, North America, and South America.

INTERNATIONAL STANDARD BIBLIOGRAPHIC DESCRIPTION (ISBD). Originating with a resolution passed at the 1969 **International Meeting of Cataloging Experts**, ISBD is a set of international standards for the content and form of bibliographic description. The first of the ISBDs, International Standard Bibliographic Description for Monographic Publications, was published by the **International Federation of Library Associations and Institutions (IFLA)** in 1971. This was followed by standards for serials, nonbook materials, maps, rare books, printed music, and electronic resources. ISBD has been adopted by national and multinational **cataloging**

codes throughout the world and is considered by many cataloging experts to be the most successful international cataloging standard. A consolidated edition that merged the texts of the seven format-specific ISBDs into a single text was published in 2011.

See also UNIVERSAL BIBLIOGRAPHIC CONTROL (UBC).

iSCHOOLS. The iSchools organization evolved from informal meetings that were held among the deans of the library and **information science** (LIS) schools at the University of Pittsburgh, Syracuse University, and Drexel University beginning in 1988. Over the years, the number of participants grew, and in 2005 they formed the iSchools Caucus. Many of the iSchools originated as traditional LIS schools, but others came from fields such as computer science, education, and information technology. As of 2012, there were 36 iSchools in 11 countries.

ITALY. In ancient Rome, libraries were generally private, with a trained staff of Greek slaves to carry out the tasks of organization and maintenance. Julius Caesar's plan to build a **public library** was carried out by his successors, and by the fourth century CE, Rome may have had as many as 29 public libraries. As elsewhere in Europe, **monastery libraries** were prevalent during the Middle Ages. With the arrival of humanism, Italian libraries became centers for learning, patronage, and prestige. The collections built by princely courts and learned men during the 15th, 16th, and 17th centuries helped lay the foundations for public libraries such as the Ambrosiana Library in Milan, the Biblioteca Marciana in Venice, and the Biblioteca Laurenziana in Florence. By the end of the 18th century, most Italian cities of any size had a civic library. Although these libraries were open to the public, they had a tradition of librarianship that was based on conservation. This tradition was reinforced by the influx of old and valuable materials from suppressed religious houses in the 1800s. Well into the 20th century, most libraries that were open to the general public housed medieval manuscripts and early printed books. The commitment to preserving Italy's bibliographical heritage was a major factor in the relatively slow development of modern librarianship. Another factor was the fragmentation caused by Italy's political and cultural history.

Prior to unification in 1861, Italy had national libraries located in the capital of each state. After unification, these libraries, together with a number of university and special libraries, became part of a national library system under state regulation and control. In 1885, the National Library of Rome and the National Library of Florence were both made centers for **legal de-**

posit and were given some authority for bibliographic control. Beginning in the 1860s, a popular library movement sprang up to provide reading material to the working class.

Italian librarians were among the first to recognize the need for special training for librarianship. University-level library **education** was first offered in 1865, but it was not until the 1920s that universities began setting up the first formal library schools. The first program was established at the University of Bologna in 1923. This was followed by programs at the universities of Padua, Rome, Florence, Milan, and Naples, as well as at the Vatican Library, which opened a school in 1934. These schools generally linked the roles of archivist and librarian in one diploma, and all of them, except the Vatican Library School, required a university degree for admission. Courses were also offered by governmental and private institutions. However, until fairly recently, the majority of Italian librarians had no special training, because specialized training was not a requirement for admission to the library civil service examination. The oldest and largest library association in Italy, the Italian Libraries Association/Associazione Italiana Biblioteche (AIB), has lobbied to upgrade librarianship since its founding in 1930, and it has maintained a list of Italian librarians who meet certain academic and professional standards since 1998. In 2013, AIB was formally recognized as representing the library profession in Italy.

In the 1970s, the government transferred responsibility for public libraries to the newly established autonomous regions. In some parts of Italy, especially in the north, this marked the beginning of a period of library modernization. The 1980s and 1990s saw increased development of university libraries, which had long suffered from inadequate space, funding, and staff. The creation of the National Library Service in the 1980s led to shared **cataloging** and interlibrary cooperation, as well as to better access through its Online Public Access Catalog (OPAC). A new Italian **cataloging** code based on **Functional Requirements for Bibliographic Records (FRBR)** was adopted by the National Library Service in 2009. At that time, nearly 4,000 state, university, public, and other libraries were part of the National Library Service network.

The 2001 opening in Bologna of the Biblioteca Salaborsa, a high-tech, multimedia library documenting contemporary culture, was considered a bright spot in Italian library development. However, plans for an ambitious European Library of Information and Culture/Biblioteca Europea di Informazione Cultura in Milan were put on hold because of economic conditions.

J

JAPAN. There were likely libraries in Japan as early as the eighth century CE, but modern librarianship dates from 19th-century efforts to adopt Western concepts and institutions. The first modern library open to the public was established by the government in Tokyo in 1872. One of its directors, Inagi Tanaka (1855–1925), received training at the Harvard University Library under **Justin Winsor**, and he was one of the founders of the Japan Library Association in 1892. The association was instrumental in the passage of the first library act in 1899, and it began offering a training course in 1903. Other courses were organized at Tokyo Imperial University in 1918 and at the Ueno Library School, which the Ministry of Education opened in 1921. The Alumni Association of Ueno Library School was a force in the development of the profession. Another important group was the Japanese League of Young Librarians, which introduced the Nippon Decimal **Classification**, the Nippon **Cataloging** Rules, and the List of Nippon Subject Headings. The Japan Society for Library and **Information Science** was founded in 1953 for researchers and educators.

At the end of World War II, several American consultants, among them **Verner Warren Clapp** of **the Library of Congress (LC)** and **Robert B. Downs** of the University of Illinois Graduate Library School, were sent to Japan to make recommendations regarding library development. Their visits led to the establishment of the National Diet Library (modeled on the Library of Congress) as well as the founding of the Japan Library School at Keio University in 1951, with assistance from the **American Library Association (ALA)** and the **Rockefeller Foundation**. The Japan Library School provided the first comprehensive university-level library training program in the country. A master's degree was added in 1967 and a PhD in 1975. The 1899 library act was amended in 1950 to support **public libraries** and to spell out minimum standards for library workers. Although the number of public libraries increased, their main function until the 1960s was to preserve materials and to provide space for students studying for entrance exams. The impetus for reform came from the Japan Library Association's 1963 report *Management of Public Libraries in Medium and Small Cities* (also known as the

Chusho report), which emphasized the circulation of books as the public library's main function. Hino City Library, which opened in 1965, provided a model with its focus on making the largest number of books available to the largest number of people. Each public school was required to have a library following the enactment of a **school library** law in 1953.

In 1964, the Ueno Library School became the National Junior College of Librarianship, and it played a central role in the **education** of librarians. It is now the College of Knowledge and **Library Sciences** in the School of Information at the University of Tsukuba. Courses in librarianship are offered at more than 250 other institutions, ranging from junior colleges to universities. Most of these are very limited courses intended to meet government requirements for **certification**. Two types of national certificates are available: *Shisho* for working in public libraries and *Shisho-kyoyu* for working in school libraries. There is no qualification system for librarians in **academic** and special libraries. The Library and Information Professions and Education Renewal (LIPER) project, conducted from 2003 to 2005, found that library education in Japan was outdated, there was little quality assurance, too many people were being awarded librarian certificates, and the gap between library and information science education in Japan and other countries was widening. Among the recommendations were a new standard curriculum and a national LIS examination.

A unique Japanese institution is the bunko library, a private **children's** library typically set up and run by volunteers. In 2006, it was estimated that there were more than 3,000 bunko libraries in homes, community centers, temples, supermarkets, and elsewhere.

JAST, LOUIS STANLEY (1868–1944). British **public library** innovator Jast was born in Halifax, Yorkshire, on August 20, 1868. In 1887, he became an assistant at the Halifax Public Library. In 1892, he was appointed as the first librarian of Peterborough Public Library, which he made into one of the first libraries in **Great Britain** to be arranged according to the **Dewey Decimal Classification (DDC)**. Later, as chief librarian of Croyden Public Library, he extended **reference services**, arranged public lectures and exhibitions, and introduced the card **catalog** and the telephone. He was active in the **Library Association (LA)**, serving as honorary secretary from 1904 to 1915. He worked at the Manchester Public Library from 1915 to 1931, first as deputy director and then as director. Based on his plans for a new central library, as detailed in his pamphlet *The Planning of a Great Library* (1926), Manchester Public Library became the largest public library in Britain.

JEFFERSON, THOMAS (1743–1829). Thomas Jefferson was the third president of the **United States** and an avid book collector. When the building housing the **Library of Congress (LC)** collection was destroyed by the British in 1814, Jefferson offered to sell his entire personal library to the government as a replacement. By that time, he had amassed more than 6,000 volumes, making his one of the largest private book collections in the world. His method for arranging the collection, a modified version of **Francis Bacon**'s hierarchical **classification** system, influenced the **Library of Congress Classification (LCC),** and his belief that LC should serve the information needs of all citizens was important in shaping the library's role.

JEWETT, CHARLES COFFIN (1816–1868). One of the founders of American librarianship, Charles Coffin Jewett was born in Lebanon, Maine, on August 12, 1816. He graduated from Brown University in 1835 and then attended the Andover Theological Seminary. In 1841, he became Brown University's first full-time librarian. One of his first tasks was to prepare a new **catalog,** for which he drew on his experience helping to revise the library catalog at Andover. Published in 1843, the *Catalogue of the Brown University Library* was recognized as a significant advance in cataloging practice. Having achieved a national reputation as a library leader, Jewett was invited to become librarian of the Smithsonian Institution in 1847. There he developed a plan for a national union catalog that was based on receiving cataloging records from individual libraries and storing them on stereotyped plates, which would be kept at the Smithsonian. The plan needed a code of cataloging standards, which Jewett created based on those of the **British Museum Library**. Although the plan met with favor from other librarians when he presented it at the **Librarians' Conference of 1853**, it was not supported by the Smithsonian and was never implemented. Following his dismissal from the Smithsonian in 1855, Jewett found employment at the **Boston Public Library,** where he served as superintendent from 1858 until his death.

See also UNITED STATES.

JOECKEL, CARLETON B. (1886–1960). Carleton B. Jeockel, who helped design the plan for federal and state aid to libraries in the **United States,** was born in Lake Mills, Wisconsin, on January 2, 1886. He graduated from the University of Wisconsin and obtained a **library science** degree from the **New York State Library School** in 1910. After working as a librarian and library science educator in California and Michigan, he received a PhD from the **Graduate Library School (GLS)** at the University of Chicago in 1934 and joined the GLS faculty in 1942. In 1945, he became a professor of librarianship at the University of California, Berkeley. Joeckel was a strong advocate for federal aid to libraries and was the principal author of a study on federal aid published by the **American Library Association (ALA)** in 1936. As a consequence, he was asked to prepare a library study for President Franklin D. Roosevelt's Advisory Council on Education, which paved the way for the passage of the **Library Services Act (LSA)** in 1956.

JONES, CLARA STANTON (1913–2012). Clara Stanton Jones, the first **African American** to serve as president of the **American Library Association (ALA)**, was born on May 14, 1913, in St. Louis, Missouri. She received a bachelor's degree from Spelman College in Atlanta, Georgia, in 1934 and a master's degree in **library science** (MLS) from the University of Michigan in 1938. She worked in several **academic libraries** in the southern **United States** before taking a position at the Detroit (Michigan) **Public Library** in 1944. She was the library's director from 1970 to 1978, making her not only the library's first **woman** and first African American director but the first African American to direct a major urban public library in the United States. During her tenure in Detroit, Jones created outreach programs to give access to citizens who had never used libraries. She served as ALA president from 1976 to 1977 and as a member of the National Commission on Libraries and **Information Science** from 1978 to 1982.

JOSEY, E. J. (1924–2009). Librarian and civil rights activist E. J. Josey was born on January 20, 2009, in Norfolk, Virginia. After graduating from Howard University in 1949, he received a master's degree in history from Columbia University and a master's degree in **library science** (MLS) from the State University of New York at Albany. His early career as a librarian included positions as director of the library of Delaware State College and librarian and associate professor at Savannah State College. Beginning in 1966, he held several library development positions in the New York State Education Department. In 1986, he joined the faculty of the University of Pittsburgh School of Library and **Information Science**. He served as **American Library Association (ALA)** president from 1984 to 1985. Josey was known as a pioneer in the cause of **African American librarianship**. His 1964 resolution, forbidding ALA officers and staff from participating in state associations that denied membership to black librarians, led to the integration of library associations in several southern states. He founded the **Black Caucus** of ALA in 1970 and edited the landmark *Black Librarian in America* (1970) and *Black Librarian in America Revisited* (1994).

See also UNITED STATES.

K

KELLOGG-ALISE INFORMATION PROFESSIONS AND EDUCA-TION RENEWAL PROJECT (KALIPER). The most extensive examination of library and **information science** (LIS) since the **Williamson report** of 1923, KALIPER was funded by the W. K. Kellogg Foundation and was conducted over two years by a team of 20 scholars from the **United States**, **Canada**, and **Great Britain**. The project report, *Educating Library and Information Science Professionals for a New Century*, was published in 2000. Among its findings were a trend toward moving beyond the traditional focus on libraries as institutions and on library-specific operations; a more user-centered perspective; investment in information technology to keep students on the cutting edge; more flexible curricula; and new degrees, particularly at the undergraduate level. The findings have been used in curricular revisions in various library schools and also as a basis for studies of LIS **education** in other countries.

KHURSHID, ANIS (1924–2008). Known as the father of modern librarianship in Pakistan, Anis Khurshid was born in Kamptee, **India**, on September 2, 1924, migrating to the newly formed Pakistan in 1947. He received a certificate in librarianship from the Karachi Library Association in 1952 and joined the staff of the Karachi University Library. In 1958, he was given the Fulbright/**Asia** Foundation scholarship for higher studies in library and **information science** at Rutgers University in New Jersey. Upon his return to Pakistan, he became part of the faculty of Karachi University's **library science** department, and he started the first master's degree in library science (MLS) program in Pakistan in 1962. Another sojourn in the **United States** resulted in his being awarded a PhD from the University of Pittsburgh in 1969. As chairman of the Department of Library and Information Science at the University of Karachi from 1979 to 1982 and again from 1984 to 1986, he worked to strengthen library science **education** in Pakistan. He also played a role in promoting **public library** development and was one of the founders of the Pakistan Library Association. He was active in librarianship on an international level and published numerous library-related articles in both Urdu and English.

KILGOUR, FREDERICK G. (1914–2006). Library **automation** pioneer Frederick G. Kilgour was born on January 6, 1914, in Springfield, Massachusetts. He graduated from Harvard University in 1935 with an undergraduate degree in chemistry, worked in intelligence during World War II, and earned a master's degree in **library science** (MLS) from Columbia University. He then served as librarian of the Yale University Medical Library. In 1967, he was hired to head the Ohio College Library Center, where he transformed what began as an intrastate consortium of libraries into the **Online Computer Library Center (OCLC)**, the largest bibliographic database in the world. He was OCLC's president and executive director until 1980. He taught at the School of Information and **Library Science** at the University of North Carolina, Chapel Hill, from 1990 to 2004. The Frederick G. Kilgour Award for Research in Library and Information Technology is presented each year in his honor.

KNAPP SCHOOL LIBRARIES PROJECT. In 1962, the **American Library Association (ALA)** received a substantial grant from the Knapp Foundation to set up demonstration libraries in five elementary and three secondary schools in the **United States**. In addition, model **education** programs for **school library** media specialists were set up at six library schools. Funding was also provided by the Knapp Foundation for the School Library Manpower Project, which developed school library job descriptions. The Knapp School Libraries Project, which lasted until 1974, helped accelerate school library growth.

KOREA. The first university library in Korea was probably established as early as 1475, but education in general was available only to the elite until reforms were introduced in the late 19th century. The largest **academic library**, the Seoul National University Library, opened in 1946. Korea's first **public libraries**, established in Seoul and Pyongyang in 1906, were privately endowed. Publicly funded libraries were introduced during the Japanese occupation but were intended to promote colonial policies. The end of Japanese control following World War II brought new opportunities only to a part of the Korean peninsula, due to a bloody civil war from 1950 to 1953 that left the country divided between South Korea (Republic of Korea) and North Korea (Democratic People's Republic of Korea). In the north, under a series of dictators, **censorship** was rife and even books themselves became rare.

In South Korea, on the other hand, considerable progress was made following the Japanese occupation. The Chosun Library Association (established in 1945 and reorganized as the Korean Library Association in 1955) offered the first library training course in 1946. Ewha Woman's University began offering a **library science** course, and in 1956, a team of Americans from Peabody Teachers College established the Department of Library Science at Yonsei University. The first editions of Korean **Cataloging** Rules and Korean Decimal **Classification** were published in 1964, modifying systems that had been developed in the 1940s. **School libraries** began to be established in South Korea in the 1950s, although few schools had libraries until the mid-1990s.

In 1976, South Korea hosted a modified Worldwide Conference of the **International Federation of Library Associations and Institutions (IFLA)**, the first time such a meeting was held in **Asia**. The national library developed Korean **Machine-Readable Cataloging** (KORMARC) in the 1980s and launched the Korean Library Information System (KOLIS), an integrated information system, in the 1990s.

The mini-library movement, a unique Korean institution, was initiated in 1960 by Dai-sup Ohm, who had reorganized the Korean Library Association in 1955. Through his efforts, libraries were constructed throughout rural South Korea to provide people with reading materials. By 1979, there were more than 34,000 mini-libraries, managed and staffed by volunteers. In contrast, there were just 118 municipal public libraries at the time. A movement in the 1980s sought to promote public libraries by eliminating entrance fees and encouraging open stacks and mobile distribution. In 2002, the government unveiled a plan to increase the number of public libraries to 750 by 2011. The first master plan for school libraries was also formulated at that time.

KRUG, JUDITH FINGERET (1940–2009). A staunch **intellectual freedom** advocate, Judith Fingeret Krug was born on March 5, 1940, in Pittsburgh, Pennsylvania. After graduating from the University of Pittsburgh, she was awarded a master's degree in **library science** (MLS) from the University of Chicago. She began her library career in 1962 as a reference librarian at the John Crerar Library in Chicago. She joined the **American Library Association (ALA)** as a research analyst in 1965 and assumed the post of director of ALA's Office for Intellectual Freedom when it was established in 1967. Beginning in 1969, she also served as founding executive director of the **Freedom to Read** Foundation. Krug created ALA's Banned Books Week in 1982, and she was involved in multiple First Amendment cases that went all the way to the **United States** Supreme Court. After her death, the Judith F. Krug Memorial Fund was established to continue her legacy as a champion of intellectual freedom.

See also WOMEN IN LIBRARIANSHIP.

KRUPSKAYA, NADEZHA (1869–1939). Nadezha Krupskaya formulated the fundamental rules and ideologies that governed the practice of librarianship in the Soviet Union. She was born February 26, 1869, in St. Petersburg and married Vladimir Ilyich Lenin in 1898. Several years of exile acquainted her with Western European libraries and with librarianship as practiced in the **United States**. Once the Soviet government was established in **Russia** in 1917, she took up the causes of eradicating illiteracy and reorganizing the educational system. Believing that libraries were important tools in spreading Soviet principles, she wrote numerous articles on **library science**, promoted library legislation, and encouraged library development. She also initiated the opening of library training programs and library science research institutions. Some aspects of her reorganization of libraries and librarianship endured even after the collapse of the Soviet system.

See also WOMEN IN LIBRARIANSHIP.

L

LATIN AMERICA. Among the first libraries in Latin America were those attached to universities that had been created by religious institutions beginning in the 16th century. During the colonial period, libraries were also established in private and professional schools, government agencies, museums, learned societies, and the homes of private collectors. Many countries established national libraries early in the 19th century, soon after independence. Also in the 19th century, **public libraries** began to appear in larger cities. The greatest promoter of public libraries was Argentinian president **Domingo Faustino Sarmiento**, whose library legislation of 1870 (the first in Latin America) influenced other nations, among them **Brazil**, Chile, and Uruguay. For the most part, libraries were based on the European model of noncirculating collections and closed stacks. Early library training courses were also based on European models, such as the **École nationale de chartes** in **France**.

Starting in the 1920s, Latin American library development was increasingly influenced by the **United States**. A number of librarians studied in the United States and returned to their countries armed with new ideas about library methods and service. US efforts to strengthen ties with Latin America resulted in the opening of binational cultural centers in a number of Latin American cities. These centers included lending libraries with collections that the **American Library Association (ALA)** helped to build. With support from the **Rockefeller Foundation**, ALA opened a Latin American Office and, in 1941, published two widely circulated Spanish-language manuals on library practice. At the invitation of the US government, ALA operated three American-style libraries in Latin America in the 1940s: the Biblioteca Benjamin Franklin (**Benjamin Franklin Library**) in **Mexico** City; the Biblioteca Americana de Nicaragua in Managua, Nicaragua; and the Biblioteca Artigas-Washington in Montevideo, Uruguay. In addition to fostering cultural relations, the purpose of these libraries was to showcase American librarianship as the model to be followed by Latin American librarians. ALA also began a series of donor-supported exchange programs that provided opportu-

153

nities for Latin American librarians to visit libraries in the United States and also for American librarians to visit Latin America as consultants on library organization and library **education**.

The first **Assembly of Librarians of the Americas**, held in Washington, D.C., in 1947, helped lay the foundation for library cooperation. Donors such as the Rockefeller Foundation and international organizations such as the Organization of American States (OAS) and the **United Nations Educational, Scientific and Cultural Organization (UNESCO)** also played a role in library development. UNESCO and OAS sponsored a conference in Brazil on public libraries in Latin America in 1951. In 1952, UNESCO and the government of Colombia opened the Medellín Pilot Public Library of Latin America, patterned after UNESCO's pilot library in New Delhi, **India**. The OAS Library Development Program, founded in 1956, supported the training of librarians and bibliographers, the creation of manuals for library staff, the development of standards, and the exchange of publications. UNESCO sponsored a conference on university library development in **Argentina** in 1962, and the OAS and UNESCO sponsored projects for centralized **cataloging** and **Machine-Readable Cataloging (MARC)**.

The first library training program in Latin America was offered in 1911 by the national library of Brazil, and the first school of librarianship was established at the University of Buenos Aires in 1922. These were the only two **library science** programs in the region until after 1940. ALA set up summer institutes in Bogota and Quito in the 1940s and also assisted in the creation of library schools in Lima and São Paulo. In 1956, the Rockefeller Foundation provided funds for the **Interamerican Library School/Escuela Interamericana de Bibliotecologia (EIBM)** at the University of Antioquia in Medellín, which drew students from all over the region. In the 1960s, EIBM sponsored a series of meetings that produced the first set of standards for Latin American library schools. In 2000, there were over 60 university-level library programs in Latin America, more than half of them located in Argentina and Brazil. Training at the postgraduate level is available in just a handful of countries. Centers for research in librarianship have been set up in Argentina, Brazil, Mexico, and a few other countries. The Centro Universitario de Investigaciones Bibliotecológicas (CUIB) in Mexico, in particular, has been a leader in the publication of librarianship literature in Spanish. In the 1980s, CUIB began producing a database of Latin American library and **information science** literature, known as INFOBILA.

Since the 1950s, libraries in Latin America have benefited from the growing awareness of the importance of Latin American materials to libraries in the United States. The **Latin American Cooperative Acquisitions Program (LACAP)**, organized by the Seminar on the Acquisition of Latin American Library Materials (SALALM) in 1959, was followed by programs such as LAMP (formerly known as the Latin American Microform Project), which the **Center for Research Libraries (CRL)** organized in 1975, and the Program for Latin American Libraries and Archives established at Harvard University in 1996. Libraries have also benefitted from efforts to establish better information services in the region. For example, the Information Society Programme for Latin America and the **Caribbean** (INFOLAC) was created in 1982 to promote cooperation among librarians, documentalists, and others in the information field. Other notable developments have been the formation of regional bodies such as the **Association of Caribbean University, Research, and Institutional Libraries (ACURIL)**; the Association of Directors of National Libraries in Latin America (ABINIA); the Inter-American Association of Agricultural Librarians and Documentalists (AIBDA); and the Latin American Forum of National Public Library Directors (FIRBIP). The publication of a Spanish translation of the second edition of *Anglo-American Cataloging Rules* (*AACR2*) in 1983 led to increased participation in international cooperative library programs.

The development of librarianship is fairly advanced in some Latin American countries, while in others it has been hampered by political and socioeconomic factors and technical isolation. University and special libraries are generally the strongest in terms of technology, budget, and professional staff. There are relatively few **school libraries** in the region. Some countries (among them Argentina, Brazil, **Cuba**, and Mexico) have efficient public libraries, but the model of service-oriented, tax-supported public libraries is not as strong in Latin America as in some other parts of the world. In several countries, public libraries have become part of the effort to further social and economic development. In Chile, for example, BiblioRedes, a network of 412 public libraries and 18 training labs, provides computer and Internet access to poor and isolated communities. Beginning in 2004, the city of Medellín in Colombia made public libraries a key part of its program to use architecture to bring about social change by constructing library parks in several poor neighborhoods.

See also AGUAYO, JORGE; BORGES, JORGE LUIS (1899–1986); CHÁVEZ CAMPOMANES, MARIA TERESA (1890–1981); MANRIQUE DE LARA, JUANA (1899–1983); PENNA, CARLOS VICTOR (1911–1998).

LATIN AMERICAN COOPERATIVE ACQUISITIONS PROGRAM (LACAP). LACAP came into being in 1959 as a way to improve the acquisition of materials from **Latin America** and the **Caribbean** by libraries in the **United States**. It was created at the urging of the members of the Seminar on the Acquisition of Latin American Library Materials (SALALM), which began meeting in 1956. LACAP was a commercial venture sponsored by an international book company in cooperation with several US research libraries. Agents traveling to Latin American countries identified and purchased recent academic publications on the libraries' behalf, so that for the first time, books were brought to the United States on a regular basis and in large numbers from nearly every Latin American country. Considered a milestone in library cooperation, LACAP was suspended in 1972, in part because the Latin American book industry became better organized.

LEAGUE OF EUROPEAN RESEARCH LIBRARIES/LIGUE DES BIBLIOTHÈQUES EUROPÉENNES DE RECHERCHE (LIBER). Founded in 1971, LIBER is the main network for research libraries in Europe. In 2012, it had 400 university, national, and other libraries from 40 countries as members.

See also CONSORTIUM OF EUROPEAN RESEARCH LIBRARIES (CERL); SCHOLARLY PUBLISHING AND ACADEMIC RESOURCES COALITION (SPARC).

LEGAL DEPOSIT. Most national libraries have built their published collections through legal deposit, the statutory requirement that one or more copies of every item published in a country be deposited in a designated national institution. The first legal deposit legislation was passed in **France** in 1537. Legal deposit became law in **Great Britain** in 1662. In the **United States**, the first deposits were received by the Department of State in 1796, and the **Library of Congress (LC)** was authorized as the depository for all copyrighted materials in 1870. The United States is one of several countries in which legal deposit is part of **copyright** legislation. In other countries, the statutory powers for legal deposit may be the subject of a separate act, or they may be included in library legislation. The Netherlands is one of the few countries in the world with no legal deposit legislation, relying instead on voluntary deposit.

Although legal deposit has been an instrument of state **censorship** and control, it is generally used as a means of developing and expanding national library collections, compiling national bibliographies, and preserving a country's cultural heritage. Over the years, nonprint publications such as sound recordings, films, microforms, CD-ROMs, and, most recently, electronic publications have been added to legal deposit laws.

LIBRARIANS' CONFERENCE, 1853. The first library conference on the North American continent was held on September 15, 1853. Publisher Charles B. Norton had suggested a national conference to exchange ideas about libraries in the July 15, 1852, edition of *Norton's Literary Gazette and Publishers' Circular*, and the idea was taken up by **Charles Coffin Jewett** of the Smithsonian Institution, among others. The meeting took place in the chapel of the University of the City of New York (later New York University). Some 80 men representing 47 libraries were in attendance, including not only Jewett but also Charles Folsom of the **Boston Athenaeum**; Edward Everett Hale of the Worcester, Massachusetts, Young Men's Christian Association (YMCA); and **William Frederick Poole** of the Chicago **Public Library**. Jewett was elected president. Although it was hoped that the meeting would be a precursor to forming a permanent organization, no subsequent meeting took place. Nevertheless, the 1853 conference set a precedent for the meeting in 1876 at which the **American Library Association (ALA)** was founded.

LIBRARY ASSOCIATION (LA). The LA of **Great Britain** was formed at the close of the first **International Conference of Librarians** held in London in 1877. In its first years of existence, the LA adopted the *Library Journal* as its official publication, but launched its own publication then called *Monthly Notes*, in 1882. The current journal, *The Library Association Record*, has been published since 1899. In 1898, the LA received a Royal Charter allowing it to award chartered (professional) status to its members.

Initially, most LA members had **academic library** backgrounds, but as the **public library** movement grew in the 1880s and 1890s, public library leaders such as **James Duff Brown**, **Louis Stanley Jast**, and **Ernest Savage** came to dominate. Responding to the need for formal training, the LA organized summer schools and correspondence courses, and it issued certificates based on examinations starting in 1885. Beginning in 1902, courses were also provided in London in collaboration with the London School of Economics. In 1919, the first full-time library school was established at the School of Librarianship at University College, London, with financial support provided by the **Carnegie** United Kingdom Trust. The LA had passed a resolution calling for the establishment of such a school, although the school's opening threatened the association's monopoly on training.

Following World War I, LA reorganization led to integration with the Scottish Library Association and various independent regional library groups. Sections were formed to represent special interests. In 1937, the Carnegie Medal, awarded by the LA each year for an outstanding book for children, was established. In 1941, the Carnegie United Kingdom Trust requested the LA to collect information regarding the effect of the war on public library service. The result was two influential reports prepared by **Lionel R. McColvin**: one on wartime problems and one on postwar development. After World War II, the proliferation of library schools caused the LA to exempt those with university degrees in librarianship from taking the professional examinations, and the examination system was eventually phased out altogether.

The LA's public library bias was a factor in the formation of the **Association of Special Libraries and Information Bureaux (ASLIB)** in 1926 and the **Standing Conference on National and University Libraries (SCONUL)** in 1950. Beginning in the 1990s, talks with ASLIB and the Institute of Information Scientists (IIS) resulted in an agreement between the LA and the IIS in 2002 to unite in a new association: the Chartered Institute of Library and Information Professionals (CILIP). Among CILIP's roles are accrediting library and **information science** courses and conferring chartered status on professionals who meet certain requirements.

See also CERTIFICATION; EDUCATION FOR LIBRARIANSHIP; NICHOLSON, EDWARD WILLIAMS BYRON (1849–1912); *RDA: RESOURCE DESCRIPTION AND ACCESS.*

LIBRARY AWARENESS PROGRAM. Beginning in the 1970s, the **United States** Federal Bureau of Investigation (FBI) conducted a Library Awareness Program to try to identify Soviet spies based on library circulation records, database searches, and photocopy usage. The FBI targeted its visits to libraries that were drawn from the directory of the **Special Libraries Association (SLA)**. When the *New York Times* brought the program to public attention in 1987, the FBI disclosed that it had been engaged in monitoring the library activities of possible spies for more than a decade. The FBI also performed 266 background checks on librarians who refused to comply with or criticized requests for confidential library use information. The Library Awareness Program was strongly challenged by the **American Library Association (ALA)**, the **Association of Research Libraries (ARL)**, and the **Medical Library Association (MLA)**, as well as other groups.

See also CENSORSHIP.

LIBRARY BILL OF RIGHTS. The history of the Library Bill of Rights began with a policy formulated at the Des Moines (Iowa) **Public Library** in 1938. Prompted by Bernard Berelson's essay "The Myth of Library Impartiality," published in *Wilson Library Bulletin*, library director Forrest Spaulding developed a Bill of Rights for the Free Public Library, which was approved by the Des Moines Public Library Board. The policy was adapted and adopted by the **American Library Association (ALA)** as the Library's Bill of Rights (later renamed the Library Bill of Rights) at the 1939 Annual Conference in San Francisco. The original Library Bill of Rights focused on unbiased selection, a balanced collection, and open meeting rooms. Over the years, it has been revised and amended, and a number of statements designated as Interpretations of the Library Bill of Rights have been added. As of

2012, there were 22 interpretations, ranging from "Access for Children and Young Adults to Nonprint Materials" to "The Universal Right to Free Expression."

See also CENSORSHIP; FREEDOM TO READ STATEMENT; INTELLECTUAL FREEDOM.

LIBRARY BUREAU. Melvil Dewey had already been selling supplies to libraries for a number of years when he established a company called the Library Bureau in 1881. The Library Bureau introduced metal bookends, card **catalog** trays, and card catalog cabinets, among other items that became standard library equipment. Dewey resigned from the Library Bureau in 1901 in a conflict with his business partners, but the business continued to expand after it began selling library card stock for commercial record-keeping. Remington Rand acquired the Library Bureau in 1927.

LIBRARY COMPANY OF PHILADELPHIA. The first American subscription library, the Library Company of Philadelphia was founded on July 1, 1731. Benjamin Franklin and other members of the Junto, a discussion group, drew up an agreement to pool their resources and establish a library so they would have access to more books than any one of them could purchase on his own. Fifty subscribers invested 40 shillings each and promised to pay 10 shillings a year. The first books arrived from London in 1732. In 1792, the library opened its reference service to the public. The Library Company of Philadelphia was the largest **public library** in the **United States** until the 1850s, and it still exists as an independent research library specializing in American culture of the 17th and 18th centuries.

See also SOCIAL LIBRARIES.

LIBRARY JOURNAL. The oldest professional library periodical in the **United States**, *Library Journal* was founded as *American Library Journal* in 1876, the result of planning by **Melvil Dewey**, Frederick Leypoldt, and **Richard R. Bowker**. It was to be published monthly out of the offices of *Publishers Weekly*, with Dewey as managing editor. In 1877, *American Library Journal* became the official organ of the **American Library Association (ALA)**. It also became, for a time, the official organ of the **Library Association (LA)** in **Great Britain**, for which reason *American* was dropped from the title. *Library Journal* ceased to be ALA's official organ in 1907, but it continues to be the most comprehensive publication for librarians in the United States.

LIBRARY OF CONGRESS (LC). In 1800, President John Adams approved a new law that appropriated $5,000 to purchase books to be used by Congress. **Thomas Jefferson** signed a law in 1802 establishing the post of librarian of Congress. The original LC was housed in the new Capitol building in Washington, D.C. After the building was burned by the British in 1814, the **United States** government accepted Thomas Jefferson's offer to sell his personal library of more than 6,000 volumes to form the basis of a new collection. Another fire in 1851 destroyed nearly two-thirds of the library's collection.

Jefferson's belief that the national legislative library should serve the information needs of all citizens was a critical factor in shaping the LC's role. It was **Ainsworth Rand Spofford**, appointed librarian of Congress in 1864, who began implementing the Jeffersonian ideal. Under his administration, the entire Smithsonian Institution Library was acquired in 1866, and in 1870, **copyright** laws were revised to require the deposit of two copies of every work copyrighted in the United States. In 1896, Spofford presided over the opening of a new building, which at the time was the largest library building in the world. During congressional hearings held in that year, Spofford, along with **Melvil Dewey**, **Boston Public Library** director **Herbert Putnam**, and other library leaders sent by the **American Library Association (ALA)**, advocated for linking the library with the broader interests of librarianship in the United States. As a result, the LC was reorganized and expanded.

In 1899, Putnam was appointed librarian of Congress. He was the first experienced librarian to hold the position, and his administration saw the beginning of a number of comprehensive services and programs that led to the standardization of library operations nationwide. Archibald MacLeish, who served as librarian of Congress from 1939 to 1944 (and whose appointment was opposed by ALA because he was not a library administrator), and Luther Evans, who served from 1945 to 1953, further expanded the library's national and international roles. Programs such as the **National Program for Acquisitions and Cataloging (NPAC)**, **Machine-Readable Cataloging (MARC)**, and **Cataloging in Publication (CIP)** were initiated under L. Quincy Mumford, who headed the LC from 1954 to 1974. In the 1970s, the LC began to shift away from its role supporting the bibliographic and **cataloging** needs of the nation's libraries to focus on acquisition and collections.

See also DIGITAL LIBRARY (DL); INFORMATION SCIENCE; LEGAL DEPOSIT; LIBRARY OF CONGRESS CLASSIFICATION (LCC); LIBRARY OF CONGRESS SUBJECT HEADINGS (LCSH); LUBETZKY, SEYMOUR (1898–2003); PROGRAM FOR COOPERATIVE CATALOGING (PCC).

LIBRARY OF CONGRESS CLASSIFICATION (LCC). The move of the **Library of Congress (LC)** to a new building in 1897 prompted a major revision of its **classification** system, which had been based on the one **Thomas Jefferson** had devised for his own library. **James C. M. Hanson**, chief of the newly created **Catalog** Division, and **Charles Martel**, Hanson's chief assistant for classification, came up with a new scheme. Because Melvil Dewey would not allow any major changes to the **Dewey Decimal Classification (DDC)**, Hanson and Martel turned instead to **Charles Ammi Cutter**'s **Expansive Classification** as their guide. In 1898, Cutter's Class Z, Book Arts, was the first schedule to be developed as Class Z, **Bibliography** and **Library Science**. The LCC was published beginning with E–F in 1901. Today it consists of 21 classes in over 40 separately published print schedules and a large database. Although originally designed for the LC collection, it has been adopted by most **academic** and research libraries in the **United States**, as well as some US **public libraries**.

See also BLISS BIBLIOGRAPHIC CLASSIFICATION; COLON CLASSIFICATION; *SEARS LIST OF SUBJECT HEADINGS*; UNIVERSAL DECIMAL CLASSIFICATION (UDC).

LIBRARY OF CONGRESS SUBJECT HEADINGS (LCSH). LCSH are a controlled vocabulary providing subject access to bibliographic records. Adapted from the *List of Subject Headings for Use in Dictionary Catalogs* published by the **American Library Association (ALA)** in 1895, LCSH were developed for the **Library of Congress (LC)** collection beginning in 1898 and were first published for general use in 1914. Although based on the LC collections, they were widely adopted, in part because of LC's **catalog card** distribution program. A number of modifications were made to fit the needs of other collections. In 1923, **Minnie Earl Sears** created *Sears List of Subject Headings* for collections in small and medium-sized libraries. Beginning in the 1960s, the Canadian Library Association and Library and Archives **Canada** developed Canadian Subject Headings to provide greater coverage of Canadian topics while remaining compatible with LCSH. Libraries in a number of other countries have adopted, translated, or adapted controlled vocabularies based on LCSH.

LCSH have been criticized for outdated and biased terminology, a cumbersome structure, and the need for highly skilled catalogers and indexers, among other issues. Some in the cataloging community have begun to suggest that LCSH be abandoned altogether. Nevertheless, LCSH constitute the most widely accepted subject heading language in the world.

LIBRARY QUARTERLY (LQ). In 1931, the **Carnegie Corporation of New York** provided financial assistance to the **Graduate Library School (GLS)** at the University of Chicago for the launch of the *Library Quarterly*, the first scholarly journal of **library science** in the **United States**. Produced and edited by GLS faculty, the *Library Quarterly* reflected the school's emphasis on research as opposed to the practical approach taken by *Library Journal* and *Public Libraries*, the other professional journals in existence at the time. For that reason, it was instrumental in developing library science as an academic discipline.

LIBRARY SCIENCE. The idea of librarianship as a science based on systems and techniques was pioneered in **Germany** in the late 18th and early 19th centuries by **Martin Schrettinger**, among others. Schrettinger, a librarian at the Munich Court Library, coined the term *library science*, which he defined as the precepts on which the practical organization of a library is based. Schrettinger also wrote the first manual of library science, published in 1808.

As it evolved in Europe in the 19th century, library science was a scholarly discipline focused on the preservation and care of library materials. In the **United States**, on the other hand, library science was about the practical aspects of the way libraries were run, underscored by the fact that the first formal library school, founded by **Melvil Dewey** in 1887, was named the **School of Library Economy**. A change to a more theoretical approach began with the establishment of the **Graduate Library School (GLS)** at the University of Chicago. The school was founded following the publication of the **Williamson report** of 1923, which called for making a distinction between clerical and professional library tasks. GLS introduced the concept of library science based on methods of investigation drawn from social and behavioral sciences and legitimized librarianship as a field for graduate research. The field's first research journal, the *Library Quarterly*, was launched by GLS faculty in 1933. Faculty member **Pierce Butler**'s classic *Introduction to Library Science*, also published in 1933, helped to promote the consideration of librarianship as a science. The term *library science* was replaced by *library and information science* beginning in the 1960s.

LIBRARY SERVICES ACT (LSA). *See* LIBRARY SERVICES AND CONSTRUCTION ACT (LSCA).

LIBRARY SERVICES AND CONSTRUCTION ACT (LSCA). In 1964, President Lyndon Johnson signed the LSCA. It expanded upon the Library Services Act of 1956, which had provided for the extension of library service to rural areas in the **United States**. The new act extended aid to all **public**

libraries, whether in rural or urban areas, and it also authorized funds for library construction and remodeling. A renewal in 1966 added funds for interlibrary cooperation and for state services to handicapped and institutionalized populations. LSCA resulted in a huge growth in public library services.

See also JOECKEL, CARLETON B. (1886–1960).

LIBRARY WAR SERVICE. In 1917, the **American Library Association (ALA)** launched its first international effort, a program under the direction of **Herbert Putnam** of the **Library of Congress (LC)** to provide library services to American Armed Forces. With **Carnegie Corporation of New York** funds, libraries were built at all of the camps that had been set up for training American soldiers. ALA conducted national fundraising drives to provide books and librarians. Another national campaign collected books to be sent to camps in the **United States** and abroad. Library services were available in 36 training camps, and books were provided to several hundred hospitals and Red Cross Houses, small military encampments, and other locations.

See also INTERNATIONAL LIBRARIANSHIP; MILAM, CARL H. (1884–1963).

LIU, GUOJUN (1899–1980). Liu Guojun, a pioneer in developing modern **library science** in **China**, began his library career at Nanking University after graduating with a bachelor's degree in philosophy and literature. In 1924, he traveled to the **United States** to study library science at the University of Wisconsin at Madison. In 1927, he became the librarian at Nanking University, succeeding American Harry Clemons, who had held the post since 1913. Several other positions followed, including chief of the national government's Library Division, until Liu became professor and (beginning in 1958) dean at the Department of Library Science at Beijing University, where he remained until 1980. Over his long career, Liu played a major role in applying Western trends in **automation** and **classification** to Chinese librarianship. In 1929, he introduced a classification for Chinese libraries which was based on the **Dewey Decimal Classification (DDC)**, and he greatly influenced schemes that were developed in China later in the 20th century. He introduced **Machine-Readable Cataloging (MARC)** into China in 1975.

LUBETZKY, SEYMOUR (1898–2003). Seymour Lubetzky, who has been called the greatest cataloger of the 20th century, was born on April 28, 1893, in Poland. After emigrating to the **United States** in 1927, he studied at the University of California at Los Angeles (UCLA) and the University of California at Berkeley. In 1934, he was awarded a Certificate in Librarianship from the UCLA library school. Articles he wrote while working as a cataloger at the UCLA library led to his being appointed as a consultant on bibliographic and **cataloging** policy by Archibald MacLeish, librarian of Congress, in 1943. Eventually, Lubetzky became chief of the Catalog Maintenance Division at the **Library of Congress (LC)**. His investigation of the **American Library Association**'s **(ALA)** *Cataloging Rules for Author and Title Entries* (1949) led to his *Cataloging Rules and Principles* (1953), which is considered one of the classics of library literature. In 1960, Lubetzky was appointed professor at the UCLA School of Library Service, and he taught there until 1969.

See also PARIS PRINCIPLES.

M

MACHINE-READABLE CATALOGING (MARC). In 1965, a conference was held at the **Library of Congress (LC)** on the conversion of bibliographic data to machine-readable form. Following the conference, LC began an experiment to produce and distribute machine-readable **catalog** records. Supported by a grant from the **Council on Library Resources (CLR)**, the Machine-Readable Cataloging Project was conducted from November 1966 to June 1968. During that time, LC distributed approximately 50,000 records for English-language monographs on magnetic tape to 16 libraries. Revisions made in the course of the pilot project resulted in the MARC II format, which was published in 1968. The MARC Distribution Service was implemented on a subscription basis in 1969. MARC was in use at LC by 1970, and within 10 years, most of the larger libraries in the **United States** had abandoned their manual card files.

MARC established the feasibility of sharing machine-readable cataloging data. It also opened the way for worldwide bibliographic standardization. While the pilot project was underway, the **British National Bibliography (BNB)** expressed interest in conducting a similar project in **Great Britain**, and in 1968, separate MARC formats were developed for Britain and the United States. Other national cataloging formats followed. The proliferation of MARC formats caused the **International Federation of Library Associations and Institutions (IFLA)** to publish Universal MARC Format (UNIMARC) in 1977 for the international exchange of machine-readable data. In the late 1990s, the US and Canadian national formats were amalgamated to become MARC 21. Since then, a number of other countries, including **Australia**, **Spain**, and Great Britain, have migrated to MARC 21. Others, such as **France**, Portugal, and **South Africa**, have developed formats that are UNIMARC based.

See also AUTOMATION; AVRAM, HENRIETTE D. (1919–2006); INFORMATION SCIENCE; UNIVERSAL BIBLIOGRAPHIC CONTROL (UBC).

MANN, MARGARET (1873–1960). Margaret Mann, the preeminent figure in **cataloging** and **classification** in the **United States** for nearly 50 years, was born in Cedar Rapids, Iowa, on April 9, 1873. In 1893, she entered the Department of Library Economy at the **Armour Institute** of Technology in Chicago. She became assistant librarian and instructor when the department was transferred to the University of Illinois in 1897. In 1902, she took a position as head cataloger of the **Carnegie** Library in Pittsburgh, where she remained until 1919. Other positions included librarian at the Engineering Societies Library in New York City and cataloging instructor at the **Paris Library School**. In 1926, she became one of the three full-time professors hired by the University of Michigan School of **Library Science** when it was inaugurated. She retired in 1938. Mann's book *Introduction to Cataloging and Classification of Books* (1930) is one of the classic texts on the topic. Since 1950, the Margaret Mann Citation has been presented by the **American Library Association (ALA)** to recognize significant achievements in cataloging and classification.
See also WOMEN IN LIBRARIANSHIP.

MANRIQUE DE LARA, JUANA (1899–1983). Mexico's first professional librarian, Juana Manrique de Lara was born in the village of El Cubo, Guanajuato, on March 12, 1899. In 1917, upon completing her studies at the Escuela Nacional de Bibliotecarios y Archiveros in Mexico City, she joined the staff of the Biblioteca Nacional. In 1921, she was named head of the Biblioteca Amado Nervo, one of the first **public libraries** opened by the new Departamento de Bibliotecas, and she made it a model for public library service. In 1924, she went to the **United States** to attend the School of the New York Public Library, and when she returned to Mexico, she was appointed library inspector. In this position, she was able to formulate and implement government library policy. In 1934, she created the first list of Spanish subject headings for Mexican libraries. The first edition of her major work *Manual del Bibliotecario Mexicano* was published in 1942. She became a member of the faculty of the Escuela Nacional de Biblioteconomía y Archivonomía when it was founded in 1945.
See also WOMEN IN LIBRARIANSHIP.

MARTEL, CHARLES (1860–1945). Charles Martel, the architect of the **Library of Congress Classification (LCC)**, was born in Zurich, Switzerland, on March 5, 1860. He moved to the **United States** in 1878, and by 1892 he was working as a cataloger at the Newberry Library in Chicago. In 1897, he took a position at the newly created **Catalog** Division of the **Library of Congress (LC)**, which was headed by **J. C. M. Hanson**. Almost immediately, Martel began to develop a new **classification** scheme for the library's collection. He supervised LCC development until 1910, providing the theoretical guidelines and working out many of the details. After serving briefly as the head of the LC Periodicals Division, Martel succeeded Hanson as chief of the Catalog Division in 1912. In the late 1920s, Martel worked with Hanson to modernize the cataloging system of the **Vatican** Library. Although he reached the mandatory retirement age in 1930, an executive order issued by President Herbert Hoover enabled Martel to continue working as a consultant on cataloging, classification, and **bibliography** at LC until 1945.

McCOLVIN, LIONEL R. (1896–1976). Lionel R. McColvin, a major force in the development of libraries in **Great Britain**, was born in Newcastle-upon-Tyne on November 30, 1896. He was only 15 when he obtained his first library post at the Croyden **Public Libraries**. By 1938, he had become chief librarian of Westminster as well as honorary secretary of the **Library Association (LA)**. In 1941, the Wartime Emergency Committee of the LA invited him to investigate the effect of the war on public library service and to report on postwar library development. *The Public Library System in Great Britain: A Report on Its Present Condition and Proposals for Post-War Reorganization* (1942), also known as the McColvin report, recommended fewer and larger public library authorities and a national system of library schools. McColvin traveled widely as a library consultant, visiting North America before the war to examine library practices and undertaking an extensive survey of libraries in **Australia** in 1946. He was active in the **International Federation of Library Associations and Institutions (IFLA)** and the **United Nations Educational, Scientific and Cultural Organization (UNESCO)**. He contributed to **children's library service** with his book *Libraries for Children*, which was published in 1961.

See also BRITISH NATIONAL BIBLIOGRAPHY (BNB).

MEDICAL LIBRARY ASSOCIATION (MLA). On May 2, 1898, the Association of Medical Librarians (later called the Medical Library Association, MLA), was formed in Philadelphia by four physicians and four librarians. The intent was to foster medical libraries and maintain an exchange of medical literature. The MLA began publishing the *Bulletin of the American Medical Library Association* in 1911. In 1948, Columbia University offered the first course on medical librarianship, and the MLA's adoption of a **certification** program in 1949 gave impetus to other library schools to establish similar courses. In 1965, the MLA supported the Medical Library Assistance Act, which brought about an expansion of medical libraries and the number of librarians with master's degrees. A new credentialing program, the Academy of Health Information Professionals, was established in 1989. In 2012, the MLA had more than 1,100 institutional members and 3,600 individual members in 43 countries.

METCALF, KEYES D. (1889–1983). Academic library leader Keyes D. Metcalf was born on April 13, 1889, in Elyria, Ohio. He worked at the Oberlin College Library from age 13 until after his graduation from Oberlin College in 1911. He then enrolled in the first class of the New York **Public Library** (NYPL) School. While a student, he joined the NYPL staff, becoming chief **reference** librarian in 1928. In 1937, he became the first trained librarian to be appointed director of Harvard University Libraries, a position he held until his retirement in 1955. His redesign of the Harvard Library system to solve problems related to size became a model for other research libraries, and his book *Planning Academic and Research Library Buildings* (1965) is considered to be a major contribution to the topic. Metcalf served as president of the **American Library Association (ALA)** from 1942 to 1943, and he was a founding member of the **American Documentation Institute (ADI)**.

METCALFE, JOHN WALLACE (1901–1982). Australian library leader John Wallace Metcalfe was born in England on May 16, 1901. His family moved to New Zealand and later settled in Sydney, **Australia**. Upon graduating from the University of New South Wales in 1923, Metcalfe took a position at the **Public Library** of New South Wales, the largest research library in Australia at the time. In 1935, he became the first Australian to be admitted by examination as a fellow of the **Library Association (LA) of Great Britain**. He was appointed principal librarian at the Public Library of New South Wales in 1942. Metcalfe was active in the Free Library Movement, which worked to create free public libraries, and he organized the Australian Institute of Librarians in 1937. In 1959, he became the first librarian of the University of New South Wales, and he created the university's School of Librarianship, which opened in 1960. He retired in 1968.

MEXICO. Modern library development in Mexico was ushered in by reform-minded bureaucrats early in the 20th century. In 1915, the government sent a number of educators to the **United States** to study educational and cultural institutions, including libraries. Beginning in 1916, the first formal training for librarians was offered at the Escuela Nacional de Bibliotecarios y Archiveros. The school only lasted two years, however, and the Mexican Revolution interrupted further reform. After the revolution, a popular library movement accompanied the government's campaign against illiteracy. To meet the growing need for librarians, scholarships were made available for study abroad. A number of the first professional Mexican librarians studied in the United States and went on to establish and teach at library schools in Mexico. The first permanent library school, the Escuela Nacional de Biblioteconomía y Archivonomía, opened in 1945.

In the 1950s, expansion of Mexico's largest institution of higher learning, the Universidad Nacional Autónoma de México (UNAM), led to an increased need for **academic** librarians. A **library science** school offering a postgraduate program was established at UNAM. The creation of the Libros del Sistema Bibliotecario de la UNAM (LIBRUNAM) database in 1978, designed to expedite **cataloging** and **classification** of materials acquired by the UNAM library system, was the first example of **automation** in Mexican **academic libraries**.

Librarians in Mexico belong to a number of organizations, most notably the Mexican Association of Librarians/Asociación Mexicana de Bibliotecarios (AMBAC), which was established in 1954 and sponsored the First Mexican Conference of Librarianship, **Bibliography**, and Exchange in 1957. After a period of decline, the public library movement was revived in the 1980s, when a new national plan led to rapid expansion. In the 1990s, academic library development was spurred by a government plan to modernize college education. At the end of the 20th century, however, too few students were graduating from library science schools to meet the growing need for librarians.

See also ASSOCIATION OF CARIBBEAN UNIVERSITY, RESEARCH AND INSTITUTIONAL LIBRARIES (ACURIL); LATIN AMERICA; CHÁVEZ CAMPOMANES, MARIA TERESA (1890–1981); MANRIQUE DE LARA, JUANA (1899–1983).

MILAM, CARL H. (1884–1963). Carl H. Milam, the longest-serving chief executive of the **American Library Association (ALA)**, was born in Harper County, Kansas, on October 22, 1884. After graduating from the University of Oklahoma, he attended the **New York State Library School** and then worked for several years in Indiana before becoming librarian at the **public library** of Birmingham, Alabama, in 1913. In 1917, he took a leave of absence in order to work in the **Library War Service**, which set up camp libraries for those serving overseas. In 1920, he was named secretary (as the chief executive was then termed) of ALA. In that position, his primary interests were library **education** and **international** library development. Milam worked to promote ALA's international efforts, which included establishing the **Paris Library School**, setting up ALA's International Relations Office, and supporting library development in **Latin America**. He also worked toward greater federal involvement in libraries and library services. Milam resigned from ALA in 1948 to become librarian of the United Nations Library, retiring from that position in 1950.

MILKAU, FRITZ (1859–1934). Considered to be one of the greatest German librarians of his day, Fritz Milkau was born on September 28, 1859, in Lötzen, in Prussia. After completing his university studies, he joined the staff of the University Library in Königsburg in 1888. In 1895, Friedrich Althoff of the Prussian Ministry of Cultural Affairs put Milkau in charge of organizing a union **catalog** of Prussian libraries, and Milkau's ideas provided the theoretical basis for the German cataloging code known as the **Prussian Instructions**. Beginning in 1902, Milkau assumed the directorships of several university libraries. In 1921, he became director of the Prussian State Library, a position that enabled him to influence **academic** and research libraries within Prussian borders and beyond. After he retired from the Prussian State Library in 1925, he was involved in library **education**, both as a **library science** professor at the University of Berlin and as the founder and director of the Institut für Bibliothekswissenschaft, which prepared library candidates for the Prussian state examinations. He was the founding editor of *Handbuch der Bibliothekswissenschaft* (1931–1942; 2nd edition, 1952–1965), a comprehensive work in library science that became a standard text in the field.

See also GERMANY.

MOLINER, MARÍA (1900–1981). María Moliner was born in Saragossa, **Spain**, on March 30, 1900. She received a degree in history from the University of Saragossa in 1921. In 1922, she passed the state examination to enter the Association of Faculty Archivists, Librarians, and Archaeologists and then held positions as a librarian and school teacher. In Valencia, where her family lived beginning in the early 1930s, she played an important role in the implementation of the Spanish government's plan to promote reading and to create, organize, and modernize **public libraries**. She established a network linking rural libraries to Valencia's central library, which provided a basis for the national library plan that she drew up in 1939. Following the Spanish Civil War, Moliner's involvement in cultural policy came to an end. In 1946, she was put in charge of the library at the Higher Technical School of Industrial Engineers, where she remained until her retirement in 1970. In the 1950s, she began work on her well-known *Diccionario de uso del español*, the third edition of which was published in 2007. A number of schools and libraries in Spain bear María Moliner's name, and, since 1998, the Spanish Ministry of Culture has conducted a campaign in her honor to encourage reading.

See also WOMEN IN LIBRARIANSHIP.

MONASTERY LIBRARIES. As urbanization and book learning waned in Western Europe during the early Middle Ages, almost all libraries were found in monasteries. Benedict of Nursia (c. 480–c. 543), founder of the Benedictine order, made reading part of the monastic routine, and Cassiodorus (c. 490–c. 585), a Roman statesman who established a monastery on his estate in southern Italy, introduced the practice of copying and translating texts.

The Benedictine requirement that there be at least one book for each of the brethren of a monastery set a minimum in terms of a collection's size. Most of the books were Christian texts, and they were frequently housed in book cupboards or *armaria*. The person in charge of the collection might be called an ***armarius***. According to rules for the library at Cluny in the 11th century, the *armarius* was second in rank to the abbot. The same room was often used as both library and scriptorium, and, in addition to keeping track of the manuscripts, it was part of the job of the librarian to provide parchment, ink, pens, pumice stones for smoothing parchment, rulers for making guidelines, and other supplies.

Most of the books in monastery libraries were theological texts, but there were some classics as well as books on grammar, medicine, and other subjects. Examples of monastery library **catalogs** from as early as the eighth century survive. Initially, these were little more than inventories, but more complex schemes emerged as collections grew. In the 12th century, monasteries began to give way to cathedral schools and universities as seats of learning, but the way monasteries organized and handled their book collections set the standards for libraries until the end of the Middle Ages.

MOORE, ANNE CARROLL (1871–1961). Anne Carroll Moore, who played a major role in shaping **children's library service** in the **United States,** was born on July 12, 1871, in Limerick, Maine. In 1895, she entered the **Pratt Institute** Library School, and after completing the program, she was hired to oversee the children's room at the Pratt Institute Free Library. In 1906, she was recruited to head the new Office of Work with Children at the New York **Public Library**, a position she held until she retired in 1941. Through the training program she organized, as well as through her publications and lectures, she created the standards for library work with children and for the selection of children's books. Beginning in 1918, she pioneered serious criticism of children's books in the articles and reviews she wrote for the *Bookman* and later for the *New York Herald Tribune* and *The Horn Book*. She was instrumental in founding the Children's Library Section of the **American Library Association (ALA),** the creation of Children's Book Week, and the formation at Macmillan publishers of the first separate department for publishing children's books.

See also WOMEN IN LIBRARIANSHIP.

MORAES, RUBENS BORBA ALVES DE (1899–1986). Brazilian library leader Rubens Borba Alves de Moraes was born in Araraquara in the state of São Paulo on January 23, 1899. He was educated in Europe, and upon his return to São Paulo he became part of a prominent group of artists and writers. After a grant from the **Rockefeller Foundation** enabled him to study library management in the **United States**, he was appointed director of the Municipal **Public Library** of São Paulo in 1935. Under his directorship, the library opened in a new modern building in 1942. Other results of his leadership were the establishment of Brazil's first course in **library science** (1936) and the founding of the São Paulo Library Association (1938). In 1945, he became the director of the National Library in Rio de Janeiro, where he introduced numerous reforms. From 1951 to 1959, he worked for the United Nations (UN), first as director of the UN Information Service in Paris and then as director of the UN Library in New York City. He taught **bibliography** at the University of Brasilia from 1963 to 1970.

MOREL, EUGÈNE (1869–1934). Eugène Morel, a major contributor to the development of **public libraries** in **France**, was born in Paris on June 21, 1869. By the time he received a law degree in 1889, he had already embarked on a literary career, and in 1892 he took a position as an assistant librarian at the **Bibliothèque nationale** because he thought it would leave time for him to pursue his writing. Instead, after a visit to **Great Britain** in 1895 introduced him to the British and American concept of the free public library, he became an advocate for the creation of libraries in France along the same lines. Morel took part in the foundation of the Association of French Librarians/Association des bibliothécaires français (ABF) in 1906, and the series of lectures he offered under the sponsorship of the ABF beginning in 1911 was the country's first library training program. Later, he lectured at the **Paris Library School** opened by the **American Library Association (ALA)** in 1923. He also cooperated in the creation of **l'Heure Joyeuse**, the **children's** library, in 1924. His book *La Librairie publique* (1910) was the first book in France devoted to public libraries.

MUDGE, ISADORE GILBERT (1875–1957). Isadore Gilbert Mudge, one of the pioneers of library **reference service**, was born on March 14, 1875, in Brooklyn, New York. After graduating from Cornell University in 1897, she entered the **New York State Library School**. Her first professional position was at the University of Illinois Library under **Katharine L. Sharp**. She was head librarian at Bryn Mawr College from 1903 to 1907. She spent most of her career at the Columbia University Library, where she worked beginning in 1911 and established a model for university library reference service. Mudge is best known as the editor of *Guide to the Study and Use of Refer-*

ence Books, taking over from Alice Bertha Kroeger, who edited the 1902 and 1908 editions. Mudge began her editorship with a supplement to the 1908 edition, followed by her first edition of what was by then called *Guide to Reference Books* (1917). In 1936, she published the sixth (her last) edition of *Guide to Reference Books*. The Isadore Gilbert Mudge Award recognizes individuals who have made a distinguished contribution to reference librarianship.

See also WOMEN IN LIBRARIANSHIP.

MUSIC LIBRARY ASSOCIATION (MLA). The professional organization of music librarianship in the **United States** and the largest such organization in the world, the MLA was established in 1931 at the **American Library Association (ALA)** Annual Conference in New Haven, Connecticut. Eva Judd O'Meara, Yale University's first music librarian, and Carleton Sprague Smith, head of the Music Division of the New York **Public Library**, arranged informal meetings during the conference for individuals who were interested in discussing problems related to music **bibliography**, and MLA was launched as a result. *Notes*, the MLA journal, began publication in 1934. In 2011, MLA became the US branch of the **International Association of Music Libraries, Archives and Documentation Centres (IAML)**.

N

NATIONAL AGRICULTURAL LIBRARY (NAL). In 1862, President Abraham Lincoln signed a law establishing the **United States** Department of Agriculture and, along with it, the Department of Agriculture Library. By 1889, when William T. Fletcher, the librarian of Amherst College, was hired to develop a **classification** scheme, the library had around 20,000 volumes. The position of librarian of the Department of Agriculture was created in 1893, and the examination that was given to applicants was prepared with the help of **Melvil Dewey**.

In 1934, the library became a pioneer in the use of microform when it launched the Bibliofilm Service, which used micrographic reproduction to distribute scientific articles on a large scale. The ***Bibliography*** *of Agriculture* was established in 1942 by **Ralph Shaw**, who served as the library's director from 1942 to 1954. In 1976, the library (by this time called the National Agricultural Library) launched Agricultural Online Access (AGRICOLA), which serves as the **catalog** and index to the collections.

See also RDA: RESOURCE DESCRIPTION AND ACCESS.

NATIONAL LIBRARY OF MEDICINE (NLM). The world's largest biomedical library, the NLM has played an important role in the history of librarianship in the **United States**. Beginning in 1836 as a collection in the office of the Surgeon General of the army, the library remained small until the shuttering of temporary hospitals at the end of the Civil War brought an influx of medical books and journals. In 1865, the army appointed one of its field surgeons, **John Shaw Billings**, to take charge. By the time Billings resigned from the army in 1895, the collection comprised 116,847 books and 191,598 pamphlets. The first comprehensive index to medical literature, *Index Medicus*, was begun by Billings in 1879.

Following recommendations made in a report that was funded by the **Rockefeller Foundation** and published by the **American Library Association (ALA)** in 1944, the library created a new **classification** system, the NLM Classification, which is used worldwide. In 1957, NLM began exploring ways to mechanize the production of *Index Medicus*. The result, the

Medical Literature Analysis and Retrieval System (MEDLARS), was released in 1964 and put NLM in the forefront of experimentation with computers for bibliographic control. In 1971, NLM launched MEDLARS Online (MEDLINE) as a resource for health professionals. In 1997, NLM announced free Internet access to MEDLINE. MEDLINEPlus, a consumer health resource, was introduced in 1998.

See also AUTOMATION; INFORMATION SCIENCE; *RDA: RESOURCE DESCRIPTION AND ACCESS.*

NATIONAL PROGRAM FOR ACQUISITIONS AND CATALOGING (NPAC). In the 1920s, the **Library of Congress (LC)** created the Cooperative **Cataloging** Project in an effort to produce increased amounts of cooperative cataloging copy. In the 1960s, this project was replaced by NPAC, sometimes referred to as the Shared Cataloging Program. NPAC was brought into being by the Higher Education Act of 1965, which authorized the transfer of funds to LC for the purchase and cataloging of scholarly materials published throughout the world. LC was also able to make use of cataloging created in certain foreign countries. In addition to building the LC collections, the program provided research libraries with cataloging information for foreign titles, thereby reducing the amount of original cataloging they had to perform. The first NPAC office was opened in London in 1966, and LC had 13 regional acquisitions centers by 1971. When funding for NPAC ran out in the 1980s, it was succeeded by the Cooperative Acquisitions Program, which required participating libraries to pay for purchases made on their behalf.

See also PROGRAM FOR COOPERATIVE CATALOGING (PCC).

NAUDÉ, GABRIEL (1600–1653). Gabriel Naudé, author of the first systematic treatment of librarianship, was born in Paris on February 2, 1600. Although he studied medicine and was appointed honorary physician to Louis XIII, he spent his working life as a scholar and librarian. In 1627, he wrote what is considered to be the first important treatise on **library science**, *Avis pour dresser une bibliothèque.* In it, he offered clearly organized principles for building library collections and was ahead of his time in advancing the idea that a library should be available for use by all. In 1642, he accepted a post as Cardinal Richelieu's librarian and after Richelieu's death joined the staff of Cardinal Mazarin. The Bibliothèque Mazarine, which he helped build into one of the largest libraries in Europe, reflected his views on how the private library of a wealthy collector should be organized and administered. It was opened to the public in 1644. When the library's collection was dispersed during the uprising known as the Fronde, Naudé went to **Sweden** to serve as royal librarian to Queen Christina. He died on his way back to **France**.

NEW YORK STATE LIBRARY SCHOOL. In 1888, **Melvil Dewey** relocated the **School of Library Economy** from Columbia College in New York City, to Albany, New York. It was renamed the New York State Library School but was perhaps better known as the Albany Library School. Although Dewey was the director, **Mary Salome Cutler Fairchild** was in charge of day-to-day operations. In 1902, the school became the first to require a college degree for admission. In 1906, it was the first to offer a master's degree in **library science** (MLS). In 1926, the school moved back to Columbia.

See also EDUCATION FOR LIBRARIANSHIP.

NICHOLSON, EDWARD WILLIAMS BYRON (1849–1912). British librarian E. W. B. Nicholson was born on March 16, 1849, in St Helier, Jersey. He graduated from Oxford University in 1872. In 1873, he was appointed librarian of the London Institution, an educational society, where he made a name for himself as an innovator. After reading accounts of the **Librarians' Conference of 1853**, held in the **United States**, he initiated the movement that resulted in the **International Conference of Librarians** and the formation of **Great Britain**'s **Library Association (LA)** in 1877. In 1881, Nicholson became the first library manager (rather than scholar) to head the **Bodleian Library**. He introduced a number of changes that modernized the library, including new management techniques, and the staff manual that he created was widely circulated as a guide to library administration and practice. His reorganization of the Bodleian Library often put him at odds with the library's governing board and staff.

NORWAY. Norwegian libraries trace their history back to the 18th century, when the Royal Norwegian Academy of Science Library was established. The first municipal library in Oslo, the Deichman Library, was established in 1785, thanks to an individual donor. The first university library came with the founding of the University of Oslo in 1811. The modern library movement began with Norwegians who traveled abroad and brought American library ideals back home, helping Norway take the lead in **public library** development in continental Europe in the early 20th century. Beginning in 1893, Hans Tambs Lyche, who had spent 12 years in the **United States**, published a series of influential articles about American librarianship. **Haakon Nyhuus** worked at the Newberry Library in Chicago and the Chicago Public Library from 1890 to 1897 and was then employed as head librarian at the Deichman Library, where he instituted numerous changes, including the **Dewey Decimal Classification (DDC)** and open shelves. In 1901, Nyhuus was appointed to a committee charged with preparing a national plan of library reform. The committee's report, *Public Book Collections in Norway: Their History and Present Condition Together with Proposals for a New Arrangement*, has been called the most important document in the library literature of Norway. Another early leader, Arne Kildal, was one of a number of Norwegians who studied at the **New York State Library School**. Kildal organized the Norwegian Library Association in 1913 and was also instrumental in the passage of the first Library Act in 1935.

Norwegians made up nearly a third of the foreign students who graduated from American library schools from 1887 to 1926. As far back as 1907, Nyhuus had written an article calling for a Norwegian library school, but formal **education** for librarianship did not exist until the Norwegian School of Librarians was established in 1940. This program merged with Oslo University College in 1994, and until 1995 was the only library and **information science** (LIS) program in Norway. Although a master's degree was introduced in 1983, most LIS education takes place at the undergraduate level.

See also SCANDIA PLAN.

NYHUUS, HAAKON (1866–1913). Norwegian library pioneer Haakon Nyhuus was born in Hedmark County near the Swedish border. In 1890, after attending school in Oslo, he traveled to the **United States** and was soon working as a **cataloging** assistant at the Newberry Library, Chicago. Two years later, he began supervising the new card catalog at the Chicago **Public Library**. Despite having become a US citizen, he returned to **Norway** in 1897 and in 1898 was hired to reorganize the Deichman Library in Oslo. His reforms, based on what he observed in the United States, included open shelves, increased hours, longer borrowing periods, and reduced age restrictions. He initiated **children's library service**, increased the number of lending stations, and opened new branches. He also introduced a **dictionary catalog** and reclassified the library's collection using the **Dewey Decimal Classification (DDC)**. In 1901, he was appointed by the Ministry of Church and Education to a committee charged with preparing a national plan of library reform. Through the committee's report, as well as through the changes he made at the Deichman Library, Nyhuus influenced library development not just in Norway but in all the Nordic countries.

O

OLCOTT, FRANCES JENKINS (1873–1963). Frances Jenkins Olcott, a pioneer in **children's library service**, was born in Paris, **France**, where her father was vice-consul-general for the **United States**. She graduated from the **New York State Library School** in 1896 and took a position at the Brooklyn **Public Library**. In 1898, she was invited to join the staff of the **Carnegie** Library of Pittsburgh, where she established an innovative children's department. She also organized the Training School for Children's Librarians, which opened in 1901. The school's initial goal was to meet the needs of the Carnegie Library, but the wider demand for trained children's librarians led the school to educate staff for other libraries as well. The first class included students from six states. Olcott served for 11 years as the director of both the children's department and the school before retiring from library work to devote herself to writing both professional literature and books for children.

See also EDUCATION FOR LIBRARIANSHIP; WOMEN IN LIBRARIANSHIP.

OLENIN, ALEXEI NIKOLAEVICH (1763–1843). Alexei Nikolaevich Olenin was born in Moscow, **Russia**. He became a prominent government official, historian, and patron of the arts before he was appointed in 1808 to the Imperial Public Library in St. Petersburg (now the National Library of Russia). As assistant director and (beginning in 1811) director, Olenin did much to shape the concept of a national library and to lay the foundation for modern Russian librarianship. In 1809, he produced the first Russian guide to bibliographic description and **catalog** creation. He created a distinct Russian section and insisted on the establishment of **legal deposit** to ensure that the Russian collection would be as complete as possible. Olenin oversaw the evacuation of the collection during Napoleon's invasion of Russia, an event that delayed the opening of the library to the public until 1814. He believed that the library should be available to anyone who wanted to use it, and the well-known scholars and literary figures whom he hired were required to participate in **reference service** and collection development based on reader requests. Olenin's long tenure at the Imperial Public Library ended only with his death.

ONLINE COMPUTER LIBRARY CENTER (OCLC). The largest bibliographic database in the world, OCLC was founded on July 5, 1967, when presidents from several universities in Ohio met on the campus of Ohio State University to establish a nonprofit organization called the Ohio College Library Center. **Frederick G. Kilgour** of Yale University was hired to create a computerized regional library system that would facilitate resource sharing, increase efficiency, and reduce per-unit **cataloging** costs. OCLC's Online Union Catalog (now WorldCat) began operation in 1971, and on August 26 of that year, Ohio University in Athens became the first library in the world to perform online cataloging. In 1977, Ohio libraries voted to expand OCLC outside Ohio. OCLC services were made available outside the **United States** beginning in 1980. The name was changed to Online Computer Library Center in 1981.

In its early years, OCLC was primarily a technical services tool supporting shared cataloging, but Kilgour envisioned other functions as well, and subsystems for interlibrary loan, serials control, acquisitions, and subject access were added. In the 1990s, OCLC began adding **reference** services such as FirstSearch. In 2008, OCLC was being used by over 69,000 libraries in 112 countries. OCLC has also become a center for research and development.

See also AUTOMATION; COUNCIL ON LIBRARY AND INFORMATION RESOURCES (CLIR); RESEARCH LIBRARIES GROUP (RLG); RESEARCH LIBRARIES INFORMATION NETWORK (RLIN).

OPEN ACCESS (OA) MOVEMENT. OA is the practice of providing peer-reviewed scholarly literature on the Internet, free of charge and free of most licensing and **copyright** restrictions. The OA movement was spurred in part by the **serials crisis** and by research libraries' advocacy for alternatives to conventional models of scholarly publication. In 2001, the Open Society Institute (OSI) brought together leaders of the OA movement for a conference in Budapest that resulted in the Budapest Open Access Initiative (BOAI). The BOAI called for the creation of open-access journals (called "gold OA") and open-access archives of articles published in other journals (called "green OA"). Because it formulated the first definition of OA, BOAI was a landmark in the history of the OA movement. The OA concept was further refined in 2003 by the Bethesda Statement on Open Access Publishing as well as the Berlin Declaration on Open Access to Knowledge in the Sciences and the Humanities. Two of the best-known examples of OA initiatives are BioMed Central and the Public Library of Science (PLOS). In support of OA, the **Association of College and Research Libraries (ACRL)** released *Principles and Strategies for the Reform of Scholarly Communication* (2003). The **International Federation of Library Associations and Institutions (IFLA)** released the *IFLA Statement on Open Access to Scholarly Literature and Research Documentation* in 2004. By 2013, more than 300 research-funding agencies and universities worldwide had adopted mandates requiring that the research they fund or support be made available publically. However, OA is opposed by many traditional publishers.

See also SCHOLARLY PUBLISHING AND ACADEMIC RESOURCES COALITION (SPARC).

OTLET, PAUL-MARIE-GHISLAIN (1868–1944). Paul Otlet, who is known as the founder of the field of **documentation**, was born in Brussels, Belgium, on August 23, 1868. Having earned a law degree in 1890, he joined the newly formed Société des études sociales et politiques in 1891. He became interested in the organization of knowledge and with a colleague, Henri La Fontaine, conceived the idea of a Universal Bibliographic Repertory, a worldwide **bibliography** on cards of all recorded knowledge. The International Institute of Bibliography (later the **International Federation for Information and Documentation, FID**) was founded by Otlet and La Fontaine to carry out this work. The **Universal Decimal Classification (UDC)**, the scheme they devised to provide subject access to the Universal Bibliographic Repertory, was published in 1905.

ÖTÜKEN, ADNAN (1911–1972). Adnan Ötüken was born in Manastir, **Turkey**. After graduating from the University of Istanbul, he studied **library science** at the Prussian State Library in Berlin from 1935 to 1939. When he returned to Turkey, he took a position at the Ministry of Education, establishing the first continuous training courses for Turkish librarians in 1942. He founded the Turkish National Library in Ankara in 1946 and was also instrumental in founding the Turkish Librarians' Association in 1949. Ötüken taught at the library school of the University of Ankara and authored the standard Turkish library science text. He prepared and presented a regular radio program on books that aired nationally during the 1940s and that extended book culture into the remotest areas of the country.

OVERSEAS LIBRARIES PROGRAMS. The **United States** government's overseas libraries programs began during World War II. The Office of War Information (OWI), which was created in 1942 to consolidate the information functions of several federal agencies, opened the first official government library outside the continental United States in the American Embassy in London. By 1945, when the OWI was terminated, there were 28 libraries in major European and British Commonwealth cities. After the war, these libraries became the responsibility of the US Department of State. In 1953, responsibility was assumed by the US Information Agency (USIA), which was formed to coordinate various US international cultural and information efforts. The USIA (the overseas arm of which was the United States Information Service, or USIS) also inherited the libraries that the **American Library Association (ALA)** had operated in **Latin America** as part of President Franklin D. Roosevelt's "Good Neighbor" program, as well as information centers set up by the American Military Government in **Germany** (where they were called Amerika Häuser) and in other zones of occupation. In all, the USIA administered 196 information centers and reading rooms in 53 countries. In addition, the USIA provided support for library programs in 34 binational centers that had been established (primarily in Latin America) to promote understanding between host countries and the United States.

According to book selection guidelines drawn up for the overseas library programs in 1948, acquisitions were grouped into three categories: descriptions of the United States, examples of American achievements in the humanities and natural and social sciences, and works supporting US foreign policy objectives. In 1953, the collections and collection policies of overseas libraries came under attack from Senator Joseph McCarthy, chairman of the Senate Permanent Subcommittee on Investigation. McCarthy sent agents to American libraries in Europe to remove books by authors who were suspected of having communist leanings, and a handful of books were burned. In response to McCarthy's attacks, ALA adopted the Overseas Libraries Statement and the **Freedom to Read Statement**. Collection priorities for the overseas libraries were altered over the years as US government agencies were reorganized and the political landscape changed.

Although the overseas libraries were often criticized for disseminating propaganda, in some countries they provided the first examples of a modern **public library** with free access, open shelves, and loan privileges. In 1980, there were overseas libraries and reading rooms in 150 foreign cities, although many of them were discontinued for budgetary reasons. The USIA libraries were phased out altogether in the 1990s and the agency was abolished in 1999. Some library functions are carried now out by the Information Resource Centers found in US embassies.

The British and the French also had overseas library programs. With the support of the French government, the Alliance Française (a private association founded in 1883) set up overseas centers that focused on language instruction but that also often included small libraries staffed by volunteers. The **British Council**, created in 1934, operated libraries around the world. Like the USIA libraries, these British and French overseas libraries played an important role in the use of books as cultural diplomacy.

See also CENSORSHIP.

P

PALMGREN, VALFRID (1877–1967). Swedish librarian Valfrid Palmgren was born in Stockholm on June 3, 1877. She received a PhD from the University of Uppsala in 1905. In 1907, while working as a library assistant at the Royal Library, she received a scholarship to travel to the **United States** in order to make a study of the **public library** system. After her return to **Sweden**, she initiated training classes at the Royal Library and established the Library for Children and Young Adults, which was the first **children's** library in Stockholm. She also published *Libraries and Popular Education*, in which she promoted **open access**, children's departments, professional staff, and service to all. She was appointed by the Swedish government to survey public libraries in Sweden, and her report formed the basis for the development of a modern public library system. In 1910, Palmgren was elected to the Stockholm city council. She moved to **Denmark** in 1911.

See also WOMEN IN LIBRARIANSHIP.

PANIZZI, ANTHONY (1797–1879). Anthony Panizzi was born on September 16, 1797, at Brescello in the Duchy of Modena in **Italy**. He became a lawyer but in 1823 fled to **Great Britain** for political reasons. After making his living as a teacher of Italian and a professor at the new University of London, he was appointed extra supernumerary librarian of the **British Museum**'s Department of Printed Books in 1831. In 1837, he was promoted to keeper of the printed books. The work of compiling an adequate **catalog** of the books led to the 1841 publication of his *Rules for the Compilation of the Catalogue* (also known as the *91 Rules*), the first modern code for author and title entry. He also enlarged the collection by soliciting funds from Parliament and enforcing the law of **legal deposit**. Panizzi was appointed principal librarian of the British Museum in 1856 and shortly thereafter opened the museum's reading room. In 1869, he was knighted by Queen Victoria for his services as a librarian.

PARIS LIBRARY SCHOOL. The Paris Library School was established in 1923 by the Temporary Board of Library Training of the **American Library Association (ALA)**. It was housed in the **American Library in Paris**, which ALA had opened in 1918 to provide reading materials to American soldiers. The school, directed by ALA Assistant Secretary **Sarah Comly Norris Bogle** and underwritten by the American Committee for Devastated **France**, began with a six-week course. This was expanded to a 36-week course in 1924. ALA provided funds for two years, after which a **Rockefeller Foundation** gift allowed the school to operate for an additional three years. More than 200 students from France and other European countries completed the program before the school closed in 1929.

See also EDUCATION FOR LIBRARIANSHIP; MOREL, EUGÈNE (1869–1934).

PARIS PRINCIPLES. Paris Principles is the common name for the Statement of Principles approved at the **International Conference on Cataloging Principles** in 1961. Drawing heavily on **Seymour Lubetzky**'s draft for a revised **cataloging** code, the Paris Principles were intended to promote international standardization in cataloging. They were adopted as the basis for numerous national codes, including the *Anglo-American Cataloging Rules (AACR)* and **Germany**'s *Rules for Descriptive Cataloging (RAK)*. The Paris Principles were replaced in 2009 by the Statement of International Cataloging Principles (ICP), which was designed for the online environment.

PENNA, CARLOS VICTOR (1911–1998). Argentine librarian Carlos Victor Penna was born on October 1, 1911, in Bahia Blanca. He graduated from the Naval School of Mechanical Engineering in Buenos Aires in 1930 and later took a position in the navy library. In 1938, he enrolled in the **library science** program at the Museo Social Argentino and, after receiving his degree in 1941, continued his **education** in the **United States** at Columbia University's School of Library Service. After his return to **Argentina**, he held several important library posts, including assistant director of the newly created Instituto Bibliotecológico (now Sistema de Bibliotecas y de Información; SISBI) at the University of Buenos Aires. His first book, *Catalogación y Clasificación de Libros*, considered to be the leading **cataloging** text in Argentina, was published in 1945. In 1951, Penna joined the **United Nations Educational, Scientific and Cultural Organization (UNESCO)** as a specialist in its Regional Office for the Western Hemisphere, headquartered in Havana. In 1964, he was transferred to Paris to be the director of the Division of Libraries, Archives, and **Documentation**.

From this position, and even after his retirement in 1971, he promoted library planning and development, not only in **Latin America** but also across the globe.

PLUMMER, MARY WRIGHT (1856–1916). Library educator Mary Wright Plummer was born on March 8, 1856, in Richmond, Indiana. In 1887, she entered the first class at the **School of Library Economy** at Columbia College and then worked as a cataloger at the St. Louis (Missouri) **Public Library** for two years. In the fall of 1890, she took a position at the **Pratt Institute** Free Library, where she created the second library studies program in the **United States** and pioneered training for library work with children. In 1895, following a leave of absence to make her second trip to visit libraries in Europe, she was made director of both the Pratt library and the library school. In 1904, she requested that the positions be separated so that she could devote her time to the school. In 1911, she left Pratt to launch a library school for the New York Public Library and remained as its head until her death. She chaired the Committee on Library Training of the **American Library Association (ALA)** 1903–1910 and was elected ALA's second **woman** president in 1915.

POOLE, WILLIAM FREDERICK (1821–1894). Bibliographer and early library leader William Frederick Poole was born on December 24, 1821, in Salem, Massachusetts. While attending Yale University, he took a job as a librarian at a student literary society, and in 1848 he compiled an index of the society's periodical collection. In 1852, he became assistant librarian at the **Boston Athenaeum** and shortly after that became librarian at the Mercantile Library Association of Boston. In 1856, he returned to the Boston Athenaeum as librarian and remained in that position for 13 years. Subsequently, he assumed positions as the first librarian at the Cincinnati (Ohio) **Public Library** and the first librarian at the Chicago Public Library. In 1876, Poole helped establish the **American Library Association (ALA).** His greatest achievement, *Poole's Index to Periodical Literature*, was published beginning in 1882. In 1887, he became head of the newly formed Newberry Library in Chicago, remaining there until his death.

  See also THE FICTION QUESTION; INTERNATIONAL CONFERENCE OF LIBRARIANS, 1877; LIBRARIANS' CONFERENCE, 1853.

POOLE'S INDEX TO PERIODICAL LITERATURE. One of the first projects of the **American Library Association (ALA)**, *Poole's Index to Periodical Literature* was the successor to an index created by **William Frederick Poole** in 1848. At its inaugural meeting in 1876, ALA asked Poole to expand the earlier index, which became a cooperative venture in which 50 libraries indexed a selected list of periodicals and then submitted the records to a central bureau, where they were compiled and arranged for printing. Beginning in 1882, *Poole's Index to Periodical Literature* was published in one volume covering the period from 1802 to 1881 and five supplements covering the years from 1882 to 1906. Publication ended in 1908 when **H. W. Wilson** began publishing *Readers' Guide to Periodical Literature*.

POWER, EFFIE LOUISE (1873–1969). Effie Louise Power, a pioneer in **children's library service**, was born on February 12, 1873, in Conneautville, Pennsylvania. Her family moved to Cleveland, Ohio, in 1881, and she began her library work in 1895 with an **apprenticeship** at the Cleveland **Public Library**. When the children's room opened in 1898, she became the first children's librarian in the Cleveland system (and one of the first people to have a library position that was devoted to children's work). In 1904, she graduated from the Training School for Children's Librarians at the **Carnegie** Library in Pittsburgh, Pennsylvania, and then, after several years of schooling and teaching, became first assistant in the Carnegie Library's children's department. In 1911, she was hired to organize the children's department at the Saint Louis (Missouri) Public Library. In 1917, she returned to Pittsburgh, where she became head of the children's department. She was director of work with children at the Cleveland Public Library from 1920 to 1937. She also taught at several library schools and continued to work, teach, and write until her death. Her groundbreaking textbook, *Library Services for Children*, was published in 1930.

See also WOMEN IN LIBRARIANSHIP.

PRATT INSTITUTE. The Pratt Institute was a technical school founded by philanthropist Charles Pratt in 1887 and located in Brooklyn, New York. In order to train assistants for work in the Pratt Institute Free Library (which also served as Brooklyn's **public library**), a training program was organized in 1890, which was the second library training school to be opened after the creation of the Columbia **School of Library Economy**. **Mary Wright Plummer** directed the program (now the School of Information and **Library Science**) from 1895 to 1911.

See also ARMOUR INSTITUTE; DREXEL INSTITUTE; EDUCATION FOR LIBRARIANSHIP.

PROGRAM FOR COOPERATIVE CATALOGING (PCC). Administered by the **Library of Congress (LC)**, PCC evolved from the National Coordinated **Cataloging** Program (NCCP), which was launched in the 1980s to combine the efforts of eight research libraries and LC to generate cataloging records of the same standard as those that LC created. NCCP lasted just four years, but the idea of creating a model for sharing high-quality catalog records resulted in the establishment of PCC in 1995. Since 1997, PCC has served as the umbrella for four projects: the Cooperative Online Serials Program (CONSER), the Name Authority Cooperative Program (NACO), the Subject Authority Cooperative Program (SACO), and the Bibliographic Record Cooperative Program (BIBCO). The oldest of these, CONSER, began in the 1970s as a project to convert manual serial cataloging into **machine-readable** records, and it developed into a cooperative cataloging program for serial titles. NACO allows participants to contribute authority records for personal, corporate, and jurisdictional names, uniform titles, and series headings to the LC/NACO Authority File. SACO enables member institutions to submit subject heading proposals for inclusion in **Library of Congress Subject Headings (LCSH)** and **classification** number proposals for inclusion in **Library of Congress Classification (LCC)** schedules. The newest program, BIBCO, was created in 1995 and focuses on catalog records for monographs. Besides the **United States**, participation in PCC programs comes primarily from **Australia**, **Canada**, and **Great Britain**.

See also NATIONAL PROGRAM FOR ACQUISITIONS AND CATALOGING (NPAC).

PROGRESSIVE LIBRARIANSHIP. Progressive librarianship, also known as activist librarianship, critical librarianship, radical librarianship, and socially responsible librarianship, has gone through several phases in the **United States**. In the 1930s and 1940s, a progressive library movement pressured the **American Library Association (ALA)** to be more responsive to issues related to segregation, library unions, and **intellectual freedom**. World War II created additional concerns. The Library Unions Round Table, which was formed in 1938, passed a resolution in 1942 that librarians should work to destroy Hitlerism. The Progressive Librarians' Council, which was in existence from 1939 to 1944, was active in assisting librarians who were European refugees.

In the 1960s, librarians and library students became involved in the ferment taking place on college campuses and elsewhere. Concern for civil and economic rights was a founding principle of the Social Responsibilities Round Table (SRRT), formally established at the ALA Midwinter Meeting in 1969. In June of that year, around 100 students and activist librarians, many of whom were SRRT members, convened at the Congress for Change to organize action to reform library **education**, librarianship, and ALA. At the Annual Conference in Atlantic City a few days later, they presented their demands that ALA democratize its structure of decision making and expand the scope of its activities beyond librarianship to include consideration of social and political issues. This challenge led to the establishment of the Activities Committee on New Directions (ACONDA) to recommend possible changes to ALA. Another factor in the activism of the 1960s was the leadership of individuals such as Eric Moon and **E. J. Josey**, both staunch champions of civil rights. As editor of *Library Journal* from 1959 to 1968, Moon took a stand on a number of issues related to social responsibility. Josey founded the ALA **Black Caucus** in 1970. **REFORMA** (The National Association to Promote Library and Information Services to Latinos and the Spanish-Speaking) and the Task Force on Gay Liberation (now the **Gay, Lesbian, Bisexual, and Transgender Round Table**) were put in place in 1971. Another wave of activism began in 1990, when new concerns about the profession's acceptance of the status quo led to the formation of the Progressive Librarian's Guild.

Outside the United States, progressive librarianship gained momentum beginning in the 1980s. Activist library groups and movements took shape in **Argentina**, Austria, **Germany**, **Great Britain**, **Mexico**, **South Africa**, **Sweden**, and elsewhere. The Social Responsibilities Discussion Group of the **International Federation of Library Associations and Institutions (IFLA)** was organized in 1997. In the 21st century, an international critical librarianship movement has developed, and an active Web community of progressive librarians has emerged.

PRUSSIAN INSTRUCTIONS. The *Instructions for the Alphabetic Catalogs of the Prussian Libraries* (known as the Prussian Instructions) was the German **cataloging** code published in 1899. It was based in part on **Karl Dziatzko**'s revision of the *Munich Cataloging Rules*, used by university libraries in Prussia, and in part on instructions created by the Royal Library for its lists of newly acquired books. These two sets of rules were reworked and merged into the Prussian Instructions, which became the definitive cataloging code in **Germany** and Austria. The Prussian Instructions also formed the basis for codes adopted by **Scandinavian** countries (with the exception of **Norway**) and a number of other **central and eastern European** countries. Following the 1961 **International Conference on Cataloging Principles**, the Prussian Instructions were replaced in Germany by the *Rules for Descriptive Cataloging/Regeln für die alphabetische Katalogisierung* (RAK), published in 1976.

See also MILKAU, FRITZ (1859–1934).

PUBLIC LIBRARIES. Public libraries are generally understood to be libraries that are publicly owned and funded and open to anyone who wants to use them. Although libraries called "public" have existed for a long time, they were public only in the sense that they were not privately owned. Often, these so-called public libraries served a limited clientele. Other types of libraries, among them **social libraries**, were the true forerunners of public libraries that provide service to all.

The modern public library had its beginnings in the passage of the **Public Libraries Act** in England in 1850 and the opening of the **Boston Public Library** in 1854. What is considered the first tax-supported public library in the world was established in Peterborough, New Hampshire, in 1833, but it was not until the late 1840s, when states in New England began passing legislation permitting communities to tax themselves for the creation of libraries, that the idea started to take hold in the **United States**. Despite some opposition to paying taxes for libraries, there were almost 6,000 public libraries in the United States by 1925. The rapid expansion of libraries supported by public funds fueled the need for trained staff and helped lead to the professionalization of librarianship.

One impetus to public library development was the mass education movement that emerged in the late 19th century. The public library concept as it evolved in the United States and **Great Britain** was rooted in reform efforts undertaken in response to the forces of industrialization, urbanization, and immigration. In the United States, Progressive-era values fostered a sense of mission to educate the masses who would come to the library to be uplifted, improved, and Americanized. A belief in education was also a factor in the philanthropy of **Andrew Carnegie**, who provided funds for the construction of more than 1,600 public library buildings in the United States, along with more than 800 libraries in other parts of the world. **Carnegie libraries** helped promote the public library idea, and Carnegie's policy of requiring communities that requested a building to contribute an annual sum of 10 percent of the money donated to build collections and hire staff was a key factor in creating a tradition of government support. Public support, in turn, contributed to the development of a concept of library service that focused on demonstrating the library's value to the community and meeting readers' needs. Thanks to pioneers such as **John Cotton Dana**, **Samuel Swett Green**, and **Justin Winsor**, the familiar features of the public library began to take shape. Hours were extended, stacks were opened, and books were circulated. **Children's library service** and **reference service** were added. In larger urban areas, branch library systems were formed. Public library development was slower in Britain, but innovations similar to those in the United States were introduced by library leaders such as **James Duff Brown** and **Louis Stanley Jast**.

The forces of nationalism, secularization, industrialization, and educational reform helped to spur public library development in many other countries. The service-based model of public librarianship that originated in Britain and the United States was adopted particularly in **Scandinavia**, while elsewhere in Europe, public libraries grew out of a tradition that was more centered on the collection. Public library development in many parts of **Africa**, **Asia**, and **Latin America** has been slow. The **British Council**, the **United Nations Educational, Scientific and Cultural Organization (UNESCO)**, and other agencies supported public library development in developing countries following World War II. UNESCO's Public Library Manifesto, describing public libraries as "a living force for education," was adopted in 1949 and revised by the **International Federation of Library Associations and Institutions (IFLA)** in 1972 and 1994.

Although public libraries are generally seen as being democratic, revisionist scholars began to offer an alternative view in the 1970s, that public libraries are elitist institutions meant to preserve the existing social order. Some scholars have also argued that attempts to establish public libraries along Anglo-American lines in developing countries were part of an effort to inculcate Western values.

See also ADULT EDUCATION; THE FICTION QUESTION.

PUBLIC LIBRARIES. One of two generally recognized American professional library periodicals in the early 20th century (the other being *Library Journal*), *Public Libraries* was first published in 1896 by the Chicago office of the **Library Bureau**, with **Mary Eileen Ahern** as its editor. Intended to meet the needs of untrained librarians staffing smaller **public libraries** in the Midwest, the journal provided information, advice, and technical instruction along with editorials, letters, and news. In 1926, the name was changed to *Libraries* to reflect a broader readership. The Illinois Library Association took over as publisher but decided to end *Libraries* when Ahern retired in 1931.

PUBLIC LIBRARIES ACT. Modern **public library** development in **Great Britain** began in 1850 with the Public Libraries Act. Liberal Member of Parliament William Ewart introduced the Public Libraries Bill after chairing the Select Committee on Public Libraries, which had been conducting hearings since 1848. Ewart was one of several reformers involved in a campaign to create a public library system. Another was **Edward Edwards** of the **British Museum Library**, who had published a report entitled "A Statistical View of Public Libraries in Europe and America" and had acted as a key witness before Ewart's committee. Ewart wanted to empower boroughs to finance free public libraries, but compromises with Conservatives in the House of Commons resulted in legislation giving towns with a population of more than 10,000 the power to levy a half-penny rate as long as more than two-thirds of taxpayers voted in favor of the levy in a referendum. The money raised could be used for buildings and staff but not for book purchase, because it was believed that adequate collections would be created by donations from members of the public. In 1853, the act was extended to Scotland and Ireland. In 1855, the population limit was lowered to 5,000 and the rate was raised to one penny. Some further limitations were removed by the Public Library Act of 1866, but it was not until 1919, when the rate limit was abolished, that the public library movement became truly established.

PUBLIC LIBRARIES IN THE UNITED STATES OF AMERICA. In 1876, the **United States** Bureau of Education published the first major government report on **public libraries**, *Public Libraries in the United States of America: Their History, Condition, and Management, Special Report*. It was an attempt to provide a comprehensive examination of all of the nation's libraries to which an individual could obtain access, including **school libraries**, special libraries, **social libraries**, and others. It included a table of statistics for 3,647 libraries with collections of 300 volumes or more. **John Shaw Billings** contributed a chapter on medical libraries and **Melvil Dewey** contributed a chapter on **cataloging**. **Ainsworth Rand Spofford** contributed chapters on binding and preservation, periodical literature, reference works, and **bibliography**. **Charles Ammi Cutter**'s *Rules for a Dictionary Catalog* made up Part II of the report and greatly influenced **cataloging** practice.

PUBLIC LIBRARY INQUIRY. The **Public Library Inquiry** was a study commissioned by the **American Library Association (ALA)** in 1946 and conducted by a team of social scientists headed by Robert D. Leigh at the University of Chicago. As part of its postwar planning, ALA had requested support from the **Carnegie Corporation of New York** for a national survey to evaluate whether the **public library** in the **United States** was achieving its objectives. The results of the study were published from 1949 to 1952 in 10 volumes, including *The Library's Public* by Bernard Berelson and **Lester E. Asheim** (1949), *The Public Library in the Political Process* by Oliver Garceau (1949), and *The Public Librarian* by Alice Bryan (1952). The general report, *The Public Library in the United States*, was published in 1950. Among the study's conclusions were that public libraries served only a small fraction of the public, and that, in terms of training, the nature of the work, and status, librarianship suffered in comparison with other professions. Among the results of the Public Library Inquiry was a new emphasis on public library standards.

PUTNAM, HERBERT (1861–1955). Herbert Putnam, the first experienced librarian to hold the position of librarian of Congress, was born in New York City on September 20, 1861. He received a BA from Harvard University in 1883 and briefly studied law at Columbia University, but in 1884 he moved to Minneapolis, Minnesota, to take a position at the Minneapolis Athenaeum.

He became librarian of the new Minneapolis **Public Library** when it absorbed the Athenaeum in 1887. In 1895, he became superintendent of the **Boston Public Library**. Putnam was one of several witnesses sent by the **American Library Association (ALA)** in 1896 to testify before Congress about the role of the **Library of Congress (LC)**. With ALA's support, he was appointed librarian of Congress by President William McKinley in 1899. Sharing the vision of **Melvil Dewey** that the national library should offer comprehensive services to other libraries in the nation, he introduced new cooperative **cataloging**, **classification**, and loan services. He also directed the **Library War Service** during World War I. After the war, he focused less on service to other libraries and more on LC's legislative, cultural, and symbolic roles. Putnam retired in 1939.

R

RANGANATHAN, SHIYALA RAMAMRITA (1892–1971). S. R. Ranganathan, who is considered to be the father of **library science** in **India**, was born August 9, 1892, in the Tanjur district of Madras. He studied mathematics and education and became a professor of mathematics. In 1924, he was offered an appointment as the first librarian at the University of Madras, and he spent time attending the School of Librarianship, University of London, in order to prepare. After returning to Madras in 1925, he developed a new **classification** system, the **Colon Classification**, which became the basis for the **British National Bibliography (BNB)** and the Indian National **Bibliography**, among others. He was instrumental in founding the Madras Library Association in 1928, and he introduced a librarianship training course in the Madras Library Association headquarters in 1929. Because of this program's success, Madras University decided to establish a certificate course in librarianship, becoming the first school of library science in an institution of higher learning in India. In 1931, Ranganathan published his **Five Laws of Library Science**, which influenced librarians all over the world. In 1933, he helped found the Indian Library Association. He remained in Madras as university librarian and head of the Library Science Department until 1944 and then went on to hold positions at several other universities. At the University of Delhi, he started India's first master's degree and PhD programs in library science. In 1959, he was appointed head of the **Documentation** Research and Training Center, which he had founded, and in 1965, he was the first librarian in India to be appointed national professor of library science. He also made contributions to various international programs related to libraries and bibliography.

RDA: RESOURCE DESCRIPTION AND ACCESS. Published jointly in 2010 by the **American Library Association (ALA)**, the Canadian Library Association, and the **Chartered Institute of Library and Information Professionals (CILIP)**, *RDA* is a set of **cataloging** standards intended to replace the ***Anglo-American Cataloging Rules, Second Edition (AACR2).*** It emerged from a conference held in Toronto, Ontario, in 1997 to consider fundamental revisions to AACR2. Following that conference, a decision was made to develop new guidelines that would be more compatible with changes in the information environment. A nationwide test of RDA was coordinated by the **Library of Congress (LC)**, the **National Agricultural Library (NAL)**, and the **National Library of Medicine (NLM)** in 2010, and implementation began in the **United States** in 2013. RDA is meant to be an international standard in line with the Statement of International Cataloguing Principles published by the **International Federation of Library Associations and Institutions (IFLA)** in 2009. As of 2013, RDA had been implemented in libraries in **Australia, Brazil, Canada, Germany, Great Britain**, Singapore, and elsewhere.

See also FUNCTIONAL REQUIREMENTS FOR BIBLIOGRAPHICAL RECORDS (FRBR).

READERS' ADVISORY SERVICE. Although activities that could be described as readers' advisory have been taking place in the **United States** since the beginning of the **public library** movement, the service got its formal start in the 1920s, when several major public libraries created full-time positions to improve the quality of reading by helping adults plan reading programs, by assisting casual readers in the selection of books, by compiling lists of recommended books, and by working with **adult education** groups. The public libraries in Cleveland and Detroit set up reader's advisory bureaus in 1922, followed by the libraries in Chicago, Cincinnati, Indianapolis, Milwaukee, and Omaha. The New York Public Library's Readers' Advisory Office opened in 1929. By 1935, there were 63 public libraries with a dedicated readers' advisory staff, but the number began to shrink during the Depression, when many libraries decided they could no longer afford to provide such personalized service. Nearly all formal readers' advisory services disappeared as the function became absorbed into adult services. The 1980s saw the beginnings of a revival, led in part by the Illinois-based Adult Reading Roundtable, which was founded in 1984. This time, the focus was less on education and more on leisure reading. Adult fiction was the priority at first, but readers' advisory now encompasses other parts of the library collection, as well as other audiences.

See also FLEXNER, JENNIE MAAS (1882–1944).

READING WITH A PURPOSE. The Reading with a Purpose program was initiated by the Commission on Library and **Adult Education** of the **American Library Association (ALA)** in 1924. Funded by a grant from the **Carnegie Corporation of New York**, the program offered guided reading courses intended to support adult self-education. From 1925 to 1933, 66 volumes were published, written by experts and covering topics such as biology, geography, philosophy, advertising, and Russian literature. Each volume typically contained an introduction of 20–30 pages, followed by an annotated list of readings in the order in which they should be read. The cost was 50 cents for a cloth cover and 35 cents for a paper cover. By the end of 1931, some 850,000 copies had been sold. Reading with a Purpose was criticized by some because it focused on classics and serious literature.

REFERENCE SERVICE. The history of library reference service in the **United States** is generally considered to have begun with **Samuel Swett Green**'s 1876 paper "Personal Relations between Librarians and Readers." In it, Green defines the four components of reference services: to instruct the reader in the use of the library, to assist readers with finding answers to their inquiries, to aid the reader in the selection of books, and to promote the library within the community. Reference emerged as part of the service-based model that had developed in **public libraries** in the United States in order to stimulate library use and support. It was also tied to the idea that the public library played a role in the pursuit of self-education. Green implemented his ideas about assistance to readers at the Worcester (Massachusetts) Public Library, where he was the director, and other public libraries followed suit. Borrowing from them, **Melvil Dewey** organized the first modern reference department at the Columbia College Library in 1884. Reference work became a regular topic of discussion at **American Library Association (ALA)** conferences beginning in 1896, and the term *reference librarian* appeared for the first time in *Library Journal* in 1897. By the start of the 20th century, reference service had become an established function. ALA published Alice B. Kroeger's *Guide to the Study and Use of Reference Books* in 1902, reflecting the fact that librarians were relying on a particular set of tools. **Isadore Gilbert Mudge** pioneered reference procedures at Columbia University beginning in 1911, providing a model for other libraries. Subject specializations began to emerge in university libraries and some large public libraries. James I. Wyer's *Reference Work: A Textbook for Students of Library Work and Librarians*, the first major reference textbook, was published in 1930.

With the introduction of electronic versions of large indexing and abstracting tools in the 1970s, the CD-ROM format in the 1980s, and the Internet in the 1990s, technology played an increasingly important role in the way information was discovered. Over time, reference service shifted from depending on sources to depending on communication and searching skills. Technology also allowed libraries to adopt new modes of communication, such as chat and instant messaging, and to provide reference service on a "24/7" basis. At the same time, technology put so much information directly into the user's hands that the value the user places on traditional reference service began to erode. Technological change and the resulting changes in user expectations triggered a reference reform movement, beginning in the 1980s and continuing into the present, with librarians questioning the utility of traditional print reference collections and debating the effectiveness of face-to-face, desk-based service models.

REFORMA. REFORMA (common name for the National Association to Promote Library and Information Services to Latinos and the Spanish-Speaking) was organized in 1971 as an affiliate of the **American Library Association (ALA)**. Its goals include the development of Spanish-language and Latino-oriented library collection; the recruitment of bilingual, multicultural library personnel; the promotion of public awareness of libraries and librarianship among Latinos; and advocacy on behalf of the information needs of the Latino community.

See also PROGRESSIVE LIBRARIANSHIP.

RESEARCH LIBRARIES GROUP (RLG). The increase in publishing and the rise in the prices of published materials in the **United States** in the last half of the 20th century caused many librarians to question whether libraries could continue to operate in isolation. One response to the problems facing research libraries was the founding of the RLG in 1974. RLG was a consortium consisting of Columbia, Harvard, and Yale universities, and the New York **Public Library**. After Harvard University dropped out, RLG expanded its membership, in time becoming the largest cooperative network among research libraries in the United States. Among its major programs, RLG built the **Research Libraries Information Network (RLIN)** and developed the RLG Conspectus for use in the evaluation of research library collections. In 1992, the **British Library** was the first library outside North America to become a member of RLG. By 2000, RLG membership had increased to 162 libraries. RLG merged with the **Online Computer Library Center (OCLC)** in 2006.

See also ASSOCIATION OF RESEARCH LIBRARIES (ARL); AUTOMATION; BIBLIOGRAPHIC AUTOMATION OF LARGE LIBRARY OPERATIONS USING A TIME-SHARING SYSTEM (BALLOTS).

RESEARCH LIBRARIES INFORMATION NETWORK (RLIN). RLIN was a bibliographic database built by the **Research Libraries Group (RLG)**. In 1978, when the Stanford University Library decided to make its **Bibliographic Automation of Large Library Operations using a Time-sharing System (BALLOTS)** available to other libraries, RLG abandoned its own plans for developing a network and adopted BALLOTS as the basis for RLIN. Reflecting the combined holdings of the members of RLG, RLIN was used for acquisitions, **cataloging**, and interlibrary loan. The first online

information about the contents of archival and manuscript collections was added in 1984. When RLG merged with the **Online Computer Library Center (OCLC)** in 2006, RLIN migrated to OCLC's WorldCat database.
See also AUTOMATION.

ROCKEFELLER FOUNDATION. Endowed by John D. Rockefeller and established in 1913, the Rockefeller Foundation played a significant role in library development. Unlike the **Carnegie Corporation of New York**, whose charter limited its philanthropic activities to the **United States** and areas of the former British Commonwealth, the Rockefeller Foundation operated internationally. In the 1920s, in addition to donating several million dollars to the New York **Public Library**, the Rockefeller Foundation aided in the construction of a new building for the library of the Imperial University of Tokyo in **Japan**, after the old building was destroyed by an earthquake. Among other library-related enterprises that the Rockefeller Foundation supported were **educating African American librarians**, copying the **Library of Congress (LC) catalog** and distributing it to 50 libraries around the world, expanding the **Bodleian Library**; development of microphotography, distributing library materials to European and Asian libraries during and immediately after World War II, and developing library education in **Asia** and **Latin America**. It also funded fellowships that allowed librarians from different countries to study library administration in the United States.

See also BRAZIL; CENTER FOR RESEARCH LIBRARIES (CRL); FARMINGTON PLAN; HAMPTON INSTITUTE LIBRARY SCHOOL; INTERAMERICAN LIBRARY SCHOOL; INTERNATIONAL LIBRARIANSHIP; NATIONAL LIBRARY OF MEDICINE (NLM); PARIS LIBRARY SCHOOL; SCHOOL OF LIBRARY SERVICE, ATLANTA UNIVERSITY.

ROSE, ERNESTINE (1880–1961). Ernestine Rose was born in Bridgehampton, New York. She received a bachelor's degree from Wesleyan University and then trained at the **New York State Library School** in Albany. In 1908, she took a position at the New York **Public Library** (NYPL), at a branch that was located in a largely Chinese neighborhood on the Lower East Side of Manhattan. She began to add Chinese books to the branch, and she continued to develop collections to meet the needs of the neighborhoods surrounding several other NYPL branches. After serving in the **American Library Association**'s **(ALA) Library War Service** during World War I, she became the head of the 135th Street branch of NYPL, known as the Harlem branch, in 1920. She hired **African Americans** as staff members, and her outreach to the community made the 135th Street branch an important part of the Harlem Renaissance. In 1925, Rose created the Division of

Negro History and Literature as a special collection at the branch, planting the seed for the world-renowned Schomburg Center for Research in Black Culture. She continued to write about and teach **library science** after her retirement from NYPL in 1942.

See also UNITED STATES; WOMEN IN LIBRARIANSHIP.

RUSSIA. Russia's first important library, the Library of the Academy of Sciences, was established by Peter the Great in 1714. The Moscow Imperial University Library, the first **academic library**, was opened in 1756. Another important event in the history of Russian librarianship was the founding of the Imperial Public Library (now the Russian National Library) in St. Petersburg in 1795. **A. N. Olenin**, its director from 1811 to 1843, made the library into a center of intellectual activity. By 1860, it was one of the largest libraries in the world, thanks in part to strict enforcement of **legal deposit**. A **public library** movement based on North American and Western European models began to take shape in the 1890s. Library activists established the Society for Librarianship, the first independent Russian library association, in 1908; published the first Russian library journal, *Bibliotekar*, from 1910 to 1915; and convened the first Russian Congress of Librarianship in 1911. The first library courses were offered at Shanyavsky People's University in Moscow in 1913; more than 1,000 librarians had graduated by 1917. Additional instruction was later provided at the Petrograd Institute of Adult Education (renamed the Krupskaya Institute of Culture in 1924).

After 1917, librarianship was shaped by Lenin and his wife, **Nadezhda Krupskaya**. They were vocal supporters of the expansion of public libraries as a way to educate the masses, but they also believed that libraries should be ideological centers that would help build socialism. Krupskaya was a driving force in formalizing library training in Russia, initiating a number of programs. In 1930, the Krupskaya Institute began a PhD program. A second institution of advanced library and bibliographical **education**, the Moscow State Library Institute, opened the same year, and postsecondary training at technical colleges continued to expand. The aim was not only to train people for library work but also to create propagandists for Marxist-Leninist ideas.

During the Soviet period, libraries were instruments of the ruling party, and the state controlled all activities in the hundreds of thousands of public, academic, **school**, government, special, and trade union libraries. Politically questionable materials were acquired by major research institutions such as the Lenin Library but were kept in *spetskhran* (special stacks). With the collapse of the Soviet system, control and financing were decentralized. Policies in the major research libraries in each of the newly independent republics had to be redefined. Libraries were free to acquire materials without regard to ideology, and materials that were hidden away in *spetskhran* were made available for public use. Library and **information science** (LIS) education was reorganized to reflect the new conditions. **Automation** of libraries began in the late 1980s and early 1990s. The Russian Library Association was established in 1994 and is the largest library association in Russia. Its activities have included working with the **Online Computer Library Center (OCLC)** to bring Russian **cataloging** rules more in line with international standards and creating the Russian **Machine-Readable Cataloging** (RUS-MARC) format, which was published in 2000.

See also EUROPE, CENTRAL AND EASTERN.

SARMIENTO, DOMINGO F. (1811–1888). Domingo Sarmiento was born on February 15, 1811, in San Juan, **Argentina**. Largely self-taught, he became a schoolteacher and a political activist. During Argentina's civil wars, he was forced into exile in Chile, and the Chilean government sent him abroad to inspect the education systems in Europe and North America. He returned to Argentina in 1852 and began a political career that culminated in his taking office as president of Argentina in 1868. Influenced by what he had witnessed on his study tours, Sarmiento instituted a variety of reforms to support mass education. The Sarmiento Law for the Development of Popular Libraries, passed in 1870, was the start of the **public library** movement in Argentina and the first law of its kind in **Latin America**, serving as a model for other countries in the region. Sarmiento was also instrumental in the establishment of the Argentine National Library in 1884.

SAVAGE, ERNEST A. (1877–1966). British **public library** pioneer Ernest Savage was born in Croyden, England, on March 30, 1877. He began working as a junior assistant at the new public library in Croyden when he was 13 years old. In 1898, he was appointed deputy to Croyden Public Library's innovative director **Louis Stanley Jast**. In 1904, Savage left Croyden to head several different libraries, becoming principal librarian of Edinburgh city libraries in 1922. He introduced open shelving and reorganized the Edinburgh Central Library into subject departments. Savage was also the driving force behind the reorganization of **Great Britain**'s **Library Association (LA)** in the 1920s, making it a more effective organization with its own headquarters and staff. As a consultant for the **Carnegie Corporation of New York**, he reported in 1934 on libraries in the West Indies. Savage retired in 1942 but continued to write on library-related topics.
See also CARIBBEAN.

SAYERS, WILLIAM CHARLES BERWICK (1881–1960). One of the shapers of modern **public** librarianship in **Great Britain**, William Charles Berwick Sayers was born in Mitcham, England, on December 23, 1881. He began his library career in 1900 at Bournemouth Public Library. In 1904, he was appointed deputy librarian of Croyden Public Library, which was headed by **Louis Stanley Jast**, and he succeeded Jast as chief librarian in 1915. Jast had made Croyden a workshop for new ideas about public librarianship, and Sayers carried on Jast's spirit of innovation. Sayers was a pioneer in **children's library service**, publishing *The Children's Library* (1913) and *Manual of Children's Libraries* (1932). The children's department that he inaugurated at Croyden served as a model for other libraries and as a training ground for children's librarians. Sayers was also a noted authority on **classification** and wrote two standard textbooks on the topic. In addition, he made a significant contribution to the development of the **Library Association (LA)**.

SCANDIA PLAN. The Scandia Plan was the first cooperative acquisitions plan for a group of countries. Launched in 1957, the Scandia Plan was a voluntary scheme involving national and university libraries in **Denmark**, **Finland**, **Norway**, and **Sweden**. Initially, the plan was administered by the Nordic Federation of Research Librarians, and the focus was on non-Nordic material. Although the Scandia Plan came to an end in 1980, the concept provided a model for other research libraries in Europe.

SCANDINAVIA. *See* DENMARK; FINLAND; NORWAY; SWEDEN.

SCHOLARLY PUBLISHING AND ACADEMIC RESOURCES CO-ALITION (SPARC). SPARC, which was created by the **Association of Research Libraries (ARL)** in 1998, is a library-based organization that focuses on encouraging the emergence of new scholarly communication models to expand the sharing of research and to reduce financial pressures on libraries. SPARC worked with the **Association of European Research Libraries/Ligue des bibliothèques européennes de recherche (LIBER)** and other European organizations to establish SPARC Europe in 2001. SPARC **Japan** was launched in 2006.
See also OPEN ACCESS (OA) MOVEMENT; SERIALS CRISIS.

SCHOOL LIBRARIES. In 2005, nearly half the library professionals in the **United States** worked in the more than 82,000 public school libraries. The history of school libraries in the United States began in 1835, when New York State allowed school districts to use tax monies to set up and maintain libraries in schools. The US Bureau of Education reported in 1876 that 21 states had made provisions for the establishment of school libraries, although the report also noted that many of the libraries were hampered by defective legislation and incompetent administration. In 1892, New York again led the way in school library development by adopting legislation requiring school districts to raise library money as a condition for receiving an allotment from the state. The legislation also required that books be kept in a school building and that a teacher be appointed to act as a librarian. Despite these steps, school libraries in the United States developed more slowly than **public libraries**, in part because of the success of the public library movement. Well into the 20th century, many schools relied on public libraries to provide services and reading materials. In 1960, the US Office of Education reported that only about 50 percent of the nation's schools had libraries and well under 50 percent were staffed by a qualified librarian. The number of schools with libraries increased to 93 percent by 1985, although dwindling support meant that in 2012, 9,000 public schools had no libraries and, of those with libraries, 22,000 had no full- or part-time certified librarians.

In part because of the effort of **John Cotton Dana** and **Melvil Dewey** (library leaders who were strong proponents of school and public library cooperation), the National Education Association (NEA) created a Library Department, the first organization for school librarians, in 1896. The National Council of Teachers of English formed a Library Section in 1913. Also in 1913, the **American Library Association (ALA)** Roundtable of Normal and High School Librarians held its first meeting. A year later, ALA approved a petition from the roundtable to form a School Libraries Section, the precursor to the American Association of School Librarians (AASL). The NEA was more effective in furthering school library development, however, appointing a committee to produce standards for school libraries in 1915. Adopted in 1918 by the NEA, *Standard Library Organization and Equipment for Secondary Schools of Different Sizes* (commonly known as the Certain standards after Charles Certain, the committee chair) established many of the basic ideas about school libraries and the role of the school librarian, and provided a model for states to follow in developing standards of their own. In 1925, the NEA and ALA collaborated to produce a second set of standards for elementary schools. The first set of K–12 school library standards, *School Libraries for Today and Tomorrow*, was produced as part of ALA's postwar planning in 1945 and marked a shift in focus from providing resources to interacting with students and teachers. *Standards for School Library Programs*, issued by AASL in 1960, emphasized the need to expand the role of the school library in education.

Federal funding for school libraries led to major growth in the 1960s. The five-year **Knapp School Libraries Project**, funded by the Knapp Foundation, helped stimulate national interest in school library development. In 1969, ALA and the NEA collaborated again on *Standards for School Media Programs*, which recognized the importance of nonprint as well as print materials and introduced terms such as *media, media specialist, media center*, and *media program*—concepts reinforced in *Media Programs: Districts* *and Schools* (1975). In 1988, AASL published *Information Power: Guidelines for School Library Media Programs*, which broadened the media specialist's responsibilities and roles. Ten years later came *Information Power: Building Partnerships for Learning*, which contained the first set of standards for information literacy. The most recent standards, *Standards for the 21st Century Learner*, were published in 2007.

A few library schools offered courses on school libraries beginning in 1917, but even after ALA adopted the master's degree as the first professional degree in 1951, most training for school librarians took place at the undergraduate level in teacher training schools. It was not until 1988 that AASL developed standards recommending graduate **education** for all library media specialists, either a degree from a program accredited by ALA or a master's degree with a specialty in school library media from an educational unit accredited by the National Council for Accreditation of Teacher Education. Professional school library media specialists must receive certification as both teachers and library media specialists, although specific requirements differ from state to state.

Outside the United States, **Australia** and **Canada** have emerged as leaders in school librarianship. In **Great Britain**, the School Library Services, set up after World War II to provided central collections as well as professional advice, is funded by local education authorities and run by public libraries. The **International Association of School Librarianship (IASL)** and the **International Federation of Library Associations and Institutions (IFLA)** are advocates for school libraries worldwide. In 2003, eight European nations adopted the Amsterdam Statement on School Libraries and Information Literacy, which calls for equal access to learning opportunities and professional training for school librarians. The IFLA/UNESCO School Library Manifesto, adopted in 1999, is used as a framework in both developed and developing countries.

See also HENNE, FRANCES E. (1906–1985).

SCHOOL OF LIBRARY ECONOMY. Having unsuccessfully put forward a plan for systematic **apprenticeship** training, **Melvil Dewey**, chief librarian at the Columbia College Library in New York City, approached the Columbia Board of Trustees in 1883 with a proposal for creating a School of Library Economy. He outlined his plans at the 1883 **American Library Association (ALA)** conference in Buffalo, New York. In 1884, Columbia College established the school and appointed Dewey as professor of library economy. It was expected that the students would be individuals already working in libraries; a college degree was not required. When instruction began on January 5, 1887, the school had 20 pupils, 17 of them **women**. Dewey developed the curriculum, which included lectures, visits to libraries, and practice sessions. He also did more than 60 percent of the teaching himself. Reflecting his concern for practical details, his lectures covered the technical aspects of **cataloging**, acquiring books and preparing them for the shelves, and planning and equipping library buildings. Columbia library staff made up the rest of the faculty, but there were frequent guest lecturers, as well. When Columbia withdrew its support, in part because of the presence of women, Dewey moved the school to the **New York State Library** in Albany in 1889.

See also EDUCATION FOR LIBRARIANSHIP.

SCHOOL OF LIBRARY SERVICE, ATLANTA UNIVERSITY. In March 1941, representatives from the **American Library Association (ALA)**, the **Carnegie Corporation of New York**, the **Rockefeller Foundation**'s General Education Board, and from several library schools and black colleges met in Atlanta, Georgia, to discuss the **education** of **African American librarians**. Following the closing of the library school at **Hampton Institute** in 1939, there was no school in the South that filled that need. As a result of the conference, the Atlanta University library school opened in September 1941, with funding from the Carnegie Corporation and the General Education Board. **Eliza Atkins Gleason** was appointed as founding dean. The school was accredited in 1943, and in 1949, it inaugurated a new program leading to a master's degree in **library science** (MLS). By the 1960s, the school, which was then called the School of Library and Information Studies and located at Clark Atlanta University, was educating more than half of all African American librarians in the **United States**. The school closed in 2004.

SCHRETTINGER, MARTIN (1772–1851). Martin Schrettinger, who coined the term *library science*, was born near Nuremberg, **Germany**, on June 17, 1772. He became a Benedictine monk and was put in charge of the **monastery** library but left in 1802 and joined the staff of the Royal Library in Munich, which had one of the largest library collections in the world. There he developed a discipline of librarianship which he called Bibliothekswissenschaft, or "library science." His books *Attempt at a Comprehensive Textbook of Library Science* (1808–1829) and *Handbook of Library Science* (1834) were influential in defining some of the principles of professional librarianship, including the purposeful organization of the library.

SCOGGIN, MARGARET C. (1905–1968). A leader in **young adult (YA) library service**, Margaret Scoggin was born in Caruthersville, Missouri, on April 4, 1905. After graduating from Radcliffe College, she worked in several branches of the New York **Public Library** (NYPL). She attended the School of Librarianship at the University of London and returned to NYPL upon receiving her degree. With the encouragement of her mentor, Mabel Williams, who was NYPL's first superintendent of work with young people, Scoggin organized the first library designed specifically for young adults: the Nathan Straus Branch Library for Children and Young People, which opened in 1941. Under her direction, the Nathan Straus Branch served as a laboratory and a model for YA librarianship. In 1952, Scoggin succeeded Williams as NYPL's superintendent of work with young people, a position she held until her retirement in 1967. Scoggin promoted YA services through her writings, radio programs, and national and international professional activities. She was the **American Library Association**'s **(ALA)** representative to the International Youth Library, which opened in Munich, **Germany**, in 1949.

See also WOMEN IN LIBRARIANSHIP.

SEARS LIST OF SUBJECT HEADINGS. *See* SEARS, MINNIE EARL (1873–1933).

SEARS, MINNIE EARL (1873–1933). Minnie Earl Sears, the creator of *Sears List of Subject Headings*, was born in Lafayette, Indiana, on November 17, 1873. She received bachelor's and master's degrees from Purdue University and was awarded a bachelor's degree in **library science** from the University of Illinois in 1900. After working as a bibliographer and cataloger at the University of Minnesota, the New York **Public Library**, and elsewhere, she joined the editorial staff of the **H. W. Wilson** Company in 1923. Wilson published her *List of Subject Headings for Small Libraries* in the same year. To create the list, she had consulted with small and medium-sized libraries throughout the **United States** before developing a modified version of the **Library of Congress Subject Headings (LCSH)** with a simplified subject vocabulary. In the third edition, the last one she edited, she added a chapter containing practical guidelines for subject heading work. In 1927, Sears left H. W. Wilson for a teaching position at the Columbia University School of Library Science. The *List of Subject Headings for Small Libraries* was renamed *Sears List of Subject Headings* after she died. It is the most widely used subject headings list in school and small public libraries in the United States.

See also CLASSIFICATION; WOMEN IN LIBRARIANSHIP.

SEMINAR ON THE ACQUISITION OF LATIN AMERICAN LIBRARY MATERIALS (SALALM). *See* LATIN AMERICAN COOPERATIVE ACQUISITIONS PROGRAM (LACAP).

SENG, SAMUEL T. Y. (1883–1976). Remembered as the father of Chinese library **education**, Samual T. Y. Seng was born in 1883. He graduated from Boone College, a small Christian school, in 1910, the same year that American teacher and librarian **Mary Elizabeth Wood** opened the Boone College Library. She chose Seng to be her assistant. In 1914, Seng went to the **United States** to study at the Library School of the New York **Public Library**, becoming the first Chinese person to attend an American library school. He received his diploma in 1916, having first reworked the **Dewey Decimal Classification (DDC)** for use in **China**. Upon his return to China, he worked with Wood to establish a school based on American models. The **Boone Library School** accepted its first class in 1920, and Seng was its director until it became part of Wuhan University in 1952. He remained with the library department until his retirement in 1965, teaching himself Russian in order to adapt to the profession's changing needs.

SERAPEUM. The first **library science** journal, *Serapeum* was started in 1840 by Emil Robert Wilhelm Naumann, school teacher and city librarian in Leipzig, **Germany**. Subtitled *Journal for Library Science, Information on Manuscripts and Older Literature*, the journal was published fortnightly and covered library holdings of manuscripts, new acquisitions, personnel changes, and reviews of books on library science or libraries. Publication ceased in 1870.

SERIALS CRISIS. What has been called the "serials crisis" had its beginnings in the 1970s, when a slowing economy in the **United States** and an end to generous federal funding for higher education caused libraries to pay attention to the high cost of periodical subscriptions. It became apparent that even the largest libraries could no longer afford to maintain comprehensive research collections, especially in the areas of science, technology, and medicine. In 1989, the **Association of Research Libraries (ARL)** published a study showing that over the previous 10 years, serials expenditures in ARL libraries had increased by around 140 percent. The rise was attributed to a number of factors, including an increase in the number and size of journals and the concentration of scientific journal publishing in the hands of a few commercial publishers. In response to the crisis, libraries began to cancel expensive journal subscriptions, migrate from print to online subscriptions, cut back on acquisitions of books and other materials, and pursue more cooperative agreements. Despite such measures, expenditures on scholarly journals at American research libraries quadrupled from 1986 to 2005. The serials crisis helped spur the creation of the **Scholarly Publishing and Academic Resources Coalition (SPARC)** as well as the **Open Access (OA) movement**.

See also ACADEMIC LIBRARIES.

SHARIFY, NASSER (1925–2013). Nasser Sharify, who has been called the father of **international librarianship**, was born on September 23, 1925, in Tehran, Iran. After his graduation from Tehran University in 1947, he joined the staff of All **India** Radio in New Delhi as an announcer and poet-in-residence. A few years later, he emigrated to the **United States**, where he received a master's degree and a PhD from Columbia University in New York City. In 1964, he helped to establish the International Library Information Center at the University of Pittsburgh, and he was its director until 1966. He then moved to the State University of New York, where he headed the office of International Librarianship, Learning Resources, and Information Services. From 1968 to 1987, he was the dean of the **Pratt Institute** Graduate School of Library and **Information Science**. During the 1970s, Sharify helped to formulate a plan for the creation of a national library in Iran. As a consultant for the **United Nations Educational, Scientific and Cultural Organization (UNESCO)**, he designed and helped establish the first school of information science in Morocco, which opened in 1974.

SHARP, KATHARINE L. (1865–1914). Library educator Katharine L. Sharp was born in Elgin, Illinois, on May 21, 1873, and graduated from Northwestern University in 1885. After working as a teacher and librarian, she applied for admission to the **New York State Library School**, receiving her **library science** degree in 1892. In 1893, at **Melvil Dewey**'s suggestion, she was hired as director of the first Midwestern library school, the Department of Library Economy at the new **Armour Institute** in Chicago. Envisioning a program that would go beyond the short technical course that was normal at the time, Sharp raised admission standards and lengthened the time of study in order to prepare leaders for the profession. In 1897, she decided to transfer the program to the University of Illinois at Urbana-Champaign, where she became head librarian and director of the Illinois State Library School. She was an advocate for the recognition of the library school as being on equal terms with other professional schools within the university, and she also promoted the requirement of a college degree for those entering the school. Lack of support and resources at the University of Illinois led to her resignation in 1907. She then became a member of the executive staff of the Lake Placid Club, which Dewey had founded.

See also EDUCATION FOR LIBRARIANSHIP; WOMEN IN LIBRARIANSHIP.

SHAW, RALPH ROBERT (1907–1972). Ralph Robert Shaw was born in Detroit, Michigan, on May 18, 1907. After graduating from Western Reserve University in Cleveland, Ohio, he studied at the Columbia University School of Library Service. Shaw was keenly interested in scientific management and the use of machines for information work, and, as director of the Gary (Indiana) **Public Library** from 1936 to 1940, he introduced such innovations as the use of photography in circulation control. In 1940, he accepted a position in the **United States** Department of Agriculture Library (later the **National Agricultural Library**), where he remained for 14 years. During that time, in addition to introducing modern library management practices, he created the *Bibliography of Agriculture* and worked on developing the Rapid Selector, the first (although ultimately unsuccessful) machine designed specifically to store, find, and reproduce bibliographic information. In 1950, he obtained a PhD at the **Graduate Library School (GLS)** of the University of Chicago, and in 1954 he joined the faculty of the Graduate School of Library Service at Rutgers University. In 1964, he became dean of library activities at the University of Hawaii. Shaw founded Scarecrow Press in 1950, and he served as president of the **American Library Association (ALA)** from 1956 to 1957.
See also AUTOMATION.

SHERA, JESSE HAUK (1903–1982). Educator and theorist Jesse Hauk Shera was born on December 8, 1907, in Oxford, Ohio. After graduating from Miami University in Ohio, he received a master's degree in English literature from Yale University. From 1928 to 1938 he worked as a bibliographer and research assistant at the Scripps Foundation for Research in Population Problems at Miami University. In 1944, he received a PhD in **library science** from the University of Chicago, joining the faculty there in 1947. In 1952, Shera became head of the **American Documentation Institute (ADI)** as well as dean of the Library School at Western Reserve University. There he established the Center for **Documentation** and Communication Research, which developed a program of teaching and research in the new field of information retrieval. Among his books are *Foundations of the Public Library: The Origins of the Public Library Movement in New England, 1629–1855* (1949) and *The Foundations of Education for Librarianship* (1972). The **American Library Association (ALA)** gives two awards in his honor: one for published research and one for doctoral research.
See also INFORMATION SCIENCE.

SHORES, LOUIS (1904–1981). Noted library educator Louis Shores was born on September 15, 1904, in Buffalo, New York. After graduating from the University of Toledo, he received a master's degree in education from the

City College of New York, followed by a degree from the School of Library Service at Columbia University. While working at Fisk University, a historically black school in Nashville, Tennessee, he conducted an important survey on library service to **African Americans**. He left Fisk in 1938 for the George Peabody College for Teachers, where he earned a PhD in **education** in addition to setting up a library school. In 1946, he became founding dean of the library school at Florida State University. His dissertation entitled "The Origins of the American College Library, 1638–1800" is a classic text in **academic library** history, and he was one of the founders of the **American Library Association**'s (ALA) Library History Round Table. The Louis Shores Award for excellence in reviewing was established in 1980.

SMITH, LILLIAN H. (1887–1983). Lillian Smith, the first trained **children's** librarian in **Canada**, was born in London, Ontario, in 1887. After graduating from the University of Toronto in 1910, she attended the Training School for Children's Librarians at the **Carnegie** Library of Pittsburgh. She worked with **Anne Carroll Moore** at the New York **Public Library** before accepting an offer in 1912 to organize a children's department at the Toronto Public Library. In 1922, the library opened Boys and Girls House (now the Lillian H. Smith Branch Library) in a separate building, with Smith as its head. She developed standards for the collection and worked closely with the schools. She also taught children's literature courses at the library school at the University of Toronto from 1928 until she retired in 1953. She was active in the Children's Services Division of the **American Library Association (ALA)** and was one of the founders of the Canadian Association of Children's Librarians. The **classification** system she designed in 1930 for children's books was in use until 1999. Her book *The Unreluctant Years: A Critical Approach to Children's Literature* (1953) became a widely used text.
See also WOMEN IN LIBRARIANSHIP.

SOCIAL LIBRARIES. Social libraries began to appear in **Great Britain** and the **United States** in the 18th century. The idea was to acquire and share materials that would satisfy the tastes of members but that were prohibitively expensive for members to purchase on their own. The first example in America was the **Library Company of Philadelphia**, which Benjamin Franklin founded in 1731. This was a subscription library of the proprietary type; members were required to purchase shares. In other cases, members did not own the collection but paid a fee in order to use it. Another type of social library, the commercial or circulating library, met the demand for fiction and other popular materials. Mudie's Select Library, which operated in Britain from 1842 to 1937, is the most famous example. As the 19th century progressed, social libraries took different forms. Some social libraries, such as the mechanics' institute libraries in Britain and apprentices' libraries in the United States, were created specifically to benefit members of the working class. Others were established for the convenience of a single gender (e.g., ladies' libraries) or to provide reading material on particular subjects. Some social libraries had functionaries described as librarians, whose job it was to loan and receive books and to keep full records of loans, borrowers, and penalties.

The social library model was carried from Britain to **Australia** early in the 19th century. Social libraries were also established in Anglophone **Africa** for the benefit of the white population. With a few exceptions, the social library model declined as the government-funded public library movement gained ground. Because they purchased books to satisfy the tastes of their members, social libraries are considered to be forerunners of **public libraries**.

See also BOSTON ATHENAEUM.

SOCIETY OF COLLEGE, NATIONAL, AND UNIVERSITY LIBRARIES (SCONUL). Representing **academic libraries** in **Great Britain**, SCONUL was established in 1950 as the Standing Conference of National and University Libraries. It originated with the **Library Association**'s **(LA)** University and Research Section, members of which were dissatisfied with the LA's **public library** focus. In 1994, it merged with the Council of Polytechnic Librarians. In 2001, it extended its membership to college libraries and adopted its current name.

SORBONNE LIBRARY. The most important medieval library in **France**, and perhaps the first **academic library**, the Sorbonne library was established in 1289 at the Sorbonne in Paris. Its benefactor, Robert de Sorbon, founded a house for poor theology students and endowed it with his collection of books when he died. The collection contained around 1,000 books by the end of the 13th century, most of them theological works. In common with many other libraries of the time, the library of the Sorbonne was divided into two collections: reference works and the best manuscripts, which were kept chained, and a small circulating library consisting of duplicate copies and books that were rarely used. Library directors were elected annually by the members of the college.

SOUTH AFRICA. In 1761, Joachim Von Dessin, an official of the Dutch East India Company who was living in South **Africa**, bequeathed his private library of around 4,000 volumes to the Dutch Reformed Church. In 1820, the collection was transferred to the new South African Library in Cape Town, which opened as one of the world's earliest tax-supported **public libraries,**

but which became a subscription library a few years later. Johannesburg Public Library opened its doors in 1890 and in 1924 began training classes to prepare individuals for the British **Library Association (LA)** examinations.

Modern library development began in 1928 when, at the request of **Matthew Miller Stirling** of the Germinston Public Library, the **Carnegie Corporation of New York** commissioned Milton J. Ferguson, state librarian of California, and Septimus A. Pitt, city librarian of Glasgow, Scotland, to investigate and report on the state of libraries in South Africa. Their visit culminated in the first South African library conference, held on November 15–17, 1928, in Bloemfontein. One outcome of the conference was the formation of the South African Library Association (SALA) in 1930. Another was a recommendation to the Carnegie Corporation to fund library services on a segregated basis for population groups other than whites. To that end, grants were made to four South African provinces: Natal, the Transvaal, the Cape, and the Orange Free State. The Carnegie Corporation also provided grants to a number of South African librarians to observe libraries in the **United States**, and these librarians brought American library practices with them when they returned. SALA began a system of examination and **certification** in 1933, following the British model. University-based **library science** programs were set up at the University of Pretoria in 1938 and the University of Cape Town in 1939.

In 1962, SALA held a national conference intended to lay the foundation for further library development, just as the 1928 conference had done. At its annual conference held immediately afterward, SALA approved a motion that limited membership to whites only. Separate associations were created for "Bantus," "Coloreds," and "Indians." One of these, the Central Bantu Library Association, became the African Library Association of South Africa (ALASA). In 1980, SALA disbanded to make way for a nonracial organization, the South African Institute for Librarianship and **Information Science** (SAILIS). This did not put an end to rifts, however, in part because SAILIS accepted only those with graduate degrees as members. In 1990, a group of white and Indian librarians formed an alternative group, the Library and Information Workers Organization (LIWO). In 1994, ALASA, LIWO, and SAILIS met at a joint workshop to address disunity in the profession. This workshop led to a move to form a new association, and the Library and Information Association of South Africa (LIASA) was launched in 1997.

For much of the 20th century, the separate development of libraries for whites, coloreds, blacks, and Indians was the norm, and library service for the white population was the priority. Some public library services were provided for nonwhite communities starting in the 1920s; for example, the Carnegie Non-European Library Service sent boxes of books to depots that were set up in rural schools, churches, and other institutions and staffed by volunteer librarians. However, such developments occurred in an environment of segregation and inequality. A public library campaign in the 1930s and 1940s led to legislation establishing free provincial public library service, but services remained segregated, the distribution of library resources was unequal, and many blacks had no exposure to libraries at all. Although the Johannesburg Public Library became the first public library to open its doors to all ethnicities in 1974, equal access was not guaranteed nationwide until the end of apartheid in 1994. After 1994, a lack of government support caused public libraries to suffer a decline. More funding has been available in recent years to build new libraries and upgrade library buildings; to buy, equip, and deliver mobile libraries and container libraries in remote areas; and to buy more library materials in indigenous languages. However, there continues to be a serious shortage of libraries in schools. In 2011, in the largest youth demonstrations in South Africa since the Soweto uprising in 1976, more than 20,000 Cape Town students joined a protest march to Parliament demanding **school libraries**. Programs such as the Mandela Day container library project, which adapts shipping containers for use as libraries, are intended to fill some of the gaps in library service to children in urban and rural areas.

Until 1999, South Africa had two national libraries: the South African Library in Cape Town (founded in 1818) and the State Library in Pretoria (founded in 1887). On November 1, 1999, the South African Library and the State Library were amalgamated to become the National Library of South Africa, which moved into a new building in Pretoria in 2008.

See also DHLOMO, HERBERT ISAAC ERNEST (1903–1956); VARLEY, DOUGLAS HAROLD (1911–2000).

SOVIET UNION. *See* RUSSIA.

SPAIN. During the Middle Ages, Spain was home to one of the largest libraries in the world, the library of Caliph al-Hakem II in Cordoba. The first **academic libraries** were established in the 13th century. The Royal Library (later the National Library) was founded in 1712. Until the 19th century, most libraries belonged to the clergy and the aristocracy, but in 1835, their collections were confiscated by the government. This action enriched university libraries and formed the nucleus of the first **public libraries**, which were created in provincial capitals. The first library training program, the Higher School of Diplomatics, was established in 1856. The first professional library organization, the Faculty of Archivists, Librarians, and Antiquarians, was created by the government in 1858 to manage and preserve the resources in public libraries that were under state control.

These libraries were mostly archival and for scholarly use. Attempts to create a system of popular libraries met with limited success until the 1930s, when steps were taken to expand the number of public libraries and supply them with books. Library development was halted during the Spanish Civil War, but 1947 saw the creation of the National Reading Service to promote reading among the general public. Public libraries were controlled by the National Reading Service until the government was decentralized in 1978. At that time, the majority of public libraries were inadequately staffed and equipped and had collections that, although of historical significance, were not of interest to the reading public.

Higher education reforms in the 1980s spurred the modernization of university libraries, including **automation**, updated facilities, additional and more qualified staff, and new information technology. In the 1990s, new public libraries were built and a number of existing public libraries were renovated. In 2001, the Spanish Ministry of Culture launched its Plan to Promote Reading, which allocated funds to public libraries in order to update collections, expand public reading areas, and provide free Internet access. Several **school library** development projects were also initiated.

Spain has a number of professional library organizations. The Spanish Federation of Associations of Archivists, Librarians, Archaeologists, Museologists and Documentalists/Federación Española de Asociaciones des Archiveros, Bibliotecarios, Archeólogos, Museólogos y Documentalistas (ANABAD) has been in existence since 1949. Fourteen library associations make up the Federation of Spanish Societies of Archives, Libraries, **Documentation** and Museology/Federación Española de Sociedades de Archivística, Biblioteconomía, Documentación y Museística (FESABID), founded in 1988. The most important academic and research library network, the Spanish Academic Libraries Network (REBIUN), was created in 1988. The public library network, Bibliographic Registry for Spanish Public Libraries (REBECA), was created in 1994.

See also MOLINER, MARÍA (1900–1981).

SPECIAL LIBRARIES ASSOCIATION (SLA). SLA is the second largest library association in the **United States** and serves a global membership. The idea of an organization of special libraries began in 1909 with Sarah B. Ball of the Business Branch of the Free **Public Library** in Newark, New Jersey, and Anna B. Sears, librarian at the Merchants Association in New York, who had been exploring closer cooperation between their libraries and other specialized libraries in the region. The SLA was formally organized at the 1909 **American Library Association (ALA)** Annual Conference following an address presented by Free Public Library of Newark's chief librarian, **John Cotton Dana**, who had created the Business Branch in Newark in 1904. The first annual meeting of the SLA was held in November of that year, with Dana presiding as president. In 2013, SLA had more than 10,000 members worldwide.

See also LIBRARY AWARENESS PROGRAM.

SPOFFORD, AINSWORTH RAND (1825–1908). Ainsworth Rand Spofford, the sixth librarian of Congress, was born in Gilmanton, New Hampshire, on September 12, 1825. He worked as a bookseller, publisher, and newspaper man in Cincinnati, Ohio. A trip to Washington, D.C., in 1861 to report on the inauguration of President Abraham Lincoln led to his career at the **Library of Congress (LC)**, first as assistant to John G. Stephenson and then as librarian of Congress starting in 1864. He believed the LC should be the national library and persuaded Congress to approve an expansion of the collection, most notably through the **copyright** law of 1870, which established **legal deposit**. In 1871, Spofford began his appeals to Congress for a new and separate building, which finally opened its doors in 1897. By that time, Spofford had already stepped down as librarian of Congress, but he stayed on as assistant librarian to his immediate successor, John Russell Young, and then to **Herbert Putnam**, who was appointed in 1899. Through Spofford's efforts, the LC was transformed from a legislative reference collection into the largest library in the **United States**.

See also THE FICTION QUESTION; *PUBLIC LIBRARIES IN THE UNITED STATES OF AMERICA.*

STEARNS, LUTIE EUGENIA (1866–1943). Lutie Eugenia Stearns was born on September 13, 1866, in Stoughton, Massachusetts. Her family moved to Milwaukee, Wisconsin, and she graduated from the Milwaukee State Normal School in 1886. After teaching for two years in Milwaukee, she joined the staff of the Milwaukee **Public Library**. In 1895, she helped to found the Wisconsin Free Library Commission, and in 1897, she became the organizer of the commission's traveling libraries, which were small, rotating collections intended to provide reading material to people living in rural areas. Stearns traveled throughout the state, lecturing and enlisting support for the traveling libraries, which eventually numbered around 1,400. She also helped Wisconsin communities apply for **Carnegie** grants to establish permanent libraries. She resigned from the Free Library Commission in 1914 to devote her time to lecturing and writing, and she became a leader in the women's suffrage movement and in the formation of women's clubs, both in Wisconsin and throughout the nation.

See also UNITED STATES; WOMEN IN LIBRARIANSHIP.

STIRLING, MATTHEW MILLER (1889–1965). Matthew Miller Stirling was born in Scotland but lived in **South Africa** from 1906 onward. While working as the town librarian at Germiston, a small town near Johannesburg, he requested that the **Carnegie Corporation of New York** send experts to investigate libraries in South Africa and to propose a system of **public library** service based on the American system. The resulting 1928 report is considered to be the start of modern South African librarianship. As administrator of the fund set up by the Carnegie Corporation for the creation of the Non-European Library Service, he became known for his promotion of reading facilities for black South Africans. He also did pioneering work in promoting school and rural library services. In 1931, Stirling was appointed head of the State Library in Pretoria, where he established many of the functions of a national central library and where he continued to spearhead library development. He served as the secretary of the South African Library Association from 1930 to 1942.

SWEDEN. The National Library of Sweden had its beginnings as the royal library in the 15th century, and the first university libraries date back to the 1600s. The first popular libraries were parish libraries organized in the 1800s. These were followed by workers' libraries and study circle libraries founded and supported by the labor and temperance movements. In 1905, a government resolution on state aid to **public libraries** was passed, although the understanding was that these libraries would serve the lower classes. The greatest promoter of state support for public libraries was **Valfrid Palmgren**. In 1907, she traveled to the **United States** to investigate public libraries, and the government then appointed her to survey public libraries in Sweden. Her report, published in 1911, recommended that public libraries should be a public service governed by local authorities and should serve the entire population, not just the lower classes. The Public Libraries Act of 1912 created a state authority responsible for inspection, library training courses, a book purchasing catalog, and subsidies to the study circle libraries, most of which eventually merged with municipal library systems. The Swedish Library Association/Sverige Allmänna Biblioteksförening (SAB) was founded 1915 and played an active role in development of the Swedish **classification** scheme in the 1920s. The current Swedish Library Association is the result of a merger in 2000 between the SAB and an association that was founded in 1921 and focused on research libraries.

The Swedish State Library School was started in Stockholm in 1926 and continued until 1972. The Stockholm Public Library maintained its own library school from 1948 to 1977. A university-level school of librarianship (now the Swedish School of Library and **Information Science**) was established in Borås in 1972, and in 1977, it became part of the University of Borås. In the general university reform of 1993, library and information science was established as an academic discipline, training programs were started at other institutions, and a master's degree was introduced. In the interest of international cooperation, The National Library announced in 2008 that it would transition from the SAB classification system to the **Dewey Decimal Classification (DDC)**, and by 2011, most Swedish university libraries had followed its lead.

See also SCANDIA PLAN.

T

TAUBE, MORTIMER (1910–1965). Mortimer Taube, a pioneer in modern methods of information retrieval, was born in Jersey City, New Jersey, on December 6, 1910. He graduated from the University of Chicago in 1933 and in 1935 was awarded a PhD from the University of California, where he also received a certificate of librarianship. After working in several **academic libraries**, he joined the staff of the **Library of Congress (LC)** in 1944 and became the head of the Science and Technology Project. He was deputy director of the Technical Information Section of the Atomic Energy Commission from 1949 to 1952. While in these positions, he developed ideas about new ways to organize scientific information so that it could be handled by machines, and his unpublished 1951 paper "Coordinate Indexing of Scientific Fields" is considered a landmark in the history of **information science**. In 1952, Taube founded **Documentation**, Incorporated, which received the first contract to provide information services to the National Aeronautics and Space Administration (NASA).

TURKEY. Turkey's library tradition is a long one, dating back to ancient times. The library at Pergamon, founded during the second century BCE when what is now Turkey was part of the Greek-speaking world, was said to rival the **Alexandrian Library**, and it became a center of learning during the Middle Ages. Most libraries of the Islamic period, which began in the 15th century, were private or were established as endowments associated with religious institutions, such as mosques. The first independent library was opened in 1678. Some libraries had sizeable staffs and well-organized collections of manuscripts. Printing appeared in Turkey in 1729, but printed books did not make their way into the endowed libraries. Reforms during the 19th century introduced institutions that were based on Western models, and the government established and maintained new libraries containing foreign-language printed books and Turkish translations. The old endowed libraries continued to exist, but many smaller collections were transferred to the Süleymaniye Library in Istanbul, which now has the world's largest collection of Islamic manuscripts. With its priceless heritage of hundreds of thousands of manuscripts held in libraries and museums, Turkey has a tradition of librarianship based on preservation.

After the establishment of the Republic of Turkey in 1923, the government promoted a more secularized and Westernized culture, including a switch from the Arabic alphabet to a modified Latin alphabet. To increase literacy, community centers called *halkevleri* (people's houses) and *halkodalari* (people's rooms) were opened in every town and were expected to have libraries where the public could find books printed in Roman characters rather than Ottoman script. Although they were closed in 1951, these centers helped lay the foundation for the modern **public library** system. Modern Turkish higher education began with the opening of Istanbul University in 1933. Fehmi Edhem Karatay, who had studied at the **École nationale de chartes** and the **Paris Library School**, was appointed director of the Istanbul University Library and established training courses for practicing librarians. **Adnan Ötüken**, who had been sent to study librarianship in **Germany** in the 1930s and later founded and directed the Turkish National Library, offered courses at Ankara University from 1942 to 1952.

The first full-fledged library school, not only in Turkey but in the Near and Middle East, was the Institute of Librarianship at Ankara University. The establishment of this school, as well as the founding of the Turkish Librarians' Association in 1949, marked the beginning of modern Turkish librarianship. The second **library science** department opened at Istanbul University in 1963, and by 2010, there were seven Turkish universities with what later came to be called departments of information and document management. The University and Research Librarians Association was founded in 1997. The Anatolian University Libraries Consortium (ANKOS) was established with 12 members in 2000, and by 2010, it had more than 100 members. Public libraries, which had previously been financed by the Turkish government, became the responsibility of local authorities in 2010.

U

UNDERGRADUATE LIBRARIES. Until the second half of the 19th century, access to **academic libraries** by lower classmen was restricted. In response, many college literary societies organized collections of their own. As policies were liberalized, some academic libraries began to set aside sections or rooms for undergraduate use. The first library built specifically for undergraduates was Harvard University's Lamont Library, which opened in 1949. The second, the undergraduate library at the University of Michigan, opened in 1958. Financial pressures eventually brought the construction of stand-alone undergraduate libraries to an end.

UNIONIZATION. The history of librarians and unions in the **United States** dates back to 1914, when **Library of Congress (LC)** employees joined the Federal Labor Union. The first **public library** union, the New York Public Library Employees Union, was granted a charter as Local Number 15590 by the American Federation of Labor on May 5, 1917. The goal of this early union included better salaries, opportunities for promotion, and civil service status for the predominantly female workforce. The union identified with the working classes and was opposed to the professionalization of librarianship as being elitist. Later, as professionalization advanced, many librarians rejected the idea of union membership on the grounds that professionals did not unionize.

The growth of unions slowed in the 1920s, and all of the early public library unions were disbanded. A new wave of unionization in the 1930s and 1940s brought library unions to a number of major metropolitan areas, including Atlanta, Boston, Cleveland, and Detroit. Chicago Public Library staff, whose attempt to organize in the 1920s had been blocked by the library administration, obtained a charter for Local 88 of the new State, County, and Municipal Employees of America Union by the end of 1937. The Library Unions Round Table was organized at the **American Library Association (ALA)** Annual Conference in Kansas City, Missouri, in 1938 to coordinate the activities of existing unions of library workers and to assist in the organization of new library unions. Ten years later, there were about 15 library unions in the United States and **Canada**, represented either by the American Federation of State, County, and Municipal Employees or the United Public Workers.

Initially, the union movement was almost entirely a public library movement. The Library Chapter of the University Federation of Teachers, organized at University of California, Berkeley, in 1965, was the first formation of a new library union in the years following World War II. The 1960s saw the growth of unions or collective bargaining organizations at the Los Angeles Public Library, the Queensborough Public Library, and others. **School** librarians also unionized in the 1960s, along with elementary and secondary school teachers, and many **academic** librarians were made part of faculty unions. To stem the tide of unionization, some ALA members pressured the association to take on a collective bargaining role. Instead, ALA adopted an official position in 1980 that recognized the principle of collective bargaining but that affirmed freedom of choice related to organizing and bargaining activities. In 2010, 23.7 percent of librarians in the United States were union members.

UNITED NATIONS EDUCATIONAL, SCIENTIFIC AND CULTURAL ORGANIZATION (UNESCO). Founded in 1945 to promote peace through dialogue and mutual understanding, UNESCO has contributed to the development of **documentation**, library, and archives services throughout the world. Initially, it focused on assistance to member states who were rebuilding their libraries after World War II, but beginning in the 1950s, its emphasis shifted to libraries in developing nations. UNESCO sponsored library seminars in **Africa**, **Asia**, **Latin America**, and several **Arab countries**; sent senior librarians as consultants to developing countries; and played a major role in the establishment of library schools. Starting in the 1970s, UNESCO gradually turned its attention away from libraries and toward broader issues related to information and knowledge. Recently, UNESCO has developed programs for expanding the pool of qualified information literacy trainers worldwide and for preserving documentary and **digital** heritage. UNESCO has worked in close cooperation with the **International Federation of Library Associations and Institutions (IFLA)** since 1947 and has formally endorsed key IFLA documents such as the **School Library** Manifesto (1999) and the Internet Manifesto (2003).

See also AUTOMATION; CENSORSHIP; CHILDREN'S LIBRARY SERVICE; CARIBBEAN; INDIA; INTERNATIONAL ASSOCIATION OF MUSIC LIBRARIES, ARCHIVES AND DOCUMENTATION CENTRES (IAML); INTERNATIONAL CONFERENCE ON CATALOGING PRINCIPLES; INTERNATIONAL LIBRARIANSHIP; INTERNATIONAL

SEMINAR ON THE DEVELOPMENT OF PUBLIC LIBRARIES IN AFRI-
CA; PENNA, CARLOS VICTOR (1911–1998); PUBLIC LIBRARIES;
UNIVERSAL BIBLIOGRAPHIC CONTROL (UBC).

UNITED STATES. The idea that libraries should make information and
resources widely available is a uniquely American contribution to the history
of librarianship. This notion stands in contrast to the tradition of preserving
materials for use by the scholarly elite.

The Harvard College Library, established in 1638, was the first library in
the American colonies. Samuel Stoddard, the first American **academic** librarian, was appointed in 1667 as the library keeper at Harvard, and he
administered the first set of library regulations in the colonies. College libraries were small, theology oriented, and relied chiefly on donations. In 1732,
the College of William and Mary became the first college library recorded as
being authorized to buy books. The first printed library **catalog** in America
was prepared at Harvard in 1723 by librarian Joshua Gee. Another early type
of library was the parish library. **Thomas Bray**, an English clergyman, promoted a scheme to establish parish libraries in order to lend religious books,
and more than 30 such libraries had been established in Maryland and other
colonies by 1699.

Sunday **school libraries** began to be established in the 1820s. New York
State became a pioneer in school district libraries when in 1835 it allowed
school districts to use tax monies to set up and maintain libraries, many of
which were open to the public. Most of the other libraries in the United States
were **social libraries**, formed by societies that were organized to acquire
collections for use by their own members, or for use by persons of a particular age, gender, interest, or vocation. Benjamin Franklin helped found what is
considered to be the first social library in America, the **Library Company of
Philadelphia** (1731), and similar libraries were opened in other cities: the
Redwood Library in Newport, Rhode Island, named after Quaker shipping
magnate Abraham Redwood (1747); the Charleston Library Society (1748);
the Providence Library Company (1753); and the New York Society Library
(1754). In the 19th century, social libraries expanded beyond their New
England and midatlantic base and included mercantile libraries, apprentices'
libraries, debating and literary society libraries, and ladies' club libraries, for
example. In addition, a small but growing number of free libraries were
supported by taxes levied by individual towns.

The **Library of Congress (LC)**, which functions as the national library of
the United States, was established in 1800. During the next 75 years, a
number of developments took place that caused libraries to increase in number and complexity and spurred the consequent rise of librarianship as a
profession. State libraries were formed, beginning with the Pennsylvania
State Library in 1816, and every state had a library located in its capital by

1876. The Morrill Land Grant Colleges Act, signed by President Abraham Lincoln in 1862, made a major contribution to the development of colleges and universities. The first national **librarians' conference** took place in New York City in 1853. **Boston Public Library**, the first large, municipally supported, freely accessible **public library** in the United States, opened its doors in 1854.

After the Civil War, increased industrialization and immigration led to an interest in mass education. Libraries in large cities began to open branches and to develop services intended to reach out to immigrants and working people, although ethnic minorities, particularly **African Americans**, remained underserved or even excluded. Pioneering librarians such as **John Shaw Billings** and **Charles Coffin Jewett** applied themselves to problems related to organizing their growing library collections and making them more accessible, setting the stage for greater codification and standardization.

In 1876, the US Bureau of Education published *Public Libraries in the United States of America*, noting the existence of around 3,600 libraries described as public, including school and asylum libraries; college libraries; theological, medical, and law libraries; prison libraries; and Young Men's Christian Association (YMCA) libraries; as well as tax-supported town libraries. The year 1876 was a watershed in the history of American libraries and librarianship in general, because, in addition to the publication of the US Bureau of Education report, it saw the publication of **Charles Ammi Cutter**'s *Rules for a Printed Dictionary Catalog*, the launch of *American Library Journal*, and the founding of the **American Library Association (ALA)**. As part of a larger pattern of occupational professionalization, the formation of ALA lent American librarianship new recognition and momentum.

A number of philanthropists endowed public research libraries in the 19th century, among them John Jacob Astor and James Lenox in New York and Walter Loomis Newberry in Chicago (the Astor and Lenox Libraries were consolidated with the Tilden Trust in 1895 to become the New York Public Library). Other philanthropists, such as Enoch Pratt in Baltimore, donated free circulating libraries to their home towns. A major event in the history of American librarianship was the opening of 1,600 public library buildings that were funded by **Andrew Carnegie**. Carnegie's philanthropy was unique in both scale and effect, leading to unprecedented growth not only in the number of libraries per se but also in the number of libraries that were publicly supported, because his gifts required that municipalities provide the money for collections and staff. This expansion helped fuel the need for trained librarians. Library training had been largely a matter of learning on the job until **Melvil Dewey** opened the first library school, the Columbia **School of Library Economy**, in 1887.

The development of academic libraries in the 19th century was spurred by the shift away from a focus on the liberal arts and religion and toward a broader curriculum that included scientific, technical, and professional education. In addition, a new model of higher education (which first emerged in **Germany**) led to the introduction of research programs and graduate study. Johns Hopkins University, founded in 1876, led the way in incorporating research as the key function of a university. These changes brought about an increasing awareness of the library's importance in supporting scholarly investigation and also to an expansion of academic library collections and services to meet new demands from researchers.

The 1923 publication of the **Williamson report**, commissioned by the **Carnegie Corporation of New York**, marked the beginning of a profound change in the library profession. The report was deeply critical of the kind of practical training for library work that was offered by programs attached to vocational schools or public libraries and called instead for a library **education** program based on theoretical principles and located in a university. Following the publication of the report, ALA began accrediting library education programs. The first research-oriented library school, the **Graduate Library School (GLS)** of the University of Chicago, was established in 1928.

Despite the growth of libraries that had occurred in the late 19th and early 20th centuries, there was still room for improvement. Adequate public library service was available to less than half the population, and most rural areas had no service at all. In addition, areas with public library service had limited book resources and personnel. President Franklin D. Roosevelt's Works Progress Administration funded some rural library demonstration projects during the Depression, but it was not until federal funding became available after World War II that real expansion occurred. "National Plan for Public Library Service," published by the ALA Committee on Postwar Planning in 1948, helped bring about the passage of the Library Services Act (LSA) of 1956, intended to improve library service in rural areas. The Academic Facilities Act of 1963 funded construction of library buildings, and the Higher Education Act of 1965 granted funds to college libraries for acquisition and networking and to research libraries for collection development in areas of national importance. Almost all academic libraries experienced growth in the 1950s and 1960s. Whereas only 15 university libraries in the United States had collections of more than 1 million volumes in 1952, there were 58 such libraries by 1970. The Medical Library Assistance Act of 1965 enabled the **National Library of Medicine (NLM)** to initiate programs designed to assist the nation's medical libraries. The Elementary and Secondary Education Act of 1965 led to an increase in the number of libraries and full-time librarians in public schools. The **Library Services and Construction Act (LSCA)** of 1966 extended the scope of the LSA to include urban areas.

Libraries of all types benefited from legislation that provided local, state, regional, and interstate networks for the coordination of resources and services. However, federal funding for libraries began to decrease in the 1970s.

The National Commission on Libraries and **Information Science** (NCLIS) was established in 1970 with ALA support to advise the president and Congress as to the nation's library and information needs and to develop and implement relevant policies and plans. NCLIS published "Toward a National Program for Library and Information Services: Goals for Action" (1975), and held two White House Conferences on Library and Information Services (1979 and 1991). In 1996, the LSCA was replaced by the Library Services and Technology Act (LSTA), which marked a shift away from library construction and toward a greater emphasis on technology, primarily in public libraries. Also in 1996, federal programs to support libraries were moved from the Department of Education to the new Institute of Museum and Library Services, which incorporated NCLIS in 2008.

See also AMERICAN ASSOCIATION OF LAW LIBRARIES (AALL); AUTOMATION; ASSOCIATION FOR INFORMATION SCIENCE AND TECHNOLOGY (ASIS&T); CENSORSHIP; CHILDREN'S LIBRARY SERVICE; MEDICAL LIBRARY ASSOCIATION (MLA); MUSIC LIBRARY ASSOCIATION (MLA); NATIONAL AGRICULTURAL LIBRARY (NAL); ONLINE COMPUTER LIBRARY CENTER (OCLC); PROGRESSIVE LIBRARIANSHIP; PUBLIC LIBRARY INQUIRY; SPECIAL LIBRARIES ASSOCIATION (SLA); UNIONIZATION; WOMEN IN LIBRARIANSHIP; YOUNG ADULT (YA) LIBRARY SERVICE.

UNIVERSAL BIBLIOGRAPHIC CONTROL (UBC). UBC was a program of the **International Federation of Library Associations (IFLA)** relating to bibliographic standardization. The idea for the program had its origins in the **International Meeting of Cataloging Experts** held in **Denmark** in 1969. In 1974, IFLA adopted UBC as one of its core programs, with the goal of making available basic bibliographical information about all publications in all countries in an internationally acceptable form. UBC was also adopted by the **United Nations Educational, Cultural and Scientific Organization (UNESCO)** as a major policy objective. The UBC program (later renamed Universal Bibliographic Control and International **Machine-Readable Cataloging**, or UBCIM) was involved in creating standards for national bibliographies, developing **International Standard Bibliographic Description (ISBD)** for **cataloging**, developing and publishing the Universal MARC Format (UNIMARC) standard for the exchange of machine-readable records among national bibliographic agencies, and extending **Cataloging-in-Publication (CIP)** programs. UBCIM ceased as a core activity in 2003, and its activities were taken over by an alliance between IFLA and the **Conference of Directors of National Libraries (CDNL)**. The new group is called the IFLA-CDNL Alliance for Bibliographic Standards (ICABS).

UNIVERSAL DECIMAL CLASSIFICATION (UDC). In 1890, Henri La-Fontaine and **Paul Otlet** of the International Institute of **Bibliography** in Brussels conceived the idea of a universal bibliography on index cards of all recorded knowledge. They looked to the **Dewey Decimal Classification (DDC)** as the basis for the bibliography's structure but made modifications, such as expanded schedules and the inclusion of nonbook materials. The adapted scheme, called the UDC or Brussels **Classification**, was published in French from 1904 to 1907. Although the universal bibliography project was abandoned in the 1930s, the development of the UDC as a classification system continued. Thanks in part to a policy that gave permission to organizations in each county or language area to act as publishers, the UDC has been translated in whole or in part into 40 languages. It is the dominant classification system in Eastern Europe and the former **Soviet Union**, as well as some countries in **Africa** and **Asia**. The UDC Consortium maintains and distributes the UDC and supports its development.

See also DOCUMENTATION; EUROPE, CENTRAL AND EASTERN.

V

VARLEY, DOUGLAS HAROLD (1911–2000). Douglas Harold Varley, a leader in **South African** librarianship, was born in London, England, and attended Oxford University. After graduating from the University College of London's School of Archives and Library Studies, he worked as a librarian in **Great Britain** until he was appointed chief librarian of the South African Public Library in Cape Town in 1938. The library operated as both a subscription lending library and a national research library. Varley instituted a number of reforms, including the extension of library services to rural areas. He also played a role in founding the first **academic library** training program in South Africa—the School of Librarianship at the University of Cape Town—in 1939. Varley was a strong advocate for the establishment of a free **public library** system as well as a state-supported national reference library. In 1954, he oversaw the separation of these two functions of the South African Public Library, which resulted in the organization of the municipally funded Cape Town Public Library and the state-supported national library, the South African Library. He directed the South African Library until 1961, when government efforts to impose apartheid caused him to resign. After serving as librarian at the University College of Rhodesia and Nyasaland, he returned to England and directed the library at Liverpool University until his retirement in 1976.

VATICAN CATALOGING RULES. In 1928, the Vatican Library began to recatalog its collections. Up until that time, there had been separate **catalogs** for each of the library's collections, and each catalog had been compiled based on its own set of rules. Funds for a new general catalog were provided by the **Carnegie** Endowment for International Peace. **J. C. M. Hanson** and **Charles Martel** of the **Library of Congress (LC)** were among the experts who were sent to **Italy** to assist with the project in its initial phases. At first, use was made of the rules set out for Italian government libraries in 1922, which were somewhat altered in order to make them more compatible with the rules of the **American Library Association (ALA)**. However, it was soon determined that an entirely new set of rules was needed, and *Norme per* *il catalogo degli stampati* was published in 1931. Drawing from both the ALA rules and **Library of Congress Classification (LCC)**, the Vatican code was considered to be the most comprehensive and best-structured cataloging code of the time. The second edition was published in 1939, and the third and last edition was published in 1949. *Rules for the Catalog of Printed Books*, an English translation of the second edition, was published in the **United States** in 1949.

VICKERY, BRIAN CAMPBELL (1918–2009). Brian Campbell Vickery, who made important contributions to the development of **information science** in **Great Britain**, was born on September 11, 1918, in **Australia**. His family moved to England and he graduated from Oxford with a degree in chemistry. His involvement with information science began in the research laboratories of an explosives factory during World War II, and after the war, he continued his research career at Imperial Chemical Industries. He played a role in the formation of the **Classification Research Group (CRG)** in 1952. In the 1960s, he helped to set up Britain's National Lending Library for Science and Technology and served as its deputy director. Later posts included head of service at the University of Manchester Institute of Science and Technology and head of research activities for the **Association of Special Libraries and Information Bureaux (ASLIB)**. In 1973, he became the director of the School of Librarianship and Archive Studies at University College, London.

W

WAPLES, DOUGLAS (1893–1978). Douglas Waples was born in Philadelphia on March 3, 1893. He studied at Haverford College and Harvard University before receiving a PhD in Educational Psychology from the University of Pennsylvania. He was a member of the faculty of the Education Department at the University of Chicago when that university opened the **Graduate Library School (GLS)** in 1926. In 1928, he accepted a post in the new school as a professor of educational method. He was one of a group of GLS scholars who established a theoretical basis for **library science**. He pioneered research on the social effects of reading in works such as *What People Want to Read About* (1931) and *People and Print: Social Aspects of Reading in the Depression* (1938). His book *Investigating Library Problems* (1939) was one of the first works on library research methodology. Waples devoted the last few years of his career to communication studies. He retired in 1957.

WEST AFRICAN LIBRARY ASSOCIATION (WALA). The first library association in West **Africa**, WALA was founded in 1954, with members from Gambia, Ghana, Nigeria, and Sierra Leone. About 40 people attended the first meeting, which was held on September 25–26, 1954, in Lagos, Nigeria. In 1962, WALA split into separate organizations: the Nigerian Library Association and the Ghana Library Association.
  See also EAST AFRICAN LIBRARY ASSOCIATION (EALA); HARRIS, WILLIAM JOHN (1903–1980); INTERNATIONAL SEMINAR ON THE DEVELOPMENT OF PUBLIC LIBRARIES IN AFRICA.

WESTERN COLORED BRANCH OF THE LOUISVILLE FREE PUBLIC LIBRARY. In 1905, the Louisville (Kentucky) Free **Public Library** opened the first public library building for **African Americans** that was not attached to a black school and did not function independently of the main library system. Headed by **Thomas Fountain Blue**, the Western Colored Branch was housed at first in three rooms in a private residence but moved in

1908 to a new **Carnegie** building. The branch offered a complete range of services, including a **children's** department headed by Rachel D. Harris. It also developed the first library training program for African Americans.

WILLIAMSON, CHARLES C. (1877–1965). Charles Williamson was born in Salem, Ohio, on January 26, 1877. He studied economics at Western Reserve University, the University of Wisconsin, and Columbia University. In 1911, he was appointed head of the new Division of Economics and Sociology at the New York **Public Library** (NYPL). In 1914, he became the municipal **reference** librarian of New York City, but he returned to NYPL a few years later. On the strength of several articles he had written for *Library Journal* in 1918–1919, the **Carnegie Corporation of New York** commissioned him to study the institutions that were offering library training. His landmark 1921 report (published in 1923 as *Training for Library Service*) led to a shift from technical training to professional **education** in a university setting. In 1921, Williamson left NYPL and joined the staff of the **Rockefeller Foundation**. In 1926, he was appointed head of the libraries and director of the School of Library Service at Columbia University. He later carried out the merger of that school with the **New York State Library School**.
See also WILLIAMSON REPORT.

WILLIAMSON REPORT. Following a 1916 report by economist Alvin Johnson that revealed the poor training received by many of the people who were staffing the **Carnegie libraries**, the **Carnegie Corporation of New York** hired **Charles C. Williamson**, then working at the New York **Public Library**, to undertake a study of library **education** and library schools. Williamson conducted his survey from 1919 to 1921 and his report *Training for Library Service*, commonly known as the Williamson report, was published in 1923. Williamson found that library education was rudimentary and was preoccupied with the techniques and details of library work almost to the complete exclusion of underlying principles. Faculty were unprepared, and only about half the library school graduates had college degrees. Among his recommendations were a shift of library education into universities, the recruitment of more qualified students, and the creation of programs at the graduate level. He also recommended the creation of standards for library education and an **accreditation** process based on those standards. As a result of the Williamson report, the curriculum was revised, training in nonacademic settings such as public libraries came to an end, and the **American Library Association (ALA)** established a system of accrediting library schools.
See also WOMEN IN LIBRARIANSHIP.

WILSON, HALSEY WILLIAM (1868–1954). Founder of the H. W. Wilson Company, Wilson was born on May 12, 1868, in Wilmington, Vermont. In 1889, while attending the University of Minnesota, he and a fellow student set up a store in their dormitory room to deal in student textbooks and supplies. As the business grew, Wilson became aware of the need for an up-to-date source for locating books in print, and he conceived the idea of the *Cumulative Book Index*, a monthly listing of new books. The index first appeared in February 1898 and sold for $1 per issue. Other indexes followed, among them the *Readers' Guide to Periodical Literature* (1901) and *Book Review Digest* (1905). The *Children's Catalog*, the first of many library collection development tools, was first published in 1908. The H. W. Wilson Company was incorporated in 1903, and in 1913 Wilson sold the bookstore and moved his publishing operation to White Plains, New York. The company found a more permanent home in the Bronx starting in 1917. It was the world's largest **reference** publishing house by the time of Wilson's death.

WILSON, LOUIS ROUND (1876–1979). Academic library leader Louis Round Wilson began his career by serving as librarian of the small collection belonging to the Methodist church in his home town of Lenoir, North Carolina. He graduated from the University of North Carolina at Chapel Hill in 1899 and was appointed librarian in 1901. He remained there for more than 30 years, building the college library into a full-fledged university library. He made the case for a new main library building, which opened in 1929, and he also established the School of **Library Science**, which opened in 1931. Wilson was offered the opportunity to become the first dean of the **Graduate Library School (GLS)** at the University of Chicago, a post he finally accepted in 1932. As dean, he added courses in librarianship as a field for research, **school** librarianship, studies in adult reading, library administration, and more. He served as president of the **American Library Association (ALA)** from 1935 to 1936. Wilson returned to Chapel Hill and rejoined the faculty of the School of Library Science in 1942.

WINSOR, JUSTIN (1831–1897). Justin Winsor, considered to be the preeminent American librarian of his time, was born in Boston, Massachusetts, on January 2, 1831. He attended Harvard University, although he left in his senior year without graduating (his degree was given to him later). After studying in Europe for several years, he returned to Boston to pursue a writing career. In 1866, he was appointed to the Board of Trustees of the **Boston Public Library**, becoming its superintendent in 1868. Winsor developed a branch system, created a shelf list in card form, and instituted Sunday hours. Interference from the Boston City Council led to his resignation, and in 1877 he accepted a position as librarian at Harvard. There, he opened stacks to students and pioneered statistical analysis in library administration. Winsor was one of the founders of the **American Library Association (ALA)** and served as its president from 1876 to 1885 and again in 1897. Because of his stature as a librarian, he lent prestige and legitimacy to the fledgling organization.

See also INTERNATIONAL CONFERENCE OF LIBRARIANS, 1877; PUBLIC LIBRARIES; UNITED STATES.

WOMEN IN LIBRARIANSHIP. Women made up 20 percent of the library profession in 1870 and 11 percent of the attendees at the first **American Library Association (ALA)** conference in 1876. What some have referred to as the feminization of librarianship began soon after, abetted by a number of early library leaders. **Justin Winsor**, speaking at the **International Conference of Librarians** in London in 1877, noted that two-thirds of the librarians at the **Boston Public Library** were women and that women were a cheap source of labor. **Melvil Dewey** made a deliberate appeal to women to attend the Columbia **School of Library Economy**, and 17 of the 20 students who were enrolled when the school opened in 1887 were women. By 1920, women accounted for more than 88 percent of the 15,297 librarians listed in the **United States** census. Encouragement from male leaders, the lack of other opportunities for educated women, women's acceptance of low salaries, the match between library work and presumptions about a woman's proper sphere, the similarities between library work and housekeeping, even Melvil Dewey's charisma, have all been cited as reasons why women flooded into the field. Nevertheless, by 1920, only two of the 35 ALA presidents had been women, and only six of the 50 largest libraries had women as directors. Women were disproportionately limited to junior positions or to spheres such as **children's** services.

In the United States, the pattern of inequity was reinforced by the changes that took place in library **education** beginning in the 1920s. Women founded and directed eight of the 10 library schools in existence before 1910, but in 1923, **Charles C. Williamson**, author of the landmark **Williamson report** on library education, wrote that the preponderance of women faculty and students lessened librarianship's prestige. In order to attract more men, he recommended that library schools be attached to universities and that a clear distinction be made between routine clerical (that is, women's) work and professional work requiring extensive specialized knowledge. Part of the discussion regarding the need to recruit more men centered around the idea that women tended to leave the profession after a few years to get married and therefore could not be considered "career" librarians. The integration of library schools into universities was a setback for women, because higher education had traditionally been dominated by men.

Thanks in part to the higher education opportunities created by the Servicemen's Readjustment Act of 1944 (better known as the GI Bill), the number of men entering the profession began to increase. The percentage of men in the profession was still small compared to the percentage of women, but, as noted in the **Public Library Inquiry** in 1952, men had a much greater chance of reaching the top and getting there faster. By 1970, although 82 percent of librarians were women, 92 percent of the chief administrators in **academic libraries** with enrollments of 3,000 or more and 61 percent of chief administrators in **public libraries** serving populations of 100,000 or more were men. Eighty-one percent of the deans and directors of accredited US library schools were men. Women's average salary was $10,874, while that of men was $14,471. The situation was similar elsewhere. In **Great Britain**, although three-quarters of the students attending library school were women, no more than a half-dozen women were chief librarians. In **Canada** in the mid-1970s, male chief librarians typically earned $4,500 more than their female counterparts. Action regarding inequity in library employment was spurred by the feminist movement of the 1960s and 1970s. ALA's Task Force on the Status of Women in Librarianship, formed within the Social Responsibilities Round Table, met for the first time in 1970. ALA's Committee on the Status of Women in Librarianship was established in 1976.

The preponderance of women in librarianship has changed little since the first decades of the 20th century and it still hovers around 82 percent. There has been some improvement in the percentage of women in higher-level positions; in 1999, 57 percent of directors of academic libraries and 65 percent of directors of public libraries in the United States were women, although this is still lower than the percentage of women in the profession as a whole. In 2010, the wage gap in some areas of the profession had closed, although women's salaries still lagged behind men's overall. Beginning in the 1990s, studies pertaining to the concerns of male librarians added an extra dimension to discussions of gender bias in librarianship.

See also AHERN, MARY EILEEN (1860–1938); AVRAM, HENRIETTE D. (1919–2006); BAKER, AUGUSTA B. (1911–1998); BARKER, TOMMIE DORA (1888–1978); BATCHELDER, MILDRED L. (1901–1998); BELPRÉ, PURA (1899–1982); BOGLE, SARAH COMLY NORRIS (1870–1932); BRADSHAW, LILLIAN MOORE (1915–2010); BRIET, SUZANNE (1894–1989); CHÁVEZ CAMPOMANES, MARIA TERESA (1890–1981); COLWELL, EILEEN HILDA (1904–2002); DELANEY, SADIE PETERSON (1889–1958); EASTMAN, LINDA ANNE (1867–1963); EDWARDS, MARGARET ALEXANDER (1902–1988); ELMENDORF, THERESA WEST (1855–1932); FAIRCHILD, MARY SALOME CUTLER (1855–1921); FLEXNER, JENNIE MAAS (1882–1944); FLORENCE, VIRGINIA PROCTOR POWELL (1897–1991); GLEASON, ELIZA ATKINS (1909–2009); GREENE, BELLE DA COSTA (1879–1950); HENNE,

FRANCES E. (1906–1985); HEWINS, CAROLINE M. (1846–1926); JONES, CLARA STANTON (1913–2012); KRUPSKAYA, NADEZHA (1869–1939); KRUG, JUDITH FINGERET (1940–2009); MANN, MARGARET (1873–1960); MANRIQUE DE LARA, JUANA (1899–1983); MOLINER, MARÍA (1900–1981); MOORE, ANNE CARROLL (1871–1961); MUDGE, ISADORE GILBERT (1875–1957); OLCOTT, FRANCES JENKINS (1873–1963); PALMGREN, VALFRID (1877–1967); PLUMMER, MARY WRIGHT (1856–1916); POWER, EFFIE LOUISE (1873–1969); ROSE, ERNESTINE (1880–1961); SCOGGIN, MARGARET C. (1905–1968); SEARS, MINNIE EARL (1873–1933); SHARP, KATHARINE L. (1865–1914); SMITH, LILLIAN H. (1887–1983); STEARNS, LUTIE EUGENIA (1866–1943); WOOD, MARY ELIZABETH (1861–1931).

WOOD, MARY ELIZABETH (1861–1931). Mary Elizabeth Wood was born in Elba, New York, on August 22, 1861. Having worked as a librarian for several years, she journeyed to Wuchang, **China**, in 1899, where her brother was serving as a missionary, and she accepted an appointment as a teacher of English at Episcopalian-operated Boone Preparatory School and College. In 1901, she began soliciting donations of books from the **United States** to set up a library for the school. In 1906, she traveled to the United States to solicit more donations and to raise funds for the Boone College Library, which opened in 1910. Recognizing the need for trained librarians, Wood arranged for two Boone graduates to study modern library practices in the United States. Wood herself was a student at the **Pratt Institute** Library School in 1908 and at the School of **Library Science**, Simmons College, from 1918 to 1919. The **Boone Library School** opened in 1920 with an American-style curriculum. In the years that followed, Wood made several more trips to the United States to promote the school and the library movement in China. She was instrumental in getting Congress to resolve that some of the indemnities that were paid to foreign embassies as part of a settlement following the Boxer Rebellion would be used to introduce a modern system of **public libraries** in China. Wood is remembered as one of the founders of modern Chinese librarianship.

See also SENG, SAMUEL T. Y. (1883–1976); WOMEN IN LIBRARIANSHIP.

WORLD'S COLUMBIAN EXPOSITION. The **American Library Association (ALA)** participated in the World's Columbian Exposition, held in Chicago in 1893, by partnering with the **United States** Bureau of Education to create a library exhibit. A committee to begin planning for the exhibit had been formed in 1890. Located in the space assigned to the Bureau, the exhibit included displays on library architecture and comparative library methods.

Innovations such as the Rudolph Continuous Indexer were on view. In addition, there was a model library containing a collection of 5,000 of the "best books" for libraries, staffed by ALA members. Half the collection was classified by **Dewey Decimal Classification (DDC)** and the other half by Cutter's **Expansive Classification**, with the two halves separated by fiction and biography sections. A publicly accessible **dictionary catalog** served as a finding aid. A list of the titles in the collection, called "Catalog of 'A.L.A. Library,'" was later published by the US Bureau of Education and was widely circulated. The majority of visitors were ALA librarians and trustees from small libraries across America, who took the latest library techniques with them when they returned home. Through the World's Congress of Librarians, which was held to coincide with the Exposition, the model library helped spread American library ideas abroad.

WORLD'S CONGRESS OF LIBRARIANS, 1893. *See* WORLD'S COLUMBIAN EXPOSITION.

Y

YOUNG ADULT (YA) LIBRARY SERVICE. Although there is some disagreement within the library profession regarding the definition of "young adult," the Young Adult Library Services Association (YALSA) of the **American Library Association (ALA)** has set the limits as ages 12 to 18. The earliest example of a library intended for YAs may have been the Brooklyn Library for Youth, which was sponsored by the Apprentice Library Association of Brooklyn and opened in 1823. It was intended for boys older than 12; girls older than 12 were only allowed to use the library for one hour per week. YA librarianship had its roots in the 1910s and 1920s, sometimes evolving from the **school** departments established in a number of **public libraries** in the **United States** prior to World War I. Separate YA departments were established as demands from high school students increased.

Mabel Williams, who is generally credited as the first librarian to set up a YA program, was recruited by **Anne Carroll Moore** to work at the New York Public Library (NYPL) in 1916, and she became Moore's assistant in charge of work with schools in 1920. Williams presided over YA services at NYPL until she was succeeded by **Margaret Scoggin** in 1952. Scoggin had previously directed the library's Nathan Straus Branch, which opened in 1941 as a laboratory for work with young people. Jean Roos, another pioneer, set up the first separate YA room, the Robert Louis Stevenson Room at the Cleveland (Ohio) Public Library, in 1925. **Margaret Alexander Edwards** organized the YA department at the Enoch Pratt Free Library in 1932. The most influential leader in the formative years of YA services, Edwards placed great emphasis on developing teen readers through individual guidance.

NYPL's *Books for the Teen Age* first appeared in 1929. In 1930, the ALA Young People's Reading Round Table (precursor to YALSA) was organized, and ALA began publishing "Books for Young People" (later "Best Books for Young Adults") in 1930. By that time, separate services for young people had been set up in Atlanta, Brooklyn, Los Angeles, Nashville, Pittsburgh, and a number of other cities. *The Public Library Plans for the Teen-Age,* published in 1948 by ALA's Committee on Post-War Planning and the Young People's Reading Round Table, provided the first set of guidelines for YA services.

Following World War II, however, what has been called the golden age of library service to YAs began to fade, in part because it was so staff intensive. Whereas in 1939 the branch libraries of NYPL had 60 YA assistants, that number dropped significantly by 1946, and in 1953 the Nathan Straus Branch was closed. YA services saw a period of growth in the 1960s, followed by more contraction as budgets were cut in the following decades. A 1988 study revealed that, although 25 percent of library users were YA, 89 percent of public libraries did not have YA librarians. Customer-focused initiatives beginning in the 1990s led to a shift in emphasis to services identified as priorities by teens themselves: homework assistance and access to new information technologies and formats. Youth participation also became an important element in planning and developing programs and services intended for them. A renewed interest in teen spaces emerged when the Los Angeles Public Library opened TeenS'cape in 1994, which was followed by Teen Central at the Phoenix Public Library in 2001.

Early YA collections generally consisted of books culled from the adult shelves, but the development of YA services helped spark the growth of literature written specifically for teens. Adolescent literature began to receive more attention in Booklist, *School Library Journal*, and other review journals. *Voice of Youth Advocates* (*VOYA*), a journal dedicated to the needs of YA librarians, was founded in 1978. The Michael L. Prinz Award to honor literary excellence in YA was established in 2000.

In many countries outside the United States, YA library services are nonexistent. The **International Federation of Library Associations and Institutions (IFLA)** published *Guidelines for Library Service for Young Adults* in 1996 in order to provide an international framework for developing such services.

See also CHILDREN'S LIBRARY SERVICE.

Appendix 1

American Library Association Accredited Library and Information Studies Master's Programs from 1925 through the Present

The following table is a list of all library and information studies programs accredited by the American Library Association from 1925 to 2013, arranged by institution and including currently and formerly accredited programs:

Institution	Accreditation Period
Alabama, University of	1972/73–present
Alabama Agricultural and Mechanical University (discontinued 1981)	1973/74–August 1982
Alberta, University of	1968/69–present
Arizona, University of	1972/73–present
Atlanta University (see Clark Atlanta University)	1941/42–June 1988
Ball State University (discontinued August 1985)	1978/79–February 1987
Brigham Young University (discontinued August 1993)	1968/69–February 1995
British Columbia, University of	1961/62–present
California–Berkeley, University of	1924/25–May 1994
California–Los Angeles, University of	1960/61–present
Carnegie Institute of Technology (discontinued 1962)	1924/25–1962
Carnegie Library of Atlanta (transferred to Emory University 1930)	1924/25–1930
Case Western Reserve University (discontinued 1986)	1924/25–December 1987
Catholic University of America	1946/47–present
Chicago, University of (discontinued 1990)	1932/33–December 1991

Clarion University of Pennsylvania	1974/75–present
Clark Atlanta University (discontinued 2005)	1941/42–May 2005
Columbia University (see also New York Public Library and New York State; discontinued June 1992)	1925/26–December 1993
Dalhousie University	1970/71–present
Denver, University of	1932/33–February 1987; 2003/04–present
Dominican University (formerly Rosary College)	1936/37–February 1957; 1960/61–present
Drexel University	1924/25–present
Emory University (see also Carnegie Library of Atlanta; discontinued August 1988)	1928/29–February 1990
Emporia State University	1930/31–February 1958; 1964/65–present
Florida State University	1951/52–present
Hampton Institute (discontinued 1939)	1926/27–1940
Hawaii, University of	1965/66–present
Illinois, University of	1924/25–present
Indiana University	1951/52–present
Iowa, University of	1969/70–present
Kent State University	1961/62–present
Kentucky, University of	1940/41–present
Long Island University	1969/70–present
Los Angeles Public Library (discontinued 1932)	1924/25–1933
Louisiana State University	1932/33–present
McGill University	1927/28–present
Maryland, University of	1965/66–present
Marywood College	1944/45–January 1956
Michigan, University of	1926/27–present
Minnesota, University of (discontinued June 1985)	1933/34–December 1986
Mississippi, University of (discontinued December 1984	Summer 1979–June 1986

Missouri–Columbia, University of	1967/68–present
Montreal, University of	1967/68–present
New Jersey College for Women (discontinued 1952)	1927/28–1953
New York–Albany, State University of	1930/31–February 1959; 1965/66–present
New York–Buffalo, State University of	1970/71–present
New York–Geneseo, State University of (discontinued August 1983)	1944/45–February 1959; 1966/67–February 1985
New York Public Library (consolidated with New York State Library School and transferred to Columbia University in 1926)	1924/25–1926
North Carolina Central University	1973/74–present
North Carolina–Chapel Hill, University of	1932/33–present
North Carolina College for Women (discontinued 1933)	1929/30–1934
North Carolina–Greensboro, University of	1980/81–present
North Texas, University of	1965/66–present
Northern Illinois, University of (discontinued May 1994)	1967/68–May 1994
Oklahoma, University of	1930/31–present
Oregon, University of (discontinued August 1978)	1966/67–January 1980
Our Lady of the Lake College	1941/42–January 1957
Peabody College for Teachers, George (merged with Vanderbilt University 1979; discontinued in August 1988)	1930/31–January 1990
Pittsburgh, University of	1962/63–present
Pratt Institute	1924/25–present
Puerto Rico, University of	1988/89–present
Queens College, City University of New York	1968/69–present
Rhode Island, University of	1969/70–present
Rutgers University	1954/55–present
St. Catherine University (formerly College of St. Catherine)	1929/30–February 1959; 2009/10–present

St. John's University	1974/75–present
St. Louis Library School (discontinued 1932)	1924/25–1933
San Jose State University	1967/68–present
Simmons College	1924/25–present
South Carolina, University of	1972/73–present
South Florida, University of	1973/74–present
Southern California, University of (discontinued 1986)	1936/37–December 1987
Southern Connecticut State University (withdrawn October 2013)	1970/71–December 2015
Southern Mississippi, University of	1978/79–present
Syracuse University	1928/29–present
Tennessee, University of	1972/73–present
Texas–Austin, University of	1951/52–present
Texas Woman's University	1936/37–present
Toronto, University of	1935/36–present
Valdosta State University	2006/07–present
Vanderbilt University (see Peabody; discontinued August 1988)	1974/75–February 1990
Washington, University of	1924/25–present
Wayne State University	1965/66–present
Western Michigan University (discontinued 1983)	1946/47–December 1984
Western Ontario, University of	1967/68–present
William and Mary, College of (discontinued 1948)	1936/37–1949
Wisconsin–Madison, University of	1924/25–present
Wisconsin–Milwaukee, University of	1974/75–present

Source: http://www.ala.org/accreditedprograms/directory/historicallist.

Appendix 2

Library Schools, Libraries, and Librarians Outside the United States

The numbers of library schools, libraries, and librarians vary greatly throughout the world. According to the *World Guide to Library, Archive and Information Science Education*, the countries listed below had the following numbers of library schools, libraries, and librarians as of 2007 (NA indicates that information was not available). Additional statistics are available at the OCLC website: http://www.oclc.org/global-library-statistics.en.html#.

Country	Library Schools	Libraries	Librarians
Albania	1	2,107	32
Algeria	3	764	58
Argentina	18	2,537	658
Australia	7	11,025	6,788
Austria	4	2,603	2,102
Azerbaijan	1	4,430	267
Bangladesh	1	217	61
Belarus	1	10,175	1,469
Belgium	12	1,157	3,704
Benin	1	125	43
Bolivia	3	549	18
Bosnia and Herzegovina	2	290	NA
Botswana	1	350	216
Brazil	43	22,545	220
Bulgaria	2	4,373	4,658
Cameroon	1	109	11
Canada	7	16,948	11,302
Chile	4	7,718	97
China	109	109,673	58,953

Colombia	5	1,942	17
Congo, Dem. Repub. of	2	141	NA
Costa Rica	2	619	76
Côte d'Ivoire	1	122	NA
Croatia	3	1,429	1,639
Cuba	3	5,661	2,533
Czech Republic	11	9,649	6,688
Denmark	1	2,210	3,394
Dominican Republic	1	554	3
Ecuador	4	1,662	2
Egypt	2	11,049	592
El Salvador	2	396	NA
Estonia	3	978	1,947
Ethiopia	1	386	15
Fiji	1	417	28
Finland	5	6,101	3,756
France	46	6,003	13,935
Gabon	1	85	2
Germany	19	11,418	15,967
Ghana	1	7,213	28
Greece	3	1,243	2,030
Guatemala	1	88	1
Guinea	1	139	NA
Holy See (Vatican City)	2	19	17
Honduras	1	511	22
Hong Kong	4	592	599
Hungary	13	5,484	10,717
Iceland	1	221	193
India	103	337,016	30,759
Indonesia	12	124,226	NA
Iran	9	8,480	627
Iraq	1	11,395	1,500

Ireland	1	1,630	939
Israel	4	3,531	2,194
Italy	77	12,403	13,628
Jamaica	1	1,156	258
Japan	11	45,824	47,090
Kazakhstan	14	10,951	8,823
Kenya	6	301	125
Korea, South	32	12,090	14,265
Kuwait	1	132	92
Kyrgyzstan	2	1,867	1,541
Latvia	1	1,942	3,331
Lebanon	2	642	88
Libya	1	41	NA
Lithuania	2	2,582	6,343
Macedonia	1	1,098	469
Malawi	1	96	85
Malaysia	3	10,175	542
Mali	1	506	16
Malta	1	141	13
Mauritius	1	113	29
Mexico	13	13,308	11,879
Moldova	1	2,898	1,714
Mongolia	1	829	333
Morocco	1	735	207
Namibia	1	1,097	115
Netherlands	9	768	4,598
New Zealand	2	2,749	1,559
Niger	1	13	NA
Nigeria	6	273	1,220
Norway	3	4,114	3,674
Pakistan	2	9,106	185
Palau	1	25	NA

Panama	2	739	NA
Papua New Guinea	1	185	1
Paraguay	1	285	137
Peru	3	2,644	88
Philippines	38	1,637	69
Poland	13	25,008	41,530
Portugal	5	1,520	2,722
Puerto Rico	2	845	384
Romania	1	11,791	15,691
Russia	45	113,984	144,123
Saudi Arabia	2	5,317	268
Senegal	1	66	98
Serbia	1	2,313	2,273
Singapore	1	424	351
Slovakia	1	8,281	1,944
Slovenia	1	1,182	1,864
South Africa	15	11,372	2,341
Spain	17	26,886	7,725
Sri Lanka	1	7,241	193
Sudan	1	4,851	NA
Sweden	7	4,590	4,534
Switzerland	11	2,422	3,114
Tanzania	2	221	1
Thailand	17	34,751	500
Tunisia	1	947	274
Turkey	4	19,631	14,693
Uganda	1	56	72
Ukraine	3	39,180	49,219
United Kingdom	18	8,438	21,286
Uruguay	1	373	223
Venezuela	2	924	222
Vietnam	5	23,962	674

Zambia	1	247	NA
Zimbabwe	1	174	12
Totals	**965**	**1,364,306**	**786,913**

Bibliography

CONTENTS

INTRODUCTION

For anyone wanting to research the history of librarianship, *American Library History: A Comprehensive Guide to the Literature*, by Michael H. Harris (Santa Barbara, CA: ABC-CLIO, 1989), is a good place to start. It identifies more than 3,000 articles, books, theses, and dissertations related to the development and function of American libraries. More recent publications are listed in "The Literature of American Library History," published biennially in *Information and Culture: A Journal of History*. "The Literature of American Library History" continues a series of literature reviews that began when Harris published "The Year's Work in American Library History" in *Journal of Library History* in 1968. These reviews appeared every year or every few years, compiled first by Harris and then by Harris and Donald G. Davis. Wayne A. Weigand took over as compiler in 1979, followed by Edward A. Goedeken in the 1990s. Since 1990, Goedeken has also compiled

"Bibliography of Writings on the History of Libraries, Librarianship, and Book Culture," which appears in each issue of the semi-annual newsletter of the American Library Association (ALA) Library History Round Table and also online at http://www.ala.org/lhrt/popularresources/libhistorybib/library-history. This bibliography is international in coverage and organizes its listings by geographic region. For materials on British library history published between 1962 and 1988, researchers can turn to the six volumes of *British Library History: Bibliography*, edited by Dennis F. Keeling (London: The Library Association, 1972–1991).

Although occasional articles on historical topics can be found in most of the journals devoted to library and information science, the major journal resource is *Information and Culture: A Journal of History*. This journal began life in 1966 as *The Journal of Library History*. Its title was changed in 1988 to *Libraries and Culture* and again in 2006 to *Libraries and the Cultural Record*. The current title, *Information and Culture: A Journal of History*, was adopted in 2012. The British counterpart is *Library and Information History*, which began publication in 1967 and was called *Library History* until 2009. It is the journal of the Library History Group of the Chartered Institute of Library and Information Professionals.

The major reference source in the history of librarianship is *Encyclopedia of Library History*, edited by Wayne A. Wiegand and Donald G. Davis (New York: Garland, 1984). David H. Stam's *International Dictionary of Library Histories* (Chicago: Fitzroy Dearborn Publishers, 2001) is notable both for its histories of individual libraries and its selection of thematic essays. General encyclopedias of library and information science can also be helpful to those researching the history of librarianship. The largest library and information science encyclopedia is *Encyclopedia of Library and Information Sciences* (Boca Raton, FL: CRC Press, 2010), the first edition of which was published in 73 volumes beginning in 1968. A smaller second edition was published in 2003, and a third edition was published in 2010. Neither the second nor third edition supersedes the first, which, although many of its entries are out of date, remains an important resource, both because it is far more comprehensive than the later editions and because of the historical background it provides. Historical perspective can also be found in the country profiles in the one-volume *ALA World Encyclopedia of Library and Information Services* (Chicago: American Library Association, 1993).

Biographical entries for librarians can be found in the *ALA World Encyclopedia of Library and Information Services*, and a few individual librarians are covered in the first edition of *Encyclopedia of Library and Information Sciences*. The major biographical reference source in library and information science is *Dictionary of American Library Biography* (Littleton, CO: Libraries Unlimited, 1978). Supplements published in 1990 and 2003 extend the coverage to librarians who died before 2000. Short entries on British librarians can be found in William Arthur Munford's *Who Was Who in British Librarianship, 1800–1985: A Dictionary of Dates with Notes* (London: Library Association, 1987). Munford's work is being updated at NewMunford (http://newmunford.wikispaces.com). Information on librarians from outside Great Britain and the United States can be difficult to find; some are given treatment in the *ALA World Encyclopedia of Library and Information Services*. A biographical encyclopedia with an international scope would be a welcome addition to the reference literature on librarianship.

The following bibliography is not exhaustive but seeks to provide an introduction to further reading in the historical development of librarianship as a profession worldwide. It consists of English-language reference works, journal articles, and monographs. For journal articles, the starting date is 1966, the year that *Journal of Library History* began publication. Some older monographs have been included, especially if they are classics.

REFERENCE TOOLS

Archives

American Library Association Archives at the University of Illinois Archives. http://archives.library.illinois.edu/ala/.

Bibliographies

Barr, Larry J., Haynes McMullen, and Steven G. Leach. *Libraries in American Periodicals before 1876: A Bibliography with Abstracts and an Index*. Jefferson, NC: McFarland, 1983.

Coleman, Sterling Joseph. *Librarianship and Information Science in the Islamic World, 1966–1999: An Annotated Bibliography*. Lanham, MD: Scarecrow Press, 2005.

Davis, Donald G., and John Mark Tucker. *American Library History: A Comprehensive Guide to the Literature*. Santa Barbara, CA: ABC-CLIO, 1989.

Harris, Michael H. "The Year's Work in American Library History." *Journal of Library History* 2, no. 4 (October 1968): 342–52.

Harris, Michael H., and Donald G. Davis. *American Library History: A Bibliography*. Austin: University of Texas Press, 1978.

Herring, Mark Youngblood. *Controversial Issues in Librarianship: An Annotated Bibliography, 1960–1984*. New York: Garland Publishing, 1987.

Huq, A. M. Abdul, and Mohammed M. Aman. *Librarianship and the Third World: An Annotated Bibliography of Selected Literature on Developing Nations, 1960–1975*. New York: Garland Publishing, 1977.

Jordan, Anne Harwell, Melbourne Jordan, and H. G. T. Cannons. *Cannons' Bibliography of Library Economy, 1876–1920: An Author Index with Citations*. Metuchen, NJ: Scarecrow Press, 1976.

Keeling, Dennis F., ed. *British Library History: Bibliography*. London: The Library Association, 1972–1991.

Young, Arthur P., and Michael H. Harris. *American Library History: A Bibliography of Dissertations and Theses*. Metuchen, NJ: Scarecrow Press, 1998.

Chronologies

Wilhite, Jeffrey M. A. *Chronology of Librarianship, 1960–2000*. Lanham, MD: Scarecrow Press, 2009.

Dictionaries, Encyclopedias, and Handbooks

Bates, Marcia J., and Mary Niles Maack. *Encyclopedia of Library and Information Sciences*, 3rd ed. Boca Raton, FL: CRC Press, 2010.

Bobinski, George S., Jesse Hauk Shera, and Bohdan S. Wynar. *Dictionary of American Library Biography*. Littleton, CO: Libraries Unlimited, 1978.

Davis, Donald G., Jr., ed. *Dictionary of American Library Biography, Second Supplement*. Westport, CT: Libraries Unlimited, 2003.

Drake, Miriam A. *Encyclopedia of Library and Information Science*, 2nd ed. New York: Marcel Dekker, 2003.

———. *Encyclopedia of Library and Information Science, Second Edition, First Update Supplement*. Boca Raton, FL: Taylor and Francis, 2005.

Feather, John, and R. P. Sturges. *International Encyclopedia of Information and Library Science*, 2nd ed. London: Routledge, 2003.

Harris, Michael H. *A Guide to Research in American Library History*. Metuchen, NJ: Scarecrow Press, 1974.

Kent, Allen, Harold Lancour, William Z. Nasri, and Jay Elwood Daily. *Encyclopedia of Library and Information Science*. New York: M. Dekker, 1968–2003.

Miller, Marilyn L., ed. *Pioneers and Leaders in Library Services to Youth: A Biographical Dictionary*. Westport, CT: Libraries Unlimited, 2003.

Munford, William Arthur. *Who Was Who in British Librarianship, 1800–1985: A Dictionary of Dates with Notes*. London: Library Association, 1987.

Stam, David H. *International Dictionary of Library Histories*. Chicago: Fitz-roy Dearborn Publishers, 2001.

Wedgeworth, Robert, ed. *ALA World Encyclopedia of Library and Information Services*, 3rd ed. Chicago: American Library Association, 1993.

Wiegand, Wayne A., ed. *Supplement to the Dictionary of American Library Biography*. Englewood, CO: Libraries Unlimited, 1990.

Wiegand, Wayne A., and Donald G. Davis. *Encyclopedia of Library History*. New York: Garland, 1984.

Directories

Cummings, Cynthia S., ed. *A Biographical-bibliographical Directory of Women Librarians*. Madison: University of Wisconsin, Madison Library School Women's Group, 1976.

Meinhold, Alexandra, ed. *World Guide to Library, Archive and Information Science Associations*, 3rd ed. Berlin/Munich: De Gruyter Saur, 2010.

Websites

American Library Association Library History Round Table. www.ala.org/lhrt.

Chartered Institute of Library and Information Professionals Library and Information History Group. www.cilip.org.uk/about/special-interest-groups/library-and-information-history-group.

The Library History Buff. www.libraryhistorybuff.com.

HISTORICAL STUDIES

General

Battles, Matthew. *Library: An Unquiet History*. New York: Norton, 2003.

Bennett, George E. *Librarians in Search of Science and Identity: The Elusive Profession*. Metuchen, NJ: Scarecrow Press, 1988.

Blair, Ann. *Too Much to Know: Managing Scholarly Information Before the Modern Age*. New Haven, CT: Yale University Press, 2010.

Bobinski, George S. *Libraries and Librarianship: Sixty Years of Challenge and Change, 1945–2005*. Lanham, MD: Scarecrow Press, 2007.

Buschman, John E., and Gloria J. Leckie, eds. *Library as Place: History, Community, and Culture*. Westport, CT: Libraries Unlimited, 2007.

Ellsworth, Dianne J., and Norman D. Stevens, eds. *Landmarks of Library Literature, 1876–1976*. Metuchen, NJ: Scarecrow Press, 1976.

Given, Lisa M., and Lianne McTavish. "What's Old Is New Again: The Reconvergence of Libraries, Archives, and Museums in the Digital Age." *Library Quarterly* 80, no. 1 (January 2010): 7–32.

Harris, Michael H. *History of Libraries in the Western World*, 4th ed. Metuchen, NJ: Scarecrow Press, 1995.

Harris, Michael H., and Stan A. Hannah. *Into the Future: The Foundations of Library and Information Services in the Post-Industrial Era*. Norwood, NJ: Ablex Publishing Corporation, 1993.

Jackson, Sidney L. *Libraries and Librarianship in the West: A Brief History*. New York: McGraw-Hill, 1974.

Lerner, Frederick Andrew. *The Story of Libraries: From the Invention of Writing to the Computer Age*. New York: Continuum, 1998.

Library History Seminar and Donald G. Davis. *Libraries and Culture: Proceedings of Library History Seminar VI, 19–22 March 1980, Austin, Texas*. Austin: University of Texas Press, 1981.

———. *Libraries and Philanthropy: Proceedings of Library History Seminar IX, 30 March–1 April 1995, University of Alabama, Tuscaloosa*. Austin: Graduate School of Library and Information Science, University of Texas at Austin, 1996.

———. *Libraries and Culture: Reading and Libraries: Library History Seminar VIII, Indiana University, Bloomington, 9–11 May 1990*. Austin: University of Texas Press, 1991.

———. *Libraries, Books and Culture: Proceedings of Library History Seminar VII, 6–8 March 1985, Chapel Hill, North Carolina*. Austin: Graduate School of Library and Information Science, University of Texas at Austin, 1986.

Library History Seminar and Harold Goldstein. *Milestones to the Present: Papers from Library History Seminar V*. Syracuse, NY: Gaylord Professional Publications, 1978.

Litwin, Rory. *Library Daylight: Tracings of Modern Librarianship, 1874–1922*. Duluth, MN: Library Juice Press, 2006.

Low, Kathleen. *Casanova Was a Librarian: A Light-Hearted Look at the Profession*. Jefferson, NC: McFarland and Company, 2007.

Rayward, W. Boyd, ed. "Pioneers in Library and Information Science." *Library Trends* 52, no. 4 (Spring 2004): entire issue.

Rovelstad, Mathilde V. "Two Seventeenth-Century Library Handbooks, Two Different Library Theories." *Libraries and Culture* 35, no. 4 (Fall 2000): 540–56.

Rubin, Richard E. *Foundations of Library and Information Science*. New York: Neal-Schuman, 2010.

Staikos, K. *The History of the Library in Western Civilization*. New Castle, DE: Oak Knoll Press, 2004.

Tevis, Ray, and Brenda Tevis. *The Image of Librarians in Cinema, 1917–1999*. Jefferson, NC: McFarland and Company, 2005.

Thompson, James. *A History of the Principles of Librarianship*. London: C. Bingley, 1977.

Tolzmann, Don Heinrich, Alfred Hessel, and Reuben Peiss. *The Memory of Mankind: The Story of Libraries since the Dawn of History*. New Castle, DE: Oak Knoll Press, 2001.

Valentine, Patrick M. *A Social History of Books and Libraries from Cuneiform to Bytes*. Lanham, MD: Scarecrow Press, 2012.

Wertheimer, Andrew B., and Donald G. Davis, Jr., eds. *Library History Research in America: Essays Commemorating the Fiftieth Anniversary of the Library History Round Table*. Washington, DC: Library of Congress, Center for the Book, 2000.

Wiegand, Wayne A. "Libraries and the Invention of Information." In *A Companion to the History of the Book*, ed. Simon Eliot and Jonathan Rose. Malden, MA: Blackwell Publishing, 2007.

Winter, Michael F. *The Culture and Control of Expertise: Toward a Sociological Understanding of Librarianship*. New York: Greenwood Press, 1988.

———. *The Professionalization of Librarianship*. Urbana: University of Illinois Graduate School of Library and Information Science, 1983.

Wright, Alex. *Glut: Mastering Information through the Ages*. Washington, DC: Joseph Henry Press, 2007.

By Country or Region

Africa

Aguolu, C. C. "Library Associations in West Africa and the Concept of a Profession." *International Library Review* 8, no. 1 (1976): 23–31.

Amadi, Adolphe O. "The Emergence of a Library Tradition in Pre- and Postcolonial Africa." *International Library Review* 13, no. 1 (1981): 65–72.

Amaeshi, Basil. *Classical Readings in African Library Development*. Lanham, MD: Scarecrow Press, 2003.

Anafulu, Joseph C. "The Standing Conference of African University Libraries, 1964–1974." *International Library Review* 8, no. 4 (1976): 397–415.

Cram, Jennifer. "Colonialism and Libraries in Third World Africa." *Australian Library Journal* 42, no. 1 (February 1993): 13–20.

Laugesen, Amanda. "'An Inalienable Right to Read': UNESCO's Promotion of a Universal Culture of Reading and Public Libraries and Its Involvement in Africa, 1948–1968." *English in Africa* 35, no. 1 (2008): 67–88.

———. "The Role of External Aid in West African Library Development." *Library Quarterly* 56, no. 1 (January 1986): 1–16.

Matogo, W. K. "Public Library Trends in East Africa, 1945–1965." *International Library Review* 9, no. 1 (1977): 67–82.

Olden, Anthony. "'For Poor Nations a Library Service Is Vital': Establishing a National Public Library Service in Tanzania in the 1960s." *Library Quarterly* 75, no. 4 (October 2005): 421–45.

———. *Libraries in Africa: Pioneers, Policies, Problems.* Lanham, MD: Scarecrow Press, 1995.

Raseroka, H. K. "Changes in Public Libraries during the Last Twenty Years: An African Perspective." *Libri* 44, no. 2 (June 1994): 153–63.

Sturges, Paul. "The Poverty of Librarianship: An Historical Critique of Public Librarianship in Anglophone Africa." *Libri* 51, no. 1 (2001): 38–48.

Sturges, Paul, and Richard Neill. *The Quiet Struggle: Libraries and Information for Africa.* London: Mansell, 1990.

Arab Countries

al-Aufi, Ali Saif, and Peter Johan Lor. "Development of Arabic Library and Information Science." *Journal of Documentation* 68, no. 4 (2012): 460–91.

al-Sharif, Abdullah M. "The Development of Professional Library Education in the Arab World." *International Library Review* 13, no. 1 (1981): 87–101.

———. "The Factors Which Affect the Development of Librarianship and Library Education in the Arab Countries." *International Library Review* 11, no. 2 (1979): 245–57.

Ali, Syed Iftekar. "Arab League Educational, Cultural and Scientific Organization (ALECSO) and Its Contribution to Middle Eastern Libraries." *International Library Review* 17, no. 1 (1985): 67–75.

Alqudsi-Ghabra, T. "Librarianship in the Arab World." *International Library Review* 20, no. 2 (1988): 233–45.

Elayyan, Ribhi Mustafa. "The History of the Arabic-Islamic Libraries: 7th to 14th Centuries." *International Library Review* 22, no. 2 (June 1990): 119–35.

Green, Arnold H. "The History of Libraries in the Arab World: A Diffusionist Model." *Libraries and Culture* 23, no. 4 (Fall 1988): 454–73.

Pantelidis, Veronica S. *The Arab World: Libraries and Librarianship, 1960–1976: A Bibliography.* London: Mansell, 1979.

Argentina

Barber, Elsa E., Nicolas M. Tripaldi, and Silvia L. Pisano. "Individual Countries or Regions: Facts, Approaches, and Reflections on Classification in the History of Argentine Librarianship." *Historical Aspects of Cataloging and Classification* 35, nos. 3–4 (July 2003): 79–105.
Parada, Alejandro E. "Towards a New History of Books and Libraries in Argentina: Background, History and Periods." *Library History* 22, no. 1 (March 2006): 55–60.
Zimmermann, A. M. P. "Libraries in Argentina: An Overview." *IFLA Journal* 30, no. 2 (2004): 108–28.

Asia

Miwa, Makiko. "Trends and Issues in LIS Education in Asia." *Journal of Education for Library and Information Science* 47, no. 3 (Summer 2006): 167–80.
Sharma, R. N. "Development of Library and Information Science Education in South Asia with Emphasis on India: Strengths, Problems and Suggestions." *Journal of Education for Library and Information Science* 46, no. 1 (Winter 2005): 77–91.
Yu, Priscilla C. "History of Modern Librarianship in East Asia." *Library History* 24, no. 1 (March 2008): 64–77.

Australia

Barker, Donald. "Reformers and Reform: Towards Free Public Libraries in Victoria." *Australian Library Journal* 56, nos. 3–4 (November 2007): 373–91.
Forum on Australian Colonial Library History, Elizabeth Morrison, and Michael Talbot. *Books, Libraries and Readers in Colonial Australia: Papers from the Forum on Australian Colonial Library History Held at Monash University, 1–2 June 1984.* Clayton, Victoria, Australia: Graduate School of Librarianship, Monash University, 1985.
Jones, David J. "Advance and Retreat: Aspects of Public Library Services in New South Wales during World War II." *Libraries and Culture* 32, no. 3 (Summer 1997): 337–48.
———. "Great Minds: Metcalfe, McColvin, and Public Libraries in Australia." *Australian Library Journal* 54, no. 4 (November 2005): 386–412.
———. "Public Library Development in New South Wales." *Australian Library Journal* 54, no. 2 (May 2005): 130–37.

Laugesen, Amanda. "Finding Another Great World: Australian Soldiers and Wartime Libraries." *Library Quarterly* 76, no. 4 (October 2006): 420–37.

Morrison, Elizabeth, and Michael Talbot, eds. *Books, Libraries and Readers in Colonial Australia: Papers from the Forum on Australian Colonial Library History Held at Monash University, 1–2 June 1984*. Clayton, Victoria, Australia: Graduate School of Librarianship, Monash University, 1985.

Pawley, Christine, Patricia Willard, and Concepción S. Wilson. "Trends and Transformations: The Changing Face of Library and Information Studies in Australia." *Journal of Education for Library and Information Science* 42, no. 4 (Fall 2001): 325–38.

Pymm, Bob. "The Trouble with Fiction." *Australian Library Journal* 44, no. 4 (November 1995): 188–94.

Reynolds, Sue. "Libraries, Librarians and Librarianship in the Colony of Victoria." *Australian Academic and Research Libraries* 40, no. 1 (March 2009): 50–64.

———. "A Nineteenth Century Library and Its Librarian: Factotum, Bookman or Professional?" *Australian Library Journal* 56, no. 4 (November 2007): 282–301.

Tilley, Christine M. "Female Librarianship in Australia." *International Library Review* 20, no. 4 (1988): 425–43.

Whyte, Jean Primrose, and David John Jones. *Uniting a Profession: The Australian Institute of Librarians, 1937–1949*. Kingston: Australian Library and Information Association, 2007.

Wilson, Concepción S., Sebastian K. Boell, Mary Anne Kennan, and Patricia Willard. "Fifty Years of LIS Education in Australia: Research Productivity and Visibility of LIS Educators in Higher Education Institutions." *Journal of Education for Library and Information Science* 53, no. 1 (January 2012): 49–68.

Bangladesh

Ahmad, N. "Education for Librarianship in Bangladesh." *International Library Review* 13, no. 1 (1981): 103–15.

Hossain, S. "Library Associations in Bangladesh." *International Library Review* 13, no. 3 (1981): 323–37.

Khan, M. H. "Public Libraries in Bangladesh." *International Library Review* 16, no. 2 (1984): 125–41.

Belgium

Mitts-Smith, Debra. "L'Heure Joyeuse: Educational and Social Reform in Post–World War I Brussels." *Library Trends* 55, no. 3 (Winter 2007): 464–73.

Brazil

Ortega, Alma C. "A History of the Fundação Biblioteca Nacional (FBN) and Its Role in the Creation of National Library Reading Initiatives in Brazil." *World Libraries* 14, no. 2 (Fall 2004): 55–67.

Burma

Khurshid, Anis. "Library Development in Burma." *Journal of Library History* 5, no. 4 (Fall 1970): 323–40.

Canada

Adams, Sue. "Our Activist Past: Nora Bateson, Champion of Regional Libraries." *Partnership: The Canadian Journal of Library and Information Practice and Research* 4, no. 1 (2009): 1–13.
Bruce, Lorne. *Free Books for All: The Public Library Movement in Ontario, 1850–1930.* Toronto: Dundurn Press, 1994.
———. "Professionalization, Gender, and Librarianship in Ontario, 1920–75." *Library and Information History* 28, no. 2 (June 2012): 117–34.
Crepeau, Isabelle. "La législation des bibliothèques publiques de Québec à travers l'histoire: Essai de synthèse." *Documentation and Bibliothèques* 45, no. 1 (1999): 25–33.
Curran, Mary, and Kewal Krishan. "The Canadian Library Association Serials Interest Group, 1980–1999." *Serials Librarian* 37, no. 3 (2000): 17–39.
Dean, Heather. "The Persuasion of Books: The Significance of Libraries in Colonial British Columbia." *Libraries and the Cultural Record* 46, no. 1 (Winter 2011): 50–72.
Delisle, C., and R. Savard. "L'ecole de Bibliothécaires (1937–1962): Discours et formation." *Documentation and Bibliothèques* 44, no. 4 (1998): 151–65.
Denis, Laurent G. "Libraries and Librarianship in Canada." *IFLA Journal* 8, no. 1 (1982): 11–41.

Edwards, Brendan Frederick R. *Paper Talk: A History of Libraries, Print Culture, and Aboriginal Peoples in Canada before 1960*. Lanham, MD: Scarecrow Press, 2005.

Edwards, Gail. "'Good Reading among Young Canadians' (c. 1900–1950): The Canadian Association of Children's Librarians, Young Canada's Book Week, and the Persistence of Professional Discourse." *Library and Information History* 28, no. 2 (June 2012): 135–49.

Fleming, Patricia, Gilles Gallichan, and Yvan Lamonde. *History of the Book in Canada*. Toronto: University of Toronto Press, 2004.

Hanson, Elizabeth. "Charles Gould, the 1900 ALA Conference and the Canadian Library Association." *Feliciter* 52, no. 3 (2006): 114–17.

Ings, Catherine, and Jennifer Joslin. "Correctional Service of Canada Prison Libraries from 1980 to 2010." *Library Trends* 59, no. 3 (Winter 2011): 386–408.

Lafortune, N., and V. Viens. "L'evolution du discours des bibliothécaires sur la lecture publique dans le Bulletin de l'ACBLF entre 1955 et 1972." *Documentation and Bibliothèques* 44, no. 4 (1998): 167–74.

Lajeunesse, Marcel. "Le bibliothécaire québécois: D'un homme de lettres a un professionnel de l'information." *Documentation and Bibliothèques* 52, no. 2 (2005): 139–48.

———. "Public Libraries and Reading in Quebec: A History of Censorship Freedom." *Library and Information History* 28, no. 1 (March 2012): 26–40.

Linnell, Greg. "The Institute of Professional Librarians of Ontario: On the History and Historiography of a Professional Association." *Canadian Journal of Information and Library Sciences* 30, nos. 3–4 (2006): 175–99.

McKechnie, Lynne (E. F.). "Patricia Spereman and the Beginning of Canadian Public Library Work with Children." *Libraries and Culture* 34, no. 2 (Spring 1999): 135–50.

McNally, Peter F. "Fanfares and Celebrations: Anniversaries in Canadian Graduate Education for Library and Information Studies." *The Canadian Journal of Information and Library Science* 18, no. 1 (April 1993): 6–22.

———. *Readings in Canadian Library History*. Ottawa, Ontario: Canadian Library Association, 1986.

Rochester, Maxine K. "Bringing Librarianship to Rural Canada in the 1930s: Demonstrations by Carnegie Corporation of New York." *Libraries and Culture* 30, no. 4 (Fall 1995): 366–90.

Stuart-Stubbs, Basil. "1927–30: The Muddle Years: History of Efforts to Organize the Canadian Library Association." *Feliciter* 46, no. 3 (2000): 148–49.

———. "1930: The Commissioners' Trail: CLA Commission of Enquiry Tour of Canadian Libraries." *Feliciter* 47, no. 3 (2001): 140–41.

————. "1933: The Commission Speaks: CLA Commission of Enquiry Tour of Canadian Libraries." *Feliciter* 48, no. 3 (2002): 126–28.

————. "1934: CLA Redux . . . Almost." *Feliciter* 49, no. 3 (2003): 161–64.

————. "1934–46: The Long Last Lap." *Feliciter* 50, no. 3 (2004): 112–15.

Caribbean

Jordan, Alma. "The Association of Caribbean University, Research and Institutional Libraries (ACURIL)." *IFLA Journal* 15, no. 3 (1989): 233–36.

Peltier-Davis, Cheryl, and Shamin Renwick, eds. *Caribbean Libraries in the 21st Century: Changes, Challenges, and Choices.* Medford, NJ: Information Today, 2007.

China

Boettcher, Cheryl. "Samuel T. Y. Seng and the Boone Library School." *Journal of Library History* 24, no. 3 (Summer 1989): 269–94.

Cheng, Huanwen. "The Effect of the Cold War on Librarianship in China." *Libraries and Culture* 36, no. 1 (Winter 2001): 40–50.

Chu, Jingli. "Librarianship in China: The Spread of Western Influences." *Library Management* 22, no. 4 (2001): 177–80.

————. "The Renaming of Library Schools in China and the Effects." *New Library World* 102, no. 7 (2001): 274–77.

Fang, Josephine Riss. "Contemporary Developments in Librarianship in China." *International Library Review* 13, no. 2 (1981): 211–19.

Feng, Qui, Huang Jungui, Li Zhe-Min, Liu Xi-Shen, and Zheng Rui. "Developing Librarianship in China, 1949–1989." *Libri* 42, no. 1 (1992): 1–19.

Kuang, Neng-fu. "Chinese Library Science in the Twelfth Century. *Libraries and Culture* 26, no. 2 (Spring 1991): 357–71.

Lee, Hur-Li Lee, and Wen-Chin Lan. "Purposes and Bibliographic Objectives of a Pioneer Library Catalog in China." *Library Quarterly* 79, no. 2 (April 2009): 205–31.

Liao, Jing. "Chinese-American Alliances: American Professionalization and the Rise of the Modern Chinese Library System in the 1920s and 1930s." *Library and Information History* 25, no. 1 (March 2009): 20–32.

————. "The Contributions of Nineteenth-century Christian Missionaries to Chinese Library Reform." *Libraries and the Cultural Record* 41, no. 3 (Summer 2006): 360–71.

————. "The Genesis of the Modern Academic Library in China: Western Influences and the Chinese Response." *Libraries and Culture* 39, no. 2 (Spring 2004): 161–74.

———. "A Historical Perspective: The Root Cause for the Underdevelopment of User Services in Chinese Academic Libraries." *Journal of Academic Librarianship* 30, no. 2 (2004): 109–15.

———. "The New Culture Movement and the Breakthrough in Chinese Academic Library Reform." *Library History* 24, no. 1 (March 2008): 37–47.

Lin, Sharon Chien. "Historical Development of Library Education in China." *Journal of Library History* 20, no. 4 (Fall 1985): 368–86.

———. *Libraries and Librarianship in China.* Westport, CT: Greenwood Press, 1998.

Nelson, Diane M., and Robert B. Nelson. "'The Red Chamber': Li Ta-chao and the Sources of Radicalism in Modern Chinese Librarianship." *Journal of Library History* 14, no. 2 (Spring 1979): 121–28.

Ning, Zhou, and Lin Lan. "Forty Years of Development of Library and Information Science Education in China." *Journal of Education for Library and Information Science* 31, no. 2 (Fall 1990): 162–69.

Ting, Lee-hsia Hsu. "Library Services in the People's Republic of China: A Historical Overview." *Library Quarterly* 53, no. 2 (April 1983): 134–60.

Tsay, Ming-yueh. "The Influence of the American Library Association on Modern Chinese Librarianship, 1924 to 1949." *Asian Libraries* 8, no. 8 (1999): 275–88.

Wang, Bing. "The Development of the Three Largest Chinese Libraries in the Twentieth Century." *Library History* 19, no. 1 (2003): 13–22.

Wen, Cheng Huan. "The Impact of American Librarianship on Chinese Librarianship in Modern Times (1840–1949)." *Libraries and Culture* 26, no. 2 (Spring 1991): 372–87.

Wu, Jianzhong, and Ruhua Huang. "The Academic Library Development in China." *Journal of Academic Librarianship* 29, no. 4 (2003): 249–53.

Xiaoying, Dong. "Transition of Library and Information Science Education in China: Problems and Perspective." *International Information and Library Review* 29, no. 1 (1997): 1–12.

Yitai, Gong, and G. E. Gorman. *Libraries and Information Services in China.* Lanham, MD: Scarecrow Press, 2000.

Yu, Priscilla C. "Leaning to One Side: The Impact of the Cold War on Chinese Library Collections." *Libraries and Culture* 36, no. 1 (Winter 2001): 253–66.

Colombia

Krzys, Richard. "Library Training in Colombia before the Inter-American Library School." *Journal of Education for Librarianship* 6, no. 4 (Spring 1966): 234–43.

Cuba

Pateman, John. "The Development of Public Libraries in Cuba since 1959." *Library History* 17, no. 3 (2001): 189–95.
Pérez-Matos, N., and Juan Carlos Fernández-Molina. "The History of Library and Information Activities in Cuba: The Relationship with Its Constitutional Periods." *Library and Information History* 26, no. 3 (September 2010): 213–24.

Denmark

Harbo, Ole. "The Development of Public Libraries in Denmark since 1964." In *Advances in Librarianship*, vol. 25, ed. Frederick C. Lynden. San Diego: Academic Press, 2001.
Skouvig, Laura. "The Construction of the Working-class User: Danish Free Public Libraries and the Working Classes, 1880–1920." *Library History* 23, no. 3 (September 2007): 223–38.

Ethiopia

Coleman, Sterling Joseph, Jr. "The British Council and UNESCO in Ethiopia: A Comparison of Linear and Cyclical Patterns of Librarianship Development." *Library History* 21, no. 2 (July 2005): 121–30.

Europe

Caidi, Nadia. "Cooperation in Context: Library Developments in Central and Eastern Europe." *Libri* 53, no. 2 (2003): 103–17.
Choldin, M. T. "Libraries in Continental Europe: The 40s and the 90s." *Journal of Documentation* 61, no. 3 (2005): 356–61.
Danilewicz, Maria. "The Post-war Problems of Continental Libraries." *Journal of Documentation* 61, no. 3 (2005): 334–40.
Dyrbye, Martin. "Anglo-Danish Library Connections in the Post-war Era: An Illustration of Cultural Aspects of the Transition from Warfare to Welfare Societies in the Years 1945 to 1964." *Library History* 24, no. 3 (September 2008): 230–39.
Virkus, Sirje, and Lawraine Wood. "Change and Innovation in European LIS Education." *New Library World* 105, no. 9 (2004): 320–29.

Finland

Ekholm, Kai. "Political Censorship in Finnish Libraries from 1944 to 1946." *Libraries and Culture* 36, no. 1 (Winter 2001): 51–57.

Mäkinen, Ilkka, ed. *Finnish Public Libraries in the Twentieth Century.* Tampere, Finland: Tampere University Press, 2001.

———. "Historical Explanations for the Success of Public Finnish Libraries (and Nordic Countries in General)." http://conference.ifla.org/past/ifla78/107-makinen-en.pdf, 2010.

———. "Libraries and Reading in Finnish Military Hospitals during the Second World War." *Library Trends* 55, no. 3 (Winter 2007): 536–50.

Saarti, Jarmo. "Libraries without Walls: Information Technology in Finnish Public Libraries from the 1970s to the 1990s." *Library History* 22, no. 1 (March 2006): 33–43.

Screen, J. E. O. "From Helsinki to Irkutsk: Military Libraries in Finland, 1812–1918." *Library and Information History* 26, no. 2 (June 2010): 139–51.

France

Benoit, Gaetan. "Eugène Morel and Children's Libraries in France." *Journal of Library History* 20, no. 3 (Summer 1985): 267–86.

Bertrand, Anne-Marie. "Inventing a Model Library 'à la française.'" *Libraries and the Cultural Record* 44, no. 4 (Fall 2009): 471–79.

Camp, Joseph. "Libraries and the Organization of Universities in France, 1789–1881." *Library Quarterly* 51, no. 2 (April 1981): 170–91.

Faye-Scribe, Sylvie. "The Cross-Fertilization of the US Public Library Model and the French Documentation Model (IIB, French Correspondent of FID) through the French Professional Associations between World War I and World War II." *Journal of the American Society for Information Science* 48, no. 9 (1997): 782–93.

———. *Histoire de la documentation en France: Culture, science, et technologie de l'information 1895–1937.* Paris: CNRS Éditions, 2000.

———. "Women Professionals in Documentation in France during the 1930s." *Libraries and the Cultural Record* 44, no. 2 (2009): 201–19.

Gicquel, Florence. "De la création à la professionnalisation de l'ADBS. Le temps des pionniers: 1963–1983." *Documentaliste* 40, no. 2 (April 2003): 94–101.

Gleyze, Alain. "Savoirs, techniques et pouvoirs: Le passe des bibliothèques universitaires de province." *Bulletin des Bibliothèques de France* 46, no. 1 (2001): 4–12.

Greenberg, Gerald S. "The Paris Commune of 1871 and the Bibliothèque Nationale." *Library Trends* 55, no. 3 (Winter 2007): 442–53.

Kibbee, Jo. "Aux Armes Citoyens! Confronting the Extreme Right in French Public Libraries." *Libri* 53, no. 4 (2003): 227–36.

Maack, Mary Niles. "Between Two Worlds: The American Library in Paris during the War, Occupation and Liberation (1939–1945)." *Library Trends* 55, no. 3 (Winter 2007): 490–512.

———. "L'Heure Joyeuse, the First Children's Library in France: Its Contribution to a New Paradigm for Public Libraries." *Library Quarterly* 63, no. 3 (July 1993): 257–81.

———. "Women Librarians in France: The First Generation." *Journal of Library History* 18, no. 4 (Fall 1983): 407–49.

Moore, Lara Jennifer. *Restoring Order: The École des Chartes and the Organization of Archives and Libraries in France, 1820–1870*. Duluth, MN: Litwin Books, 2008.

Oliver, Bette W. "The Bibliothèque Nationale from 1792 to 1794: Becoming a National Institution during the French Revolution." *Libraries and the Cultural Record* 42, no. 1 (Winter 2007): 48–56.

Patte, Genevieve. "Children's Libraries in France." *International Library Review* 6, no. 4 (1974): 435–48.

Poulain, Martine, ed. *Histoire des bibliothèques françaises*. Paris: Promodis, 1992.

———. *Livres pilles, lectures survállées: Les bibliothèques françaises sous l'Occupation*. Paris: Éditions Gallimard, 2008.

———. "Retourner à Tocqueville: Pour comprendre l'histoire comparée des bibliothèques américaines et françaises au XIXe siècle." *Bulletin des Bibliothèques de France* 47, no. 5 (2002): 66–73.

Stasse, François. *La véritable histoire de la Grande Bibliothèque*. Paris: Éd. du Seuil, 2002.

Wenzel, Sarah G. "From Revolution to Evolution: The Transformation of the Bibliothèque Nationale into the Bibliothèque Nationale de France, through the Lens of Popular and Professional Reports." *Library Quarterly* 69, no. 3 (July 1999): 324–38.

Germany

Boese, Engelbrecht. *Das Öffentliche Bibliothekswesen im Dritten Reich*. Frankfurt: Boch and Herchen, 1997.

Bunzel, Jürgen, and Roswitha Poll. "German Academic Libraries: Tradition and Change." *Journal of Academic Librarianship* 28, no. 6 (November 2002): 418–25.

Buzás, Ladislaus. *German Library History, 800–1945.* Jefferson, NC: McFarland, 1986.

Ferret, Christine. "Les bibliothécaires de République Démocratique Allemande: entre compromis et résistance." *Bulletin des Bibliothèques de France* 42, no. 4 (1997): 59–66.

Fligge, Jorge. "Bremen, Danzig, Hamburg und Lubeck: Hanseatische Stadtbibliotheken–Gleiche Wurzeln, Verschiedene Wege." *BuB-Journal* 55 (February 2003): 74–79.

Garrett, Jeffrey. "Redefining Order in the German Library, 1775–1825." *Eighteenth-century Studies* 33, no. 1 (Fall 1999): 103–23.

Habermann, Alexandrea, and Peter Kittel. *Lexikon Deutscher Wissenschaftlicher Bibliothekare: Die Wissenschaftlichen Bibliothekare der Bundesrepublik Deutschland (1981–2002) und der Deutschen Demokratischen Republik (1948–1990).* Frankfurt am Main: Vittorio Klostermann, 2004.

Krosta, Frank. *Die Universitätsbibliothek Bonn in der Zeit des Nationalsozialismus: Personal, Erwerbung, Benutzung.* Munich: Martin Meidenbauer, 2008.

Kunoff, Hug. *The Foundations of the German Academic Library.* Chicago: American Library Association, 1982.

Minter, Catherine J. "The Classification of Libraries and the Image of the Librarian in Nineteenth- and Early Twentieth-century Germany." *Library and Information History* 25, no. 1 (March 2009): 3–19.

Richards, Pamela Spence. "German Libraries and Scientific and Technical Information in Nazi Germany." *Library Quarterly* 55, no. 2 (April 1985): 151–73.

Stieg, Margaret F. "Catholic Libraries and Public Libraries in the Third Reich: A Reciprocal Relationship." *Catholic Historical Review* 77, no. 2 (April 1991): 235–59.

———. "The Richtungstreit: The Philosophy of Public Librarianship in Germany before 1933." *Journal of Library History* 21, no. 2 (Spring 1986): 261–76.

Vodosek, Peter. "Innovation and Ideology: Walter Hofmann's Library in Desden-Plauen and Leipzig." *Library History* 23, no. 1 (March 2007): 63–76.

———. "The Usual Delay: Public Libraries in Nineteenth Century Germany." *Library History* 17, no. 3 (November 2001): 197–202.

Great Britain

Black, Alistair. "Arsenals of Scientific and Technical Information: Public Technical Libraries in Britain during and Immediately after World War I." *Library Trends* 55, no. 3 (Winter 2007): 474–89.

————. "False Optimism: Modernity, Class, and the Public Library in Britain in the 1960s and 1970s." *Libraries and Culture* 38, no. 3 (Summer 2003): 201–13.

————. *A New History of the English Public Library: Social and Intellectual Contexts, 1850–1914*. London: Leicester University Press, 1996.

————. "Organizational Learning and Home-grown Writing: The Library Staff Magazine in Britain in the First Half of the Twentieth Century." *Information and Culture: A Journal of History* 47, no. 4 (Fall 2012): 487–513.

————. *The Public Library in Britain: 1914–2000*. London: British Library, 2000.

————. "Skeleton in the Cupboard: Social Class and the Public Library in Britain through 150 Years." *Library History* 16, no. 1 (2000): 3–12.

————. "The Victorian Information Society: Surveillance, Bureaucracy, and Public Librarianship in 19th Century Britain." *Information Society* 17 (January–March 2001): 63–80.

Black, Alistair, and Dave Muddiman. *Understanding Community Librarianship: The Public Library in Post-modern Britain*. Aldershot, UK: Avebury, 1997.

Black, Alistair, Dave Muddiman, and Helen Plant. *The Early Information Society: Information Management in Britain before the Computer*. Aldershot, UK: Ashgate, 2007.

Black, Alistair, and Christopher Murphy. "Information, Intelligence, and Trade: The Library and the Commercial Intelligence Branch of the British Board of Trade, 1834–1914." *Library and Information History* 28, no. 3 (September 2012): 186–201.

Bowman, J. H. "Classification in British Public Libraries: A Historical Perspective." *Library History* 21, no. 3 (September 2005): 143–73.

Ellis, Alec. "English Public Libraries: Years of Crisis, 1914–1919." *Journal of Library History* 22, no. 3 (Summer 1987): 272–84.

————. *Library Services for Young People in England and Wales: 1830–1970*. Oxford: Pergamon Press, 1971.

Hoare, Peter, and Alistair Black, eds. *Cambridge History of Libraries in Britain and Ireland*. Cambridge: Cambridge University Press, 2007.

Hung, Margaret. "A Guerrilla War in World War II: How the Library Association Fought the War Office and the Army—and Lost." *Library History* 24, no. 2 (June 2008): 167–88.

Jenkinson, Penelope. "Travelling Hopefully: Progress and the Nineteenth-century Public Library." *Library History* 15, no. 1 (1999): 23–32.

Johansen, Michelle. "A Fault-Line in Library History: Charles Goss, the Society of Public Librarians, and 'The Battle of the Books' in the Late Nineteenth Century." *Library History* 19, no. 2 (July 2003): 75–91.

Kelly, Thomas. *Early Public Libraries: A History of Public Libraries in Great Britain before 1850*. London: Library Association, 1966.

———. *A History of Public Libraries in Great Britain, 1845–1975*. London: Library Association, 1977.

Kerslake, Evelyn. "'They Have Had to Come Down to the Women for Help!': Numerical Feminization and the Characteristics of Women's Library Employment in England, 1871–1974." *Library History* 23, no. 1 (March 2007): 17–40.

Manley, K. A. "The Official Library Journal Wars of the 1870s and '80s." *Library History* 12 (1996): 106–17.

McNicol, Sarah. "Library Co-operation in the Inter-war Period: Lessons from History." *Library History* 21, no. 2 (July 2005): 83–89.

Muddiman, Dave. "The Public Library in an Age of Inclusion: Edward Sydney, Harold Jolliffe and the Rise and Fall of Library Extension, 1927–1972." *Library History* 18, no. 2 (2002): 117–30.

Munford, William Arthur. *A History of the Library Association, 1877–1977*. London: Library Association, 1976.

Peatling, Gary Kenneth. "Historical Perspectives on Problem Patrons from the British Public Library Sector, 1850–1919." *Reference Librarian* 36, nos. 75–76 (2002): 33–43.

———. "Public Libraries and National Identity in Britain, 1850–1919." *Library History* 20, no. 1 (March 2004): 33–77.

Plant, Helen. "Women's Employment in Industrial Libraries and Information Bureaux in Britain, ca. 1918–1960." *Library History* 20, no. 1 (March 2004): 49–63.

Ravenwood, Clare, and John Feather. "Censorship and Book Selection in British Public Librarianship, 1919–1939: Professional Perspectives." *Library and Information History* 26, no. 4 (December 2010): 258–71.

Sturges, R. P., and Alison Barr. "The 'Fiction Nuisance' in Nineteenth-century British Public Libraries." *Journal of Librarianship and Information Science* 24 (March 1992): 23–32.

Tedd, Lucy A. "Library Management Systems in the UK: 1960s–1980s." *Library History* 23, no. 4 (2007): 301–16.

Whatley, Herbert Allan. *British Librarianship and Information Science, 1966–1970*. London: Library Association, 1972.

Greece

Gerolimos, Michalis. "Library Education in Greece: History, Current Status and Future Prospects." *Library Review* 60, no. 2 (2011): 108–24.

Krikelas, James. "Academic Libraries in Greece." *International Library Review* 16, no. 3 (1984): 235–46.

India

Patel, Jashu, and Krishan Kumar. *Libraries and Librarianship in India.* Westport, CT: Greenwood Press, 2001.

Toney, Bernard J. "Indian Library Science Training, 1911–1965." *Journal of Education for Library and Information Science* 8, no. 2 (1976): 115–23.

Umapathy, K. S. "Education for Librarianship in India." *International Library Review* 9, no. 3 (1977): 289–301.

Wani, Zahid Ashraf. "Development of Public Libraries in India." *Library Philosophy and Practice* 10, no. 1 (2008): 1–10.

Indonesia

Fitzpatrick, Elizabeth B. "The Public Library as Instrument of Colonialism: The Case of the Netherlands East Indies." *Libraries and the Cultural Record* 43, no. 3 (Summer 2008): 270–85.

Sulistyo-Basuki, L. "The Rise and Growth of Libraries in Pre-war Indonesia." *Library History* 14, no. 1 (1998): 55–64.

Iran

Hariri, Mehrangiz, and Hussein Davoodifar. "Continuing Library/Information Science Education in Iran: The Assessment of Irandoc Short Courses (1982–1986)." *International Library Review* 20, no. 1 (1988): 19–28.

Hayati, Zouhayr, and Rahmatollah Fattahi. "Education for Librarianship in Iran before the 1979 Islamic Revolution: A Historical Review of American Roles and Influences." *Library Review* 54, no. 5 (2005): 316–27.

Ireland

Cullen, Clara. "'Dublin Is Also in Great Need of a Library Which Shall Be at Once Accessible to the Public and Contain a Good Supply of Modern and Foreign Books': Dublin's Nineteenth-century 'Public' Libraries." *Library History* 23, no. 1 (March 2007): 49–61.

Italy

Carpenter, Ray L. "Contrasting Developments in Italian Libraries." *International Library Review* 8, no. 1 (1976): 33–49.

Del Bono, G. "Library Science in Italy since 1945." *Libraries and Culture* 25, no. 3 (Summer 1990): 406–32.

Peruginelli, Susanna. "A Brief History of Library Automation in Italy." *Libraries and Culture* 25, no. 3 (Summer 1990): 446–60.

Japan

Domier, Sharon. "From Reading Guidance to Thought Control: Wartime Japanese Libraries." *Library Trends* 55, no. 3 (Winter 2007): 551–69.
Welch, Theodore F. *Libraries and Librarianship in Japan.* Westport, CT: Greenwood Press, 1997.

Korea

Lee, Pongsoon, and Young Ai Um. *Libraries and Librarianship in Korea,* Westport, CT: Greenwood Press, 1994.

Latin America

Kim, Byong-Ju. "The History of the Development of School Libraries in the Republic of Korea." *School Libraries Worldwide* 6, no. 1 (January 2000): 95–100.
Historia de las Bibliotecas Nacionales de Ibero-América: Pasado y Presente. Mexico City: UNAM, Coordinación de Humanidades: Instituto de Investigaciones Bibliográficas, Centro Universitario de Investigaciones Bibliotecológicas, 1995.
Lozano Rivera, Uriel. "La Escuela Interamericana de Bibliotecología: 45 Años Formando Lideres en la Gestion de la Información y el Conocimiento para Colombia y América Latina." *Revista Interamericana de Bibliotecología* 25 (July/December 2002 supp.): entire issue.
Maymí-Sugrañes, Héctor J. "The American Library Association in Latin America: American Librarianship as a Modern Model during the Good Neighbor Policy Era." *Libraries and Culture* 37, no. 4 (Fall 2002): 307–38.

Malaysia

Rasmussen, Radha. "Education for Librarianship in Malaysia: 1955–1975." *Journal of Library History* 13, no. 2 (Spring 1978): 131–47.

Mexico

Castillo, Angel, and Carlos Martínez. "Library Science in Mexico: a Discipline in Crisis." *Progressive Librarian*, no. 31 (2008): 29–36.
Jones, Phillip. "'Indispensable in a Civilized Society': Manuel Payno's 'Las Bibliotecas de México.'" *Libraries and the Cultural Record* 42, no. 3 (Summer 2007): 268–90.
———. "The Mission of 'Little Star': Juana Manrique de Lara's Contributions to Mexican Librarianship." *Libraries and the Cultural Record* 45, no. 4 (Fall 2010): 469–90.

New Zealand

Ollson, Arthur. "Sixty Years of New Zealand Libraries: A Chronicle 1937 to 1997." *New Zealand Library and Information Management Journal* 52, no. 1 (October 2010): 6–19.
Trade, J. E. "Sordid Duplicity or Cross-cultural Misunderstanding? The Fate of Andrew Carnegie's Gifts for Free Public Libraries in New Zealand." *Library History* 16, no. 1 (2000): 13–34.
Verran, David. "New Zealand Mechanics' Institutes and Their Effect on Public Library Development." *Australian Public Libraries and Information Services* 18 (September 2005): 113–20.

Nigeria

Agboola, A. T. "Five Decades of Nigerian University Libraries: A Review." *Libri* 50, no. 4 (December 2000): 280–89.
Aguolu, C. C. "The Foundations of Modern Libraries in Nigeria." *International Library Review* 9, no. 4 (1977): 461–83.
Onadiran, G. T., and R. W. Onadiran. "Public Library Services in Nigeria." *International Library Review* 13, no. 4 (1981): 409–33.

North America

Dale, Doris Cruger. *A Directory of Oral History Tapes of Librarians in the United States and Canada*. Chicago: American Library Association, 1986.
Jackson, Sidney L., Eleanor B. Herling, and E. J. Josey. *A Century of Service: Librarianship in the United States and Canada*. Chicago: American Library Association, 1976.
Samek, Toni. "The Canadian-American Library Frontier, 1944–1946: Providing a Context." *Épilogue*, nos. 13–14 (1992): 18–28.

Norway

Lindsay, Margot. "Librarianship in an Occupied Country: Norway 1940–1945." *Library History* 11 (1995): 49–62.

Pakistan

Anwar, Muhammad. "Political and Professional Inputs in Public Library Development in Pakistan." *Pakistan Library Bulletin* 28 (March–June 1997): 1–9.

Haider, Syed Jalaluddin. "First Conference of Pakistan Library Association (PLA): An Event of Great Significance." *Pakistan Library and Information Science Journal* 39 (March 2008): 2–10.

Philippines

Hernández, Vicente S. "Trends in Philippine Library History." *Libraries and Culture* 36, no. 2 (Spring 2001): 329–44.

Poland

Gorny, Miroslaw. "From the Old-fashioned Library to the Public Library: Changes in the Cultural Functions of Polish Academic Libraries." *Advances in Library Administration and Organization* 27 (2009): 109–22.

Sroka, Marek. "Soldiers of the Cultural Revolution: The Stalinization of Libraries and Librarianship in Poland, 1945–1953." *Library History* 16, no. 2 (November 2000): 105–25.

Romania

Dragulanescu, Nicolae. "Emerging Information Society and History of Information Science in Romania." *Journal of the American Society for Information Science and Technology* 53 (January 1, 2002): 41–46.

Russia and the Soviet Union

Greening, Joyce Martin. "The Years in the Life of Russian Libraries." *International Information and Library Review* 27, no. 2 (1995): 113–27.

Kimmage, Dennis. "Glasnost in Soviet Libraries; Part One of Two." *American Libraries* 19, no. 7 (1988): 570.

Klim, Irina. "The Impact of American Librarianship on Libraries of Communist and Postcommunist Russia." In *Advances in Librarianship*, vol. 24, ed. Elizabeth A. Chapman and Frederick C. Lynden. San Diego: Academic Press, 2000.

Knutson, Ellen. "New Realities: Libraries in Post-Soviet Russia." *Library Trends* 55, no. 3 (Winter 2007): 716–29.

Leich, Harold M. "The Society for Librarianship and Russian Librarianship in the Early Twentieth Century." *Journal of Library History* 22, no. 1 (Winter 1987): 42–57.

Main, Steven J. "The Creation and Development of the Library System in the Red Army during the Russian Civil War (1918–1920): A Historical Introduction." *Library Quarterly* 65, no. 3 (July 1995): 319–32.

Melent'eva, Julia P. "Youth Services in Russian Libraries in an Era of Social Change." *Libraries and Culture* 33, no. 1 (Winter 1998): 69–75.

Raymond, Boris. *Krupskaia and Soviet Russian Librarianship, 1917–1939.* Metuchen, NJ: Scarecrow Press, 1979.

Richardson, John V. "The Origin of Soviet Education for Librarianship: The Role of Nadezhda Konstantinovna Krupskaya, Lyubov' Borisovna Khavkina-Hamburger, and Genrietta K. Abele-Derman." *Journal of Education for Library and Information Science* 41, no. 2 (Spring 2000): 106–28.

Smith-Peter, Susan J. "Provincial Public Libraries and the Law in Nicholas I's Russia." *Library History* 21, no. 2 (July 2005): 103–19.

Stuart, Mary. "'The Ennobling Illusion': The Public Library Movement in Late Imperial Russia." *Slavonic and East European Review* 76, no. 3 (July 1998): 401–40.

———. "The Evolution of Librarianship in Russia: The Librarians of the Imperial Public Library, 1808–1868." *Library Quarterly* 64, no. 1 (January 1994): 1–29.

———. "'A Potent Lever for Social Progress': The Imperial Public Library in the Era of the Great Reforms." *Library Quarterly* 59, no. 3 (July 1989): 199–222.

Volodin, Boris. "Foreign Libraries in the Mirror of Soviet Library Science during the Cold War." *Libraries and Culture* 36, no. 1 (Winter 2001): 204–10.

———. "History of Librarianship, Library History, or Information History: A View from Russia." *Library Quarterly* 70, no. 4 (October 2000): 446–67.

Scandinavia

Hannesdóttir, Sigrún Klara. *The Scandia Plan: A Cooperative Acquisition Scheme for Improving Access to Research Publications in Four Nordic Countries.* Metuchen, NJ: Scarecrow Press, 1992.

Kaegbein, Paul, and Magnus Torstensson, eds. "The History of Reading and Libraries in the Nordic Countries." *Libraries and Culture* 28, no. 1 (Winter 1993): entire issue.

South Africa

Bell, Fiona. "The Carnegie Corporation Decides on Racially Segregated Libraries in South Africa in 1928: Negrophilist or Segregationist?" *Library and Information History* 25, no. 3 (September 2009): 174–89.

Cobley, Alan G. "Literacy, Libraries, and Consciousness: The Provision of Library Services for Blacks in South Africa in the Pre-apartheid Era." *Libraries and Culture* 32, no. 1 (Winter 1997): 57–80.

Dick, Archie L. "Ethnic Identity and Library Development in Apartheid South Africa: The Cape Library Association, 1960–1975." *Libri* 58, no. 1 (2008): 1–62.

Kalley, Jacqueline A. *Apartheid in South African Libraries: The Transvaal Experience.* Lanham, MD: Scarecrow Press, 2000.

Lor, Peter Johan. "A Distant Mirror: The Story of Libraries in South Africa." *Daedalus* 125, no. 4, Books, Bricks, and Bytes (Fall 1996): 235–65.

Owens, Irene. "South African Libraries from Pre-apartheid to Apartheid in the 1960s and 1970s: The Beginning of the End." *Library Management* 23, nos. 1–2 (2002): 53–58.

Raju, J. "LIS Education and Training in South Africa: A Historical Review." *South African Journal of Library and Information Science* 71, no. 1 (2005): 74–78.

Walker, Clare M. "Library Associations in South Africa, 1930–2005." *Library Management* 27, nos. 1–2 (2006): 26–37.

Spain

Cuadrado, A. G. "Aproximación a la Organización Bibliotecaria Española en el Siglo XVIII." *Investigación Bibliotecológica: Archiva, Bibliotecológia, e Información* 11 (July–December 1997): 102–36.

Orera, Luisa Orera. "El Sistema Bibliotecario Español." *Scire* 2 (July–December 1996): 99–120.

Turkey

Erünsal, İsmail E. "A Brief Survey of the Development of Turkish Library Catalogues." *Libri* 51, no. 1 (March 2001): 1–7.
———. "Ottoman Foundation Libraries in the Age of Reform: The Final Period." *Libri* 54, no. 4 (December 2004): 247–55.
İcimzoy, A. Oğuz, and İsmail E. Erünsal. "The Legacy of the Ottoman Library in the Libraries of the Turkish Republic." *Libri* 58, no. 1 (March 2008): 47–57.
Müller, Hildegard. "German Librarians in Exile in Turkey, 1933–1945." *Libraries and Culture* 33, no. 3 (Summer 1998): 294–305.

Ukraine

Haigh, Maria. "Escaping Lenin's Library: Library and Information Science Education in Independent Ukraine." *International Information and Library Review* 39, no. 2 (2007): 72–79.

United States

"The First 100 Years." *American Libraries* 38 (June–July 2007): 60–75.
"100 of the Most Important Leaders We Had." *American Libraries* 30 (December 1999): 38–46.
Anderson, Sarah A. "'The Place to Go': The 135th Street Branch Library and the Harlem Renaissance." *Library Quarterly* 75, no. 4 (October 2003): 384–421.
Appelt, Kathi, and Jeanne Cannella Schmitzer. *Down Cut Shin Creek: The Pack Horse Librarians of Kentucky*. New York: HarperCollins, 2001.
Augst, Thomas, and Kenneth E. Carpenter. *Institutions of Reading: The Social Life of Libraries in the United States*. Amherst: University of Massachusetts Press, 2007.
Augst, Thomas, and Wayne A. Wiegand, eds. "The Library as an Agency of Change." *American Studies* 42 (Fall 2001): entire issue.
Barrett, Kayla, and Barbara A. Bishop. "Integration and the Alabama Library Association: Not So Black and White." *Libraries and Culture* 33, no. 2 (Spring 1998): 141–61.
Bobinski, George S. "The Golden Age of US Librarianship, 1945–1970." *Wilson Library Bulletin* 53 (January 1984): 338–44.
Boyd, Donald C. "The Book Women of Kentucky: The WPA Pack Horse Library Project, 1936–1943." *Libraries and the Cultural Record* 42, no. 2 (Spring 2007): 111–28.

Brewster, Beverly. *American Overseas Library Technical Assistance, 1940–1970*. Metuchen, NJ: Scarecrow Press, 1976.

Bundy, Mary Lee, and Frederick J. Stielow. *Activism in American Librarianship, 1962–1973*. New York: Greenwood Press, 1987.

Carmichael, James V., Jr. "Southern Librarianship and the Culture of Resentment." *Libraries and Culture* 40, no. 3 (Summer 2005): 324–52.

Cresswell, Stephen. "The Last Days of Jim Crow in Southern Libraries." *Libraries and Culture* 31, nos. 3–4 (Summer–Fall 1996): 557–73.

Dain, Phyllis. *The New York Public Library: A History of Its Founding and Early Years*. New York: New York Public Library, 1972.

Dain, Phyllis, and John Young Cole. *Libraries and Scholarly Communication in the United States: The Historical Dimension*. New York: Greenwood Press, 1990.

Davis, Donald G. *Winsor, Dewey, and Putnam: The Boston Experience*. Urbana: University of Illinois Graduate School of Library and Information Science, 2002.

DeGruyter, Lisa. "The History and Development of Rural Public Libraries." *Library Trends* 28, no. 4 (Spring 1980): 413–23.

Ditzion, Sidney Herbert. *Arsenals of a Democratic Culture: A Social History of the American Public Library Movement in New England and the Middle States from 1850 to 1900*. Chicago: American Library Association, 1947.

Du Mont, Rosemary Ruhig. "Race in American Librarianship: Attitudes of the Library Profession." *Journal of Library History* 21, no 3 (Summer 1986): 488–509.

———. *Reform and Reaction: The Big City Public Library in American Life*. Westport, CT: Greenwood Press, 1977.

Francoeur, Stephen. "Prudence and Controversy: The New York Public Library Response to Post-war Anti-communist Pressures." *Library and Information History* 27, no. 3 (September 2011): 140–60.

Freeman, Robert S., and David M. Hovde. *Libraries to the People: Histories of Outreach*. Jefferson, NC: McFarland and Co., 2003.

Gambee, Budd. "The Great Junket: American Participation in the Conference of Librarians, London, 1877." *Journal of Library History* 2, no. 1 (Winter 1967): 9–44.

———. *Return Engagement: The Role of American Librarians at the Second International Library Conference, London, 1897*. Urbana: University of Illinois Graduate School of Library Science, 1977.

Garrison, Dee. *Apostles of Culture: The Public Librarian and American Society, 1876–1920*, 2nd ed. Madison: University of Wisconsin Press, 2003.

Glynn, Tom. "The Professionalization of a Calling: Mission and Method at the New York Library Club, 1885–1901." *Libraries and the Cultural Record* 41, no. 4 (Fall 2006): 438–61.

Gorman, Robert M. "Blazing the Way: The WPA Library Service Demonstration Project in South Carolina." *Libraries and Culture* 32, no. 4 (Fall 1997): 427–55.

Graham, Patterson Toby. *A Right to Read Segregation and Civil Rights in Alabama's Public Libraries, 1900–1965.* Tuscaloosa: University of Alabama Press, 2006.

Harris, Michael H. "Portrait in Paradox: Commitment and Ambivalence in American Librarianship, 1876–1976." *Libri* 26, no. 4 (1976): 281–301.

———. "The Purpose of the American Public Library: A Revisionist Interpretation of History." *Library Journal* 98 (15 September 1973): 2509–14.

———. *Reader in American Library History.* Washington, DC: Microcard Editions, 1971.

Harris, Steven R. "Civil Rights and the Louisiana Library Association: Stumbling toward Integration." *Libraries and Culture* 38, no. 4 (Fall 2003): 322–50.

Holley, Edward G., and Robert F. Schremser. *The Library Services and Construction Act: An Historical Overview from the Viewpoint of Major Participants.* Greenwich, CT: JAI Press, 1983.

Hovde, David M. "YMCA Libraries on the Texas Border, 1916." *Libraries and Culture* 32, no. 1 (Winter 1997): 111–24.

Jaeger, Paul T., Ursula Gorham, Lindsay C. Sarin, and John Carlo Bertot. "Libraries, Policy, and Politics in a Democracy: Four Historical Epochs." *Library Quarterly* 83, no. 2 (April 2013): 166–81.

Jones, Plummer Alston. *Libraries, Immigrants, and the American Experience.* Westport, CT: Greenwood Press, 1999.

Karetzky, Stephen. *Not Seeing Red: American Librarianship and the Soviet Union, 1917–1960.* Lanham, MD: University Press of America, 2002.

Kramp, Robert Scott. *The Great Depression: Its Impact on Forty-six Large American Public Libraries: An Inquiry Based on a Content Analysis of Published Writings of Their Directors.* Duluth, MN: Library Juice Press, 2010.

Kraske, Gary E. *Missionaries of the Book: The American Library Profession and the Origins of United States Cultural Diplomacy.* Westport, CT: Greenwood Press, 1985.

Leigh, Robert D. *The Public Library in the United States: The General Report of the Public Library Inquiry.* New York: Columbia University Press, 1950.

Lincove, David A. "Propaganda and the American Public Library from the 1930s to the Eve of World War II." *RQ* 33, no. 4 (Summer 1994): 510–23.

Liu, Mengxiong. "The History and Status of Chinese Americans in Librarianship." *Library Trends* 49, no. 1 (Summer 2000): 109–37.

Maack, Mary Niles. "Gender, Culture and the Transformation of American Librarianship, 1890–1920." *Libraries and Culture* 33, no. 1 (Winter 1998): 51–61.

McMullen, Haynes. *American Libraries before 1876.* Westport, CT: Greenwood Press, 2000.

McReynolds, R. "A Heritage Dismissed; Librarians in Search of Their Place in American Popular Culture, 1876–1950." *Library Journal* 110 (1 November 1985): 25–31.

Miksa, Francis L. "The Making of the 1876 Special Report on Public Libraries." *Journal of Library History* 8, no. 1 (Winter 1973): 30–40.

Molz, Redmond Kathleen. "From the Territorial Frontier to the Frontier of Science: Library Service in the United States of America." *IFLA Journal* 11, no. 2 (1985): 91–105.

———. *National Planning for Library Service, 1935–1975.* Chicago: American Library Association, 1984.

Novotny, Eric. "'Bricks without Straw': Economic Hardship and Innovation in the Chicago Public Library during the Great Depression." *Libraries and the Cultural Record* 46, no. 3 (Summer 2011): 258–75.

———. "Library Services to Immigrants: The Debate in the Library Literature, 1900–1920, and a Chicago Case Study." *Reference and User Services Quarterly* 42, no. 4 (Summer 2003): 342–52.

Passet, Joanne E. "'Order Is Heaven's First Law': Itinerant Librarians and Bibliographic Control, 1887–1915." *Library Quarterly* 60, no. 1 (January 1990): 23–43.

———. "Reaching the Rural Reader: Traveling Libraries in America, 1892–1920." *Libraries and Culture* 26, no. 1 (Winter 1991): 100–18.

Patterson, Lotsee. "History and Status of Native Americans in Librarianship." *Library Trends* 49, no. 1 (Summer 2000): 182–93.

Pawley, Christine, and Louise S. Robbins, eds. *Libraries and the Reading Public in Twentieth-century America.* Madison: University of Wisconsin Press, 2013.

Preer, Jean. "Promoting Citizenship: How Librarians Helped Get Out the Vote in the 1952 Presidential Election." *Libraries and the Cultural Record* 43, no. 1 (Winter 2008): 1–28.

———. "The Wonderful World of Books: Librarians, Publishers, and Rural Readers." *Libraries and Culture* 32, no. 4 (Fall 1997): 404–26.

Raber, Douglas. *Librarianship and Legitimacy: The Ideology of the Public Library Inquiry.* Westport, CT: Greenwood Press, 1997.

Robbins, Louise S. *The Dismissal of Miss Ruth Brown: Civil Rights, Censorship, and the American Library.* Norman: University of Oklahoma Press, 2000.

Rubenstein, Ellen. "From Social Hygiene to Consumer Health: Libraries, Health Information, and the American Public from the Late Nineteenth Century to the 1980s." *Library and Information History* 28, no. 3 (September 2012): 202–19.

Schlup, Leonard. *Librarianship in Gilded Age America: An Anthology of Writings, 1868–1901.* Jefferson, NC: McFarland, 2009.

Scott, Edith. "The Evolution of Bibliographic Systems in the United States, 1876–1945." *Library Trends* 25, no. 1 (Summer 1976): 293–309.

Seavey, Charles A. "The American Public Library during the Great Depression." *Library Review* 52, no. 8 (2003): 373–78.

Solon, Kasia. "Present in Its Absence: Law Librarians and Technology at the Founding of AALL." *Law Library Journal* 98 (Summer 2006): 515–30.

Spencer, Gwladys. *The Chicago Public Library: Origins and Backgrounds.* Chicago: University of Chicago Press, 1943.

Stone, Elizabeth W. *American Library Development, 1600–1899.* New York: H. W. Wilson Company, 1977.

Swain, Martha. "A New Deal in Libraries: Federal Relief Work and Library Service, 1933–1943." *Libraries and Culture* 30, no. 3 (Summer 1995): 265–83.

Thompson, Charles Seymour. *Evolution of the American Public Library, 1653–1876.* Washington, DC: Scarecrow Press, 1952.

Utley, George Burwell. *The Librarians' Conference of 1853, a Chapter in American Library History.* Chicago: American Library Association, 1951.

Wiegand, Wayne A. "The Development of Librarianship in the United States." *Libraries and Culture* 24, no. 1 (Winter 1989): 99–109.

———. *Main Street Public Library: Community Places and Reading Spaces in the Rural Heartland, 1876–1856.* Iowa City: University of Iowa Press, 2011.

———. "Tunnel Vision and Blind Spots: What the Past Tells Us about the Present; Reflections on the Twentieth-century History of American Librarianship." *Library Quarterly* 69, no. 1 (January 1999): 1–33.

Williams, Robert V. "The Documentation and Special Libraries Movements in the United States, 1910–1960." *Journal of the American Society for Information Science* 48, no. 9 (September 1997): 775–81.

Winger, Howard W., ed. "American Library History, 1876–1976." *Library Trends* 25, no. 1 (July 1976): entire issue.

Young, Arthur P. "Reception of the 1876 Report on Public Libraries." *Journal of Library History* 12, no. 1 (Winter 1977): 50–56.

Yugoslavia

Cveljo, Katherine. "Libraries and Education for Librarianship in Yugoslavia: A Bibliographic Overview." *International Library Review* 9, no. 3 (1977): 319–50.

SPECIFIC TOPICS

Academic Libraries

Bales, Stephen E. "Tracing the Archetypal Academic Librarian." *Library Philosophy and Practice.* http://unllib.unl.edu/LPP/bales.pdf.

Bostick, Sharon L. "The History and Development of Academic Library Consortia in the United States: An Overview." *Journal of Academic Librarianship* 27, no. 2 (March 2001): 128–30.

DeVinney, Gemma S. "Academic Librarians and Academic Freedom in the United States: A History and Analysis." *Libri* 36, no. 1 (1986): 24–39.

Hamlin, Arthur T. *The University Library in the United States, Its Origins and Development.* Philadelphia: University of Pennsylvania Press, 1981.

Hardesty, Larry L., John P. Schmitt, and John Mark Tucker. *User Instruction in Academic Libraries: A Century of Selected Readings.* Metuchen, NJ: Scarecrow Press, 1986.

Johnson, Edward R. "Subject-divisional Organization in American University Libraries, 1939–1974." *Library Quarterly* 47, no. 1 (1977): 23–42.

Johnson, Richard David. *Libraries for Teaching, Libraries for Research: Essays for a Century.* Chicago: American Library Association, 1977.

Kaser, David. "A Century of Academic Librarianship as Reflected in the Literature." *College and Research Libraries* 37, no. 2 (March 1976): 110–27.

Miller, Catherine. "Academic Library Reform and the Ideal of the Librarian in England, France, and Germany in the Long Nineteenth Century." *Library and Information History* 29, no. 1 (March 2013): 19–37.

Miller, Ruth H. "Electronic Resources in Academic Libraries, 1980–2000: A Historical Perspective." *Library Trends* 48, no. 4 (Spring 2000): 645–70.

Moran, B. B. "The Unintended Revolution in Academic Libraries: 1939 to 1989 and Beyond." *College and Research Libraries* 50, no. 1 (January 1989): 25–41.

Shiflett, Orvin Lee. *Origins of American Academic Librarianship.* Norwood, NJ: Ablex Publishing Corporation, 1981.

Stueart, Robert D. *Academic Librarianship: Yesterday, Today, and Tomorrow.* New York: Neal-Schuman Publishers, 1982.

Thompson, James. *University Library History: An International Review*. New York: K. G. Saur, 1980.

Tucker, John Mark. "User Education in Academic Libraries: A Century in Retrospect." *Library Trends* 29, no. 1 (Summer 1980): 9–27.

Weber, David C. "A Century of Cooperative Programs among Academic Libraries." *College and Research Libraries* 37, no. 3 (1976): 205–21.

Wiegand, Wayne A., ed. *Leaders in American Academic Librarianship, 1925–1975*. Pittsburgh: Beta Phi Mu, 1983.

Acquisitions

Ishimoto, Carol F. "The National Program for Acquisitions and Cataloging: Its Impact on University Libraries." *College and Research Libraries* 34, no. 2 (March 1973): 126–36.

Wagner, Ralph D. *A History of the Farmington Plan*. Lanham, MD: Scarecrow Press, 2002.

Adult Services

Birge, Lynn E. *Serving Adult Learners: A Public Library Tradition*. Chicago: American Library Association, 1981.

Burt, Laura. "Vivian Harsh, Adult Education, and the Library's Role as Community Center." *Libraries and the Cultural Record* 44, no. 2 (Spring 2009): 234–55.

Heim, Kathleen M. "Adult Services within the American Library Association: A Historical Examination of the Move to Synthesis." *RQ* 30, no. 3 (Spring 1991): 386–94.

Lee, Robert Ellis. *Continuing Education for Adults through the American Public Library, 1833–1964*. Chicago: American Library Association, 1966.

African Americans in Librarianship

Dawson, Alma. "Celebrating African-American Librarians and Librarianship." *Library Trends* 49, no. 1 (Summer 2000): 49–87.

Jackson, Andrew P., Julius Jefferson, and Akilah Nosakhere, eds. *The 21st-century Black Librarian in America: Issues and Challenges*. Lanham, MD: Scarecrow Press, 2012.

Jenkins, Betty L. "A White Librarian in Black Harlem." *Library Quarterly* 60, no. 3 (July 1990): 216–31.

Josey, E. J. *The Black Librarian in America*. Metuchen, NJ: Scarecrow Press, 1970.

———. *The Black Librarian in America Revisited*. Metuchen, NJ: Scarecrow Press, 1994.

Josey, E. J., and Marva L. LeLoach, eds. *Handbook of Black Librarianship*, 2nd ed. Lanham, MD: Scarecrow Press, 2000.

McPheeters, Annie L. *Library Service in Black and White: Some Personal Recollections, 1921–1980*. Metuchen, NJ: Scarecrow Press, 1988.

Phinazee, Annette L. *The Black Librarian in the Southeast: Reminiscences, Activities, Challenges: Papers Presented for a Colloquium*. Durham, NC: The School, 1980.

Sutton, Allison M. "Bridging the Gap in Early Library Education History for African Americans: The Negro Teacher-Librarian Training Program (1936–1939)." *Journal of Negro Education* 74, no. 2 (Spring 2005): 138–50.

Tucker, John Mark. "Let the Circle Be Unbroken: The Struggle for Continuity in African-American Librarianship, 1970–1995." *Libraries and Culture* 31, nos. 3–4 (1996): 645–55.

———. *Untold Stories: Civil Rights, Libraries, and Black Librarianship*. Champaign, IL: Publications Office, Graduate School of Library and Information Science, 1998.

Whitmire, Ethelene. "Breaking the Color Barrier: Regina Andrews and the New York Public Library." *Libraries and the Cultural Record* 42, no. 1 (Winter 2007): 409–21.

Wilkin, Binnie Tate. *African American Librarians of the Far West: Pioneers and Trailblazers*. Lanham, MD: Scarecrow Press, 2006.

African Americans, Library Service to

Battles, David M. *The History of Public Library Access for African Americans in the South, or, Leaving Behind the Plow*. Lanham, MD: Scarecrow Press, 2009.

Cook, Karen. "Struggles Within: Lura G. Currier, the Mississippi Library Commission, and Library Services to African Americans." *Information and Culture: A Journal of History* 48, no. 1 (Winter 2013): 134–56.

Cresswell, Stephen. "The Last Days of Jim Crow in Southern Libraries." *Libraries and Culture* 31, nos. 3–4 (1996): 557–73.

Fultz, Michael. "Black Public Libraries in the South in the Era of De Jure Segregation." *Libraries and the Cultural Record* 41, no. 3 (Summer 2006): 337–59.

Graham, Patterson Toby. "Public Librarians and the Civil Rights Movement: Alabama, 1955–1965." *Library Quarterly* 71, no. 1 (January 2001): 1–27.

Jones, Reinette F. *Library Service to African Americans in Kentucky, from the Reconstruction Era to the 1960s*. Jefferson, NC: McFarland and Co., 2002.

Lipscomb, Carolyn E. "Race and Librarianship: Part I." *Journal of the Medical Library Association* 92, no. 3 (July 2004): 299–301.

———. "Race and Librarianship: Part II." *Journal of the Medical Library Association* 93, no. 3 (July 2005): 308–10.

Malone, Cheryl Knott. "Autonomy and Accommodation: Houston's Colored Carnegie Library, 1907–1922." *Libraries and Culture* 34, no. 2 (Spring 1999): 95–112.

———. "Louisville Free Public Library's Racially Segregated Branches, 1905–35." *Register of the Kentucky Historical Society* 93, no. 2 (Spring 1995): 159–79.

———. "Unannounced and Unexpected: The Desegregation of Houston's Public Library in the Early 1950s." *Library Trends* 55, no. 1 (Winter 2007): 665–74.

Willet, Holly G. "*Rifles for Watie*: Rollins, Riley, and Racism." *Libraries and Culture* 36, no. 4 (Fall 2001): 488–505.

American Library Association

American Library Association, and Maynard J. Brichford. *Guide to the American Library Association Archives*. Chicago: American Library Association, 1979.

Dalton, Margaret Stieg. "The International Relations Office, 1956–1972." *Library Trends* 55, no. 3 (Winter 2007): 609–22.

Luyt, Brendan. "The ALA, Public Libraries and the Great Depression." *Library History* 23, no. 2 (June 2007): 85–96.

Preer, Jean L. "'This Year—Richmond!' The 1936 Meeting of the American Library Association." *Libraries and Culture* 39, no. 2 (Spring 2004): 137–60.

Shiflett, O. Lee. "The American Library Association's Quest for a Black Library School." *Journal of Education for Library and Information Science* 35, no. 1 (Winter 1994): 68–72.

Skallerup, Harry R. "The Steamship Named ALA." *Libraries and Culture* 39, no. 2 (Fall 2004): 446–51.

Thomison, Dennis. *A History of the American Library Association, 1876–1972*. Chicago: American Library Association, 1978.

Wiegand, Wayne A. "American Library Association Executive Board Members, 1876–1917: A Collective Profile." *Libri* 31, no. 1 (1981): 153–66.

———. *The Politics of an Emerging Profession: The American Library Association, 1876–1917*. New York: Greenwood Press, 1986.

Wiegand, Wayne A., and Sarah Wadsworth. "By Invitation Only: The American Library Association and the Woman's Building Library of the World's Columbian Exposition, Chicago, 1893." *Signs: Journal of Women in Culture and Society* 35, no. 3 (Spring 2010): 699–722.

Ancient Libraries

Blum, Rudolf. *Kallimachos: The Alexandrian Library and the Origins of Bibliography.* Madison: University of Wisconsin Press, 1991.
Canfora, Luciano. *The Vanished Library.* Berkeley: University of California Press, 1989.
Houston, George W. "Tiberius and the Libraries: Public Book Collections and Library Buildings in the Early Roman Empire." *Libraries and the Cultural Record* 43, no. 3 (Summer 2008): 247–69.
Posner, Ernst. *Archives in the Ancient World.* Cambridge, MA: Harvard University Press, 1972.
Thompson, James Westfall. *Ancient Libraries.* Berkeley: University of California Press, 1940.
Too, Yun Lee. *The Idea of the Library in the Ancient World.* New York: Oxford University Press, 2010.
Webb, Kerry. "'The House of Books': Libraries and Archives in Ancient Egypt." *Libri* 63, no. 1 (2013): 21–32.

Associations

Anuar, Hedwig. "The Why and How of CONSAL as a Regional Library Association." *IFLA Journal* 15, no. 3 (1989): 237–42.
Bradley, Carol June. "The Music Library Association: The Founding Generation and Its Work." *Notes* Second Series 37, no. 4 (1981): 763–822.
Greider, Antoinette Paris. "IAALD: The First Fifty Years." *Quarterly Bulletin of the International Association of Agricultural Information Specialists* 51, no. 1 (2006): 15–23.
Muddiman, Dave. "A New History of ASLIB, 1924–1950." *Journal of Documentation* 61, no. 3 (2005): 402–28.
Musisi, J. S., and J. L. Abukutsa. "Evolution of the Library Association of Kenya." *International Library Review* 10, no. 4 (1978): 345–53.
Richards, Pamela Spence. "ASLIB at War: The Brief but Intrepid Career of a Library Organization as a Hub of Allied Scientific Intelligence, 1942–1945." *Journal of Education for Library and Information Science* 29, no. 4 (Spring 1989): 279–96.
Swaby, Joan E. "Regional Cooperation: The Role of COMLA in International Librarianship." *IFLA Journal* 15, no. 3 (1989): 243–45.

Wagstaff, John. "The International Association of Music Libraries (IAML): Past, Present, and Future." In *Advances in Librarianship*, vol. 24, ed. Elizabeth A. Chapman and Frederick C. Lynden. San Diego: Academic Press, 2000.

Yamashita, Kenneth A. "Asian/Pacific American Librarians Association—A History of APALA and Its Founders." *Library Trends* 49, no. 1 (Summer 2000): 88–109.

Automation

Black, Alistair. "Mechanization in Libraries and Information Retrieval: Punched Cards and Microfilm before the Widespread Adoption of Computer Technology in Libraries." *Library History* 23, no. 4 (December 2007): 291–99.

Borgman, Christine L. "From Acting Locally to Thinking Globally: A Brief History of Library Automation." *Library Quarterly* 67, no. 3 (July 1997): 215–49.

Bourne, Charles P., and Trudi Bellardo Hahn. *A History of Online Information Services, 1963–1976*. Cambridge, MA: MIT Press, 2003.

Bowman, J. H. "Classification in British Public Libraries: A Historical Perspective." *Library History* 21, no. 3 (November 2005): 143–73.

———. "OPACS: The Early Years, and User Reactions." *Library History* 23, no. 4 (December 2007): 317–29.

———. "Retrospective Conversion: The Early Years." *Library History* 23, no. 4 (December 2007): 331–40.

Brown-Syed, Christopher. *Parents of Invention: The Development of Library Automation Systems in the Late 20th Century*. Santa Barbara, CA: Libraries Unlimited, 2011.

Burke, C. "The Ford Foundation's Search for an American Library Laboratory." *IEEE Annals of the History of Computing* 24, no. 3 (2002): 56–74.

Crawford, John, ed. "The History of Library Automation in the UK." *Library History* 23, no. 4 (December 2007): entire issue.

Gay, Ruth. "The Machine in the Library." *The American Scholar* 49, no. 1 (Winter 1980): 66–77.

Hopkinson, Alan. "Library Automation in Developing Countries: The Last 25 Years." *Information Development* 25, no. 4 (November 2009): 304–12.

Marcum, Deanna B. "Automating the Library: The Council on Library Resources." *IEEE Annals of the History of Computing* 24, no. 3 (2002): 2–13.

McCallum, Sally H. "MARC: Keystone for Library Automation." *IEEE Annals of the History of Computing* 24, no. 2 (2002): 34–49.

Naylor, Bernard. "Early Developments in the Automation of Higher Education Libraries." *Library History* 23, no. 4 (December 2007): 283–90.

Peay, Wayne J., and Paul Schoening. "Estelle Brodman and the First Generation of Library Automation." *Journal of the Medical Library Association* 96, no. 3 (July 2008): 262–67.

Primich, Tracy, and Caroline Richardson. "The Integrated Library System: From Innovation to Relegation to Innovation Again." *Acquisitions Librarian* 18, nos. 35–36 (2006): 119–33.

Rau, Erik P. "Managing the Machine in the Stacks: Operations Research, Bibliographic Control and Library Computerization, 1950–2000." *Library History* 23, no. 2 (June 2007): 151–68.

Rayward, W. Boyd. "A History of Computer Applications in Libraries: Prolegomena." *IEEE Annals of the History of Computing* 24, no. 2 (2004): 4–15.

Smith, K. Wayne. "OCLC: Yesterday, Today and Tomorrow." *Journal of Library Administration* 25, no. 4 (1998): 251–70.

Tedd, Lucy A. "Computer-based Library Systems: A Review of the Last Twenty-one Years." *Journal of Documentation* 43, no. 2 (1987): 145–65.

Carnegie Corporation and Carnegie Libraries

Bobinski, George S. *Carnegie Libraries: Their History and Impact on American Public Library Development*. Chicago: American Library Association, 1969.

Jones, Theodore. *Carnegie Libraries across America: A Public Legacy*. Washington, DC: Preservation Press, 1997.

Maurizi, D. "Carnegie and His Legacy: The Little Libraries That Could." *Public Libraries* 40, no. 6 (November–December 2001): 346–48.

Radford, Neil A. *The Carnegie Corporation and the Development of American College Libraries, 1928–1941*. Chicago: American Library Association, 1984.

Rochester, Maxine K. "American Philanthropy Abroad: Library Program Support from the Carnegie Corporation of New York British Dominions and Colonies Fund in the 1920s and 1930s." *Libraries and Culture* 31, no. 2 (Spring 1996): 342–63.

———. "The Carnegie Corporation and South Africa: Non-European Library Services." *Libraries and Culture* 34, no. 1 (Winter 1999): 27–51.

Sullivan, Peggy. "Carnegie Fellowships for Librarians 1929–1942: A Microcosm of Carnegie Corporation and American Library Association Joint Enterprise." *Libraries and Culture* 3, no. 2 (Spring 1996): 437–46.

Van Slyck, Abigail Ayres. *Free to All: Carnegie Libraries and American Culture, 1890–1920*. Chicago: University of Chicago Press, 1995.

Cataloging and Classification

Baker, Barry B. *Cooperative Cataloging: Past, Present, and Future.* New York: Haworth Press, 1993.

Banush, David. "Cooperative Cataloging at the Intersection of Tradition and Transformation: Possible Futures for the Program for Cooperative Cataloging." *Cataloging and Classification Quarterly* 48, nos. 2–3 (2010): 247–57.

Beall, J., and J. S. Mitchell. "History of the Representation of the DDC in the MARC Classification Format." *Cataloging and Classification Quarterly* 48, no. 1 (2010): 48–63.

Beghtol, Clare. "Exploring New Approaches to the Organization of Knowledge: The Subject Classification of James Duff Brown." *Library Trends* 52, no. 4 (Spring 2004): 702–18.

Blake, Virgil L. P. "Forging the Anglo-American Cataloging Alliance: Descriptive Cataloging, 1830–1908." *Cataloging and Classification Quarterly* 35, nos. 1–2 (September 2002): 3–22.

Carpenter, Michael, and Elaine Svenonius. *Foundations of Cataloging: A Sourcebook.* Littleton, CO: Libraries Unlimited, 1985.

Dahlberg, Ingetraut. "Major Developments in Classification." In *Advances in Librarianship*, vol. 7, ed. Melvin John Voight and Michael H. Harris. New York: Academic Press, 1977.

Ducheyne, S. "'To Treat the World': Paul Otlet's Ontology and Epistemology and the Circle of Knowledge." *Journal of Documentation* 65, no. 2 (2009): 223–44.

Frost, Carolyn O. "The Bodleian Catalogs of 1674 and 1738: An Examination in the Light of Modern Cataloging Theory." *Library Quarterly* 46, no. 3 (July 1976): 248–70.

Galeffi, Agnese. "Biographical and Cataloging Common Ground: Panizzi and Lubetzky, Kindred Spirits Separated by a Century." *Library and Information History* 25, no. 4 (December 2009): 227–46.

Hickey, Doralyn J. "The Search for Uniformity in Cataloging: Centralization and Standardization." *Library Trends* 25, no. 3 (Winter 1977): 565–86.

Hopkins, Judith. "The 1791 French Cataloging Code and the Origins of the Card Catalog." *Libraries and Culture* 27, no. 4 (Fall 1992): 378–404.

Joachim, Martin D., ed. *Historical Aspects of Cataloging and Classification.* Binghamton, NY: Haworth Press, 2003.

Knapp, Patricia B. "The Subject Catalog in the College Library: The Background of Subject Cataloging." *Library Quarterly* 14, no. 2 (April 1944): 108–18.

Knowlton, Steven A. "Criticism of Cataloging Code Reform, as Seen in the Pages of *Library Resources and Technical Services* (1957–66)." *Library Resources and Technical Services* 53, no. 1 (January 2009): 15–24.

Lehnus, Donald J. *Milestones in Cataloging: Famous Catalogers and Their Writings, 1835–1969.* Littleton, CO: Libraries Unlimited, 1974.

Madison, Olivia. "The Origins of the IFLA Study on Functional Requirements for Bibliographic Record." *Cataloging and Classification Quarterly* 39, nos. 3–4 (2005): 15–37.

Maxwell, Margaret F. "The Genesis of the Anglo-American Cataloging Rules." *Libri* 27, no. 1 (1977): 238–62.

McIlwaine, I. C. "Universal Bibliographic Control and the Quest for a Universally Acceptable Subject Arrangement." *Cataloging and Classification Quarterly* 48, no. 1 (2010): 36–47.

———. "The Universal Decimal Classification: Some Factors Concerning Its Origins, Development, and Influence." *Journal of the American Society for Information Science* 48 (April 1997): 331–39.

Miksa, Francis L. *The Development of Classification at the Library of Congress.* Urbana: University of Illinois Graduate School of Library and Information Science. 1984.

———. "The Legacy of the Library Catalogue for the Present." *Library Trends* 61, no. 1 (Summer 2012): 7–34.

———. *The Subject in the Dictionary Catalog from Cutter to the Present.* Chicago: American Library Association, 1983.

Myall, Carolynne, and Ruth C. Carter, eds. *Portraits in Cataloging and Classification: Theorists, Educators, and Practitioners of the Late Twentieth Century.* New York: Haworth Press, 1998.

Osborn, Andrew Delbridge. "From Cutter and Dewey to Mortimer Taube and Beyond: A Complete Century of Change in Cataloguing and Classification." *Cataloging and Classification Quarterly* 12, nos. 3–4 (1991): 35–50.

Rodriguez, Robert D. "Classification and Subject Indication: Highlights of the Anglo-American Debate, 1850–1950." *Libri* 31, no. 4 (1981): 322–40.

Seikel, Michele, and Thomas Steele. "How MARC Has Changed: The History of the Format and Its Forthcoming Relationship to RDA." *Technical Services Quarterly* 28 (July–September 2011): 322–34.

Spicher, Karen M. "The Development of the MARC Format." *Cataloging and Classification Quarterly* 21, nos. 3–4 (1996): 75–90.

Stone, Alva T., ed. "The LCSH Century: One Hundred Years with the Library of Congress Subject Headings System." *Cataloging and Classification Quarterly* 29, nos. 1–2 (2000): entire issue.

Tillet, Barbara. "Catalog It Once for All: A History of Cooperative Cataloging in the United States Prior to 1967 (before MARC)." *Cataloging and Classification Quarterly* 17, nos. 3–4 (1993): 3–38.

Wiegand, Wayne A. "The 'Amherst Method': The Origins of the Dewey Decimal Classification Scheme." *Libraries and Culture* 33, no. 2 (Spring 1998): 175–95.

Winship, Michael. "The Library of Congress in 1892: Ainsworth Spofford, Houghton, Mifflin and Company, and *Uncle Tom's Cabin.*" *Libraries and the Cultural Record* 45, no. 1 (January 2010): 85–91.

Wright, Wyllis E. "The Anglo-American Catalog Rules: A Historical Perspective." *Library Resources and Technical Services* 20, no. 1 (Winter 1976): 37–38.

Yee, Martha M. "Attempts to Deal with the 'Crisis in Cataloging' at the Library of Congress in the 1940s." *Library Quarterly* 57, no. 1 (January 1987): 1–31.

———. "'Wholly Visionary': The American Library Association, the Library of Congress, and the Card Distribution Program." *Library Resources and Technical Services* 53, no. 2 (April 2009): 68–78.

Censorship

Asato, Noriko. "The Origins of the Freedom to Read Foundation: Public Librarians' Campaign to Establish a Legal Defense against Library Censorship." *Public Library Quarterly* 30, no. 4 (October 2011): 286–306.

Curry, Ann. "The Library Association Record and Censorship: A Content Analysis." *Libri* 47, no. 4 (1997): 214–23.

Geller, Evelyn. *Forbidden Books in American Public Libraries, 1876–1939: A Study in Cultural Change.* Westport, CT: Greenwood Press, 1984.

Knuth, Rebecca. *Libricide: The Regime-Sponsored Destruction of Books and Libraries in the Twentieth Century.* Westport, CT: Praeger, 2003.

Mediavilla, Cindy. "The War on Books and Ideas: The California Library Association and Anti-communist Censorship in the 1940s and 1950s." *Library Trends* 46, no. 2 (Fall 1997): 331–47.

Moon, Eric. *Book Selection and Censorship in the Sixties.* New York: Bowker, 1969.

Robbins, Louise S. *Censorship and the American Library: The American Library Association's Response to Threats to Intellectual Freedom, 1939–1969.* Westport, CT: Greenwood Press, 1996.

———. *The Dismissal of Miss Ruth Brown: Civil Rights, Censorship, and the American Library.* Norman: University of Oklahoma Press, 2000.

Stielow, Frederick J. "Censorship in the Early Professionalism of American Libraries, 1876–1923." *Journal of Library History* 18, no. 1 (Winter 1983): 37–54.

Von Merveldt, Nikola. "Books Cannot Be Killed by Fire: The German Freedom Library and the American Library of Nazi-banned Books as Agents of Cultural Memory." *Library Trends* 55, no. 3 (Winter 2007): 523–35.

Woods, L. B. *A Decade of Censorship in America: The Threat to Classrooms and Libraries, 1966–1975.* Metuchen, NJ: Scarecrow Press, 1979.

Children's Librarianship

Bader, Barbara. "Cleveland and Pittsburgh Create a Profession." *Horn Book Magazine* 88 (May–June 2012): 27–34.

———. "Realms of Gold and Granite." *The Horn Book Magazine* 75 (September–October 1999): 524–31.

Doll, Carol A. "Audiovisual Materials and Programming for Children: A Long Tradition." *Journal of Youth Services in Libraries* 6, no. 1 (Fall 1992): 53–62.

Eddy, Jacalyn. *Bookwomen: Creating an Empire in Children's Book Publishing, 1919–1939.* Madison: University of Wisconsin Press, 2006.

Fenwick, Sara Innis. "Library Service to Children and Young People." *Library Trends* 25, no. 1 (Summer 1976): 329–60.

Hamilton-Honey, Emily. "Guardians of Morality: Librarians and American Girls' Series Fiction, 1890–1950." *Library Trends* 60, no. 4 (Spring 2012): 765–85.

Hand, Shane. "Transmitting Whiteness: Librarians, Children, and Race, 1900–1930s." *Progressive Librarian* 38–39 (Spring 2012): 34–63.

Jenkins, Christine. "The History of Youth Services Librarianship: A Review of the Research Literature." *Libraries and Culture* 35, no. 1 (Winter 2000): 103–40.

———. "Professional Jurisdiction and ALA Youth Services Women: Of Nightingales, Newberys, Realism, and the Right Books, 1937–1945." *Library Trends* 44, no. 4 (Spring 1996): 813–39.

Kimball, Melanie A. "Seeing the World from Main Street: Early Twentieth-century Juvenile Collections about Life in Other Lands." *Library Trends* 60, no. 4 (Spring 2012): 675–93.

Long, Harriet G. *Public Library Service to Children: Foundation and Development.* Metuchen, NJ: Scarecrow Press, 1969.

Lukenbill, W. Bernard. "Helping Youth at Risk: An Overview of Reformist Movements in American Public Library Services to Youth." *New Review of Children's Literature and Librarianship* 12, no. 2 (November 2006): 197–213.

McDowell, Kate. "Children's Voices in Librarians' Words, 1890–1930." *Libraries and the Cultural Record* 46, no. 1 (Winter 2011): 73–101.

McDowell, Kate, and Caroline Nappo. "Evolution in Children's Science Books: Recommendations and Library Collections, 1863–1956." *Library Trends* 60, no. 4 (Spring 2012): 655–74.

Smith, Karen Patricia, ed. "Imagination and Scholarship: Contributions of Women to American Youth Services and Literature." *Library Trends* 44, no. 4 (Spring 1996): entire issue.

Smith, Rita J. "Just Who Are These Women? Louise Seaman Bechtel and Ruth Marie Baldwin." *Journal of Youth Services in Libraries* 11, no. 2 (Winter 1998): 161–70.

Thomas, Fanette H. "Early Appearances of Children's Reading Rooms in Public Libraries." *Journal of Youth Services in Libraries* 4, no. 1 (Fall 1990): 81–85.

Tolson, Nancy. "Making Books Available: The Role of Early Libraries, Librarians and Booksellers in the Promotion of African-American Children's Literature." *African American Review* 32, no. 1 (Spring 1998): 9–16.

Welch, Cindy C. "Children's Stories through the Air: Librarian-Broadcasters, 1922–1941." *Library Quarterly* 82, no. 2 (April 2012): 141–59.

Cold War Librarianship

Anghelescu, Hermina G. B., and Martine Poulain. "Books, Libraries, Reading, and Publishing in the Cold War: Proceedings of an International Conference, 11–12 June 1998, Centre Sèvres, Paris." *Libraries and Culture* 36, no. 1 (Winter 2001): entire issue.

Jenkins, Christine. "ALA Youth Services Librarians and the CARE-UNESCO Children's Book Fund: Selecting the Right Books for Children in Cold War America." *Libraries and Culture* 31, no. 1 (Winter 1996): 209–34.

McReynolds, Rosalee, and Louise S. Robbins. *The Librarian Spies: Philip and Mary Jane Keeney and Cold War Espionage.* Westport, CT: Praeger Security International, 2009.

Pawley, Christine. *Reading Places: Literacy, Democracy, and the Public Library in Cold War America.* Amherst: University of Massachusetts Press, 2010.

Preer, Jean. "The American Heritage Project: Librarians and the Democratic Tradition in the Early Cold War." *Libraries and Culture* 28, no. 2 (Spring 1993): 165–88.

Richards, Pamela Spence. "Cold War Librarianship: Soviet and American Library Activities in Support of National Foreign Policy, 1946–1991." *Libraries and Culture* 36, no. 1 (Winter 2001): 193–203.

Robbins, Louise S. "After Brave Words, Silence: American Librarianship Responds to Cold War Loyalty Programs, 1947–1957." *Libraries and Culture* 30, no. 4 (Fall 1995): 345–65.

Documentation

Farkas-Conn, Irene Sekely. *From Documentation to Information Science: The Beginnings and Early Development of the American Documentation Institute-American Society for Information Science*. New York: Greenwood Press, 1990.

Rayward, W. Boyd. "The International Exposition and the World Documentation Congress, Paris 1937." *Library Quarterly* 53, no. 3 (July 1983): 254–68.

————. "The UDC and FID—A Historical Perspective." *Library Quarterly* 37, no. 3 (July 1967): 259–78.

Williams, Robert V. "The Documentation and Special Libraries Movements in the United States, 1910–1960." *Journal of the American Society for Information Science* 48, no. 9 (September 1977): 775–81.

Education and Training for Librarianship

Brundin, Robert E. "Sydney B. Mitchell and the Establishment of Graduate Education for Librarianship." *Libraries and Culture* 29, no. 2 (Spring 1994): 166–85.

Carroll, C. Edward. *The Professionalization of Education for Librarianship, with Special Reference to the Years 1940–1960*. Metuchen, NJ: Scarecrow Press, 1970.

Churchwell, Charles D. *The Shaping of American Library Education*. Chicago: American Library Association, 1975.

Dalton, Margaret Stieg. *Change and Challenge in Library and Information Science Education*. Chicago: American Library Association, 1992.

Davis, Donald G., Jr. "Ninety Years of Education for the Profession: Reflections on the Early Years." *Journal of Education for Library and Information Science* 46, no. 3 (Summer 2005): 266–70.

Eaton, Gale. "The Education of Alice M. Jordan and the Origins of the Boston Public Library Training School." *Libraries and the Cultural Record* 46, no. 1 (Winter 2011): 26–49.

Hansen, Debra Gold. "Professionalizing Library Education, the California Connection: James Gillis, Everett Perry, and Joseph Daniels." *Library Trends* 52, no. 4 (Spring 2004): 963–87.

Houser, Lloyd J., and Alvin M. Schrader. *The Search for a Scientific Profession: Library Science Education in the US and Canada*. Metuchen, NJ: Scarecrow Press, 1977.

Kinnell, Margaret. "From Autonomy to Systems: Education for the Information and Library Professions, 1986–1999." *Journal of Documentation* 56, no. 4 (July 2000): 399–411.

Lynch, Beverly P. "Library Education: Its Past, Its Present, Its Future." *Library Trends* 56, no. 2 (Spring 2008): 931–53.

Martin, Robert Sidney, and Orvin Lee Shiflett. "Hampton, Fisk, and Atlanta: The Foundations of the American Library Association and Library Education for Blacks, 1925–1941." *Libraries and Culture* 31, no. 2 (Spring 1996): 299–325.

Shera, Jesse Hauk. *The Foundations of Education for Librarianship*. New York: Becker and Hayes, 1972.

Sugimoto, Cassidy R., Terrell G. Russell, and Sheryl Grant. "Library and Information Science Doctoral Education: The Landscape from 1930–2007." *Journal of Education for Library and Information Science* 50, no. 3 (Summer 2009): 190–202.

Sullivan, Peggy. "ALA and Library Education: A Century of Changing Roles and Actors, Shifting Scenes and Plots." *Journal of Education for Library and Information Science* 26, no. 3 (1986): 143–53.

Swigger, Boyd Keith. *The MLS Project: An Assessment after Sixty Years*. Lanham, MD: Scarecrow Press, 2010.

Vann, Sarah K. *Training for Librarianship before 1923: Education for Librarianship Prior to the Publication of Williamson's Report on Training for Library Service*. Chicago: American Library Association, 1961.

———. *The Williamson Reports: A Study*. Metuchen, NJ: Scarecrow Press, 1971.

Wheeler, Maurice B. *Unfinished Business: Race, Equity, and Diversity in Library and Information Science Education*. Lanham, MD: Scarecrow Press, 2005.

White, Carl Milton. *A Historical Introduction to Library Education: Problems and Progress to 1951*. Metuchen, NJ: Scarecrow Press, 1976.

Wilson, Anthony M., and Robert Hermanson. "Educating and Training Library Practitioners: A Comparative History with Trends and Recommendations." *Library Trends* 46, no. 3 (Winter 1998): 467–99.

Evaluation of Libraries

Kyrillidou, Martha, and Colleen Cook. "The Evolution of Measurement and Evaluation of Libraries: A Perspective from the Association of Research Libraries." *Library Trends* 56, no. 4 (Spring 2008): 888–909.

Historiography

Aspray, William. "The History of Information Science and Other Traditional Information Domains: Models for Future Research." *Libraries and the Cultural Record* 46, no. 2 (Spring 2011): 230–48.

Davis, Donald G., Jr. "International Trends in Library History." *Libraries and the Cultural Record* 45, no. 1 (Winter 2010): 123–29.

Goedeken, Edward A. "The Library Historian's Field of Dreams: A Profile of the First Nine Seminars." *Libraries and Culture* 35, no. 1 (Winter 2000): 161–72.

———. "Our Historiographical Enterprise: Shifting Emphases and Directions." *Libraries and the Cultural Record* 45, no. 3 (Summer 2010): 350–58.

Harris, Michael H., and Stanley A. Hannah. "Why Do We Study the History of Libraries? A Meditation on the Perils of Ahistoricism in the Information Era." *Library and Information Science Research* 14, no. 2 (April–June 1992): 123–30.

Maack, Mary Niles. "International Dimensions of Library History: Leadership and Scholarship, 1978–1998." *Libraries and Culture* 35, no. 1 (Winter 2000): 66–76.

Ollé, James G. *Library History*. London: Clive Bingley, 1979.

Pawley, Christine. "History in the Library and Information Science Curriculum: Outline of a Debate." *Libraries and Culture* 40, no. 3 (Summer 2005): 223–38.

Shiflett, Orvin Lee. "Clio's Claim: The Role of Historical Research in Library and Information Science." *Library Trends* 32, no. 4 (Spring 1984): 385–406.

Image of Librarians

Adams, Katherine C. "Loveless Frump as Hip and Sexy Party Girl: A Reevaluation of the Old-Maid Stereotype." *Library Quarterly* 70, no. 3 (July 2000): 287–301.

Dilevko, Juris, and Lisa Gottlieb. "The Portrayal of Librarians in Obituaries at the End of the Twentieth Century." *Library Quarterly* 74, no. 2 (April 2004): 152–80.

Newmeyer, Jody. "The Image Problem of the Librarian: Femininity and Social Control." *Journal of Library History* 11, no. 1 (Winter 1976): 44–67.

Radford, Marie L., and Gary P. Radford. "Librarians and Party Girls: Cultural Studies and the Meaning of the Librarian." *Library Quarterly* 73, no. 1 (January 2003): 54–69.

Stevens, N. D. "The Image of the Librarian: How the Past May Illuminate the Future." *Urban Library Journal* 10, nos. 1–2 (Fall 1997–Winter 1998): 23–27.

Tevis, Ray, and Brenda Tevis. *The Image of Librarians in Cinema, 1917–1999*. Jefferson, NC: McFarland and Company, 2005.

Information Science

Apostle, Richard A., and Boris Raymond. *Librarianship and the Information Paradigm*. Lanham, MD: Scarecrow Press, 1997.

Bensman, Stephen J. "Urquhart and Probability: The Transition from Librarianship to Library and Information Science." *Journal of the American Society for Information Science and Technology* 56, no. 2 (January 15, 2005): 189–214.

East, Harry. "Professor Bernal's 'Insidious and Cavalier Proposals': The Royal Society Scientific Information Conference, 1948." *Journal of Documentation* 54, no. 3 (1998): 294–302.

Hahn, Trudi Bellardo, and Michael Buckland, eds. *Historical Studies in Information Science*. Medford, NJ: Information Today, 1998.

Herner, Saul. "A Brief History of Information Science." *Journal of the American Society for Information Science* 35, no. 3 (1984): 157–63.

Metcalfe, John Wallace. *Information Retrieval, British and American, 1876–1976*. Metuchen, NJ: Scarecrow Press, 1976.

Rayward, W. Boyd. "The History and Historiography of Information Science: Some Reflections." *Information Processing and Management* 32, no. 1 (January 1996): 3–17.

———. "The Origins of Information Science and the International Institute of Bibliography/International Federation for Information and Documentation (FID)." *Journal of the American Society for Information Science* 48, no. 4 (1997): 289–300.

Intellectual Freedom

Cohen, Henry, and Mary Minow. "Intellectual Freedom in Libraries: Then and Now." In *Advances in Librarianship*, vol. 30, ed. Danuta A. Nitecki and Eileen Abels. Amsterdam: Academic Press, 2006.

Krug, Judith F. "ALA and Intellectual Freedom: An Historical Overview." In *Intellectual Freedom Manual*, 6th ed., pp. 3–32. Chicago: American Library Association, 2002.

Latham, J. M. "Wheat and Chaff: Carl Roden, Abe Korman, and the Definitions of Intellectual Freedom in the Chicago Public Library." *Libraries and the Cultural Record* 44, no. 3 (Summer 2009): 279–98.

Oboler, Eli M. *Defending Intellectual Freedom: The Library and the Censor*. Westport, CT: Greenwood Press, 1980.

Robbins, Louise S. "Champions of a Cause: American Librarians and the Library Bill of Rights in the 1950s." *Library Trends* 45, no. 1 (Summer 1996): 28–49.

————. "The Overseas Libraries Controversy and the Freedom to Read: US Librarians and Publishers Confront Joseph McCarthy." *Libraries and Culture* 36, no. 1 (Winter 2001): 27–39.

————. "Segregating Propaganda in American Libraries: Ralph Ulveling Confronts the Intellectual Freedom Committee." *Library Quarterly* 63, no. 2 (April 1993): 143–65.

Samek, Toni. *Intellectual Freedom and Social Responsibility in American Librarianship, 1967–1974*. Jefferson, NC: McFarland, 2001.

————. "The Library Bill of Rights in the 1960s: One Profession, One Ethic." *Library Trends* 45, no. 1 (Summer 1996): 50–60.

International Federation of Library Associations and Institutions

Anderson, Dorothy Pauline. "IFLA's Programme of Universal Bibliographic Control: Origins and Early Years." *IFLA Journal* 26, no. 3 (2000): 209–14.

Koops, Willem R. H., and Joachim Wieder, eds. *IFLA's First Fifty Years: Achievement and Challenge in International Librarianship*. München: Verlag Dokumentation, 1977.

Lor, Peter Johan. "The IFLA-UNESCO Partnership, 1947–2012." *IFLA Journal* 38, no. 4 (December 2012): 269–82.

International Librarianship

Bliss, Nonie J. "The Emergence of International Librarianship as a Field." *Libri* 43, no. 1 (1993): 39–52.

Byrd, Cecil K., ed. "The Influence of American Librarianship Abroad." *Library Trends* 20, no. 3 (Winter 1972): entire issue.

Lee, Mordecai. "Clara M. Edmunds and the Library of the United States Information Service, 1934–1948." *Libraries and the Cultural Record* 42, no. 3 (Summer 2007): 213–30.

Rayward, W. Boyd. "The Evolution of an International Library and Bibliographic Community." *Journal of Library History* 16, no. 2 (Spring 1981): 449–62.

Richards, Pamela Spence. *The History of Reading and Libraries in the United States and Russia: Proceedings of an International Conference, 19–21 June 1996, Vologda, Russia*. Austin: Graduate School of Library and Information Science, University of Texas, 1998.

————. "Soviet–American Library Relations in the 1920s and 1930s: A Study in Mutual Fascination and Distrust." *Library Quarterly* 68, no. 4 (October 1998): 380–405.

Simmons, Wendy A. "Three Decades of Challenges and Changes in US Embassy Libraries around the World." In *Advances in Librarianship*, vol. 29, ed. Danuta A. Nitecki and Eileen Abels. Amsterdam: Academic Press, 2005.

Thompson, Anthony. "UNESCO, IFLA and FID: Their Contribution to the Development of International Comparative Librarianship." *Focus On International Library and Information Work* 37, no. 3 (December 2006): 90–94.

Witt, Steven. "Merchants of Light: The Paris Library School, Internationalism, and the Globalization of a Profession." *Library Quarterly* 83, no. 2 (April 2013): 131–51.

Law Librarianship

Butler, A. Hays. "Frederick Hicks's Strategic Vision for Law Librarianship." *Law Library Journal* 98, no. 2 (Spring 2006): 367–79.

Healey, Paul D. "Go and Tell the World: Charles R. McCarthy and the Evolution of the Legislative Reference Movement, 1901–1917." *Law Library Journal* 99, no. 1 (Winter 2007): 33–53.

Houdek, Frank G. "AALL History through the Eyes of Its Presidents." *Law Library Journal* 98, no. 2 (Spring 2006): 299–347.

———. "Frequently Asked Questions about AALL's First Hundred Years." *Law Library Journal* 98, no. 1 (Winter 2006): 157–67.

Solon, Kasia. "Present in Its Absence: Law Librarians and Technology at the Founding of AALL." *Law Library Journal* 98, no. 3 (Summer 2006): 515–30.

Lesbian, Gay, Bisexual, and Transgender (LGBT) Librarianship

Carmichael, James V. *Daring to Find Our Names: The Search for Lesbigay Library History*. Westport, CT: Greenwood Press, 1998.

———. "'They Sure Got to Prove It on Me': Millennial Thought on Gay Archives, Gay Biography, and Gay Library History." *Libraries and Culture* 35, no. 1 (Winter 2000): 88–102.

Gittings, Barbara. *Gays in Library Land: The Gay and Lesbian Task Force of the American Library Association: The First Sixteen Years*. Philadelphia, PA: B. Gittings, 1990.

Johnson, Matt. "Transgender Subject Access: History and Current Practice." *Cataloging and Classification Quarterly* 48, no. 8 (November 2010): 661–83.

Kester, Norman G. *Liberating Minds: The Stories and Professional Lives of Gay, Lesbian, and Bisexual Librarians and Their Advocates*. Jefferson, NC: McFarland, 1997.

Passet, Joanne E. "Hidden in Plain Sight: Gay and Lesbian Books in Midwestern Public Libraries, 1900–1969." *Library Trends* 60, no. 4 (Spring 2012): 749–64.

Librarians, Selected Individual

Asheim, Lester

Hamilton, Beth A., and Joel M. Lee. *As Much to Learn As to Teach: Essays in Honour of Lester Asheim*. Hamden, CT: Linnet Books, 1979.

Baker, Augusta

Bader, Barbara. "Augusta Baker: Reformer and Traditionalist, Too." *The Horn Book Magazine* 27 (May–June 2011): 18–25.

Belpré, Pura

Hernandez Delgado, Julio L. "Pura Teresa Belpré: Storyteller and Pioneer Puerto Rican Librarian." *Library Quarterly* 62, no. 4 (October 1992): 425–40.

Núñez, Victoria. "Remembering Pura Belpré's Early Career at the 135th Street New York Public Library: Interracial Cooperation and Puerto Rican Settlement during the Harlem Renaissance." *Centro Journal* 21, no. 1 (Spring 2009): 52–77.

Billings, John Shaw

Chapman, Carleton B. *Order Out of Chaos: John Shaw Billings and America's Coming of Age*. Boston: Boston Medical Library in the Francis A. Countway Library of Medicine, 1994.

Bishop, William Warner

Sparks, Claud Glenn. *Doyen of Librarians: A Biography of William Warner Bishop*. Metuchen, NJ: Scarecrow Press, 1993.

Bostwick, Arthur

Yu, Priscilla C., and Donald G. Davis, Jr. "Arthur Bostwick and Chinese Library Development: A Chapter in International Cooperation." *Libraries and Culture* 33, no. 4 (Fall 1998): 389–406.

Brett, William Howard

Ring, Donald R. "Fighting for Their Hearts and Minds: William Howard Brett, the Cleveland Public Library, and World War I." *Journal of Library History* 18, no. 1 (Winter 1983): 1–20.

Briet, Suzanne

Buckland, Michael K. "The Centenary of 'Madame Documentation': Suzanne Briet, 1894–1989." *Journal of the American Society for Information Science* 46, no. 3 (April 1995): 235–37.
Maack, Mary Niles. "'The Lady and the Antelope:' Suzanne Briet's Contribution to the French Documentation Movement." *Library Trends* 52, no. 4 (Spring 2004): 719–47.

Butler, Pierce

Richardson, John V., and Pierce Butler. *The Gospel of Scholarship: Pierce Butler and a Critique of American Librarianship.* Metuchen, NJ: Scarecrow Press, 1992.

Cutter, Charles Ammi

Cutter, Charles A., and Francis L. Miksa. *Charles Ammi Cutter, Library Systematizer.* Littleton, CO: Libraries Unlimited, 1977.

Dana, John Cotton

Mattson, Kevin. "The Librarian as Secular Minister to Democracy: The Life and Ideas of John Cotton Dana." *Libraries and Culture* 35, no. 4 (Fall 2000): 499–513.
Winser, Marian Manley. "John Cotton Dana and the Special Libraries Association." *Special Libraries* 87, no. 4 (1996): 293–97.

Dewey, Melvil

Dewey, Melvil, and Sarah K. Vann. *Melvil Dewey, His Enduring Presence in Librarianship*. Littleton, CO: Libraries Unlimited, 1978.
Lee, Mordecai. "Clara M. Edmunds and the Library of the United States Information Service, 1934–1948." *Libraries and the Cultural Record* 42, no. 3 (Summer 2007): 213–30.
Miksa, Francis L. "Melvil Dewey: The Professional Educator and His Heirs." *Library Trends* 34, no. 3 (Winter 1986): 359–81.
Stevenson, Gordon, and Judith Kramer-Greene. *Melvil Dewey, the Man and the Classification: A Seminar*. Albany, NY: Forest Press, 1983.
Wiegand, Wayne A. *Irrepressible Reformer: A Biography of Melvil Dewey*. Chicago: American Library Association, 1996.
———. "'Jew Attack': The Story behind Melvil Dewey's Resignation as New York State Librarian in 1905." *American Jewish History* 83, no. 3 (1995): 359–79.
———. "Wresting Money from the Canny Scotsman: Melvil Dewey's Designs on Carnegie's Millions, 1902–1906." *Libraries and Culture* 31, no. 2 (Spring 1996): 380–94.

Edwards, Edward

Black, Alistair. "Edward Edwards and Modernity: Personality, Progress and Professionalism." *Library History* 12 (1996): 77–92.
Manley, K. A. "Edward Edwards: A Humble Librarian at Oxford." *Library History* 7, no. 3 (January 1986): 73–89.

Florence, Virginia Proctor Powell

Gunn, Arthur Clinton. "A Black Woman Wants to Be a Professional: The Struggle of Virginia Proctor Powell Florence." *American Libraries* 20, no. 2 (February 1989): 154–57.

Greene, Belle Da Costa

Ardizzone, Heidi. *An Illuminated Life: Belle Da Costa Greene's Journey from Prejudice to Privilege*. New York: Norton, 2007.

Hasse, Adelaide

Beck, Clare. *The New Woman as Librarian: The Career of Adelaide Hasse.* Lanham, MD: Scarecrow Press, 2006.

Henne, Frances E.

Cameron, Eleanor. "The Inimitable Frances." *The Horn Book Magazine* 67 (March–April 1991): 180–85.
Henne, Frances. *Frontiers of Library Service for Youth: Essays Honoring Frances E. Henne, Professor Emeritus, Columbia University, School of Library Science.* New York: The School, 1979.
Kester, Diane D., and Plummer Alston Jones, Jr. "Frances Henne and the Development of School Library Standards." *Library Trends* 52, no. 4 (Spring 2004): 952–62.

Hofmann, Walter

Rabe, Roman. "Das umstrittene Volksbibliotheksmodell: Walter Hofmann und die Freie Öffentliche Bibliothek Dresden-Plauen." *BuB-Journal* 58 (May 2006): 394–400.
Vodosek, Peter. "Innovation and Ideology: Walter Hofmann's Library Work in Dresden-Plauen and Leipzig." *Library History* 23, no. 1 (March 2007): 63–76.

Jewett, Charles Coffin

Harris, Michael H., ed. *The Age of Jewett: Charles Coffin Jewett and American Librarianship, 1841–1868.* Littleton, CO: Libraries Unlimited, 1975.

Josey, E. J.

Josey, E. J., and Ismael Abdullahi. *E. J. Josey: An Activist Librarian.* Metuchen, NJ: Scarecrow Press, 1992.

Leibniz, Gottfried Wilhelm

Carlquist, Erik. "Leibniz and the 'Core of Books': A 17th Century Librarian on Abstracting." *Library History* 11 (1995): 31–36.

Hartbecke, Karin, ed. *Zwischen Fürstenwillkür und Menschheitswohl: Gottfried Wilhelm Leibniz als Bibliothekar*. Frankfurt am Main: Vittorio Klostermann, 2008.

Mann, Margaret

Grotzinger, Laurel. "Margaret Mann: The Preparatory Years." *Journal of Library Education* 10, no. 4 (Spring 1970): 302–15.

McColvin, Lionel

Black, Alistair. "National Planning for Public Library Service: The Work and Ideas of Lionel McColvin." *Library Trends* 52, no. 4 (Spring 2004): 902–23.
Kerslake, Evelyn. "No More the Hero: Lionel McColvin, Women Library Workers, and Impacts of Othering." *Library History* 17, no. 3 (2001): 181–87.

Moliner, María

Alarcón, María R. Osuna. "María Moliner and Her Contribution to the History of Spain's Public Libraries." *Libraries and the Cultural Record* 44, no. 2 (Spring 2009): 220–33.

Moore, Anne Carroll

Bader, Barbara. "Only the Best: The Hits and Misses of Anne Carroll Moore." *The Horn Book Magazine* 73 (September–October 1997): 520–29.
McElderry, Margaret K. "Remarkable Women: Remembering Anne Carroll Moore and Company." *School Library Journal* 38, no. 3 (1992): 156–62.
Sayers, Frances Clarke. *Anne Moore: A Biography*. New York: Atheneum, 1972.

Morel, Eugène

Benoît, Gaëtan M. *Eugène Morel: Pioneer of Public Libraries in France*. Duluth, MN: Litwin Books, 2008.

Murray, Daniel Alexander Payne

Walker, Billie E. "Daniel Alexander Payne Murray (1852–1925), Forgotten Librarian, Bibliographer, and Historian." *Libraries and Culture* 40, no. 1 (Winter 2005): 25–37.

Naudé, Gabriel

Clarke, Jack A. *Gabriel Naudé, 1600–1653*. Hamden, CT: Archon Books, 1970.

Otlet, Paul

Rayward, W. Boyd. *The Universe of Information: The Work of Paul Otlet for Documentation and International Organizations*. Moscow: Published for the International Federation of Documentation (FID) by the All-Union Institute for Scientific and Technical Information (VINITI), 1975.
———. "Visions of Xanadu: Paul Otlet (1868–1944) and Hypertext." *Journal of the American Society for Information Science* 45, no. 4 (May 1994): 235–50.

Panizzi, Anthony

Glasgow, Eric. "Panizzi and His Allies." *Library History* 17, no. 2 (2001): 133–42.
———. "Sir Anthony Panizzi." *Library Review* 50, no. 5 (2001): 251–54.
Miller, Edward. *Prince of Librarians: The Life and Times of Antonio Panizzi of the British Museum*. London: Deutsch, 1967.

Plummer, Mary Wright

Maack, Mary Niles. "'No Philosophy Carries So Much Conviction as the Personal Life': Mary Wright Plummer as an Independent Woman." *Library Quarterly* 70, no. 1 (January 2000): 1–46.

Power, Effie Louise

Kimball, Melanie A., Christine A. Jenkins, and Betsy Hearne. "Effie Louise Power: Librarian, Educator, Author." *Library Trends* 52, no. 4 (Spring 2004): 924–51.

Putnam, Herbert

Putnam, Herbert, and John D. Knowlton. *Herbert Putnam: A 1903 Trip to Europe*. Lanham, MD: Scarecrow Press, 2005.

Wiegand, Wayne A. "Herbert Putnam's Appointment as Librarian of Congress." *Library Quarterly* 49, no. 3 (July 1979): 255–82.

Ranganathan, S. R.

Roe, George. "Challenging the Control of Knowledge in Colonial India: Political Ideas in the Work of S. R. Ranganathan." *Library and Information History* 26, no. 1 (March 2010): 18–32.

Sharma, Ravindra N. "Ranganathan's Impact on International Librarianship through Information Technology." *Libri* 42, no. 3 (1992): 258–67.

Rankin, Rebecca Browning

Seaver, Barry W. *A True Politician: Rebecca Browning Rankin, Municipal Reference Librarian of the City of New York, 1920–1952*. Jefferson, NC: McFarland, 2003.

Rose, Ernestine

Jenkins, Betty L. "A White Librarian in Black Harlem." *Library Quarterly* 60, no. 3 (July 1990): 216–31.

Sayers, Frances Clarke

Heins, Ethel L. "Frances Clarke Sayers: A Legacy." *The Horn Book Magazine* 66 (January–February 1990): 99–109.

Sharp, Katharine

Grotzinger, Laurel Ann. *The Power and the Dignity: Librarianship and Katharine Sharp*. New York: Scarecrow Press, 1966.

Shera, Jesse

Budd, John M. "Jesse Shera, Sociologist of Knowledge?" *Library Quarterly* 72, no. 4 (October 2002): 423–40.

Grossman, Hal B. "Without Reserve: Jesse Shera in the *Wilson Library Bulletin* and Elsewhere, 1961–1970." *Library and Information History* 26, no. 2 (June 2010): 152–69.

Wright, H. Curtis. *Jesse Shera, Librarianship, and Information Science.* Provo, UT: School of Library and Information Sciences, Brigham Young University, 1988.

Shores, Louis

Marshall, John David. *Louis Shores, Author-Librarian: A Bibliography.* Tallahassee: Gamma Chapter, Beta Phi Mu, School Of Library Science, Florida State University, 1979.

Shiflett, Orvin Lee. *Louis Shores: Defining Educational Librarianship.* Lanham, MD: Scarecrow Press, 1996.

———. "Louis Shores and Library History." *Libraries and Culture* 35, no. 1 (Winter 2000): 35–40.

Smith, Lillian

Johnston, Margaret E. "Lillian H. Smith." *The Horn Book Magazine* 58 (June 1982): 325–32.

Smith, Lillian H., Adele M. Fasick, Margaret Johnston, and Ruth Osler. *Lands of Pleasure: Essays on Lillian H. Smith and the Development of Children's Libraries.* Metuchen, NJ: Scarecrow Press, 1990.

Spofford, Ainsworth Rand

Ostrowski, Carl. "The Choice of Books: Ainsworth Rand Spofford, the Ideology of Reading, and Literary Collections at the Library of Congress in the 1870s." *Libraries and the Cultural Record* 45, no. 1 (Winter 2010): 70–84.

Stearns, Lutie

Pawley, Christine. "Advocate for Access: Lutie Stearns and the Traveling Libraries of the Wisconsin Free Library Commission, 1895–1914." *Libraries and Culture* 35, no. 3 (Summer 2000): 434–58.

Varley, Douglas Harold

Coates, Peter. "Douglas Harold Varley: A Life's Work in Librarianship Part
I." *Quarterly Bulletin of the National Library of South Africa* 55, no. 4
(June 2001): 166–78.
———. "Douglas Harold Varley: A Life's Work in Librarianship Part II."
Quarterly Bulletin of the National Library of South Africa 56, no. 1 (Sep-
tember 2001): 20–31.

Wilson, Louis Round

Martin, Robert S. "Louis Round Wilson and the Library Standards of the
Southern Association, 1926–1929." *Journal of Library History* 19, no. 2
(Spring 1984): 259–81.
Tauber, Maurice F. *Louis Round Wilson, Librarian and Administrator.* New
York: Columbia University Press, 1967.

Winsor, Justin

Cutler, Wayne, and Michael H. Harris, eds. *Justin Winsor: Scholar Librarian.* Littleton, CO: Libraries Unlimited, 1980.

Wood, Mary Elizabeth

Winkelman, John H. "Mary Elizabeth Wood (1861–1931): American Mis-
sionary-Librarian to Modern China." *Journal of Library and Information
Science* 8, no. 1 (1982): 62–76.
Zheng, Jing, et al. "The Queen of the Modern Library Movement in China:
Mary Elizabeth Wood." *Library Review* 59, no. 5 (2010): 341–49.

Libraries, Selected Individual

Boston Athenaeum, The

Wendorf, Richard, ed. *The Boston Athenaeum: Bicentennial Essays.* Boston:
Athenaeum, 2009.

Library of Congress

Cole, John Y. *Encyclopedia of the Library of Congress: For Congress, the Nation and the World.* Washington, DC: Library of Congress; Lanham, MD: Bernan Press, 2004.

————. "The Library of Congress Becomes a World Library, 1815–2005." *Libraries and Culture* 40, no. 3 (Summer 2005): 385–98.

Conaway, James. *America's Library: The Story of the Library of Congress, 1800–2000.* New Haven, CT: Yale University Press in association with the Library of Congress, 2000.

Robbins, Louise S. "The Library of Congress and Federal Loyalty Programs, 1947–1956: No 'Communists or Cocksuckers.'" *Library Quarterly* 64, no. 4 (October 1994): 365–85.

Rosenberg, Jane A. *The Nation's Great Library: Herbert Putnam and the Library of Congress, 1899–1939.* Urbana: University of Illinois Press, 1993.

Thorin, Suzanne E., and Robert Wedgeworth. "Librarians of Congress: A Look Back at a Century of Controversies and Triumphs Surrounding the National Library's Leaders." *American Libraries* 38, no. 6 (June–July 2007): 86–90.

Library Science and Information Schools

Allen, Walter C., and Robert F. Delzell. *Ideals and Standards: The History of the University of Illinois Graduate School of Library and Information Science, 1893–1993.* Urbana-Champaign: The School, 1992.

Cramer, Clarence Henley. *The School of Library Science at Case Western Reserve University: Seventy-five Years, 1904–1979.* Cleveland, OH: The School, 1979.

Grotzinger, Laurel. "The University of Illinois Library School, 1893–1942." *Journal of Library History* 2, no. 2 (Spring 1967): 129–41.

Miksa, Francis L. "The Columbia School of Library Economy, 1887–1888." *Journal of Library History* 23, no. 3 (Summer 1988): 249–80.

Paris, Marion. *Library School Closings: Four Case Studies.* Metuchen, NJ: Scarecrow Press, 1988.

Richardson, John V. *The Spirit of Inquiry: The Graduate Library School at Chicago, 1921–51.* Chicago: American Library Association, 1982.

Literacy and Reading

Karetzky, Stephen. *Reading Research and Librarianship: A History and Analysis.* Westport, CT: Greenwood Press, 1982.

Medical Librarianship

Brodman, Estelle. "Education and Attitudes of Early Medical Librarians to Their Work: A Discussion Based on the Oral History Project of the Medical Library Association." *Journal of Library History* 15, no. 2 (Spring 1980): 167–82.

Connor, Jennifer. *Guardians of Medical Knowledge: The Genesis of the Medical Library Association.* Chicago: Medical Library Association, 2000.

Humphreys, Betsy L. "Adjusting to Progress: Interactions between the National Library of Medicine and Health Sciences Librarians, 1961–2001." *Journal of the Medical Library Association* 90, no. 1 (January 2002): 4–20.

Jacobson, Susan. "Present at the Creation: The Founding and Formative Years of the Association of Academic Health Sciences Libraries." *Journal of the Medical Library Association* 91, no. 2 (April 2003): 149–54.

McClure, Lucretia W. "Introduction: Personal Recollections of the Contributions of Estelle Brodman: An Enduring Legacy for Health Sciences Librarianship." *Journal of the Medical Library Association* 96, no. 3 (July 2008): 239–41.

Medieval Libraries

Guthrie, Lawrence S. "An Overview of Medieval Library Cataloging." *Cataloging and Classification Quarterly* 15, no. 3 (1992): 93–100.

Thompson, James Westfall. *The Medieval Library.* Chicago: University of Chicago Press, 1939.

Music Librarianship

Bradley, Carol June. *American Music Librarianship: A Biographical and Historical Survey.* New York: Greenwood Press, 1990.

Online Computer Library Center (OCLC)

Lees, Janet. "OCLC in Europe, the Middle East and Africa, 1998–2008." *Journal of Library Administration* 49, no. 6 (2009): 603–11.

Smith, K. Wayne. *OCLC, 1967–1997: Thirty Years of Furthering Access to the World's Information.* New York: Haworth Press, 1998.

Preservation

Baker, Nicholson. *Double Fold: Libraries and the Assault on Paper*. New York: Random House, 2001.
Darling, Pamela. "From Problems Perceived to Programs in Practice: The Preservation of Library Resources in the USA, 1956–1980." *Library Resources and Technical Services* 25, no. 1 (January–March 1981): 9–29.
Higginbotham, Barbara Buckner. *Our Past Preserved: A History of American Library Preservation, 1876–1910*. Boston: G. K. Hall, 1990.

Public Libraries

Black, Alistair. "Libraries for the Many: The Philosophical Roots of the Early Public Library Movement." *Library History* 9, nos. 1–2 (1991): 27–36.
Davies, David William. *Public Libraries as Culture and Social Centers: The Origin of the Concept*. Metuchen, NJ: Scarecrow Press, 1974.
Goldstein, Daniel. "The Spirit of an Age: Iowa Public Libraries and Professional Librarians as Solutions to Society's Problems, 1890–1940." *Libraries and Culture* 38, no. 3 (Summer 2003): 214–35.
Harris, Michael H. "The Purpose of the American Public Library: A Revisionist Interpretation of History." *Library Journal* 98, no. 16 (September 15, 1973): 2509–14.
Hayes, Emma, and Anne Morris. "Leisure Role of Public Libraries: A Historical Perspective." *Journal of Librarianship and Information Science* 37, no. 2 (September 2005): 75–81.
Latham, Joyce M. "Clergy of the Mind: Alvin S. Johnson, William S. Learned, the Carnegie Corporation, and the American Library Association." *Library Quarterly* 80, no. 3 (July 2010): 249–65.
Lincove, David A. "Propaganda and the American Public Library from the 1930s to the Eve of World War II." *RQ* 33, no. 4 (Summer 1994): 510–23.
Malone, Cheryl Knott. "Towards a Multicultural American Public Library History." *Libraries and Culture* 35, no. 1 (Winter 2000): 78–87.
Martin, Lowell A. *Enrichment: A History of the Public Library in the United States in the Twentieth Century*. Lanham, MD: Scarecrow Press, 1998.
McCrossen, A. "'One Cathedral More' or 'Mere Lounging Place for Bummers'? The Cultural Politics of Leisure and the Public Library in the Gilded Age." *Libraries and Culture* 41, no. 2 (Spring 2006): 169–88.
Muddiman, Dave. "The Public Library in an Age of Inclusion: Edward Sydney, Harold Jolliffe and the Rise and Fall of Library Extension, 1927–1972." *Library History* 18, no. 2 (July 2002): 117–30.

Raber, Douglas. *Librarianship and Legitimacy: The Ideology of the Public Library Inquiry*. Westport, CT: Greenwood Press, 1997.

Shera, Jesse H. *The Foundations of the Public Library: The Origins of the Public Library Movement in New England, 1692–1855*. Chicago: University of Chicago Press, 1949.

Snape, Robert. *Leisure and the Rise of the Public Library*. London: Library Association, 1995.

Wiegand, Wayne A., ed. "Windows on the World: Analyzing Main Street Public Library Collection." *Library Trends* 60, no. 4 (Spring 2012): entire issue.

Readers' Advisory

Crowley, Bill. "Rediscovering the History of Readers' Advisory Service." *Public Libraries* 44, no. 1 (January–February 2005): 37–41.

Dilevko, Juris, and Candice F. C. Magowan. *Readers' Advisory Service in North American Public Libraries, 1870–2005: A History and Critical Analysis*. Jefferson, NC: McFarland and Company, 2007.

Luyt, Brendan. "Regulating Readers: The Social Origins of the Readers' Advisor in the United States." *Library Quarterly* 71, no. 4 (October 2001): 443–66.

Reference Services

Cheney, Frances Neel, Edwin S. Gleaves, and John Mark Tucker. *Reference Services and Library Education: Essays in Honor of Frances Neel Cheney*. Lexington, MA: Lexington Books, 1983.

Katz, William. *From Cuneiform to Computer: A History of Reference Services*. Lanham, MD: Scarecrow Press, 1990.

Landesman, Margaret. "Getting It Right: The Evolution of Reference Collections." *Reference Librarian* 44, nos. 91–92 (2005): 5–22.

Miller, William. "Reference Services over the Past Century: Moving from the Center to the Fringes." *Reference Librarian* 48, no. 2 (2007): 3–7.

Rettig, James. "Reference Service: From Certainty to Uncertainty." In *Advances in Librarianship*, vol. 30, ed. Danuta A. Nitecki and Eileen Abels. Amsterdam: Academic Press, 2006.

Richardson, John V., Jr. "Teaching General Reference Work: The Complete Paradigm and Competing Schools of Thought, 1890–1990." *Library Quarterly* 62, no. 1 (January 1992): 55–89.

Rothstein, Samuel. "Across the Desk: 100 Years of Reference Encounters." *Canadian Library Journal* 34, no. 5 (October 1977): 391–99.

Straw, Joseph E. "From Magicians to Teachers: The Development of Electronic Reference in Libraries: 1930–2000." *Reference Librarian* 35, no. 74 (2001): 1–12.

Tyckoson, David A. "Issues and Trends in the Management of Reference Services: A Historical Perspective." *Journal of Library Administration* 51, no. 3 (April 2011): 259–78.

School Libraries

Butler, Rebecca P. "Contending Voices: Intellectual Freedom in American Public School Libraries, 1827–1940." *School Libraries Worldwide* 5, no. 1 (1999): 30–39.

Knuth, Rebecca. "Factors in the Development of School Libraries in Great Britain and the United States: A Comparative Study." *International Information and Library Review* 27, no. 3 (1995): 265–82.

Latrobe, Kathy Howard. *The Emerging School Library Media Center: Historical Issues and Perspectives*. Englewood, CO: Libraries Unlimited, 1998.

Lowrie, Jean E. *School Libraries: International Developments*. Metuchen, NJ: Scarecrow Press, 1972.

Michie, Joan, and Barbara A. Holton. *Fifty Years of Supporting Children's Learning: A History of Public School Libraries and Federal Legislation from 1953–2000*. Washington, DC: National Center for Education Statistics, 2005.

Midland, Susan. "From Stereopticon to Google: Technology and School Library Standards." *Teacher Librarian* 35, no. 4 (April 2008): 30–33.

Pender, Kevin. "Historical Influences on the Development of American School Libraries to 1978." *Audiovisual Librarian* 10 (October 15, 1984): 200–204.

Wiegand, Wayne A. "The Rich Potential of American Public School Library History: Research Needs and Opportunities for Historians of Education and Librarianship." *Libraries and the Cultural Record* 42, no. 1 (Winter 2007): 57–74.

Serials Librarianship

Goedeken, Edward A. "The Serials Librarian: A Brief History and Assessment." *The Serials Librarian* 49, no. 4 (2006): 157–73.

Special Libraries and Services

Christianson, Elin B. *Daniel Nash Handy and the Special Library Movement.* New York: Insurance Division, Special Libraries Association, 1980.

Johns, Ada Winfred. *Special Libraries: Development of the Concept, Their Organization, and Their Services.* Metuchen, NJ: Scarecrow Press, 1968.

Library of Congress. *That All May Read: Library Service for Blind and Physically Handicapped People.* Washington, DC: National Library Service for the Blind and Physically Handicapped, Library of Congress, 1983.

Terminology

Shapiro, Fred R. "Contributions to the History of Library Terminology." *Library Quarterly* 59, no. 2 (April 1989): 95–115.

Unionization

Shanley, Catherine. "The Library Employees' Union of Greater New York, 1917–1929." *Libraries and Culture* 30, no. 3 (Fall 1995): 235–64.

United Nations Educational, Scientific and Cultural Organization (UNESCO)

Parker, J. Stephen. *UNESCO and Library Development Planning.* London: Library Association, 1985.

War and Librarianship

Becker, Patti Clayton. *Books and Libraries in American Society during World War II: Weapons in the War of Ideas.* New York: Routledge, 2005.

Davis, Donald G. "Wars in American Libraries: Ideological Battles in the Selection of Materials." *Libraries and Culture* 33, no. 1 (Winter 1998): 40–47.

Hung, Margaret. "A Guerrilla War in World War II: How the Library Association Fought the War Office and the Army—And Lost." *Library History* 24, no. 2 (June 2008): 167–88.

Kimball, Melanie A. "From Refuge to Risk: Public Libraries and Children in World War I." *Library Trends* 55, no. 3 (Winter 2007): 454–63.

Maack, Mary Niles. "'I Cannot Get Along without the Books I Find Here': The American Library in Paris during the War, Occupation, and Liberation, 1939–1945." *Library Trends* 55, no. 3 (Winter 2007): 490–512.

Richards, Pamela S. "Information Science in Wartime: Pioneer Documentation Activities in World War II." *Journal of the American Society for Information Science* 39, no. 5 (September 1988): 301–6.

———. "The Quest for Enemy Scientific Information, 1939–1945: Information History as Part of Library History." *Library History* 9, nos. 1–2 (1991): 5–14.

Russell, Dale C. "Promotion of Public Libraries in the Second World War." *Library History* 15, no. 1 (1999): 41–48.

Stielow, Frederick J. "Librarian Warriors and Rapprochement: Carl Milam, Archibald MacLeish, and World War II." *Libraries and Culture* 25, no. 4 (Fall 1990): 513–33.

Wiegand, Wayne A. *"An Active Instrument for Propaganda": The American Public Library during World War I.* New York: Greenwood Press, 1989.

Winston, Mark D., and Susan Quinn. "Library Leadership in Times of Crisis and Change." *New Library World* 106, nos. 9–10 (2005): 395–415.

Young, Arthur P. *Books for Sammies: The American Library Association and World War I.* Pittsburgh, PA: Beta Phi Mu, 1981.

Zgonjanin, Sanja. "The Prosecution of War Crimes for the Destruction of Libraries and Archives during Times of Armed Conflict." *Libraries and Culture* 40, no. 2 (Spring 2005): 128–44.

Women in Librarianship

Bailey, Joanne Passet. "'The Rule Rather Than the Exception': Midwest Women as Academic Librarians, 1875–1900." *Journal of Library History* 21, no. 4 (Fall 1986): 673–92.

Baum, Christina D. *Feminist Thought in American Librarianship.* Jefferson, NC: McFarland, 1992.

Carmichael, James V., Jr. "Atlanta's Female Librarians, 1883–1915." *Journal of Library History* 21, no. 2 (Spring 1986): 376–99.

———. "Women in Southern Library Education, 1905–1945." *Library Quarterly* 63, no. 2 (April 1992): 169–216.

Corwin, Margaret Ann. "An Investigation of Female Leadership in Regional, State, and Local Library Associations." *Library Quarterly* 44, no. 2 (April 1974): 133–44.

Cummings, Cynthia S. *A Biographical-Bibliographical Directory of Women Librarians.* Madison: University of Wisconsin, Madison Library School Women's Group, 1976.

Daniels, Caroline. "The Feminine Touch Has Not Been Wanting: Women Librarians at Camp Zachary Taylor, 1917–1919." *Libraries and the Cultural Record* 43, no. 3 (Fall 2008): 286–307.

Garrison, Dee. "The Tender Technicians: The Feminization of Public Librarianship, 1876–1905." *Journal of Social History* 6, no. 2 (Winter 1972–1973): 131–59.

Grotzinger, Laurel A., James V. Carmichael, and Mary Niles Maack. *Women's Work: Vision and Change in Librarianship*. Urbana: University of Illinois Graduate School of Library and Information Science, 1994.

Hahn, Trudi Bellardo, and Diane L. Barlow, eds. "Women Pioneers in the Information Sciences, 1900–1950." *Libraries and the Cultural Record* 44, no. 2 (Spring 2009): entire issue.

———. "Women Pioneers in the Information Sciences, Part II." *Libraries and the Cultural Record* 45, no. 2 (Spring 2010): entire issue.

Hansen, Debra Gold, Karen F. Gracy, and Sheri D. Irvin. "At the Pleasure of the Board: Women Librarians and the Los Angeles Public Library, 1880–1905." *Libraries and Culture* 34, no. 4 (Fall 1999): 311–46.

Harris, Roma M. *Librarianship: The Erosion of a Woman's Profession*. Norwood, NJ: Ablex Publishing Corporation, 1992.

Heim, Kathleen M. *The Status of Women in Librarianship: Historical, Sociological and Economic Issues*. New York: Neal-Schuman, 1983.

Hildenbrand, Suzanne. "Library Feminism and Library Women's History: Activism and Scholarship, Equity and Culture." *Libraries and Culture* 35, no. 1 (Winter 2000): 51–65.

———. *Reclaiming the American Library Past: Writing the Women In*. Norwood, NJ: Ablex Publishing Corporation, 1996.

Kerslake, Evelyn. "Constructing Women in Library History: Responding to Julia Taylor's 'Left on the Shelf.'" *Libraries and Culture* 34, no. 1 (Winter 1999): 52–63.

Kerslake, Evelyn, and Janine Liladhar. "Angry Sentinels and Businesslike Women: Identity and Marital Status in 1950s English Library Career." *Library History* 17, no. 2 (2001): 83–90.

Kerslake, Evelyn, and Nickianne Moody, eds. *Gendering Library History*. Liverpool: Media Critical and Creative Arts, Liverpool John Moores University and the Association for Research in Popular Fictions, 2000.

Kruger, Betsy, and Catherine A. Larson, eds. *On Account of Sex: An Annotated Bibliography on the Status of Women in Librarianship, 1998–2002*. Lanham, MD: Scarecrow Press, 2006.

Kruger, Betsy, Catherine A. Larson, and Allison A. Cowgill. *On Account of Sex: An Annotated Bibliography on the Status of Women in Librarianship, 1993–1997*. Lanham, MD: Scarecrow Press, 2000.

Maack, Mary Niles. "Toward a History of Women in Librarianship: A Critical Analysis with Suggestions for Further Research." *Journal of Library History* 17, no. 2 (Spring 1982): 164–85.

———. "American Bookwomen in Paris during the 1920s." *Libraries and Culture* 40, no. 3 (Fall 2005): 399–415.

McCook, Kathleen de la Peña, and Katharine Phenix. *On Account of Sex: An Annotated Bibliography on the Status of Women in Librarianship, 1977–1981*. Chicago: American Library Association, 1984.

McDowell, Kate. "Surveying the Field: The Research Model of Women in Librarianship, 1882–1898." *Library Quarterly* 79, no. 3 (July 2009): 279–300.

Myers, Margaret, and Mayra Scarborough. *Women in Librarianship: Melvil's Rib Symposium: Proceedings of the Eleventh Annual Symposium Sponsored by the Alumni and Faculty of the Rutgers University Graduate School of Library Service*. New Brunswick, NJ: Bureau of Library and Information Science Research, Rutgers University Graduate School of Library Service, 1975.

Passet, Joanne E. *Cultural Crusaders: Women Librarians in the American West, 1900–1917*. Albuquerque: University of New Mexico Press, 1994.

———. "Women Academic Librarians on the Western Frontier, 1900–1920." *Library Quarterly* 60, no. 4 (October 1990): 320–36.

Phenix, Katharine, and Kathleen de la Peña McCook. *On Account of Sex: An Annotated Bibliography on the Status of Women in Librarianship, 1982–1986*. Chicago: American Library Association, 1989.

Taylor, Julia. "Left on the Shelf? The Issues and Challenges Facing Women Employed in Libraries from the Late Nineteenth Century to the 1950s." *Library History* 11 (1995): 96–107.

Webber, Nigel. "Prospect and Prejudice: Women and Librarianship, 1880–1914." *Library History* 6, no. 5 (1983): 153–62.

Weibel, Kathleen, Kathleen de la Peña McCook, and Dianne J. Ellsworth. *The Role of Women in Librarianship, 1876–1976: The Entry, Advancement, and Struggle for Equalization in One Profession*. Phoenix, AZ: Oryx Press, 1979.

Young Adult Librarianship

Atkinson, Joan. "Pioneers in Public Library Service to Young Adults." *Top of the News* 43, no. 1 (Fall 1986): 27–44.

Bernier, Anthony, Mary K. Chelton, and Christine A. Jenkins. "Two Hundred Years of Young Adult Library Services History: The Chronology." *Voice of Youth Advocates* 28, no. 2 (June 2005): 106–11.

Campbell, Patricia J. *Two Pioneers of Young Adult Library Services*. Lanham, MD: Scarecrow Press, 1998.

Craver, Kathleen W. "Social Trends in American Young Adult Library Service, 1960–1969." *Libraries and Culture* 23, no. 1 (Winter 1988): 18–28.

About the Author

Mary Ellen Quinn received a BA from the University of Michigan, an MA in English from the University of Toronto, and an MLS from the University of Michigan. She worked as a librarian at the Jacksonville Public Library in Florida from 1976–1979 and at the Chicago Public Library in Illinois from 1979–1997. From 1997–2011, she worked at the American Library Association as the editor of the Reference Books Bulletin section of *Booklist*, the association's review journal. She was also the managing editor of *Booklist Online* from 2006–2011. She has published numerous articles related to library collection development and reference publishing, including Reference Books Bulletin's annual encyclopedia update. She wrote the "Librarian's Library" column in *American Libraries* from 2007–2011. In 2001, she received the Louis Shores Award for excellence in book reviewing for libraries.